The Putney Debates of 1647

In the autumn of 1647, soldiers and officers of Oliver Cromwell's New Model Army held discussions near London on the constitution and future of England. Would there be a king and Lords, or not? Would suffrage be limited to property-holders? Would democratic changes lead to anarchy?

Three generations of scholars examine the debates in their multiple contexts: the Putney debates themselves, the nature and history of the debate text that has come down to us, the immediate concerns of the army, the role of Leveller and other democratic ideas, the wider ramifications for politics and gender of the issues underlying Putney, and the place of the debates and the Levellers in nineteenth- and twentieth-century historical consciousness. Though frequently anthologised and widely read, the debates receive here their most sustained and varied scrutiny, resulting in a much richer appreciation of the very words reported to have been spoken by Oliver Cromwell, Henry Ireton, Thomas Rainborough and the others, on those three tense and exhilarating days.

MICHAEL MENDLE is Professor of History, University of Alabama

The Putney Debates of 1647
The Army, the Levellers and the English State

Edited by

Michael Mendle

CAMBRIDGE
UNIVERSITY PRESS

PUBLISHED BY THE PRESS SYNDICATE OF THE UNIVERSITY OF CAMBRIDGE
The Pitt Building, Trumpington Street, Cambridge, United Kingdom

CAMBRIDGE UNIVERSITY PRESS
The Edinburgh Building, Cambridge CB2 2RU, UK
40 West 20th Street, New York, NY 10011-4211, USA
10 Stamford Road, Oakleigh, VIC 3166, Australia
Ruiz de Alarcón 13, 28014 Madrid, Spain
Dock House, The Waterfront, Cape Town 8001, South Africa

http://www.cambridge.org

First published 2001

Printed in the United Kingdom at the University Press, Cambridge

Typeface Plantin 10/12   *System* QuarkXPress™   [SE]

A catalogue record for this book is available from the British Library

ISBN 0 521 65015 1 hardback

Contents

List of illustrations   *page* vii
Notes on the contributors   viii
Editor's acknowledgements   x
Textual note and abbreviations   xi

1 Introduction   1
   MICHAEL MENDLE

Part 1 The Putney debates: the artefact

2 The survival of the manuscript   19
   LESLEY LE CLAIRE

3 Reading, and writing, the text of the Putney debates   36
   FRANCES HENDERSON

Part 2 The Putney debates and their contexts

4 The debates from the perspective of the army   53
   AUSTIN WOOLRYCH

5 The army, the state and the soldier in the English civil war   79
   BARBARA DONAGAN

6 The case of the armie truly re-stated   103
   JOHN MORRILL AND PHILIP BAKER

7 Putney's pronouns: identity and indemnity in the great debate   125
   MICHAEL MENDLE

8 The *Agreements of the people* and their political contexts,
   1647–1649   148
   IAN GENTLES

9   From Reading to Whitehall: Henry Ireton's journey   175
    BARBARA TAFT

Part 3 Levellers and 'Levellerism' in history and historiography

10 'The poorest she': women and citizenship in early modern
    England   197
    PATRICIA CRAWFORD

11 The Leveller legacy: from the Restoration to the Exclusion
    Crisis   219
    TIM HARRIS

12 Puritanism, liberty and the Putney debates   241
    WILLIAM LAMONT

13 The Levellers in history and memory, c. 1660–1960   256
    BLAIR WORDEN

14 The true Leveller's standard revisited: an afterword   283
    J. G. A. POCOCK

    Index   292

Illustrations

The opening page of the Putney debates (after the title page),   cover
    Worcester College, Oxford, Ms. 65.
    By kind permission of Worcester College, Oxford
From a 1667 pack of playing cards, *The knavery of the Rump.*   *page* 212
    By the kind permission of Guildhall Library: Worshipful Company of
    Makers of Playing Cards Collection.

Notes on the contributors

Philip Baker is currently working for the University of Oxford as a Research Editor with the *New dictionary of national bibliography*. He is completing a Cambridge doctoral dissertation on 'The origins and early history of the Levellers, c. 1635–c. 1647'.

Patricia Crawford teaches history at the University of Western Australia. Her recent publications include, with Sara Mendelson, *Women in early modern England 1550–1730* (Oxford, 1998), and with Laura Gowing, *Women's worlds in seventeenth-century England: a sourcebook* (Oxford, 2000).

Barbara Donagan is a research scholar at the Huntington Library. Her articles, which form part of a larger study of the English civil war, address its law and practice, and the crises of conscience involved in the resort to arms.

Ian Gentles is the author of *The New Model Army in England, Ireland and Scotland* (Oxford, 1992) and is currently at work on a book on the English revolution in the three kingdoms. He teaches history at Glendon College, York University (Toronto).

Tim Harris, professor of history at Brown University, has written extensively on Restoration and later Stuart politics and popular culture. He is editing a collection of essays entitled *The politics of the excluded in early modern England* and is at work on a book entitled *British revolutions: the making of the modern nation, 1660–1707*.

Frances Henderson recently completed her doctoral thesis at Oxford University, where in 1996–8 she was appointed Research Associate at Worcester College. She has published a number of articles relating to the use of shorthand by the army secretariat during the English civil wars.

William Lamont is currently research professor of history at the University of Sussex. Three earlier studies of English Puritanism were reprinted in 1991 as *Puritanism and the English revolution* (3 vols., Aldershot). His *Puritanism and historical controversy* was published in 1996 (Montreal). At present he is completing *The Muggletonian history 1652–1979*.

Lesley Le Claire was formerly librarian of Worcester College, Oxford. A dramatised version she made of the Putney debates was performed in Oxford and later in the church at Putney. It has since been used by the BBC and by various university history departments.

Michael Mendle is professor of history at the University of Alabama. His writings on seventeenth-century British political thought include *Henry Parker and the English civil war* (Cambridge, 1995). He is at work on a study of the construction, preservation and later discovery of the primary sources of seventeenth-century history.

John Morrill FBA is professor of British and Irish history at Cambridge University and is fellow and vice-master of Selwyn College. He has published widely on early modern state formation and on the political and religious dynamics of the English – and British – revolutions of the mid-seventeenth century.

J. G. A. Pocock is professor emeritus of history at the Johns Hopkins University and convenor of the Steering Committee of the Folger Institute Center for the History of British Political Thought. He has recently published essays on the War of the Three Kingdoms and Thomas May's *History of the Parliament.*

Barbara Taft is coeditor of *The writings of William Walwyn* (Athens, GA, 1989) and has written articles about seventeenth-century English politics and political thought that have appeared in British and American publications.

Austin Woolrych FBA served in the British army for over six years before going to university. When Lancaster University opened he was its first professor of history. His books include *Soldiers and statesmen: the General Council of the Army and its debates, 1647–1649* (Oxford, 1987).

Blair Worden FBA is professor of early modern history at the University of Sussex and is currently a British Academy research professor. His books include *The Rump Parliament* (Cambridge, 1974) and *The sound of virtue: politics in Philip Sidney's 'Arcadia'* (New Haven, CT, 1996).

Editor's acknowledgements

This volume had its genesis in a conference on the Putney debates at the Folger Shakespeare Library, held in 1997, their 350th anniversary. Most of the papers in this volume were delivered, in preliminary form, at that conference. I wish to thank the Folger Shakespeare Library and its director, Werner Gundersheimer, its educational arm, the Folger Institute and its chair, Barbara Mowat, and the immediate sponsoring body, the Folger Institute's Center for the Study of British Political Thought for the opportunity to celebrate and study Putney and its multiple contexts. Members of the Folger Institute staff, especially Lena Orlin and Kathleen Lynch, the two executive directors in whose tenure the planning and the programme itself took place, were magnificent, taking the enormous burden of the non-scholarly preparation wholly off my back and lightening the weight of the rest. The steering committee of the Center, then composed of John Pocock, Gordon Schochet and Lois Schwoerer, were always supportive. The editors and staff of the Cambridge University Press – especially Bill Davies – provided expert advice and continuing support. Katy Cooper, the volume's copy-editor, worked wonders in bringing all to order and uniformity. Dr Joanna Parker, Librarian of Worcester College, was most helpful in arranging for the photograph of Putney debates manuscript acknowledged below.

I gratefully acknowledge the permissions of Worcester College, Oxford to use the cover illustration of the first page of Putney debates text in Worcester College Ms. 65, and of the Guildhall Library, Worshipful Company of Makers of Playing Cards Collection, for the illustration that appears on p. 212.

Above all, I wish specially to thank the contributors, from whom I learned beyond recompense, and whose professionalism was exceeded only by their encouragement and generosity.

Textual note and abbreviations

The Putney debates have been published in full in two modern editions, each of which has been reprinted more than once, and both of which are repeatedly cited in the text and notes that follow. In the case of *Puritanism and liberty*, the history is somewhat complicated.

CP   *The Clarke papers: selections from the papers of William Clarke . . .*, ed. C. H. Firth, Camden Society, new series, vols. 49, 54, 61, 62 (1891–1901). The debates are found in volume I, pp. 226–418. The entire series was reprinted in London and New York: Johnson Reprint Company, 1965; volumes I and II, with a new preface by Austin Woolrych, were reprinted in one volume by the Royal Historical Society in 1992.

P&L   *Puritanism and liberty, being the Army debates (1647–9) from the Clarke manuscripts with supplementary documents*, ed. with an introduction by A. S. P. Woodhouse, foreward by A. D. Lindsay (1938). That edition was reissued with minor changes to the prefaces (but not the introduction) in 1950 and 1951, as a self-described 'second edition'. A true second edition, with a new preface by Ivan Roots, appeared in 1974; the same, with revisions to the preface and bibliography, was reissued as a third edition in 1986, and again in 1992. However, the basic text and pagination of Woodhouse's introduction and his edition of the debates and other documents were unchanged, so for that purpose the editions are interchangeable. Woodhouse's introduction was paged with arabic numerals within square brackets, the sources by arabic numbers alone. That convention is followed here.

OTHER ABBREVIATIONS

BIHR   *Bulletin of the Institute for Historical Research*
BL   British Library
CJ   *Commons Journals*
CSPD   *Calendar of state papers, domestic*

EHR   *English Historical Review*
HJ   *Historical Journal*
HMC   Historical Manuscripts Commission
JBS   *Journal of British Studies*
LJ   *Lords Journals*
PRO   Public Record Office
TRHS   *Transactions of the Royal Historical Society*

While a distinction is in principle to be made between the published texts of the *Agreement of the people*, and other references to the Agreement (without italics) considered simply as an idea or proposal, in practice the distinction is hard to sustain, particularly with reference to the Putney and Whitehall debates. Therefore, all references will be in italics.

In addition, I have standardised to the usual form, *The heads of the proposals*, although the initial edition was titled *The heads of proposals*.

1 Introduction

Michael Mendle

By the middle of the twentieth century, the events at the centre of this volume, the debates of the army held at Putney late in October and on the first day of November 1647, became a fixture of the popular consciousness of the seventeenth century. The rights of the 'the poorest hee' spoken for by Colonel Rainborough stand only a little beneath Oliver, the regicide and Restoration in the British public imagination. But it is rather astonishing that this ever happened. The debates at Putney, laced with undercurrents of unrest and possible sedition and mutiny, received scant treatment in the newsbooks of the day, and what little emerged was the work of Pollyanna. *The Moderate Intelligencer* for 28 October–4 November reported that on the 28th, 'A great assembly was this day at Putney Church, where was debated matters of high concernment . . . there was resolution taken to meet the next day and proceed, and first to put up supplications to God for a good issue'. For 29 October, the newsbook reported that: 'the Councell sate this day at *Putney*, whose proceedings . . . was to appoint a Committee to agree upon something, and bring it in . . .'.[1] Other newsbooks were even more coy: the debates of 28 and 29 October were not 'thought fit to mention untill the further sense of the Generall Councell be knowne', 'not thought fit to be presented to the publique view', 'not thought fit to be communicated'.[2] It was, all in all, close to a news blackout.[3] Shortly after the tense days of recorded debate, the Leveller organisation managed to emit a printed text of *An agreement of the people* and a few other pieces of that kidney, yet no direct account of the proceedings ever surfaced in the press or, indeed, any sustained manuscript account.

---

[1] *The Moderate Intelligencer*, no. 137, 28 Oct.–4 Nov. 1647, 1345–6.

[2] Successively, *A Perfect Diurnall*, no. 222, 25–30 Oct. 1647, 1787; *The Perfect Weekly Account*, no. 43, 26 Oct.–2 Nov. 1647, sig. S2v; *The Kingdomes Weekly Intelligencer*, no. 232, 26 Oct.–2 Nov. 1647, 715.

[3] See Austin Woolrych, *Soldiers and statesmen* (Oxford, 1987), 226 and nn. 44, 243, for the sparseness, circumspectness and mincing delicacy of contemporary news accounts of the proceedings at Putney. By contrast, however, *An agreement of the people* was widely available as a text and in summary, with two early free-standing editions and several summaries or substantial extracts in the newsbooks.

Only after the Restoration, in 1662, did Sir William Clarke transcribe his shorthand notes and produce what became part of Clarke Ms. 65 of the library of Worcester College, Oxford. As deftly recounted in this volume by Lesley Le Claire, that volume and its fellows lay almost entirely unnoticed by a historian until Charles Firth followed up a suggestion of the college librarian, Henry Pottinger. The result, of course, was Firth's edition, for the Camden Society, of the Clarke papers. The first volume, containing the debates at Putney as well as those at Reading (July 1647) and Whitehall (1648) and much other material, appeared in 1891. Yet printed publication hardly made the debates an item of public currency. While Firth provided an exemplary and sustained 'Preface' (or, rather, introduction) of some seventy pages to the volume, replete with detailed and page-referenced discussion of the sources within, there was no table of contents, running heads or index.[4] Unintroduced document followed unintroduced document, occasionally so seamlessly that a reader needed to read with care simply to see where one item ended and another began. A greyer and more imposing volume could scarcely be imagined, nor one more physically approximating Thomas Carlyle's caricature of the output of 'the Dryasdust Publishing Societies'.[5] Two other great seventeenth-century sources, Sir Simonds D'Ewes' diary of the Long Parliament and the Thomason tracts at the British Museum, as it then was, had already been canonised (and both owed much to the propaganda activities on their behalf by Thomas Carlyle),[6] but Firth undertook no such public campaign on behalf of the Putney debates.

And, indeed, nowhere in the preface did Firth refer precisely to 'the Putney Debates' or 'the Putney debates', and nor did the text itself.[7] Firth clearly appreciated their significance[8] but the pages with their first heading ('Att the generall Councill of Officers att Putney. 28 October, 1647') in simple Roman type were not perceived as a unit or topos. 'The Putney debates' did not yet exist.

They were (and remain) a 'tough read'. In chapter 3 Frances Henderson trains her unique mastery of Clarke's shorthand upon the

---

[4] The index to the first volume appeared in the second, published in 1894.

[5] 'An election to the Long Parliament', 392, 393. For Carlyle's attitudes to the book clubs, Heather Henderson, 'Carlyle and the book clubs: a new approach to publishing?,' *Publishing History* 6 (1980), 37–62. See also Philippa Levine, *The amateur and the professional: antiquarians, historians and archaeologists in Victorian England, 1838–1886* (Cambridge, 1986), 41–5.

[6] These activities are discussed in my forthcoming study of the construction and preservation of the historical memory of the seventeenth century, *Bottling the air: keeping and finding the seventeenth century.*

[7] But see *CP,* I:vii (the first page of the 'Preface'), where Firth describes the volume containing 'the debates of the Council of the Army in 1647' as 'the most valuable of all'.

[8] See Blair Worden's essay, chapter 13, in this volume.

debates-as-text, revealing many of the causes of what all readers from Firth forward have known – that Clarke's text ranges from the pellucid and seemingly nearly echoic to the irremediably obscure. Many of the speeches on the second day of debate – 'franchise day' – are so rich in idiom, in repetition and cadence, in turns of phrase that might easily be omitted with no loss of basic sense, that is hard not to feel the thrill of time-transport. Others are fragmentary and crabbed (as Dr Henderson shows, not least to Clarke), and seemed to Firth to require significant editorial conjecture, either by way of textual addition or by revising the order of sentences (see, for example, the last twenty pages of the recorded debates, *CP,* I:387–406).

Yet the debates were readable, and did make their way into wider historical consciousness. Samuel Rawson Gardiner, in his *History of the great civil war 1642–1649* (first edition 1898–1901), took careful account of 'a meeting of the Army Council . . . in Putney Church', though his remarks, the highly analytic table of contents, running heads, and the index knew nothing of the 'Putney debates' under that or a similar name.[9] Both G. P. Gooch's *English democratic ideas in the seventeenth century* (first published in 1898) and T. C. Pease's *The Leveller movement* (1916) treated them in some detail. But, again, they were not yet, *tout court*, 'the Putney debates'. Gooch referred to 'Clarke's reports of the debates at Putney', as well as to 'the Putney meetings' and the discussions 'in the Council at Putney' and 'in the great meeting at Putney'. This seems close enough, but it did not quite stick. Pease wrote of the debates at Putney without once mentioning the venue. With minor changes of wording they are either 'the army-council debates' or debates 'in the Council of the Army'.[10] Clearly the critical and transformative moment was the initial publication, in 1938, of A. S. P. Woodhouse's *Puritanism and liberty*, a volume commercially available to non-Camden subscribers, and prepared with an eye to accessibility. William Lamont's essay in this volume (chapter 12), which joins Blair Worden's (chapter 13) in exploring the ideological and cultural underpinnings of interest in the Levellers, particularly traces the impact of Woodhouse's volume. As Professor Lamont points out, Woodhouse reified – and perhaps at the same time embalmed – those long blocks of grey text. Like Adam, Woodhouse gave names to things created but not

[9] *History of the great civil war 1642–1649* (4 vols; first edn. 1898–1901; repr. 1965), III:382, and IV:index.

[10] G. P. Gooch, *English democratic ideas in the seventeenth* century (1898, 2nd edn 1927), 129, 132, 136. T. C. Pease, *The Leveller movement* (1916, repr. 1965), 210, 215, 217, 218, 227. Perhaps it should be noted that Eduard Bernstein's *Cromwell and communism*, trans. H. J. Stenning (1930), referred to 'the "Conferences of Putney"' (p. 67) but the accompanying note makes clear that this was not a settled usage, since it refers to the same discussions through a circumlocution.

yet (clearly) distinguished: the Reading debates, the Putney debates, the Whitehall debates. The Putney debates were subdivided in the table of contents by date, creating the all-but-irresistible urge to give the debates a dramatic structure, the first, second and third days metamorphosing into a play in three acts, a choice neither as automatic nor as innocent of consequence as it might seem, since the debates continued for days later, even though Clarke preserved almost nothing of their contents.

Woodhouse also felt obliged to go well beyond what Firth had done by way of editorial intervention.[11] Firth had sometimes added a word or phrase merely to improve style, acting as a kind of Victorian essay master. Woodhouse's interpolations were far less restrained. I remember, as a beginning research student first exposed to the debates through *Puritanism and liberty*, my wonderment at the editorial telepathy that allowed Woodhouse to read the mind of the debaters so perfectly as to supply not one or two words but whole extended phrases – would I ever manage to become as adept? Later scholars have generally, and rightly, recoiled from Woodhouse's excesses. While Olivier Lutaud's translation of parts of the debates into French understandably included glosses in the manner of stage directions,[12] most English-speaking scholars have resorted to the use of Firth's more austere edition. Gerald Aylmer's useful documentary collection, *The Levellers in the English revolution*, courageously took the minimalist step of publishing large extracts of the debates with only the tiniest amount of textual intervention.[13]

It was, however, Woodhouse's edition that most people encountered, especially in the long interval between 1891 (or whenever the stock of the volume ran out) and 1965, when the Camden volume was first reprinted.[14] Modernised in spelling and punctuation, seemingly clairvoyant in its editorial emendation, and titled, trussed and divided, the debates were accessible, if not to Everyman, then to a considerable university public. That readership was probably enhanced by an order of magnitude through frequent anthologisation.

Yet the world that had embraced the Putney debates – from the naively, affirmatively democratic centre to the various Lefts – had become on their

[11] In fairness to Woodhouse, his editorial conventions and apparatus allowed for a more accurate reconstruction of the manuscript than did Firth's, and he denied that his was 'a less conservative text', *P&L*, [12].

[12] Olivier Lutaud, *Les Niveleurs, Cromwell, et la république* (1967); for example, a speech of Cromwell's in reply to one of Wildman's is tagged 'Cromwell (intervient, après un long silence: ton d'abord contrôlé, puis saccadé, furieux)'. The corresponding pages of Firth's edition are *CP*, I:269–71, of *P&L* (which Lutaud used as the basis of his edition), 30–2.

[13] Gerald Aylmer (ed.), *The Levellers in the English revolution* (1975).

[14] The paperback reissue of 1992 of volumes. I and II, under the aegis of Austin Woolrych, has regrettably gone out of print.

350th anniversary in 1997 in some ways as much a period piece as the debates themselves, and as necessary of historical reconstitution: the world turned upside down had become, finally, the world we had lost.[15] Happily, the recovery of the historiographical Putney is one of the tasks undertaken here, directly by William Lamont and more broadly by Blair Worden. But had time wrong-footed the anniversary? At the Folger Library conference, which was the occasion of the first presentation of many of the essays presented here, it might have seemed so. Much more was said about the contexts and ramifications than the debates themselves. Was it that there was no more to say, that the debates had been talked to death? Or, instead, was the stillness a marker of reticence, as if the things that most needed utterance were embarrassing or self-convicting – the little heresies that engender their own hypocrisies of silence? Had the twin tsunamis of revisionism – Conrad Russell's on the front end of the seventeenth century, Jonathan Clark's on the rear – ruined the liberal and Left interpretative paradigms from which the occasion had gained meaning? Had Mark Kishlansky's pace-setting studies of the New Model Army, however modified by the subsequent researches of Ian Gentles and Austin Woolrych, toppled the colossus, and shown how *little* Putney was in its own day?[16] Or was something even broader afoot – a cultural shift that had finally brought academe into loose synchrony with the wider neo-capitalist culture of the 'Anglo' world? How could Putney's 'poorest hee' expect to compete with the glitz and ever-present low-level eroticism of court studies? Had contemporary waves of disorder attuned modern historians not to the oppressiveness but the fragility of institutions, and awakened them to the anarchic tendencies in Leveller radicalism, an element seldom missed by hostile contemporaries, and far less easy to refute than the largely groundless charges of deliberate (rather than accidental) communism? Most worrisome to some, had Ireton been right?

As is the way of such things, fortunately, the embarrassment of the

---

[15] The third edition (1998) of R. C. Richardson's *The debate on the English revolution* is rich in the nostalgia-driven elucidation of post-World War II scholarship up to the moment of the revisionists. See also the excellent introduction and bibliography in Andrew Sharp (ed.), *The English Levellers* (Cambridge Texts in the History of Political Thought, 1998), vii–xxxiv.

[16] Conrad Russell, *The causes of the English civil war* (Oxford, 1990); *The fall of the British monarchies, 1637–1642* (Oxford, 1991); and many of the essays collected in *Unrevolutionary England, 1603–1642* (London, 1990). J. C. D. Clark, *Revolution and rebellion* (London, 1986). Mark Kishlansky, 'The army and the Levellers: the roads to Putney', *HJ* 22(4) (1979), 795–824; 'Consensus politics and the structure of debate at Putney', *JBS* 20(2) (1981), 50–69; 'Ideology and politics in the parliamentary armies, 1645–9' in John Morrill (ed.), *Reactions to the English civil war* (London, 1982), 163–83; *The rise of the New Model Army* (Oxford, 1979); 'What happened at Ware?', *HJ* 25 (1984), 827–39.

moment added impetus to the re-evaluation. The essays here, both those first presented at the conference and subsequently commissioned, devote appropriate attention both to the debates proper and their immediate circumstances, and to wider contexts. Those who write here have no party line to follow, are adherents of no single interpretive school, and, perhaps most notably, span several scholarly generations. Some disagree with others, both in the seemingly small but occasionally critical matters of attribution of key texts as well as in larger questions of historical hermeneutics. They concur, though, in sensing that not only has the last word not been said about Putney, but also that the kaleidoscope of time reveals as it also obscures, that re-examination of the debates and their multiple contexts and implications, including the variety of reactions to them, is a project necessary precisely as the easy consensus that permitted the repeated anthologisation of the same brief passages of an extended source document has dissolved. The contributors consider much that is relatively familiar, but also much that is quite new.

It is striking how little, until this volume, the text of the debate has itself been subjected to critical examination – a necessary but often routine procedure in editorial presentation, though here greatly complicated by the text's status as a transcription from underlying shorthand notes that have not survived. Dr Eric Sams, who used cryptographic techniques to crack Clarke's shorthand found elsewhere in Clarke's papers, reported briefly on it in his contribution to the introductory booklet accompanying the Harvester Press microfilm edition of the Clarke papers.[17] But it has been left to Frances Henderson, and to her uniquely, to master Clarke's system; in this volume (chapter 3) she applies her knowledge to a consideration of the text of the debates. She has uncovered evidence of Clarke's own difficulties in 1662 in deciphering the notes of 1647, not all of which perhaps he personally took. Shorthand practice was a rapidly developing art in the mid-seventeenth century. Unlike nineteenth- and early twentieth-century systems, it was clearly dependent upon exceptional mental gifts: a highly retentive memory as well as great powers of concentration. Leading practitioners boasted of decades of expertise. Thus it is impossible to generalise from one case to all. Yet Clarke's own apparent stumbles in transcription should alert us to regard virtually every passage with caution; not least, to consider where on the spectrum of possibility a given speech or remark is to be placed, from near-verbatim transcription through wearied and occasionally failing attempts to catch a gist. How far Clarke 'smoothed' his text is also a live question. By the time he tran-

---

[17] *Sir William Clarke manuscripts 1640–1664* (Brighton, 1979), 29–34.

scribed his notes, extended and apparently polished coverage of trials had created models and implicit standards. There was the late king's trial, which Clarke probably took or arranged to be taken in shorthand; there was, in the same year, Lilburne's 1649 trial; nearer to hand, the trials of the regicides, in the first of which Clarke himself had appeared as star witness.

Lesley Le Claire (chapter 2) provides a sensitive study of Clarke, as well as the fullest recounting of the history of his books and manuscripts. He is, as she says, a 'mysterious' man. A consummate bureaucrat trained to hear but not much to be seen, and an apparently adept trimmer, Clarke left surprisingly little trace of himself amidst all his collections, apart from frequent notations of book prices, both asked and paid. Le Claire reports a startling exception, a marginal notation in Clarke's copy of Charles' scaffold speech indicating his own presence upon that stage; was similar risk-taking entailed in Clarke's decision to transcribe the Putney debates? Did he, like George Thomason, have the ability to separate his own commitments from his collecting activities?[18] In either case, affirmative answers suggest a determination to preserve a record for posterity, undoubtedly the strongest motive for collection of tracts and political manuscripts in the seventeenth century.

For Firth, amongst whose works were two studies in military history,[19] the Putney debates, as the discussions at Reading and the more structured debates at Whitehall, were inseparable from their military venue. They were, to be sure, more than simply of military interest, but they were the discussions of soldiers. Something of that ethos was lost in the Woodhouse edition. Rightly (and Firth would have been last to disapprove), Woodhouse supplied a great deal of non-military documentary material; he and others who embarked upon the construction or reconstruction of the civil party of the Levellers set out to broaden, even to universalise, the context of Putney. It may fairly be said that until the work of Mark Kishlansky that mindset dominated the field. But it was Kishlansky's work that firmly restored the military setting to the Putney debates, and in the process markedly lowered both the civilian and the 'radical' profile of the supporters of *An agreement of the people*, the Leveller draft constitution that was the proximate 'cause' of the need for the discussions at Putney. Very powerfully, Kishlansky situated the debates at

---

[18] Amongst the curiosities of Clarke's bound books is a printed indulgence blank (Worcester College BB. 1. 14, no. 7). One can only speculate what it meant to this godly man. The volume otherwise largely consists of anti-papist polemic from 1584 to 1648.

[19] *Cromwell's army* (first edn 1902; repr. 1962); with Godfrey Davies, *The regimental history of Cromwell's army* (1940).

Putney within the matrix of army loyalty and discipline, its acute sense of honour (and, with that, responsibility), the political and military imperatives before and after Putney, and the abortive uprising (if that is what it was) at Ware.[20]

Two contributors to this volume have elsewhere powerfully added to the appreciation of the military setting of the Putney debates, even as they resisted the sole application of Kishlansky's occasionally Occamist evidentiary razor. Both Austin Woolrych and Ian Gentles allow for a greater degree and a somewhat earlier onset of ideological division within the army, both see religious motives more actively in play, and as a consequence view the debates as a more menacing occasion than does Kishlansky. It must be said, however, that Kishlansky's interpretive structure remains something that no student of Putney can afford to dismiss, and few do. For this volume, Woolrych has contributed an essay (chapter 4) of exceptional clarity treating, from the army's perspective, the political narrative in the months leading up to the Putney debates as well as a reconstruction of the dynamics of the debate itself; any further treatment here would be an exercise in arrogance as much as supererogation. Barbara Donagan's analysis of the army's relation to parliament (chapter 5), to civilian law and to accepted military practice (the laws of war), exposes the more sensitive spots of what could otherwise be a functioning relationship and, particularly in the matter of soldiers' indemnity, provides the fullest treatment yet of the background to the precise constitutional crux that, Michael Mendle (chapter 7) argues, the Leveller draft constitution *An agreement of the people* was intended to resolve.

Indeed, one of the distinctive features of this volume is the centrality that several contributors attribute to the issue of indemnity, which constituted what for the soldier was probably the most difficult element in the transition from war to peace. In 1977 John Morrill identified indemnity as a principal issue in the 'Army of Revolt of 1647'; the issue was further reprised in articles by Robert Ashton and Ann Hughes, and received further analytic and statistical treatment that also placed indemnity in the broader context of army–civilian relations in Ian Gentles' *New Model Army*.[21] But although the indemnity issue was long appreciated as a live

[20] Kishlansky, *Rise of the New Model Army*; 'What happened at Ware; 'Consensus politics' 'The army and the Levellers'. Professor Kishlansky's conclusions about the events at Ware have been rigorously challenged, especially by Professor Woolrych, *Soldiers and statesmen*, 283–6.

[21] John Morrill, 'The army revolt of 1647', first published in A. Duke and C. Tamse (eds.), *Britain and the Netherlands*, vol. VI (1977) and republished in Morrill, *The nature of the English revolution* (London, 1993), 307–31; Robert Ashton, 'The problem of indemnity, 1647–1648' in Colin Jones et. al. (eds.), *Politics and people in revolutionary England* (Oxford, 1986), 117–40; Ann Hughes, 'Parliamentary tyranny? Indemnity proceedings

one at Putney, it was construed as an ignoble and particularist deviation from the 'larger' concerns of the day. Readers can see how integral, however, indemnity was to those grander interests.

Studies of the Levellers as well as of the army are heavily text-centred. The London Levellers were, to a great extent, media creatures; archival resources, apart from those found in the army debates of 1647 and 1648 and related documents, are rather scarce. They are known in very considerable measure through their own writings; even tracts and accounts hostile to the Levellers, in responding to their press output, paradoxically affirmed the centrality of the Levellers' own self-presentation. The army too was, in 1647, heavily press-oriented. Its several representations and addresses, like those of the 1642 'war of words' between the king and the Houses of Parliament, were public displays. Surviving army accounts show the outlays for press propaganda; to take one notable example, the publication of the New Model chaplain Joshua Sprigge's apolgia-cum-history of the army, *Anglia rediviva*, was subsidised by army funds.[22] Radicals and leadership elements also had to communicate with the troops, which could also take printed form.

In such a logocentric but manifestly interested setting, there is little room for the death-of-the-author school of criticism. Necessary as accurate attribution is in studies of the Levellers and army opinion, it is notoriously difficult to do. Anonymous tracts abound; occasionally tracts were wilfully or ignorantly misattributed at the time of publication;[23] outright fraud was not unknown.[24] Few modern attempts at reattribution have won wide assent; scholarly prudence has also prompted frequent assertions of multiple authorship, which usually can neither be proved or disproved and sometimes have the air of attribution by majority vote. John Morrill and Philip Baker (chapter 6), thus, have been bold to argue with the conventional attribution to John Wildman of *The case of the armie truly*

---

and the impact of the civil war', *Midland History* 11 (1986), 49–78; Gentles, *New Model Army*, 120–39.

[22] £150 of army funds were used to reimburse the London bookseller John Partridge 'for the Losses hee sustained by Anglia Rediviva' (Chequers Ms. 782 at Chequers Court, included in microfilm edition of Clarke papers, item 4/8, reel 17, fol. 42v, dated 5 May 1657 [*sic*, for 1647]).

[23] For one example, see p. 128 below.

[24] As, for one example among many, the massive fraud perpetuated by Edward Hyde in authoring *Two speeches made in the House of Peers, on Munday the 19 of December, for, and against Accommodation, the one by the earl of Pembroke, the other by the Lord Brooke* (London, 1642[/43]). For the episode see Clarendon, *Life* (3 vols., Oxford, 1827), I:161–3 and Graham Roebuck, *Clarendon and cultural continuity: a bibliographical study* (New York, 1981), 79–80. The fraud still has its victims: see Conrad Russell, *The causes of the English civil war* (Oxford, 1990), 23, 58, 142; I count myself amongst the duped.

stated, an important, somewhat inflammatory tract nearly contemporaneous with *An agreement of the people*. *The case of the armie* clearly distressed Cromwell and Ireton at Putney; their assumption that John Wildman was the author has been taken at face value. Morrill and Baker make a case for Edward Sexby, a soldier perhaps more at the hub of a hypothetical flow-chart of army political activity than any other, but an individual who at this time, unlike in the 1650s, is rather a shadowy figure. Sexby fancied himself, it seems, as a master army propagandist;[25] he clearly was in touch with London radical elements; as a favoured agitator who had become a new agent, he had surprisingly close links to the military leadership, and had certainly not been hurt financially by that relationship.[26] Subject as he was to contrary pulls and of a mercurial temperament to boot, it is easy to see him both as the author or principal author of *The case of the armie truly stated*, which on Morrill and Baker's reading is an army-focused (if at spots Leveller-influenced) document, and the hothead and *enragé* of the debates. The Morrill–Baker argument makes new sense of the turns of rhetoric in the debates. So far as they could, Ireton and Cromwell would want to pin what they found objectionable in *The case of the armie* on the civilian outsider, rather than on Sexby, who even if they suspected his authorship was not lightly to be alienated; in other matters, though, they gave greater respect to *The cases of the armie*'s less sweeping demands than to the constitutional earthquake of *An agreement*. The fly in the ointment of this strategy was Sexby himself, whose sense of offence at the social insults of Ireton scraped at the thin skin of army solidarity.

Henry Ireton's role is probably most in need of re-examination. Barbara Taft's essay (chapter 9) in one way, Ian Gentles' (chapter 8) in another, examine this Socrates of the debates. Like the Athenian, Ireton's mien antagonised those around him; like him, too, this thinker of considerable adroitness, lucidity and intellectual sophistication left virtually nothing in print behind him, save for a letter from Ireland and, notably but characteristically, his anonymous contributions to army formulas for settlement. Ireton is, of course, remembered for his unyielding assertion at Putney that property in land or, to much the same effect, what amounted to a 'freehold' of trading rights, was the foundation of civil society. The latter point is often not fully appreciated. Far from being a gesture of inclusion towards the non-landed bourgeoisie, Ireton's equation of land and membership in a closed, if municipal, corporation with

---

[25] See below, p. 127.

[26] Gentles, *New Model Army*, 176 and n. 275; some attention might also be focused on the payment of £296 made in November 1647 to 'seuerall Agitators for Ext. expenses' (Chequers Ms. 782, fol. 44v). The parallel entry in the accounts in *Publications of the Thoresby Society*, 11 (1904), 145 identifies the payees as 'Agents'. Neither account specifically puts a date on the transactions.

trading privileges was as cruel a slap as any at the radicals. Amongst the strongest planks in the Leveller (as it would soon be called) platform was the demand for 'free trade'. This was not an issue having to do with tariffs and customs duties, as the term is usually taken today; rather, it was about the right of those who lacked heritable, limited trading privileges to set up and conduct their business. Undoubtedly Ireton's restriction cut to the quick of soldiers of raised political consciousness and ordinary background: what the property-restricted franchise meant to them was the denial of the prospect of their gaining entry, by political means, to the charmed circle of those permitted to trade. The intellectual springs of Ireton's vision have yet to be positively identified. Richard Tuck, plausibly, finds Grotius lurking in the shadows.[27] Whether or not that can be more definitively established, it is an intriguing suggestion, for Ireton who far more obviously than the Levellers can be described as a 'possessive individualist'[28] can also, in the manner of Grotius, be seen as a sort of 'possessive communitarian', in finding civil society and property to be Siamese twins.[29]

But no less than the army radicals, Ireton was tentered on a frame of contrary hopes and fears, and Ireton's political role was not bounded by the lines in the sand that he drew at Putney. As Barbara Taft shows, Ireton was a committed religious Independent; he was also a firm adherent of the radical version of the case that parliament's adherents took with them to war in 1642. Even at Putney he did not flinch from the position that the people could do anything that their safety required (although he also believed that the king and House of Lords possessed similar rights).[30] His outlook seems close in many respects in the spring and summer of 1647 to those with whom he would so differ in the autumn. But as author of, or at least the army's point man for, *The heads of the proposals*, he was also the icon of their sense of betrayal. Tactless in debate, as quick to choler as Sexby, he also felt the urge to compromise, to nurture and sustain consensus. Barbara Taft's essay, tracing Ireton's words, as reported by Clarke, across the army discussions at Reading, Putney and Whitehall reports on

---

[27] Richard Tuck, *Philosophy and government 1572–1651* (1993), 246, where Selden is also noted as a possible influence. A problem for a 'Grotian' Ireton may ultimately be theological, for the Arminian (and naturalistic) commitments of Grotius cannot easily be squared with Ireton's puritanism. It may be that Ireton's assertions at Putney that he would accede to the destruction of king, Lords and property if he saw the hand of God going about it may represent his attempt to square the circle of natural society and providential activity; *CP*, I:296, 306, 322, 405. Earlier, Tuck canvassed the possible connection to Selden: '"The ancient law of freedom": John Selden and the civil war' in John Morrill (ed.), *Reactions to the English civil war* (1982), 137–61, at 156.

[28] The phrase, of course, of C. B. Macpherson, *The political theory of possessive individualism* (Oxford, 1962).   [29] See Tuck, *Philosophy and government*, 174–7, 178–9.

[30] *CP*, I:389–91 and ch. 7 below.

this most enigmatic character. Ian Gentles traces a similar evidentiary base, with an eye to the several subsequent revisions of the *Agreement of the people*. His essay demonstrates, first, the unmistakable hold a founding constitutional agreement had for the politically aware and, secondly, that the franchise issue, exquisitely sensitive in the recorded debates at Putney but negotiable then and afterwards, was not in the fore of the subsequent attempts to fashion a foundation agreement. Gentles urges us to refocus upon the 'reserves', the powers withheld from the otherwise omnicompetent parliament. The reserves – a remarkable and crisply terse feature of the first *Agreement* – had degenerated in the third *Agreement* to something like a radicals' political wish-list. From one angle, the reserves appear as an emergent liberalism, a Bill of Rights before the fact; from another a programme of libertarianism and decentralisation, as Gentles describes it, that bordered on the nationally anarchic. Has the day come when the Levellers are perceived not primarily as proto-liberals or proto-socialists, but as the progenitors of contemporary America's citizen militias? A cursory websearch reveals that, apart from the predictable academic niches, the memory of the Levellers is kept alive by the British Libertarian Alliance and a Colorado-based outfit interested in the legalisation of marijuana and (because of a court case connected with drug use) jury nullification.[31]

To ask of the influence of Putney in the later seventeenth century is the historian's analogue to the Zen master's puzzle of the sound of one hand clapping. Even 'the Levellers' as a category seems to have little resonance in the era of Restoration and exclusion. But two essays in this volume suggest that the question of Leveller 'influence' is intrinsically *mal posé*. To focus solely upon the most *outré* of Leveller positions – the universal franchise and destruction of king and House of Lords – is to miss two things. First, the Levellers could be rather flexible on the former issue; on the second matter individual Levellers disagreed and changed their minds, with respect to the king (there appears to be a greater consistency of hostility towards the Lords). To look in those places for a Leveller legacy is to buy into a caricature. Yet there were parts of the Leveller platform that were only an assertive and less compromising version of enduring universalising rhetorics – the birthright of Englishmen, the legal equivalency of all free men – which could and did link up with royalist assertions of the rule of law in the face of parliamentary and then army tyranny. It is not surprising, therefore, that the most influential of all Leveller-inspired or Leveller-related documents was not *An agreement of the people* but John

---

[31] See the links at www.libertarian.org and www.levellers.org.

Lilburne's 1649 trial, in which Lilburne thumped that common-law Bible, Edward Coke's *Institutes*, at his judges.

But that is not all. The Levellers did not invent, did not monopolise, but did very much expand the range of popular political activity in London in the 1640s, just as they created a model for their century of the irrepressible pamphleteer. In this, unsurprisingly, they were sometimes matched by and sometimes associated with that other world of clandestine and semi-clandestine activists, the royalists. And, obviously, they did not spring from thin air. Richard Overton had before him the model of the Marprelate tracts, and, nearer to hand, the future Levellers drew upon the mass political activities of 1641 and 1642, when indeed such Leveller stalwarts as Lilburne, Overton, William Walwyn and the radical printer William Larnar cut their political teeth. Allowing these qualifications their full due, the public imagination grasped at the Levellers as activists who did not care to vet the social qualifications of their supporters and whose message was of political inclusion.

In this different light, the Levellers' influence emerges from the shadows; their ideas and actions were part of a larger matrix, which at times they expanded. As Patricia Crawford shows (chapter 10), active, participatory citizenship, like the myth of the freeborn Englishman, had a dynamic of inclusion that scraped against other logics of limitation and restriction; like the Christian sense of the spiritual equality of male and female, bond and free, the Leveller message, necessarily loosely construed, could not entirely be kept away from women. Perhaps it is better to say that Leveller notions and the participatory activities of non-elite women (if not quite the 'poorest shes') were part of the same universalising broth. And the Leveller political 'technology' co-ordinating press and crowd showed itself remarkably durable, much readier for use than the rusty musket over the hearth or the moth-eaten uniform in the chest. For all the differences, the 'Protestant joiner' of the exclusion era, Stephen College, is the political child of John Lilburne; in particular, College used (obviously with less success) Lilburne's 1649 trial both as a text in law and a model for behaviour.[32] Tim Harris' treatment (chapter 11) of popular political activity from the Levellers' heyday into the era of

---

[32] See *The arraignment, tryal and condemnation of Stephen Colledge for high-treason* (London, 1681). At 4–5, 7, 13, Lilburne's 1649 trial (also Stafford's) was repeatedly raised by College and replied to by North, LCJ and Sgt Jeffries, on the matters of counsel at trial, use of notes, and pleading guilty or not guilty; Coke was also used in Lilburne's fashion, mixed with talk of birthright. College's social background was an above- and below-the-table issue. See, for example, 24 (continued at 86, 93) on whether joiners should have pistols, a 'right' that College defends. The 'old' *Dictionary of national biography* article on College concludes with judgement of the man from his portrait: 'Although the features are plebeian, with high cheek-bones, coarse nose and mouth, long upper lip, and massive chin, he has an intelligent expression of eye, and is dressed above his station.'

Restoration and exclusion is a roadmap showing both the dead ends and the continuities. He stresses both activism and large notions of popular sovereignty. A recent essay by Quentin Skinner, while not addressing this issue directly, so reopens the notion of participatory politics that the social and cultural walls undoubtedly separating the high republicans and aristocratic Whig constitutionalists on one side and the populists on the other can now be seen to have some large chinks.[33]

The largely unreported discussions at Putney after Clarke's account of three days seemed to move toward compromise. But underlying passions did not go away, and Cromwell and Fairfax faced a difficult situation at the army rendezvous at Corkbush Field near Ware on 15 November. Mutinous troops had pinned a text of the *Agreement* to their hats. Once, certainly, and perhaps twice on that difficult day Oliver Cromwell ventured into the midst of them and personally tried to pluck the offending papers off their hats.[34]

Cromwell's actions can be fully explained by the exigencies of the moment. The leadership wanted soldiers to sign a remonstrance that, in effect, repudiated the *Agreement*; the taunting gesture of a mass of soldiers wearing the scorned *Agreement* as a badge of livery was in a military as well as political sense intolerable to Fairfax no less than to Cromwell. Perhaps, though, there is a story behind the story. The debates at Putney are battles of texts – *physical* texts. The army's 'book of declarations' was the source text of the 'engagements' that were the focus of the first day's debate. To the agents, they were also the memorial of the failure to keep them in the soldiers' interests, the source of the despair of *The case of the armie truly stated*.[35] Both books were also present in Putney Church and the quartermaster-general's quarters, the site of the second day's meetings.[36] But most inflammatory and most available of all was the *Agreement* itself. The constant references to it made by all the principal speakers as 'this paper' or 'that paper' suggest that it was in nearly every hand. Its physicality is to be sensed throughout. Cromwell on 28 October spoke tellingly of the utter absurdity, as he saw it, of crediting a press artefact of the last twenty-four hours (perhaps) with the standing of a constitution to alter the 'very Governement of the Kingedome . . . since itt was a Nation':

---

[33] Quentin Skinner, *Liberty before liberalism* (Cambridge, 1998).

[34] Woolrych, *Soldiers and statesmen*, 282–84, and Gentles, *New Model Army*, 223–4, review the evidence for these episodes, which were challenged by Kishlansky, 'What happened at Ware?' It is the second instance, with respect to Robert Lilburne's regiment, that is in dispute.

[35] *A declaration of the engagements, remonstrances, representations* (Oxford, 1647). Thomason dated this item [BL E. 409(25)] as 27 September 1647.

[36] Woolrych, *Soldiers and statesmen*, 230.

How do wee know if whilst wee are disputing these thinges another companie of men shall gather together, and shall putt out a paper as plausible perhaps as this? I doe nott know why itt might not be done by that time you have agreed upon this, or gott hands to itt, if that be the way. And not onely another, and another, butt many of this kinde.[37]

And on 29 October, the day of the franchise debate, Ireton in exasperation but perhaps also in contempt said something that suggests that, on that day as well, the *Agreement* had already moved from text to emblem:

Wee speake to the paper, and to that matter of the paper, nott to persons; and I hope noe man is soe much engaged to the matter of the paper, I hope our persons, and our hearts, and judgements are not [so] *pinn'd to papers*, butt that wee are ready to heare what good or ill consequences will flow from it.[38]

It is at least possible that the *Agreement*, obviously available as text, was also already pinned to the hats of its supporters.[39] One must suppose that would have added to the sense of outrage that Cromwell felt at Corkbush Field.[40]

That corporeality, the physicality of the *Agreement* in the debates, is easy for modern onlookers of the debates to pass by, but it was the epicentre of the tension of the occasion. That all the freeborn men of England should subscribe to '*this* paper' spoke to a boldness (though likely one born of fear) no less remarkable than similar moments of putting pen to paper: the regicides' death warrant, the American Declaration of Independence. In one respect it was more: this was not to be the work of a few but, in principle, of all. The failure does not detract from the significance of the attempt, and the record of the occasion when it was so passionately discussed, for all its many imperfections, will never want for readers and admirers.

---

[37] *CP*, I:236, 237.   [38] Ibid., I:310, emphasis added.

[39] Assuming, that is, that hats were worn inside Putney Church, which, given the Independent and sectarian commitments of most present, seems likely.

[40] Another intriguing if remote possibility is that the pinned *Agreements* at Corkbush Field were a taunting response to Ireton's comment at Putney.

Part 1

The Putney debates: the artefact

2 The survival of the manuscript

Lesley Le Claire

When Milton's fallen angels picked themselves up after their long tumble into Hell, the first thing they did was to sit down and have a formal debate on policy along very parliamentary lines: and those leisure moments that Milton considerately provides for them were also beguiled with philosophical discussion.

> Others apart sat on a Hill retir'd
> In thoughts more elevate and reason'd high
> Of Providence, Foreknowledge, Will, and Fate,
> Fixt Fate, free will, foreknowledge absolute,
> And found no end, in wandring mazes lost.[1]

Indeed, a recent essayist has argued persuasively that *Paradise lost* constituted 'a course in political education' with Milton as a sort of Socratic educator.[2] Be this as it may, it is not surprising that the fallen angels should have the habit of argument; their author belonged to a questioning and debating world. Even soldiers in that world ultimately were to reject their traditional role of blind obedience, refusing simply to do or die and demanding, in no uncertain terms, the right to reason why. At the end of the first civil war, as a formula for peace grew increasingly elusive, the grievances of the New Model Army – financial, religious, political – steadily rose to the surface. In 1647 they bubbled over and were voiced in meetings of the General Council of the Army at Putney. But posterity would never have known the precise nature of the arguments which raged back and forth if, in the midst of the army, there had not been a recording, rather than a fallen, angel: William Clarke was one of the junior army secretaries whose function was to take shorthand notes of the Council meetings and years later, after the Restoration, he transcribed these notes into longhand. It is thanks to him that we know that three and a half centuries ago, the soldiers of Cromwell's army, having beaten their so-called betters

[1] John Milton, *Poetical works*, ed. Douglas Bush (London, 1966), 244 (*Paradise lost*, Book II, ll. 557–61).

[2] M. A. Radzinowicz, 'The politics of *Paradise lost*' in K. Sharpe and S. N. Zwicker (eds.), *The politics of discourse* (Berkeley, 1987), 204–29, at 206.

in battle, had lost their respect for rank and birth and found themselves, to their own amazement, questioning the very foundations of the constitution and the powers of the Crown. Even so, what Austin Woolrych has called 'the blessed fact of [the] survival' of his manuscript[3] is indeed a considerable miracle – or, rather, a series of miracles. The story behind it is not only intriguing in itself but also throws light on some dim corners of Oxford in the last three centuries. It is a compound of several elements – a rather crusty librarian, a devoted scholar, a series of appalling college rows, a cultivated benefactor, a loyal widow – and, above all, the personality of the recording angel himself, William Clarke.

The Clarke papers were discovered in Worcester College, Oxford, towards the end of the nineteenth century. At that time, the college was small, undistinguished and on the face of it rather poor. There were only about twelve fellows and they seem to have been largely unaware of the riches lying dormant in their library. Certainly for several years there is no record of anything being spent on its upkeep. But they did have a librarian, Henry Pottinger, who seems, by all accounts, to have been a man of some eccentricity. A bibliomaniac rather than a bibliophile, he had poacher's pockets made in his coats to accommodate the books he purchased – some of which, one cannot help feeling, were acquired for the sole reason that no one could ever possibly wish to read them. He was furious when the Franco-Prussian war broke out – not because he was interested in the rights and wrongs of that conflict, but because it meant he could no longer haunt the bookshops and *quais* of Paris.[4] And yet, whatever his quirks, he had at least two admirable qualities: he both knew his library and, in the manner of all good librarians, made it his business to share his knowledge with interested scholars. He showed biographers of both William Laud[5] and Richard Deane[6] material relevant to their studies – and then, most importantly, he mentioned, quite casually perhaps, to a young historian of his acquaintance that there was some stuff in a cupboard in Worcester that might be worth his attention. The historian was Charles Firth.

To say the least, it was an odd juxtaposition of personalities – Pottinger the elderly antiquary and Firth the rather fiery young scholar. Firth had been trained in the rigorous school of Stubbs and was the friend and amanuensis of the great narrative historian of the English civil war, Samuel Rawson Gardiner. He was already engaged in his life-long battle

[3] Austin Woolrych, *Soldiers and statesmen: the General Council of the Army and its debates 1647–1648* (Oxford, 1987), 1.
[4] C. H. Wilkinson,'Worcester College Library', *The Transactions of the Oxford Bibliographical Society* 1 (Oxford, 1922–3), 65.
[5] W. H. Hutton, *William Laud* (London, 1895).
[6] J. B. Deane, *The life of Richard Deane* (London 1870).

to free the history faculty in Oxford from the taint of being 'an easy school for rich men'.[7] Pottinger, on the other hand, was convinced that young Firth was flogging a dead horse. Indeed in his submission to the University Commission of 1881, Pottinger insisted gloomily that Oxford had always been 'the place where research gets persecuted'. To support his theory he cited the fate of William Prynne. Describing him, rather curiously, as 'the man to whom we owe nearly all our knowledge of early constitutional history', he pointed out that the reward for his pains was not only to have his ears chopped off, but also, unkindest cut of all, to be deprived of his BA degree.[8] So there is a certain irony that it should be Pottinger who placed in Firth's hands the documentary evidence that was to establish the latter's reputation as one of the leading research historians of his day.

It was, of course, the sort of discovery that is the stuff of scholars' dreams. One can well imagine Firth's growing excitement as the full significance of the treasure-trove dawned on him. He found himself confronted with some forty-seven volumes. Of these, several are smallish quartos bound in leather – pocket-books, really – containing contemporary rough notes, often in shorthand; the rest are large folios, mostly bound in rather tattered vellum, containing fair copies made later. The Putney manuscript belongs to the second category, although it is a medium-sized folio bound in leather. A number of them had been listed in a catalogue of manuscripts in Oxford colleges drawn up some years earlier, but H. O. Coxe, the compiler of the catalogue, obviously did not realise their importance and in any case had not been shown all of them. They were no doubt mixed up with other material. Indeed, more than a century later, they were still in some disarray. Certainly Firth gives full acknowledgement to Pottinger's discovery of some additional volumes, 'including', he writes, 'the most valuable of all, that containing the debates of the Council of the Army in 1647'.[9]

Firth immediately set about creaming the manuscripts for the edition printed by the Camden Society in 1891 and 1894. With scholarly generosity, he showed his pre-publication drafts and proofs to Gardiner in time for his old friend and mentor to incorporate the first account of the Putney debates into the final volume of his *History of the great civil war*. Whatever cooler judgements modern revisionist scholarship may have pronounced on this whole area of English history, there is no doubt that Gardiner shared Firth's initial euphoria of discovery. He was to write:

[7] C. H. Firth, *Modern history in Oxford 1841–1918* (Oxford, 1920), 7.   [8] Ibid., 20.
[9] *CP,* I:viii.

Mr Firth's discovery of the Clarke Papers throws every other accession of material into the shade . . . Taken altogether they bring strongly out the conservative and hesitating side of Cromwell's character, whilst they also bring us, as we have never been brought before, into the very heart of that army in the midst of which Cromwell lived and moved, and enable us to trace the movements of political thought which afterwards developed themselves in the constitutional experiments of the Commonwealth.[10]

Editing Clarke's documents was no easy task: a comparison of Firth's text with the originals demonstrates how meticulously he approached it. No further attempt was made until half a century later and even then it was only the famous debates that were tackled by A. S. P. Woodhouse in an edition under the title *Puritanism and liberty*. The date – 1938 – was perhaps significant. There was a growing awareness of another looming threat to English liberty and democracy. Woodhouse's edition is particularly useful for the clarity of its introduction, but his editing is freer than Firth's and occasionally his tampering with the text is questionable. For example, he suggests that when Rainborough demands to know why, just because a man is poor, he should be 'pressed', the reading should be '[op]pressed',[11] whereas clearly the sense in that company is 'pressed into military service'. Forty years after *Puritanism and liberty*, the Harvester Press produced a microfilm edition of all Clarke's manuscripts from 1640 to 1664 under the direction of Gerald Aylmer, whose admirable introductory booklet complements both Firth and Woodhouse.[12]

It is interesting that Firth's courage seems to have failed him when it came to tackling Clarke's shorthand even though, as Frances Henderson has pointed out, there was increasing interest in compressed writing systems in the eighteenth and nineteenth centuries.[13] On the other hand, he, like his successors, probably felt that the task required a particular and rarefied intelligence. So it was not until the 1970s that Clarke's shorthand code was cracked by the distinguished cryptanalyst, musicologist and brilliant challenger of orthodox Shakespearean scholarship, Dr Eric Sams. The subsequent immense task of translation and commentary was then undertaken by Frances Henderson and forms the subject of her chapter in this book.[14]

The reason for Clarke's papers falling into the hands of Worcester College, Oxford, is perhaps the most curious part of the whole story. It is

---

[10] S. R. Gardiner, *History of the great civil war 1642–1649* (4 vols., London, 1891), III:vi.

[11] *P&L*, 59. For further consideration of Woodhouse's edition, see ch. 12, below.

[12] G. E. Aylmer, *Sir William Clarke manuscripts 1640–1664* (Brighton, 1979).

[13] Frances Henderson, 'The hidden hand of William Clarke', *Worcester College Record* (Oxford, 1998), 70–3.

[14] Eric Sams, 'Sir William Clarke's shorthand' in Aylmer, *Sir William Clarke manuscripts*, 29–34. Henderson, ch. 3 below.

at this point that the college rows already mentioned played their part. It is true that the official history of the university has done much to correct the commonly held view that the intellectual life of eighteenth-century Oxford was at an abysmally low ebb. Of course, there *were* serious and cultivated men in the university – William Clarke's son George was one such – and in the context of the present study, historians have reason to be grateful that in 1724, twelve years before George's death, the Regius Professorship of Modern History – Firth's chair – was established under King George I. Nevertheless, there are times when it is difficult not to feel that the scathing criticisms of the young Gibbon, priggish adolescent though he may have been, were fully justified.[15] It was undoubtedly a deeply contentious time in Oxford. A contemporary writer remarks, 'we see Whigs engaged against Whigs, Tories against Tories, Masters against Doctors and Heads of Houses, Senior Fellows against Junior Fellows, one college against another college and many colleges against themselves'.[16] All Souls was one such college at war with itself, an internal strife for which it was to pay a high price. George Clarke was a fellow of All Souls from the age of twenty until his death fifty-six years later. He had quite an important public career: among other offices, he acted as judge-advocate general for the last two decades of the seventeenth century; he was secretary to Prince George of Denmark (the husband of Queen Anne), and finally became a lord of the admiralty. But on the death of Queen Anne, he largely retired from public life to Oxford, although he remained member of parliament for the University. Very much the virtuoso and man of taste, his interests ranged far and wide but, of these, architecture took pride of place. He was the personal friend of many contemporary architects and not only collected their designs, but also about a third of the drawings of Inigo Jones. Indeed, it has been argued that it was Clarke quite as much as Burlington and Colen Campbell who turned the face of English architecture towards the Palladian style. His interest was practical as well as theoretical. From 1703 until his death in 1736 he was continuously involved as consultant and designer of Oxford buildings. In 1703 he offered to build, at his own expense, a set of lodgings for All Souls, to be his for life and thereafter to act as a residence for the warden. These buildings were part of his grand neo-Gothic design for the college and was largely realised by his friend Hawksmoor. 'God send us', runs an entry in the Warden's Register for 1706, 'more such ample Benefactours' – a devout prayer that heads of similar modern institutions would undoubtedly echo. In the case of All Souls, the prayer was certainly answered, but

---

[15] E. Gibbon, *Memoirs of my life*, ed. B. Radice (London, 1984), 75–91.
[16] L. S. Sutherland and L. G. Mitchell (eds.), *The history of the University of Oxford. V. The eighteenth century* (Oxford, 1986), 100.

as the years passed Clarke's own generosity diminished as he grew increasingly disillusioned by internecine feuds within the college. In the way of men of affluence, he almost made a hobby of frequent tinkering with his will, but in 1728 his distaste for this quarrelsome atmosphere drove him into a radical alteration of his bequests. He was already involved in building schemes for several other colleges. Howard Colvin calls him one of the academic amateurs 'who, Vitruvius in hand, had done his best to rescue the buildings of the University from the unlettered conservatism of the master masons'.[17] In addition to All Souls, Christ Church, Queen's, Brasenose and Magdalen were all on the receiving end of his ministrations, to their great benefit and his considerable enjoyment. His plans for Worcester College were already well advanced and it was this struggling foundation on the edge of the city that he chose as the recipient of his main benefaction. He not only left the college money for future building, but he also left it his magnificent library. All Souls has never quite forgiven him, but Worcester, on the other hand, understandably, refers to him as 'almost our founder'. A considerable part of his library – and this, of course, is what is relevant to the present narrative – consists of books and papers inherited from his father.

William Clarke is a more mysterious figure than his son. He was born about 1623. What form his early education took is not clear, but we know he was admitted a student of the Inner Temple in 1646 and was later called to the bar although he never practised as a lawyer. He seems to have acquired his secretarial skills under the eye of John Rushworth, who had been one of the under-clerks of the Commons, and he was certainly a member of the army secretariat by the mid-1640s. From 1647 to 1650 he was secretary to the General Council of the Army. In 1650, he accompanied Cromwell on his Scottish campaign and remained in Scotland after Cromwell's return south. He was based in Scotland for the whole of the interregnum, acting as secretary to successive senior officers in command there. His longest spell of duty was under General Monck from 1654 to 1660. The relationship between the two men was clearly one of mutual respect. When Robert Lilburne (the rather less radical brother of John Lilburne) handed over his command to General Monck in 1654, he warmly recommended Clarke to him as one who would be 'most useful and servissable'[18] and so indeed Monck found him. Clarke was with Monck on his march south in January 1660 to restore a civilian government, a move which, whether intended or not, was to result in the Restoration. Initially Clarke's association with Monck plus his new-found

---

[17] H. Colvin, *A catalogue of architectural drawings of the 18th and 19th centuries in the library of Worcester College, Oxford* (Oxford, 1964), xviii.

[18] J. D. Griffith Davies, *Honest George Monck* (London, 1936), 135.

royalism (which in all probability arose not so much from conviction as from an understandable instinct for self-preservation) profited him greatly – but a few years later they were to be the death of him. He was given a knighthood and the great lodge and sixty acres of land in Marylebone Park; in 1661 he was appointed secretary-at-war; he had also become father of a hopeful son – but then, on 5 June 1666, there is a bleak little entry in the diary of Samuel Pepys, 'Some say that Sir William Clarke is dead of his leg being cut off.'[19] The poor man was indeed dead. He was one of the many casualties suffered by the English fleet during the bloody four-day battle of the second Dutch war. A modern biographer of Pepys ranks this battle with Dunkirk and the Armada fight as 'one of the longest, fiercest and most desperate actions ever fought in home waters'.[20] Clarke was with Monck (now the duke of Albemarle) on his flagship when a cannon ball shattered his leg and he died two days later. He was forty-three. But despite the hubbub of recrimination which broke out after this costly defeat, Albemarle (who was largely blamed) found time to commend the widow and child of his old friend and colleague to the favour of the king, describing him as 'a faithful and indefatigable servant of the state'. He could not, he said, 'express too much kindness to his memory'.[21]

Pepys knew William Clarke slightly and is one of the few people to give us a contemporary view of him. At one point he refers to him as one of Albemarle's 'sorry instruments',[22] but this is a piece of Pepysian gossip – he is repeating the view of his patron, the earl of Coventry; their malice is really directed at Albemarle, whom they both disliked and mistrusted, rather than at Clarke. Elsewhere Pepys speaks of Clarke with something approaching affection as 'a brisk blade'[23] and 'a very civil man'.[24] In fact there were considerable similarities between the two men. Both were highly trusted and competent civil servants; both were upwardly mobile in society; both, interestingly, used the same shorthand primer – Shelton's *Tachygraphy* – and both, in Pepys's phrase, were 'in all things curious',[25] as demonstrated by their multifaceted libraries. The cataloguer of Pepys' library was to write:

Were the diary non-existent and were no other source of knowledge available, a judgment of Pepys's character formed upon a consideration of the contents of his library would reveal him to be a man of great breadth of interest and catholicity of taste, an inquisitive scholar conversant with more languages than his own, and a person in whom a love of order and neatness in detail was paramount.[26]

[19] R. Latham and W. Matthews (eds.), *The diary of Samuel Pepys* (11 vols., London, 1970–83), VII:135.   [20] R. Ollard, *Pepys: a biography* (London, 1974), 151.
[21] *CP,* I:ix.   [22] Latham and Matthews, *The diary of Samuel Pepys*, VII:151.
[23] Ibid., VII:84.   [24] Ibid., IX:317.   [25] Ibid., II:188.
[26] F. Sidgwick, *Bibliotheca Pepysiana. A descriptive catalogue of the library of Samuel Pepys, II* (London, 1914), i.

These words could have been written with equal truth about William Clarke – especially since in his case a personal diary *is* non-existent[27] and there are not many other sources of knowledge. But the same love of order was also paramount in him and drove him, after the Restoration when perhaps he had more leisure, into organising his papers and books in a remarkably methodical way. One might have expected a man who had prospered under the new regime to be tempted to distance himself from his previous associations, but instead he undertook the long and immensely tedious task of transcribing his rough notes and shorthand into fair copies, destroying the originals as he did so. Working through his notes chronologically, he had reached 1650 at the time of his death, – so the material for the next ten years when he was in Scotland survived in its original state. On the face of it, it largely consists of letters to and within Scotland with minutes of courts martial and notes about the Assessment (or 'Sesse'), the direct tax on property levied in Scotland to help maintain the English army. This levy was clearly deeply resented and extremely difficult to administer. However, it is in these manuscripts that the bulk of the surviving shorthand is to be found and it is for this period, therefore, that the final results of Frances Henderson's research will be so important.

The instinct for book collecting often begins early. On the title-page of a short treatise on oratory, published in Padua in 1574, there is written in a childish hand, 'William Clarke his book, March 10 1630'. Five years later he has added the wistful note, 'non possum scribere Italianum, nec possum bene legere'. Whether the bookish little boy ever became fluent in Italian is not known, but his interest in the language must have continued because at some point he acquired Florio's great dictionary. And he acquired much else. Poetry, drama, historical romances, voyages and travels, military science, natural history, alchemy, law, finance and political theory are all represented. Inevitably, there is an enormous number of sermons, but there is comic and satirical literature too; he had an eye for a humorous, not to say bawdy, cartoon. Matthew Seccombe,[28] who made a comprehensive survey of the whole collection some years ago when he was working on the Wing STC, tends to regard some of his books as the typical furniture of a gentleman's library. This is a little severe, perhaps, although it is perfectly true that books are often bought without being

---

[27] William Clarke did keep a brief, official diary relating to the events of his last service at sea, 23 April–1 June 1666 (BL Add. Ms. 14286).

[28] No one who has struggled through the tangled undergrowth of seventeenth-century pamphlets can fail to be grateful to Dr Seccombe for the paths he has cut through it. I learned a great deal from him some years ago when he was working on pamphlet and newsbook collections in Oxford and elsewhere. Worcester College Library has a particular cause for gratitude in that he bequeathed to it the card catalogue he made of the college's Wing entries.

read. But as representing the wide-ranging tastes of a cultivated man in the mid-seventeenth century, it is an interesting collection by any standards. It is also a great deal more: it is difficult to believe that it was merely a polite interest or an official sense of duty that motivated the acquisition of so much of the background literature to the events through which he lived and the remarkable outburst of political ideas that sprang from them, 'a body of political theory which questioned every traditional assumption about political and social hierarchy'.[29] Indeed, it is not too large a claim to say that it is possible to trace the growth of that body of political theory along the shelves of Clarke's library. His legal background and parliamentary connections doubtless predisposed him towards the purchase of seminal texts; at a time when most of his countrymen were still comfortable to the point of complacence with the English recipe for the balanced polity of 'mixed monarchy', he seems to have been reading Machiavelli. Critics of the Crown, reluctant to level personal accusations against the king, often took refuge in the 'evil counsellors' argument, pointing the finger at men like the earl of Strafford and Laud; Clarke, perhaps testing the validity of this argument, later bound together a whole volume of material devoted to Strafford and made a fair copy from rough transcripts of the trial of Archbishop Laud. His books become steadily more republican in tone, from the comparatively moderate writings of Henry Parker to the sermons that quoted the Bible to justify resistance to an ungodly ruler, and then on to the justifications made by government propagandists such as Anthony Ascham and Marchamont Nedham for the trial and execution of the king and the establishment of the republic. As one would expect, he has Milton's *The tenure of kings and magistrates* and his *Eikonoklastes,* which both appeared in 1649. In fact several of Milton's writings 'of the left hand' are in his collection and some of the early poems. Sadly, he died a year before the appearance of *Paradise lost* but he would have recognised many elements of the great debate and wondered perhaps, as others have done since, that Milton should not only have given Satan the best tunes but also the most cogent republican arguments.[30] His preoccupation with evolving constitutional ideas and the problem of obedience continued during the Commonwealth and Protectorate. The theory of political obligation defined in part by Ascham and Nedham was swept to its brilliant if bleak conclusion in 1651 with the

---

[29] A. Woolrych, 'Political theory and political practice' in C. A. Patrides and Raymond B. Waddington (eds.), *The age of Milton: backgrounds to seventeenth-century literature* (Manchester, 1980), 34–71, at 47.

[30] But see Blair Worden's explanation in his 'Milton's republicanism and the tyranny of heaven' in G. Bock, Q. Skinner and M. Viroli (eds.), *Machiavelli and republicanism* (Cambridge, 1990), 225–45.

publication of the most famous political treatise of all, Thomas Hobbes' *Leviathan*, of which Clarke acquired the beautiful first edition. He also acquired James Harrington's much more liberal *The commonwealth of Oceana*, which appeared in 1656.

It could be argued that the books cited above merely indicate the interest of an intelligent man who was involved in the business of government and wished to keep abreast of contemporary political thought. Moreover, most of these writers, however republican or anti-royal, are not in any sense democratic. But a closer examination of Clarke's remarkable pamphlet collection brings a sense of a distinct change of gear in the mid-1640s and the realisation that he was not only abreast of his peers, but in some ways ahead of them. He collected some 6,000 pamphlets and broadsides and at some point bound them into volumes – for the most part in a loosely thematic way. Of course, other men were making similar collections, George Thomason in London for example, and John Rushworth, Clarke's friend and mentor, although sadly, his was dispersed on his death. But one of the striking aspects of Clarke's collection is the amount of Leveller material it contains. However much modern historians may disagree about the nature and importance of the Leveller movement, the fact remains that a cool, level-headed, contemporary observer sensed that 'the combination of radical journalism and pamphleteering, ideological zeal, political activism, and mass organisation that prevailed in England from 1646 to 1649'[31] was an astonishing phenomenon. The writings of prominent figures in the movement – Richard Overton, William Walwyn and, of course, John Lilburne – are all represented. Of the eighty pamphlets written by John Lilburne, Clarke had nearly seventy, bound in a single volume with other material which is very revealing of Lilburne's strange and passionate career and of what has been aptly called his 'boundless capacity for identifying his own sufferings with the cause of liberty'.[32] He even has pamphlets which indicate his awareness of the Diggers, the fringe group on the left of the Leveller movement whose leader was the agrarian communist Gerrard Winstanley. In fact, there is one pamphlet by Winstanley which has not been found anywhere else, *England's spirit unfoulded, or, an incouragement to take the engagement*, which is interesting as being one of the most political of Winstanley's statements and shows that despite attempts by the Commonwealth government to suppress the Digger experiment, he still felt the republican regime was the country's best hope.[33]

---

[31] G. E. Aylmer (ed.), *The Levellers in the English revolution* (London, 1975), 9.

[32] F. D. Dow, *Radicalism in the English revolution 1640–1660* (Historical Association Studies, Oxford, 1985), 38.

[33] G. E. Aylmer (ed.), '*England's spirit unfoulded* . . . A newly discovered pamphlet by Gerrard Winstanley,' *Past and Present* 40 (July 1968), 3–15.

But perhaps the most important aspect of Clarke's collection is the way it can be seen to extend the themes of the manuscripts. The manuscript of the Laud trial and the volume of Strafford pamphlets have already been mentioned. For the crucial year of 1647 there is one large group of pamphlets in which the rising tension between parliament and army crackles through the volume like a forest fire in the undergrowth as increasingly angry edicts from parliament against petitions from the soldiers are interspersed with the actual petitions themselves. In another unique pamphlet there is a pathetic *cri de coeur* from a man called James Pitson: 'I beseech your honours to pardon my boldness in writing', he says, 'but I have waited these two years for my money out of purse, and have spent as much in waiting as the money is worth and have had nothing to live on these twelve months whereby to maintain myself and my family but what I have borrowed, and am now speedily to go for Ireland and have nothing to leave my family in my absence'; there could hardly be a more graphic description of the seed-bed in which Leveller ideas took root. Again, anyone with an ear for language can hear echoes of the rhetoric of Lilburne behind the democratic eloquence of Wildman, Rainborough and Sexby at Putney. Similarly, the Scottish pamphlets of the 1650s reflect the preoccupations with matters of law and order to be found in the manuscripts for the same period. Some years ago, this material provided a moment of very real excitement. Among a volume of pamphlets for 1650, Clarke has inserted a little manuscript letter in very faded ink in his own unmistakeable hand. It is dated Musselburgh, 3 August.[34] Closer reading revealed that it was that most famous of Cromwellian manifestoes to the ministers of the Kirk, 'Is it therefore infallibly agreeable to the Word of God all that you say? I beseech you in the bowels of Christ think it possible that you may be mistaken.' It is a reproof to bigots for all time and it seems clear that Clarke was with Cromwell before the battle of Dunbar and had taken dictation of the letter. The sheer physical misery of that campaign is well documented. The Lammas floods were at their height and Cromwell's supply ships had great difficulty making port at Dunbar. His troops lacked tents and were ravaged by dysentry: 'Our bodies [were] enfeebled with fluxes, our strength wasted with watchings; want of drink, wet and cold being our constant companions, much impaired our strength and courage and made altogether useless above 2,000 men which at severall times we were forced to send to Berwick.'[35] It is a tribute both to Clarke's professionalism and to his sense of the importance of the letter that despite these terrible conditions, he remained true to his training and scrupulously made and kept a copy.

[34] I am most grateful to Dr Seccombe for drawing my attention to this pamphlet.
[35] *Mercurius politicus*, 12–19 September 1650, 227 – a newsbook in Clarke's collection.

There is one other very remarkable pamphlet which must be mentioned as indicative of Clarke's rare knack for finding himself at the centre of things. In his copy of the well-known account of the execution of Charles – *King Charls his speech made upon the scaffold at White-hall-gate, immediately before his execution* – he has placed a small asterisk beside the phrase 'a Gentleman that touched the Ax' and in the opposite margin another asterisk with his own initials, 'W.C.'. It was a trick Rushworth also used to hint at *his* attendance at some momentous event.[36] In this instance, it reveals an interesting ambivalence in Clarke. He was very well aware of the horrible fate of men whose presence on that scaffold could damn them as regicides and yet at the same time, without wishing to broadcast his presence there, he wanted posterity to know. No doubt he had been required to take notes of the proceedings and, for the same reason, it is also clear that he was present at the king's trial: proof positive of his recording role on that occasion is found in the testimony he was called on to give at the trial of regicides in 1660 when he admitted to seeing several of the accused at the trial of the king, adding in the case of Harrison, 'as I took notice of it in a Book'.[37]

The question remains, why was Clarke taking all this trouble to put his material in order? Perhaps not for the first time, he had thoughts of emulating his friend John Rushworth by producing his own 'Historicall Collections', aiming, like Rushworth, 'whilst things were fresh in memory, to separate Truth from Falsehood'.[38] But here again, one can compare him to Pepys who, in similar fashion, amassed notes throughout his long life in the hope, never realised, of writing a great history of the navy. Sadly, the cannon ball across the deck of the *Royal Charles* put an end to the possibility that Clarke might do the same thing for the army, but it is interesting that the man who married Clarke's widow, Samuel Barrow, who had been chief physician to the army in Scotland and later physician in ordinary to Charles II, did think seriously of writing a history of the period[39] and therefore may well have realised the importance of his predecessor's archive and been instrumental in its preservation. But all that can be said with certainty about Clarke is that he had a very real sense of the importance of events as they were happening and of the need to record them.

[36] F. Henderson, ' "Posterity to judge" – John Rushworth and his "Historicall Collections" ', *Bodleian Library Record* 15 (1996), 250.

[37] [Nottingham, Heneage Finch, earl of], *An exact and most impartiall accompt of the indictment, arraignment, trial, and judgment (according to law) of twenty nine regicides* (London, 1660). This pamphlet in Clarke's collection had escaped my notice and I am most grateful to Michael Mendle for drawing my attention to it.

[38] Henderson, ' "Posterity to judge" '. Frances Henderson's article is an admirable account of Rushworth's methods, aims, critics and the possible tampering with his text by later, 'politically correct' editors.

[39] C. H. Firth (ed.), *Stuart tracts 1603–1693* (Westminster, 1903), xxviii.

Clarke indicates on the fair copy of the Putney manuscript that he began his transcription in 1662. Fifteen years had elapsed – fifteen enormously eventful years – since as a young man of twenty-four he had sat at the meeting in Putney scribbling down the speeches of the debaters as fast as he could, and in several cases he was now listening to the voices of ghosts. But without any fanfare or introduction, page after page of his elegant longhand (there are very few crossings-out) recreate the extraordinary atmosphere in Putney Church, the mixture of fear and religious exaltation, of logical argument and angry protest. The cross-currents of the ideas running through the literature he had collected are all met in the whirlpool of Putney. It is true that sometimes the speeches are interminably long; sometimes, like the fallen angels, the debaters are 'in wandering mazes lost', occasionally the historical myths which so often underpin the arguments meet one another head-on – as when Ireton, echoing Sir Edward Coke, refers to 'the Civill Constitution of this kingedome, which is originall and fundamentall, and beyond which I am sure noe memory of record does goe',[40] and is challenged with the interjection 'Nott before the Conquest', that contradictory myth, so much loved by the Levellers, of the Norman yoke which supposedly had suppressed the old Anglo-Saxon freedoms. But despite the confusion, words and phrases leap off the page and personalities emerge in vivid colours. The apocalyptic style of William Goffe nearly always has a sympathetic reception – 'hee hath never spoke butt hee hath touched my heart'[41] says Ireton, but one feels that it is Cromwell, weary and depressed and fearing anarchy, whose heart is more deeply touched; when Goffe declares that a voice from heaven has revealed to him that they sinned against the Lord 'in tampering with his enemies',[42] he replies hesitantly, 'I am one of those whose heart God hath drawne out to wait for some extraordinary dispensations, according to those promises that hee hath held forth of things to be accomplished in the later time',[43] but at the same time he warns against trusting in imagined visions. It is easy for the modern mind to underestimate the religious theme at Putney, especially since the long prayer meeting is not reported in full. The fear that haunts them all is that if God is not with them, then he is with some other party and the desire for a seeking after God is never far away.

On several occasions, the friction between Cromwell and Rainborough manifests itself. When Cromwell, with his characteristic distaste for abstractions, points to the practical difficulties of implementing the soldiers' demands for their natural and inalienable rights, Rainborough rounds on him with a soldier's reply: if difficulties had scared them, they

---

[40] *CP,* I:300.   [41] Ibid., I: 256.   [42] Ibid., I: 374.   [43] Ibid., I: 378.

would never have gone to war in the first place – and then, blithely discarding precedent, that foundation rock of constitutional law, he declares, 'if writinges bee true, there hath bin many scufflinges betweene the honest men of England and those that have tyranniz'd over them' and therefore if people, freemen as they are, find the old laws do not suit them, there is no reason why they should not be changed to new.[44] Ireton emerges as the most brilliant of the debaters – and the most intellectually arrogant: when he argues lucidly, but at great and tactless length, in favour of a property qualification for all voters, he provokes a most bitter outcry from Sexby:

> Wee have engaged in this Kingedome and ventur'd our lives and itt was all for this: to recover our birthrights and priviledges as Englishmen, and by the arguments urged there is none . . . itt seemes now except a man hath a fix't estate in this Kingedome, hee hath no right in this Kingedome – I wonder wee were soe much deceived! If wee had nott a right to the Kingedome, wee *were* meere mercinarie souldiers.[45]

There are sudden, touching, human moments – as when the trooper Robert Everard says humbly, 'Though I have many impediments in my speach, yett I thanke you that you will heare mee speake . . . For my parte I am butt a poore man, and unacquainted with the affaires of the Kingedome, yett this message God hath sent mee to you, that there is great expectation of suddaine destruction.'[46] A little earlier than this, cutting across all the talk, comes an even blunter insistence on the need for speedy action – a grim little reminder of the background to the whole discussion – 'if wee tarry longe', says Captain Audley, 'the kinge will come and say who will be hang'd first'.[47] The king casts a very long shadow over the proceedings at Putney. It is one of the first occasions that 'the man of blood'[48] is used to describe him and the debaters are fearfully conscious of the smell of treason in the air. Finally, from that hot-headed middle-class champion of the underdog, Colonel Rainborough, there comes the famous and most explicit statement of all – 'words that still ring in our ears after three and a half centuries'[49] – 'I thinke that the poorest hee that is in England hath a life to live as the greatest hee, and therfore truly, Sir, I thinke itt's cleare, that every man that is to live under a Governement ought first by his owne consent, to putt himself under that Governement.'[50]

---

[44] Ibid., I:245.
[45] Ibid., I:326. I have italicised 'were' because Sexby is harking back to the famous, proud boast of the New Model that they were not 'mere mercenary soldiers' as expressed in *The declaration of the army*, 14 June 1647, 46.   [46] *CP,* I:285–6.   [47] Ibid., I:265.
[48] Ibid., I:383.
[49] Ian Gentles, *The New Model Army in England, Ireland and Scotland 1645–1653* (Oxford, 1992), 209.   [50] *CP,* I:301.

And in the short run, it all came to nothing. As these echoes from the past resonated through Clarke's mind, he must also have remembered the aftermath for, yet again, he was there, watching from the sidelines. The mutiny at Ware was the sad, but perhaps inevitable, postscript to the excitement of Putney and Clarke wrote his eyewitness account on the same day that it happened. The story is well known. On 15 November General Fairfax held a review at Corkbush Field, near Ware. It was to be the first of three. Initially there was no trouble, the soldiers expressing their loyalty to their senior officers. But then, against orders, the regiments of Harrison and Robert Lilburne appeared on the field. They had driven away most of their officers and had copies of *An agreement of the people* stuck in their hats. They were shouting for 'England's freedom! Soldiers' rights!' Fairfax and Cromwell acted swiftly to suppress this mutiny. A council of war was called on the field and three of the mutineers were tried and condemned to death. Only one of them, chosen by lot, paid the penalty, being shot to death by his comrades at the head of his regiment. On the face of it, Clarke's account of the incident is very much what one would expect from a good civil servant; it is dispassionate and official and tallies with Fairfax's report to parliament. He clearly sees the necessity to restore discipline. The army was in real danger of becoming an armed mob. As Austin Woolrych points out, 'for soldiers to march to the General's rendezvous against orders and without their officers was a highly mutinous act. . . Mutiny on this occasion, which was designed as a great public reaffirmation of the army's unity and discipline in face of the threat posed by the king's flight, was particularly serious, and the treatment of its perpetrators was remarkably (though characteristically) lenient.'[51] But there is a certain dryness of tone when Clarke says that after the summary shooting of their colleague, the soldiers were then 'sensible of their error'. There is, after all, nothing like a swift execution for concentrating the minds of the onlookers. And it is also interesting that he thinks it worth mentioning that the disconsolate figure of John Lilburne, who had just been released from one of his many imprisonments, was in the background – 'John Lilburne came this day to Ware: but things not succeeding at the Rendez-vous according to expectation, came not further.'[52]

George Clarke was barely six years old when his father was killed and can hardly have known him. No doubt his mother taught him to revere his

---

[51] Woolrych, *Soldiers and statesmen*, 285.

[52] William Clarke, *A full relation of the proceedings at the rendezvous of that brigade of the army that was held at Cork-bush Field in Hartford parish on Monday last* (15 November 1647). Reprinted in Francis Baron Maseres (ed.), *Select tracts relating to the civil wars in England* (2 vols., London, 1815), I:lviii.

memory and we owe a double debt of gratitude to her in that she preserved as her son's inheritance not only the precious manuscripts, but
also the books that give us a key to the temper and quality of her
husband's mind. But whether William's mind would always have been in
tune with his son's had he lived to see him reach man's estate is another
matter. It is true that, like his father, George held the office of secretary-
at-war and had some direct military experience – he attended William III,
for example, at the battle of the Boyne. He also collected some interesting
Irish siege plans, although one feels that he looked at them with an architectural eye. But on the whole he lived in a very much more elegant and
cushioned world than his father and in a very different intellectual
climate. It is a far cry from campaigns on bleak Scottish moorlands to
Palladian villas basking in the sunlight of the Restoration, from soldiers
arguing fiercely and earnestly about the rights of man at Putney to sophisticated virtuosi discussing questions of taste at Oxford high tables. Nor is
it known what George felt about the company his father kept during the
war or the radical content of his library. As a collector himself, he does
seem to have had a sense of the importance of the pamphlets because he
tried to persuade the Bodleian Library to buy the Thomason collection,[53]
which suggests that he realised the two sets were complementary and that
scholars would benefit by having them in one place. But he almost certainly differed from his father in his attitude to Charles I. As a connois-
seur, he would naturally feel sympathy for a king whom Rubens described
as 'le plus grand amateur de peinture du monde' and who had been
patron of the architect he admired above all others. He was by no means a
Jacobite Tory but the martyrisation of Charles I had been a growth industry throughout his formative years. He himself had acquired several icons
of the blessed memory – for example, the subscription set engraved by
George Vertue of 'The True Portraitures and Characters of the Royal
Martyr King Charles the First and the several Noble, Loyal, and
Reverend Worthies . . . That Suffered for the Royal Cause'.[54] He
bequeathed to All Souls the melancholy portrait by or after Edward
Bower of Charles I at his trial, a portrait which moved his friend, the poet
Thomas Tickell, to write a poem 'Inscribed to George Clarke, Esq.'.[55] It
must be said that Tickell's loyalty to 'Charles, the good, the great' is con-
siderably stronger than his poetic inspiration. So there is a rather delight-

[53] Ian Philip, *The Bodleian Library in the seventeenth and eighteenth centuries* (Oxford, 1983),
76.
[54] Timothy Clayton, *The English print 1688–1802* (London and New Haven, 1997), 61.
[55] It was Timothy Clayton who reminded me of the existence of this poem and its dedica-
tion. I am most grateful to him for much interesting information about George Clarke as
a collector and for highly enjoyable discussions about the contrasting worlds of both
Clarkes.

ful irony that all this material, together with the magnificent Inigo Jones drawings, the great symbol of the other side of the civil war, the royal patronage that was to cost Charles I – and his people – so dear, should lie so long in the quiet dust of Worcester College cheek by jowl with the Putney debates. Inigo Jones died in 1652, 'through grief, as is well known', said his loyal pupil John Webb, 'for the fatal calamity of his dread master'.[56] George Clarke probably took the piety of this remark at face value and approved. But if he ever knew of it, he maintained a discreet silence about the role of his own father when the royal actor played his last part in front of the Banqueting House and the curtain came down on the masque to end all masques.

William Clarke's widow raised a memorial tablet to him in Harwich Church and a nineteenth-century historian has made sure that we shall not forget his name. But curiously, it was a nineteenth-century poet who unwittingly, but quite uncannily, captured his elusive quality. Robert Browning died shortly before Firth's great discovery and so, of course, knew nothing about William Clarke. But he knew a great deal about observers of human affairs and wrote lines that could well have formed Clarke's epitaph:

> He glanced o'er books on stalls with half an eye
> And fly-leaf ballads on the vendor's string,
> And broad-edge, bold-print posters by the wall.
> He took such cognisance of men and things.
> If any beat a horse, you felt he saw,
> If any cursed a woman, he took note,
> Yet stared at nobody . . .
> We had among us not so much a spy
> As a recording chief inquisitor .[57]

[56] J. Summerson, *Inigo Jones* (London, 1966), 137.
[57] R. Browning, 'How it strikes a contemporary' in *Poetical Works 1833–1864*, ed. Ian Jack (Oxford, 1970), 634.

Reading, and writing, the text of the Putney
debates

Frances Henderson

Since their publication in the first volume of Sir Charles Firth's edition of
The Clarke papers over a hundred years ago,[1] the Putney debates have continued to hold a particular fascination for generations of historians and
politicians. More than that, they have become part of that select group of
English historical events – 1066 and all that – which have captured the
imagination of a much wider audience, few of whom would claim to be
either historians or politicians. As the present collection of essays shows,
much has been and continues to be written about the debates, and their
text has been scrutinised and rescrutinised for fresh clues and new
insights. There have been both a further edition and several published
selections from them,[2] and they have inspired both broadcast and live
dramatisations. Their almost miraculous survival along with many other
official papers of the army secretary Sir William Clarke (1624?–66) is
described by Lesley Le Claire elsewhere in this volume.[3]

Yet while the content of the manuscript has over the years been subjected to the most minute examination, little attention has been paid to
how it came into existence, to what its original form might have been and
to how that original form may then have evolved. When Sir Charles Firth
first came across the debates some time around 1890, he surmised that
this remarkably vivid and apparently verbatim account would originally
have been taken down by William Clarke himself in shorthand during the
debates.[4] Clarke's earliest notes of the debates have not survived, and we
are left to guess what form they might have taken. The only remaining
record is his fair copy, 'incepit Aug[us]t 8th 1662' (as he noted) – written,
that is, some fifteen years after the event. It seems that during the more
leisured days of the Restoration Clarke was systematically putting his official working papers in order, copying out in his elegant hand only those he
wished to preserve and discarding all of the originals, whether or not he

---

[1] *CP,* I:226–418.
[2] *P&L,* and, for example, G. E. Aylmer in *The Levellers in the English revolution* (London,
1975) and Andrew Sharp (ed.), *The English Levellers* (Cambridge, 1998).
[3] See ch. 2, above.   [4] *CP,* I:xlviii.

had retained a copy of them. By the time he met his unforeseen death in June 1666 he had completed the process only up to March 1651. Thirteen working notebooks covering the next fourteen years (during much of which time he was based in Scotland as secretary to successive commanders-in-chief of the English army there) give a very good idea of what the earlier examples would have consisted of. They contain copies of orders, correspondence and memoranda (both official and personal), of official documents and of printed pamphlets. While many of these have been written *en clair* by several hands, including Clarke's own, they are interspersed throughout by numerous shorthand passages – all of them written by Clarke himself. It was these which alerted Sir Charles Firth to Clarke's command of shorthand and led him to deduce that this was how the Putney meetings, among others, must have been recorded. Students of the debates, most often reading from the edition that Firth published in 1891, have usually accepted this theory without question – correctly, as it now turns out. Based on this belief, they have felt safe to treat the text as a reasonably full and accurate record of the debates, despite its shortcomings, which are most often attributed to Clarke's inefficiency as a shorthand writer rather than to the possible inadequacies of the system upon which he had to rely.[5] But just how far can we depend upon Clarke's account, given the limitations which would have been imposed upon him by the primitive shorthand systems of his day?

The manuscript

For reasons that are not entirely clear, Firth made, as far as we can tell, no attempt to decipher any of Clarke's shorthand.[6] It was not until 1973 that Eric Sams established that Clarke favoured one of the most widely used of seventeenth-century systems, Thomas Shelton's *Tachygraphy* [1635].[7] One of eleven systems known to have been published by 1642 (by which time Clarke seems to have learnt his shorthand), *Tachygraphy* was in favour for many years despite being overtaken by more efficient systems; an extremely basic version of it was, for example, still being used (by Thomas Jefferson) in 1792. Despite Dr Sams' valuable lead, Clarke's shorthand notes retained their secrets until I began my own transcription of them in the mid-1980s. Initially this was a laborious process which involved establishing equivalents for Clarke's many personal variations on

[5] *P&L*, [12].
[6] It is curious that Firth appears to have made no attempt to have the notes deciphered. I have speculated upon this in 'The hidden hand of William Clarke', *Worcester College Record* (1997), 70–3.
[7] E. Sams, 'Sir William Clarke's shorthand' in G. E. Aylmer (ed.), *Sir William Clarke manuscripts 1640–1664* (Brighton, 1979), 29–34, at 30.

Shelton's scheme. Now, having transcribed some 230,000 words, I believe that I can justifiably claim some familiarity with Clarke's shorthand. In particular, I have had to address problems of transcription from this truncated form of writing similar to those which, rereading his notes after many years, Clarke must also have experienced. This prompted me to embark upon a detailed examination of his longhand record of the Putney debates to see whether I could find any clues to demonstrate conclusively that they had originally been taken down in shorthand, and perhaps learn something of the technical difficulties that might have led to the many deficiencies of the text. I was not to be disappointed.

As he wrote his fair copy in the late summer of 1662, Clarke marked many words by underlining them – either as single words or as groups in short phrases.[8] At first sight his reason for doing so is not clear. A few of the phrases might have conceivably been marked in this way in order to emphasise their importance, for example '[if a man bee] Engag'd hee must performe his Engagements', or 'unlesse God bee first sought'.[9] However, in most cases there is no obvious explanation for Clarke to have drawn attention to particular words or passages; indeed, many of the single words are of no apparent significance, for example, 'an', 'are', 'be', 'end'.[10]

As I worked through the manuscript it did not take me long to realise exactly why Clarke had used this device. In almost every case the underscored passage consisted of words which in their shorthand form I, too, had found difficult to interpret in my own transcription of Clarke's surviving shorthand notes. The reason for this was usually either because in Shelton's system (or Clarke's adaptation of it) they were allocated symbols that had more than one possible equivalent, or because they could easily be confused with closely similar signs. In the examples which I have given above, for instance, 'an' might also be read as '2', 'to', 'too', 'any', 'from', 'des-', 'dis-', 'upon'; 'are' could as easily be 'or' or 'were', and 'end' might alternatively stand for 'do', 'did' or 'effect'. As a further illustration, Clarke used an identical outline for 'his' (underlined in the Putney manuscript seven times), 'in' (fifteen times) and 'our' (four times).

In transcribing Clarke's shorthand, I have usually found that the context pointed to the correct reading. Where it did not, my solution has been to provide all likely alternatives so that the reader might make his or her own selection. Evidently Clarke, possibly believing that his notes would not be read by anyone other than himself, chose to mark such doubtful equivalents by underlining them.

[8] I counted some 607 such words.
[9] Worcester College Ms. 65, fols. 10r and 14v respectively.
[10] See, for example, fols. 8r, 10v, 27v, 39r and 70v.

The case is further strengthened by the many alterations and insertions added by Clarke to the 1662 manuscript. For example, 'turned' has replaced the identical 'called', 'before' is superimposed upon the identical 'hold' and 'principles' is written over the almost indistinguishable 'particulars'. Other problematic words have clearly been inserted at a later stage. All of these are represented by shorthand outlines for which, without having Clarke's advantage (albeit after some fifteen years) of being able to call on personal memory, I have myself had difficulty in selecting the intended equivalent.

In total, the markings and alterations tell us that Clarke appears to have had doubts about 294 individual symbols, some of them repeated many times.[11] The most frequently recurring of these are 'be' (sixteen examples), 'it' (twenty-four examples), 'of' (fourteen examples), 'the' and 'to' (both with twenty examples).

Clarke used the same conventions in his longhand transcripts of other major events recorded in the same way – the army debates at Reading in July 1647, and at Whitehall between December 1648 and March 1649, and the proceedings of the High Court of Justice that tried the earls of Holland and Cambridge, Lords Goring and Capel, and Sir John Owen in February–March 1649. All combine brief paragraphs of descriptive reportage with lengthier passages of 'verbatim' material. The annotations usually occur in passages quoting actual speech and, as in the Putney debates, most are attached to words which for technical reasons present difficulties when being transmitted from Shelton's shorthand.[12]

Early shorthand systems

Now that we are able to say with some certainty that the manuscript provides some clear indications that *at some stage* (although we cannot say when) a longhand copy was taken from original shorthand notes, we must, in order to gain a further understanding of Clarke's *modus operandi*, examine the shorthand systems of the mid-seventeenth century and ask to what extent did they satisfy the demands of their practitioners. And – especially important for our enquiry – were they sufficiently streamlined to enable (as was often claimed) the faithful reproduction of verbatim speech? If they were not, what steps were taken to compensate for their inadequacies in this respect?

[11] I counted well over 700 underlined or altered words, appearing either as single words or as components of short phrases.

[12] Worcester College Mss. 65, 70. In Clarke's record of the trial of Archbishop Laud (November 1643–January 1645), although the proportion of verbatim speech to reportage is lower than in the other examples, the same conventions for marking problematic words are used (Worcester College Ms. 71).

Most seventeenth-century practitioners did not, as is often believed, invent their own systems but learned a ready-made method either from primers or directly from a shorthand teacher. Early in the century, brachygraphy (shorthand) was considered by some to be one of the most important calligraphic arts to be taught by London writing masters.[13] As with other extracurricular subjects such as French, mathematics, fencing, dancing and riding,[14] shorthand was taught in the university towns, and in London around the Inns of Court. In the editions of Thomas Shelton's *Tachygraphy* printed by the University Press at Cambridge in 1635, 1641 and 1647, the title page advertised that the method had been 'approved by both Unyversities'; on one copy a seventeenth-century owner added, 'and especially by Cambridge'.[15] Shorthand was also widely taught in schools, as the visiting Polish scholar Jan Comenius noted in 1641.[16] Without doubt it was the newly fashionable accomplishment of the educated man – rather like the personal computer in our own day.[17] There is nothing to indicate how William Clarke learned his *Tachygraphy*, and no primer survives among his collection of printed books at Worcester College.

The earliest modern shorthands were invented in England towards the end of the sixteenth century. First to appear in print were two approximately contemporary methods invented by Timothy Bright and Peter Bales respectively.[18] Like the Tironian notes of republican Rome that inspired them, these pioneering schemes were based on logographic principles, and doubtless like the *notae* were destined to fail because of the strain imposed upon the user's memory by the enormous numbers of individual symbols upon which they depended.[19]

[13] John Stow, *The annales, or generall chronicle of England* (London, 1615), 984 (appendix).
[14] K. Wrightson, *English society 1580–1640* (London, 1982), 192.
[15] W. J. Carlton, *Bibliotheca Pepysiana. A descriptive catalogue of the library of Samuel Pepys. IV. Shorthand books* (London, 1940), vii.
[16] R. F. Young, *Comenius in England* (Oxford and London, 1932), 65.
[17] This was an image which it preserved until the mass introduction of the typewriter into the office in the late nineteenth century, when it was promoted as a suitable accomplishment for the female 'typewritists' whose nimble fingers were felt to make them more suitable for this occupation than men.
[18] T. Bright, *Characterie. An arte of short, swifte and secrete writing by character* (London, 1588); Bales, *The writing schoolemaster: conteining three bookes in one: the first teaching swift writing; the second, true writing; the third, faire writing* (London, 1590). Though visually dissimilar, the two systems shared some characteristics. Bales' system was very likely in use before that of Bright, who, however, was the first to secure the royal patent to publish his system – probably through his patron, William Cecil, Lord Burghley.
[19] Some 13,000 were listed by Janus Gruterus in his *Inscriptionum antiquarum appendix una cum XXIV indicibus accuratissimus* (Heidelberg, 1602). For the links between Tironian notes and early modern shorthands, see V. Salmon, *The works of Francis Lodwick* (London, 1972), 62 and J. Knowlson, *Universal language schemes in England and France* (Toronto and Buffalo, 1975), 19.

The first truly viable shorthand, the part-alphabetic, part-phonetic *Art of Stenographie*, was published anonymously in 1602. Devised by John Willis and built on completely new precepts, it went far towards solving the principal drawbacks of its predecessors. By substantially reducing the number of symbols required and grouping them as in conventional orthography, Willis's scheme was at once more effective, more flexible and more manageable. It was an immediate success and was followed by a stream of (usually derivative) 'improved' methods, each claiming to offer major advantages over previous methods. Inventors and writing-masters were keen to promote the benefits of learning shorthand, foremost among them its use for both secrecy and speed, although such claims were only partially justified.

From the outset, one of shorthand's most successful functions was as a means of privacy or concealment. Relatively simple for someone familiar with the method to decrypt, its contracted form nevertheless rendered shorthand sufficiently secure (then as now) to permit its use as an informal and convenient cipher;[20] it even possessed an additional advantage over conventional ciphers in that it did not require a prearranged key. Although the distinction between shorthand and cipher would become more pronounced later in the seventeenth century, the inventor of the first published system, Timothy Bright, expressly claimed his *Characterie* to be a means of 'secrete writing', and this aspect was also stressed by later inventors.[21] Fifty or so years later Thomas Shelton would write that many of his pupils considered this to be *Tachygraphy*'s main advantage, particularly 'divers Merchants and Factors, who have in forraigne parts used Bibles and Testaments, written in this hand, where they durst not make use of those that are printed'.[22]

Shorthand regularly served as an informal cipher during the English civil wars and interregnum, and both Clarke and his colleagues in the parliamentary army secretariat habitually used Shelton's *Tachygraphy* for concealing sensitive information and for writing to each other in private.[23] And, of course, throughout the century it was also used to protect many personal diaries from prying eyes – most famously, perhaps, by Samuel Pepys.[24]

Its concise format also made shorthand ideal for personal memoranda

[20] [John Falconer], *Cryptomenysis patefacta* (London, 1685), 89; John Davys, *An essay on the art of decyphering* (London, 1737), 16.

[21] Knowlson, *Universal language schemes*, 19.

[22] Thomas Shelton, *A tutor to tachygraphy* (London, 1642), sig. A3r.

[23] *CP,* I:28, 31; Historical Manuscripts Commission, *Report on the manuscripts of F. W. Leyborne-Popham Esq.* (1899), 79.

[24] R. Latham and W. Matthews (eds.), *The diary of Samuel Pepys* (11 vols., London, 1970–83).

and it was utilised for everything from astrological charts to household accounts. It was particularly convenient for marginal and other annotations, as can be seen in many seventeenth-century libraries. Clarke's colleague John Rushworth employed it to mark up his collection of newsbooks and pamphlets during the preparation of his four-volume history of the civil wars, the *Historical collections* (1659–1701).[25] William Clarke's library is no exception. On 7 May 1661, for example, he noted in shorthand the birth of his son George in a printed almanac, and there are numerous other examples among his printed books.

In situations where speed was not important, therefore, the earliest shorthand systems offered undoubted benefits over ordinary handwriting, but they were less successful in meeting some of the other claims made for them. Foremost among these was their supposed ability to record verbatim speech. Although this was almost invariably advertised as one of shorthand's chief advantages, at least two early inventors qualified their assertions in this respect by stipulating that the speaker must deliver his words 'treatably'.[26]

Although secretary hand was by now being rapidly superseded by the faster round hand, especially in administrative and commercial circles,[27] conventional handwriting was presumably even less well equipped to record verbatim speech than it is today. Despite the shortcomings that it displayed in practice, shorthand undoubtedly fascinated observers by its supposed ability to capture the spoken word, not only in recording speeches and the proceedings of meetings, but also in the dictation of letters and other documents to secretaries and clerks.[28] There are, however, many indications that the claims were exaggerated.

First, it was customary to rely, whenever possible, on more than one note-taker. This had earlier been the custom in republican Rome where, because of the inadequacy of the Tironian notes, the custom was to place several *notarii* in different parts of the senate; later they would compare notes and concoct a final, collective, fair copy.[29] This Roman expedient

---

[25] F. Henderson, ' "Posterity to judge" – John Rushworth and his "Historicall Collections" ', *Bodleian Library Record* 15 (1996), 247–59.

[26] Bales, *The arte of brachygraphie . . . that is to write as fast as a man speaketh treatably* (London, 1597); [J. Willis], *The art of stenographie*, sig. A2v.

[27] K. Thomas, 'The meaning of literacy in early modern England' in G. Baumann (ed.), *The written word: literacy in transition* (Oxford, 1986), 97–131, at 111.

[28] Edmond George Petty-Fitzmaurice, 1st baron Fitzmaurice, *The life of Sir William Petty 1623–1687* (London, 1895), 49–50. There are many examples in William Clarke's papers to show that he took dictation in this way.

[29] Plutarch, *Lives*, trans. B. Perrin (Cambridge, MA and London, 1919), VIII:289–91. This belies some claims that the *notarii* were able to write more swiftly than the words could be spoken (Martial, *Epigrams*, trans. W. C. A. Ker (Cambridge, MA and London, 1920), II:513, Epigram 207, 'A shorthand writer'; Ausonius, *Works*, trans. H. G. E. White (Cambridge, MA and London, 1919), I:27).

was known in seventeenth-century England and was imitated in order to cope with the demands of recording parliamentary proceedings, trials and executions. Thomas Burton (who developed his own system of 'speed writing' rather than using a formal shorthand) related in his *Diary* how on 25 January 1658 he was instructed by the Speaker to take notes of Cromwell's lengthy speech on that day. Immediately afterwards he compared notes with John Smyth, clerk of the Commons, and John Rushworth (both of whom used conventional shorthands), the speech being so long that they were unable to complete their joint transcript until the following morning.[30] To take another example, we know that three shorthand writers (one of whom was William Clarke) were present on the scaffold during the execution of Charles I.[31] (Images of the scene rarely show a scribe and then only one, kneeling on one knee and resting a pad on the other; marks on the pad resemble shorthand rather than ordinary writing.[32]) Even the provision of more than one note-taker was sometimes not enough to ensure success. The published version of the earl of Derby's scaffold speech in October 1651 specifically mentioned the presence of two clerks but none the less the newsbook *Mercurius Politicus* noted, perhaps with a hint of sarcasm, 'as near as it could be taken in short-hand'.[33]

When circumstances dictated that only one set of notes could be taken, the text would be carefully checked and revised, often by the speaker. When Charles I attempted to arrest five MPs in the House of Commons on 4 January 1642, the king observed that John Rushworth was busily recording his extempore speech – even although expressly forbidden to record any proceedings other than orders and reports.[34] Rushworth was immediately afterwards summoned to Whitehall where the king edited and corrected his notes (perhaps with not only Rushworth's accuracy in mind), before they were printed on the following day.[35] In 1680, when

---

[30] The speech is printed in Burton's *Diary* (4 vols., London, 1828) II:351–71.

[31] *England's black tribunall* (London, 1660), 65. It was Lesley Le Claire who first noticed that on his own copy of *King Charles his speech made upon the scaffold at Whitehall-Gate* (1649) Clarke had indicated his presence on the scaffold by adding his initials in two places. It is confirmed in print by the 1703 edition of *England's black tribunall* (p. 47) printed by Henry Playford, a distant relation of Clarke. Clarke also attended the king's trial in Westminster Hall (*A complete collection of state trials*, V:985–1073), and it is more than likely that he recorded the version of that event published in three parts as *A perfect narrative of the whole proceedings of the High Court of Justice* (London, 1649). It was licensed by Clarke's brother-in-law Gilbert Mabbott, and printed for John Playford.

[32] Ashmolean Museum, Oxford, Sutherland Collection: C 111.198.

[33] *The Earle of Darbys speech on the scaffold* (London, 1651), 6; *Mercurius Politicus* 72 (16–23 Oct. 1651), 1151.

[34] *Proceedings of the Short Parliament of 1640*, ed. E. S. Cope (London, 1977), 41, 203.

[35] John Forster, *The arrest of the five members by Charles the First* (London, 1860), 187–92, 251–2.

Samuel Pepys took down in shorthand Charles II's own description of his escape after the battle of Worcester in 1651, he required two lengthy sessions with the king, and even so there were many alterations and deletions in his notes.[36]

Naturally, accuracy and completeness would depend to a considerable extent on the rate at which any speech was delivered, for which little evidence has survived, although one contemporary of Oliver Cromwell suggested that the Lord Protector spoke slowly and distinctly.[37] To cite another rare example, Stephen Egerton complained (of a sermon taken in Bright's *Characterie*) that the transcript had many faults despite the fact that he was 'constrained thorough the straightnes of [his] breast, & difficulty of breathing, to speake more laysurely then most men doe'.[38]

Although it was claimed to be possible to memorise sermons without the aid of written notes, it is in this context that shorthand was most usually mentioned. Indeed, Samuel Hartlib believed that the need to discover faster methods of writing was connected with the beginning of more powerful preaching in England,[39] while the large number of Englishmen taking down sermons in shorthand (or appearing to do so) greatly impressed Comenius in 1641.[40] Much later in the century, Samuel Jeake used a method passed on by his father for the same purpose.[41] It may well be that when sermons were said to have been recorded in this way, rather than capturing every word in shorthand the writer would write down as much as he could, amplifying it later from memory, with varying degrees of success. Daniel Dyke, publishing his late father's sermons, felt it necessary to inform the reader that these were not 'the corrupted matter of broken notes, penned from the mouth of a preacher, mingled perhaps with the weake conceits of some illiterate Stenographer',[42] while Milton's nephew, John Phillips, wrote in satirical vein:

> There *Will* writes Short-hand with a pen of brasse,
> Oh how he's wonder'd at by many an asse
> That see him shake so fast his wartie fist
> As if he'd write the Sermon 'fore the Priest

[36] *Charles II's escape from Worcester*, ed. William Matthews (London, 1967).
[37] Richard Fleckno[e], *The idea of his highness Oliver Late Lord Protector* (London, 1659), 14–15.
[38] *A Lecture preached by Maister Egerton at the Blacke-friers 1589 taken by Characterie by a young practitioner in that facultie: and now againe perused, corrected and amended by the Author* (London, 1603), sig. [A5]v. I am grateful for this and the reference given in n. 42 below to Dr James Rigney.
[39] Salmon, *Works of Francis Lodwick*, 62.   [40] Young, *Comenius in England*, 65.
[41] M. Hunter and A. Gregory, *An astrological diary of the seventeenth century, Samuel Jeake of Rye 1652–1699* (Oxford, 1988), 25, 279.
[42] [Jeremiah Dyke], *Divers select sermons on severall texts* (London, 1640), sig. A5.

Has spoke it . . .
Nay I could see that many Short hand wrote,
Where listning well, I could not hear a jote.[43]

There are many such contemporary comments about the custom of (supposedly) recording sermons in shorthand. What researchers do not find is evidence from informed but disinterested commentators to suggest that the practice was successful. One surviving example of what purports to be an entire sermon written in shorthand by Jeremiah Rich around 1650 is contained in a tiny leather-bound volume some five-eighths of an inch square.[44] It consists of just over 1,900 outlines, or words, which may be somewhat shorter than might be expected for the average seventeenth-century sermon. Although Rich, in a refinement of his system, introduced the practice of representing by a single outline 'set-piece' phrases such as might have been used in a sermon, its value must necessarily have been somewhat limited.

A further indication lies in the increasing emphasis placed on speed in the titles of the primers which appeared from the mid-seventeenth century onwards, each one in turn claiming to be – at last – the answer to capturing verbatim speech. *The penns dexterity* by Jeremiah Rich (1659), William Hopkins's *The flying pen-man* (1670) and both William Mason's *A pen pluck'd from an eagles wing* (1672) and his third, improved system, *La plume volante* (1707), all testify to a continued striving after this goal – an emphasis which continues to this day, after some five hundred or so intervening systems.

What caused these primitive systems to be so cumbersome in comparison with today's more streamlined methods? Even after John Willis produced his much-improved invention *Stenographie* in 1602, there were fundamental flaws to slow the writer down. The differential relative positioning of disjunct consonants to indicate medial vowels, the backward slope of some consonants, and the placing of some signs to the left of their antecedents continuously disrupted the flow of writing from left to right. My own experiments with Shelton's *Tachygraphy* confirm that such features would have posed a serious drawback. (On the other hand, I have found that the need to pause regularly to gather ink is largely offset by the lightness of the quill travelling over the page, and may have been less of a hindrance than is sometimes believed.)

Modern writers have tended to be disparaging about Clarke's abilities as a shorthand writer. Sir Charles Firth noted that Clarke was 'not a very skilful note-taker'.[45] In his revised edition of the Putney debates, A. S. P.

---

[43] *A satyre against hypocrites* (1655), 5, 9.   [44] Bodleian Library, Ms. Eng. misc. g. 2.
[45] *CP,* I:xii–xiii.

Woodhouse, probably correctly, attributed defects in Clarke's record of the Putney debates to 'a frenzied effort on the part of the stenographer to catch up with the speaker', noting in support of this that 'No speech of any length is wholly free from . . . defect.'[46] Given the limitations of the techniques at his disposal, however, it is clear that Clarke's final copy of the debates is surprisingly complete. More recently, Austin Woolrych referred to the 'crude shorthand' that Clarke used to record the debates.[47] Even though perceptively identifying the defects of the method rather than of the writer, the statement still requires some modification. As we have seen, mid-seventeenth century shorthands, although considerably more successful than the original methods of Bales and Bright, were still crude and slow. Although by the autumn of 1647 Clarke was an experienced and skilful note-taker (much more so than in 1643–5, when his transcript of Laud's trial holds many gaps and many fewer passages of verbatim speech),[48] it is none the less virtually impossible that working alone in *Tachygraphy* he could have kept pace with more than a few minutes of speech, particularly in the heated atmosphere of the debates. This would be difficult enough using the greatly refined methods of today, and the most likely explanation for the comprehensiveness of Clarke's account is that he was acting as part of a team of perhaps three shorthand writers at Putney as on other occasions. Indeed, a careful reading of the manuscript does produce a few slender clues – no more – to indicate that this was in fact the case.

More than one note-taker?

The most persuasive piece of evidence to indicate that Clarke did not work alone is provided by the only example that survives of a transcript which he would have made at, or very close to, the time of recording an event in shorthand – his fragmentary notes on the trial of John Lilburne in October 1649.[49] These alone, of all the proceedings that we believe Clarke to have recorded in shorthand, appear to be a direct transcript of his shorthand notes rather than in the form of a fair copy made as he tidied up his official papers in the 1660s. We may assess their completeness by comparing them with a much fuller, printed version of the trial which was circulated at the time.[50] This states that it was taken in shorthand, although by whom is not known.[51] Only six of Clarke's double-

---

[46] *P&L*, [12]. Woodhouse also observed the defectiveness of Clarke's punctuation, unaware that Clarke omitted almost all punctuation when writing shorthand.

[47] A. Woolrych, 'Looking back on the Levellers', *The Historian* 34 (1992), 3–8, at 5.

[48] Worcester College Ms. 71.   [49] Worcester College Ms. 181, fols. 160–5.

[50] [Clement Walker], *The triall, of Lieut. Collonell John Lilburne* (London, 1649).

[51] In 1903 the note-taker was wrongly identified as Jeremiah Rich by A. T. Wright, *Jeremiah Rich* (London, 1911), 38.

sided folios now exist but, from his own enumeration of them, there were originally many more, and they probably covered the entire duration of the trial. These remaining excerpts are almost word-for-word identical to the published version, so that there need be no doubt that they represent a true record of some of what was said. *However*, such passages as are found are by no means as complete as any of the other similarly-recorded proceedings which survive among Clarke's papers. Their longest continuous passages consist of only some half-dozen lines, and even then will typically contain short gaps. The most likely inference must be that Clarke would have relied upon the notes of other shorthand writers to complete his own defective record.

A second clue lies in the corrupt nature of the manuscript itself, with its many repetitions, gaps and *non sequiturs* – often commented on and usually, as we have seen, attributed to Clarke's lack of shorthand skill. While this (or rather, as I have suggested, the shortcomings of *Tachygraphy*) might account for breaks and discrepancies in the account, it is hard to find a satisfactory explanation for the many repeated or contradictory phrases, such as 'such kind of Action, Action of that nature' or 'Itt is made noe wonder of, Itt is made a wonder of'.[52] It is inherently unlikely that Clarke would have had either time or opportunity to backtrack and record any passages a second time while making his shorthand record of the debates. One very plausible explanation is that he was copying from a tangled conflation of two or more separate sets of notes – put together shortly after they were taken down in 1647, or (perhaps less likely) at the time of making his fair copy fifteen years later.

Clarke's overall ability and competence in composing lucid passages of prose are not in doubt and are amply demonstrated not only throughout his manuscripts but also in the many official documents that he wrote for subsequent publication.[53] In other words, had he been working only from his own shorthand notes in 1662, it is almost unthinkable that he would produce such a defective final version; it would have been far more in line with his usual practice for him to correct and refine them as he went along, arriving at a text which met his usual high standards – the standards of one who had trained as a barrister.[54]

Thirdly, there are at least two different styles of reporting. Much of the first three days of debate consists of what are clearly passages of actual

---

[52] Worcester College Ms. 65, fols. 29v and 22r respectively.

[53] For example, [W.C.], *The intentions of the army, discovered in a letter from a gentleman* (London, 1647).

[54] A description of a portrait of the duke of Albemarle which is dedicated to Clarke clears all doubt that he and the William Clarke called to the bar in 1653 were one and the same (Aylmer, *Sir William Clarke manuscripts*, 9); A. Globe, *Peter Stent London printseller circa 1642–1665* (Vancouver, 1985), 48.

speech. Occasionally these are replaced by shorter sections of reportage, where speeches are considerably condensed and written in the third person, much as the minutes of a meeting might be recorded today. As an example, in the proceedings for 1 November there are fourteen such passages, of which no less than seven relate to Rainborough. Even these brief reports contain an unusually high number of examples of Clarke's underscoring – that is, words about which he felt some doubt. A variety of plausible explanations suggest themselves. Were Rainborough's words inaudible for some reason? Did he speak too quickly? (It is certainly difficult to imagine that he spoke too quietly.) Did he possess a local dialect too pronounced for his words to be fully intelligible? This did not seem to pose a problem in the earlier days of the debates. Or, supposing that the shorthand writers did work in teams at Putney, as we know that they did elsewhere, how would they do this? Would each be allocated a particular speaker, or group of speakers, to record? In such circumstances, if the writer appointed to 'track', say, Rainborough and certain others was absent from the meeting during all or part of it, this might explain the anomaly. Alternatively, was there a set of full notes to which for some reason Clarke did not have access, having to rely on a much briefer record? Although such questions will probably never be answered, it is at least possible to speculate that the very different style of some of the reporting and also the pattern of omissions indicate at least one additional set of notes to Clarke's own.

Finally, in two, and possibly three, places there are tiny corrections in a second, contemporary script, clearly demonstrating that at least one person other than Clarke was checking through the fair copy.[55] I have been unable to identify the hand, although I can say that it is not that of Clarke's colleague John Rushworth – as we have seen, another shorthand writer, and one who may have been present during at least part of the debates. One cannot even say with certainty whether the annotations were added during Clarke's lifetime, but they may be another sign that Clarke's version was being compared with a second set of notes, and possibly even by their writer.

Using such tiny threads of evidence, the number of note-takers at Putney can only be speculated upon. The most compelling indication that Clarke would not have been acting alone is quite simply that it would not, I believe, have been physically possible for one man relying on the archaic and inadequate shorthand systems of the earlier seventeenth century to make such a complete record of these lengthy and lively debates.

---

[55] Worcester College Ms. 65, fols. 23r, 23v and 91r.

Modern editors

The first person known to have read through the debates in modern times was, of course, Sir Charles Firth, who, as we have seen, was well aware of the manuscript's many deficiencies and thought carefully about the reasons for them. When it came to reproducing the text for publication, Firth's difficulty was to produce a script which was at once readily intelligible and yet faithful to Clarke's somewhat intractable original.[56] The resulting edition, with its admirable introductory summary of the debates,[57] bears out Firth's consummate skill as both editor and historian. Readers wishing to catch the flavour or feel the drama of the debates will find all that they require in the 1891 edition, but Firth's emendations were sweeping. While he made only such alterations to the manuscript as, in his own words, he felt were 'absolutely necessary'[58] in order to clarify its meaning, these were none the less extensive and are by no means invariably signalled in the text. For example while alterations of fifty-three words are pointed out in footnotes, some fifty-five are not. Similarly, while most of almost 500 words or phrases inserted by Firth are marked by enclosure within square brackets, others have been added silently. About three times as many passages have been transposed without comment as have been indicated in footnotes, and punctuation has been altered in some forty-five instances. In the majority of these cases, the sense of Clarke's original is more clearly brought out, but in some the meaning is altered or reversed, for example when the word 'not' is omitted.[59] In one particularly striking instance, Firth without comment attributed a lengthy speech to Henry Ireton. The speech is not, perhaps, characteristic of Ireton and is not credited to him in the manuscript, where it appears to be a continuation of the preceding speech (delivered by an unidentified agitator).[60] In his full edition of the major part of the debates, setting out to identify Firth's emendations, A. S. P. Woodhouse adopted the attribution without observation, although he was sufficiently cautious to enclose the name of Ireton (provided by Firth as 'Comm. Gen.') within square brackets.[61]

Woodhouse based his text on a close comparison of Firth's edition with Clarke's manuscript, and found it no easier to deal with the complexities of the manuscript than had Firth himself. Although Woodhouse's stated

---

[56] Firth's *cri de coeur* that a certain passage is 'past amending' (*CP*, I:267 n. b) reveals the difficulties he faced.   [57] *CP*, I:xlviii–liv.   [58] Ibid., I:lxxvi.

[59] Ibid., I:382; Worcester College Ms. 65, fol. 74r.

[60] Worcester College Ms. 65, fol. 59r-v; *CP* I:349–51. I must thank Dr Clive Holmes' group of final-year Oxford undergraduates, who independently questioned the attribution from their reading of *The Clarke papers*, for their stimulating insights on this point.

[61] *P&L*, 88.

intention was to clarify the latter, his version requires a very clear head indeed in order to differentiate between his own and the 1891 edition, and between those and Clarke's original text.

What, in conclusion, does all of this mean for those of us who wish to make a detailed study of the Putney debates today? It seems that if we are to come closest to the most accurate account of them, then it is to the manuscript that we must turn. But we must do so with caution. This would apply to any document which had reached us via the medium of seventeenth-century shorthand,[62] regardless of the writer's degree of expertise, but the pedigree of the Worcester College manuscript is particularly labyrinthine and shrouded in uncertainty. We must guard against treating it as we might a transcript made from the considerably more efficient shorthands of our own day, almost as if it were a tape-recording; it is quite simply not safe to do so. More than that, an awareness of its complex genesis and history is essential if we are to make any assessment of its text. We must, for instance, ask ourselves from what sort of notes was William Clarke working as he wrote his final copy – the only copy we now have – and were they in shorthand or in longhand? Were they, as seems most probable (and particularly in the light of his patchy record of John Lilburne's trial of 1649), a compilation of several sets of notes taken in shorthand and amalgamated into longhand at the time of the debates, or was Clarke working from several sets of longhand notes? Alternatively, as has always been thought, but as seems unlikely in our present state of knowledge, was he working from a single set of notes taken by himself at Putney? It seems improbable that we will ever be certain of the answer to these questions, but as we read and write about the debates, as well as pore over their meaning and context, there is a further lens through which we should focus our attention: that of the inadequacies of the tool upon which William Clarke would have had to rely, Thomas Shelton's *Tachygraphy*, and its very real consequences for the first person to read and to write the Putney debates as we know them – William Clarke himself.

[62] The same point was made in 1901 by C. L. Stainer in the preface to his edition of *Speeches of Oliver Cromwell 1644–1655* (London and New York, 1901).

Part 2

The Putney debates and their contexts

4   The debates from the perspective of the army

Austin Woolrych

The famous debates at Putney which William Clarke recorded between 28 October and 1 November 1647 have commonly been regarded primarily as a chapter in the history of the Leveller movement. This is fully understandable, because the most interesting ideas discussed on those days were Leveller ideas, and the documents that gave rise to the recorded debates were part of a Leveller-led campaign to indoctrinate the army and harness its power in the realisation of Leveller ideals of government. If the emphasis in what follows is more on the significance of the debates in the history of the New Model Army, it does not imply any disparagement of the Levellers' contribution, but rather a recognition that the ideological and military aspects of the confrontation are inseparable. Most leading Levellers believed that the most promising way – perhaps the only way at that time – to inaugurate a commonwealth after their own hearts was to convert the soldiery *en masse* and employ their pressure to coerce or dissolve the present parliament.

Yet the recorded debates, in which the Levellers strove against Ireton and Cromwell for the hearts and minds of the soldiers and the more junior officers, began and ended in a military institution, the General Council of the Army, which had been constituted nearly five months earlier for quite another purpose. It had been debating the settlement of the kingdom on and off since mid-July, but on very different lines from those now proposed by the Levellers. For months, the army commanders had had their own agenda for the General Council, and to them the Leveller campaign from October onward was a disturbing interruption of it – a bid indeed to wrest control from them and alter radically the whole political direction that the army, under their guidance, had been taking. The objectives of Fairfax, Cromwell and Ireton were in some vital respects incompatible with those of the Leveller spokesmen at Putney, so we are witnessing a crucial contest for power as well as a clash of constitutional principles. Since the king and the parliament already lay very much at the army's mercy, the outcome of the contest was of incalculable importance for the whole kingdom. It may therefore help to start by sketching its larger political context, starting in the spring of 1647, which was a formative stage in the development of both the political conscious-ness of the army and the political programme of those London-based rad-icals who would soon be known as the Levellers.

The New Model Army had then been in existence for two years. As a body it had so far scrupulously refrained from political activity, despite the tendency of presbyterians both religious and political to portray it as a hotbed of sectaries and radicals.[1] This is not to say it that it lacked politi-cal awareness, for the majority of its officers must have been very con-scious of the long drawn out controversy in both Houses of Parliament that had attended its formation, largely because of presbyterian fears of arming known independents. Below officer level, there was a strong con-trast in political sophistication between infantry and cavalry. Most of the foot soldiers were pressed men, drawn from the lower reaches of society; many were illiterate, and a fair number had earlier fought for the king and enlisted after being taken prisoner. The cavalry troopers, on the other hand, were men of some small substance – yeomen, independent crafts-men and others of the 'middling sort' – who were not only literate but highly aware of the issues at stake during the war and since its conclusion. Most were volunteers, and many had taken up arms because (as Cromwell said) they knew what they fought for, and loved what they knew. But Fairfax, their general, was as little of a political animal as a man in his station of life could be, and he was averse to soldiers exceeding their military function. The Self-Denying Ordinance of 1645 had required members of both Houses of Parliament to resign their military commis-sions when the New Model was formed, but Cromwell had been granted a series of temporary exemptions from it, and as finally enacted it had not debarred officers from being elected to parliament in the future. Cromwell was joined in the Commons, through by-elections between 1645 and 1647, by his fellow-officers Commissionary-General Ireton, Major-General Philip Skippon, and Colonels Charles Fleetwood, Thomas Harrison and Richard Ingoldsby. But this was a small military presence in a house of nominally more than 500 members, and before the confrontation that began in March 1647 it did not figure as a distinct army interest.

From then on, however, two main grievances drew the army as a body

---

[1] Henceforth the capitalised form Presbyterian will be used when referring to the church and churchmen of that denomination and presbyterian when the appellation carries the loose political sense current at the time. It characterised politicians who were constitu-tionally and socially conservative, desirous of a negotiated settlement with the king, sus-picious (at least) of the New Model Army, in favour of a single national church and opposed to religious toleration. Religious Independents will be distinguished similarly from political independents.

into the political arena. One was the shabby treatment that the parliament was according to its soldiers, starving them of their pay, failing to provide them with adequate indemnity from prosecution for acts committed under the stress of war (such as commandeering horses or doing damage to property for defensive reasons), and making little provision either for those incapacitated by their wounds or for the widows and orphans of the fallen. The other major grievance was the growingly obvious intention of the presbyterian-dominated parliament to liquidate the New Model Army by constituting an expeditionary force for Ireland exclusively from its ranks and disbanding most of the rest. There was, of course, a strong case for reducing the land forces in England after the first civil war had been won, and a no less strong need to recover Ireland from the rebel confederation that had been controlling the greater part of the country for too many years. But in the spring of 1647 the New Model accounted for less than half the troops afoot in England and Wales, being outnumbered by the various regional forces and the many garrisons that were still under arms. The question was which units to disband first. A substantial standing force needed to be kept up, for the king was giving no satisfaction over the peace terms that parliament was offering him, and many Scots as well as Irish were prepared to go on fighting for him. It made no military sense to lay the axe first to the New Model, whose fighting quality and corporate morale far outshone those of the provincial forces.

As for the reconquest of Ireland, there was a prima facie case for employing the most militarily effective forces that England possessed, but to draw exclusively on the New Model's regiments was very reasonably seen by their officers and men as unjust. Many veterans, including most of the cavalrymen, had enlisted as volunteers to fight a specific enemy, and had had no thought of serving outside their own country. Some were willing to go to Ireland, some were not, but if they went, they wanted to fight alongside their old comrades under the officers they knew.

That was not what the presbyterian politicians who currently dominated parliament had in mind. Their motives, in planning as they did for the reduction of the home forces and the reconquest of Ireland, were transparently political,[2] and resentment of this fact was strongly to colour the debates at Putney. They wanted to weaken their political opponents, the independents, who were the army's allies, and they feared (as they had reason to) that the army and the independents would stand together against any partisan deal that they, the presbyterians, might strike with

---

[2] Mark A. Kishlansky has defended the presbyterians' plans in *The rise of the New Model Army* (Cambridge, 1979), esp chs. 6 and 7. My reasons for disagreeing with his reading are explained and documented more fully in my *Soldiers and statesmen: the General Council of the Army and its debates, 1647–1648* (Oxford, 1987), chs. 1 and 2.

the king. The same political motives shone through their proposals regarding the standing force to be kept up in England. They decided, and carried it through the Commons by a bare ten votes, that it should consist only of 5,400 cavalry and 1,000 dragoons, with no regular infantry except the soldiers in a small number of garrisons. This was manifestly inadequate, with peace terms still to be settled, widespread unrest in the country, and the king ready to exploit any opportunity; a new civil war lay in fact little more than a year away. Even this token force was to include only five New Model regiments, including those of Fairfax and Cromwell, whom even the party of Denzil Holles and Sir Philip Stapleton dared not insult. All the votes on these decisions divided the House along party lines. So did three resolutions that the presbyterians carried on 8 March: that no officer in England except Fairfax should rank higher than colonel (which would have meant, for a start, demoting Cromwell, Skippon and Ireton), that MPs should hold no military commands in England (which would have forced several to choose between their parliamentary and military careers), and that all officers serving in England must take the Solemn League and Covenant and conform to the parliamentary settlement of religion. Many had, of course, volunteered to fight for parliament long before there was any question of imposing a Presbyterian state church on the country. The implication of the last vote was that it was acceptable for Independent or Baptist officers to go and fight in Ireland, but they were not to be tolerated at home.

Overt dissatisfaction in the army began in mid-March with a spontaneous petitioning movement among the soldiery, originating in the cavalry regiments stationed in East Anglia. It was just under way when parliament sent three commissioners to Fairfax's headquarters to enlist officers and their men for service in Ireland. These parliament-men, all of Holles' faction, were disconcerted to encounter a collective unwillingness among the officers whom Fairfax convened to meet them to make any commitment until they were satisfied on a number of points: who was to command those who went to Ireland, how far they could be assured of regular pay and support, which regiments were to be kept up in England, and what provision parliament was making for all the men's arrears of pay and for their indemnity for acts committed in war. Meanwhile, sympathetic officers had persuaded the discontented soldiers to embody their grievances in a single, collective petition, and to address it not to parliament but to Fairfax. Probably under their moderating influence, its tone was impeccably respectful and it confined itself to the soldiers' legitimate concerns as soldiers. These were chiefly indemnity for acts done in war, security for their arrears of pay, provision for the maimed and for their fallen comrades' widows and children, and that there should be no compulsion on those who had enlisted as volunteers to serve outside the kingdom.[3] Before it was presented to Fairfax, however, the three commissioners got hold of a copy while they were with the army, and they divulged it to the Commons on 27 March. The House promptly commanded Fairfax to suppress it, and he gave orders that it should go no further.

Two days later, however, the Commons received intelligence not only that the petition was still circulating for signatures (which was probably true), but, far more dubiously, that the petitioning campaign was being directed by a whole group of senior officers, including Ireton. The House exploded in anger, and late in the evening Holles drafted a declaration which was passed without a division. The Lords, too, passed it next day. It expressed parliament's 'high dislike' of the petition, and warned that all who went on promoting it 'shall be looked upon as enemies of the state and disturbers of the public peace'.[4] Parliament also resolved to proceed at once with disbanding almost all of the New Model except such as would take service in Ireland.

This Declaration of Dislike, as it came to be called, deeply offended the army's sense of honour and would be bitterly recalled at Putney six months later. Holles probably thought he had caught the army wrong-footed and sought to exploit the situation to its discredit, but he badly failed to anticipate its response. It may seem strange that he could persuade experienced politicians to overreact so disastrously, but part of the explanation is that the army petition came before the House little more than a week after another petition that contained the fullest statement so far of the aims of those who would soon be known as the Levellers. The proximity in time of the two documents seems to have been sheer coincidence, for there is no sound evidence that the Levellers inspired the army petition, which contains not a trace of specifically Leveller doctrine. The Levellers had made a few converts in the army, but not many as yet; the newswriters who reported during April that the army was 'one Lilburne throughout' were thoroughly mistaken. Like many conservative souls, they jumped to the conclusion that what they saw as two contemporaneous strains of subversion had a single source. Both Houses of Parliament had been shocked and shaken by the Levellers' demands in what came to be known as their 'Large Petition'. So far John Lilburne, William Walwyn, Richard Overton and their associates were known chiefly for their quarrels with particular parliamentary leaders and their articulation of specific

[3] 'The Petition of the officers and soldiers in the army' is printed in *A declaration of the engagements, remonstrances, desires and resolutions from Sir Thomas Fairfax and the Generall Councel of the Army* (27 September 1647, hereafter *Army declarations*), 1–2.
[4] *CJ* V:129.

grievances, especially those felt by the 'middling sort', though Lilburne had already called for annual parliaments, and all three were evolving a doctrine of natural rights inherent in all the sons of Adam. Parliaments, they had already argued, existed only to defend the rights and liberties of the sovereign people who betrusted them, and had no lawful power to domineer over them. The gist of the Large Petition, which made it so offensive to most MPs, was that the present parliament was oppressing the people in ways all too similar to those that it had charged against the personal rule of Charles I, not least in the matter of religious persecution. The range of its attacks, and the radical implications of such demands as those for a codification of the laws (in English), a very large freedom of religion, the abolition of tithes and the dissolution of the Merchant Adventurers' Company, added to the outrage with which it was received. But the Levellers had not yet advanced far towards a positive prescription for a democratic commonwealth. Their ideas regarding the franchise and parliamentary reform, and their identification of specific, indefeasible natural rights that not even the people's democratically elected representatives might encroach upon, were still to come. Their promulgation of all these in October was to make the Putney debates uniquely exciting.

Fairfax continued to obey the parliament's ban on the army petition and for several weeks his officers and men held their peace, despite repeated attempts by parliamentary commissioners to drive a wedge through their ranks by enlisting all they could for Ireland and segregating them from the rest. But in mid-April the soldiers of the eight cavalry regiments that were quartered in Essex and East Anglia began spontaneously to elect representatives to act for them in securing the redress of their grievances. They called them adjutators or agitators or agents; the words all meant the same to them, but 'agitator' tended to stick, especially among those who viewed their emergence with alarm. It was natural that the movement should arise among the more educated and politically conscious cavalry troopers, but it spread strikingly soon to the foot regiments, all of which elected their own agitators during May. This tallies with other evidence that a number of officers, mostly junior, acted in concert with the agitators from the start. At any rate the agitators soon had a well-knit organisation of their own, operating throughout the army, with a central council, and with ready access to printing presses that published their pamphlets and petitions. This organisation was viewed by the army commanders with a mixture of sympathy for the grievances that it articulated and concern over its readiness to initiate military actions, such as preventing the train of artillery from being taken over by emissaries from the parliament, without any reference to the army's formal chain of command. The most spectacular example of independent action was the abduction of the king from Holmby House on 3 June, for although Comet Joyce was in command, the party that he led was got together by the agitators' organisation and the decision to remove the king, rather than risk letting him be removed by agents of the parliament, was taken by Joyce and his men collectively.[5]

Just before Joyce carried off the king, Fairfax and his council of war took the momentous decision to defy parliament's order for the disbandment of his army. The last straw had been its attempt to turn the men off with just six weeks' pay on account and little security for the rest, though their arrears ranged from eighteen to forty-three weeks, the longest being in the cavalry. Parliament had ordered the regiments to widely separated places to be paid off, so as to prevent any concerted resistance, but with Fairfax's concurrence all but a few distantly stationed units marched to a single rendezvous near Newmarket. Fairfax was dismayed to learn that the king, too, was on his way to Newmarket and at first tried to return him to Holmby, but Charles very firmly preferred the army's custody to that of the parliament, and for a while possession of the royal person was to prove a considerable advantage.

The muster of officers at the general rendezvous was not complete. A minority of about in one in four in the senior ranks (from colonel down to captain), and perhaps one in five overall, declined to participate and left Fairfax's army, either because they positively wished to continue their military careers in Ireland or because they were unwilling to disobey the commands of parliament.[6] There had always been a minority of political presbyterians in the New Model, and their withdrawal from the service at this stage narrowed the range of political views that would be expressed at Putney. But all the officers and men who did join in the general rendezvous subscribed there a document called *The solemn engagement of the army*, which was to be much invoked at Putney. It was more than a manifesto; it was, rather, a military covenant, with conscious parallels in the Scottish National Covenant and the Solemn League and Covenant. Ireton was probably its main author, in consultation with at least some of the agitators. All who signed or assented to it pledged each other, and promised parliament and the kingdom, that they would obediently disband *when* they had received redress of their grievances and *when* the politicians who had abused the army had been removed from power. But they would not disband or be divided until these ends had been achieved,

---

[5] Woolrych, *Soldiers and statesmen*, 106–14; Ian Gentles, *The New Model Army in England, Ireland and Scotland, 1645–1653* (Oxford, 1992), 169–71.

[6] Kishlansky in *Rise of the New Model Army*, 218–21, overstates the proportion of officers who withdrew from the service at this stage. Gentles provides a corrective in *New Model Army*, 167–8, and cf. Woolrych, *Soldiers and statesmen*, 133–6.

to the satisfaction of a new General Council of the Army (as it was soon to be called) which was to include two officers and two soldiers chosen from each regiment.[7] In effect, this gave formal recognition to the agitators and brought them within the regular chain of command, stretching from the Lord General downward, for it was for Fairfax to decide when to summon the General Council. But the army commanders' desire to consult and involve all ranks was genuine, and the balancing of the rank-and-file agitators with elected officers should not be seen as a device to tame them. We know of more committed political radicals among the officer-representatives in the summer of 1647 than among the original soldier-agitators.

Nine days after launching its *Solemn engagement,* the army published an important *Declaration,* stating its political objectives more precisely. This was another of the public 'engagements' that would be argued over at Putney, and it emanated, after such consultation as time permitted, from Fairfax's regular council of war and not from the newly created General Council of the Army, which had not yet met.[8] It vindicated the right of the army, which was 'not a mere mercenary army, hired to serve any arbitrary power of a state', to stand up in defence of the people's rights and liberties, as well as its own. It demanded that both Houses of Parliament should be purged of members found unfit for their trust; the army had already launched impeachment proceedings against eleven MPs whom it particularly blamed for its mistreatment. It called for a fixed limit to the duration of this and all future parliaments, and for the seats in the Commons to be radically reapportioned so as 'to render the parliament a more equal representative of the whole'. When the king had given the royal assent to these and other reforms his own rights should be settled, 'so farre as may consist with the Right and Freedome of the Subject'.

When this *Declaration* (sometimes called *A representation*) was promulgated in mid-June, the army was on the move towards London, fearing that the presbyterians were preparing a counter-force with which to resist it. One reason why the document was not submitted to the full General Council was doubtless that in so pressing a situation time precluded a lengthy debate. But it should be remembered that the General Council had been erected for a limited purpose, namely to register the army's satisfaction or otherwise with what parliament should offer by way of redress of its grievances. Since parliament had as yet offered very little,

---

[7] Text in *Army declarations,* 23–7 and in John Rushworth, *Historical collections* (8 vols., London, 1680–1701), V:510–12. The essential parts are printed in *P&L* (1938), 401–3.

[8] Text in W. Haller and G. Davies (eds.), *The Leveller tracts, 1647–1653* (New York, 1994), 56–61; excerpts in *P&L,* 403–9. For provenance see Woolrych, *Soldiers and statesman,* 126–30.

there was no reason why Fairfax should summon the full body of representative officers and agitators. But something of a stand-off took place after his forward units took up positions a mere ten miles from the capital. He moved his headquarters back from Uxbridge to Reading, and there a fresh group of commissioners, whom parliament had lately sent to negotiate, asked that the army should present a consolidated statement of its desires regarding a national settlement. Ireton was deputed to prepare this, with Colonel John Lambert to assist him, and the result was the famous document that came to be known as *The heads of the proposals.* Ireton was its main draftsman, but there is evidence that he worked in close consultation with Lord Wharton, one of the parliamentary commissioners at headquarters, and probably with Viscount Saye and Sele, who visited the army in mid-July.[9] What resulted was a comprehensive scheme for a settlement that (it was hoped) could be presented to parliament and the nation in the name not only of the whole army but of the powerful party of moderate independents which included Sir Henry Vane and Oliver St John in the Commons as well as Saye, Northumberland and Wharton in the Lords.

This alliance greatly strengthened the prospects of *The heads of the proposals* receiving public acceptance, despite the opposition of the presbyterians and the Scots, and if the king could be brought to agree to them they would offer a better hope of a lasting peace than anything yet advanced by parliament.[10] Compared with parliament's own propositions they were more generous to Charles, and offered far more in the way of positive reforms, including some that the Levellers had been advocating. They called for biennial parliaments sitting for a minimum of 120 days and a maximum of 240, with a wholesale redistribution of seats in the Commons so as to disfranchise rotten boroughs and increase the proportion of county members. They proposed that no one should be forced to take the Solemn League and Covenant, and that all acts that imposed penalties for not coming to church or for meeting for worship elsewhere should be repealed. They set checks upon the king's future control over ministerial appointments and his disposal of the armed forces, but would have taken them away from him altogether for only ten years. They were much more moderate than the parliament in the confiscations that they

---

[9] See J. S. A. Adamson, 'The English nobility and the projected settlement of 1647', *HJ* 30 (1987), 567–602. Mark A. Kishlansky challenged his interpretation in 'Saye what', *HJ* 33 (1990), 917–37, but Adamson defends it, in essentials convincingly, in *HJ* 34 (1991), 231–55. I continue to believe that Ireton was the main author of *The heads of the proposals,* but I am persuaded by Adamson's evidence that Wharton, Saye and other leading independents were closely consulted in their preparation.

[10] Text in S. R. Gardiner (ed.), *Constitutional documents of the Puritan revolution* (3rd edn, Oxford, 1906), 316–26.

would have imposed on the defeated royalists' estates, and many of the particular reforms that they espoused matched those proposed by the Levellers.

But these statesmanlike proposals appeared at a time when relations between the agitators and the high command were becoming strained. The Levellers had no desire to see a concordat between the generals and the king, and in the three months since the agitators had first appeared they had been targeting them with some limited success. The more radical agitators had been dismayed by the army's abandonment of its advance on London, and were pressing that it should be resumed. At this juncture, Fairfax was persuaded to summon the full General Council of the Army for the first time on 16 July. The debate that day was focused on a formidable 'humble petition and representation' from the agitators, and it lasted until midnight. The petitioners called for an immediate march on London, with the object of getting the eleven impeached MPs removed from parliament, the City militia restored to safe hands, the re-enlistment of disbanded soldiers (called reformadoes) stopped, the payment of long-overdue assessments enforced, and John Lilburne and other Leveller leaders released from prison. But Cromwell urged repeatedly that for the army to resort to force prematurely would be self-defeating, though neither he nor Ireton was unsympathetic to the agitators' objectives in themselves. Ireton argued persuasively that the army was not intent on power as such but on securing the kingdom's liberties, so before it took further action it should be ready to inform the public as to 'what wee would do with that power if we had itt in our hands'.[11] Eventually it was agreed that the agitators' requests, including that for the release of Lilburne and his associates, should be transmitted to parliament, with a demand for an answer within four days, but not to back it with a threat to march on London.

Next day the generals had even more important business to put before the General Council, namely the full text (as it then stood) of *The heads of the proposals* themselves. It is striking testimony of the importance that they attached to the assent of the army as a whole that they chose to submit this long and complex document to the debate of private soldiers and junior officers before it was read in complete form to the parliamentary commissioners or shown to the king. William Allen, one of the most prominent and articulate of the agitators, recognised the 'great weight' of the matters before them and asked for plenty of time for debating them, but meanwhile he supported a motion by Ireton that a committee should work over them before the full General Council moved further towards

[11] *CP,* I:182.

approving them. The committee, it was agreed, should consist of twelve officers appointed by Fairfax and twelve agitators – another sign of the respect accorded to the latter.

The hopes and expectations were that the committee would prepare matters for the General Council's debate, that *The heads of the proposals,* amended if need be, would receive the army's formal approval, and that negotiations would quickly follow with the parliament and the king. But the process was interrupted later in July by violent disturbances in London, where the army was widely hated and feared. A great mob of citizens, apprentices and reformadoes, whipped up by hostile members of the City Corporation, Presbyterian ministers and presbyterian politicians, invaded both Houses of Parliament and forced them to vote to bring the king back to London at once, before any terms had been agreed with him. The independent peers and MPs took refuge with the army, which at the request of both Speakers marched into London to quash this attempted counter-revolution, which collapsed well before Fairfax's troops entered the capital. Before the army set off, Ireton and other officers went to the king and begged him to give his immediate assent to *The heads of the proposals,* which had been shown to him just after the initial debate on them at Reading. If he had honestly accepted them then as the basis on which he would be restored to his regal authority, there is little doubt that Fairfax and his army would have escorted Charles himself back to his capital, as well as the fugitive peers and MPs. But Charles, slippery as ever and ill advised by his friends, put off giving an answer until he had seen whether the counter-revolutionaries in London would do his business for him at a cheaper rate, and even when they collapsed he declined to commit himself. Thereby he not only lost his best chance of recovering his throne on honourable terms, and without further bloodshed, but he seriously damaged his reputation in the army. The significance of the episode for the Putney debates is that whereas most of the army had so far been quite well disposed towards him, from now on many of its members thought him so incorrigible and untrustworthy that they should have no further dealings with him. Some, such as Colonel Rainborough, were already tinged with republicanism, but probably rather more turned against him on religious grounds, seeing him as a man of blood, bent on defying the judgement that God had delivered against him and his cause in battle. Cromwell and Ireton on the other hand, and with them Fairfax, felt obliged to go on pursuing the path of negotiation that *The heads of the proposals* had opened up. Those terms had hardly been considered by parliament yet, and Charles had at least stated publicly that he preferred them to the parliament's Propositions of Newcastle.

Fairfax's entry into London early in August effectively demonstrated the army's strength and discipline, and served to crack the whip at both the parliament and the City. But neither he nor Cromwell and Ireton intended a military occupation of the capital, let alone a takeover of government, and early in September he established his headquarters at Putney, just over six miles upstream from London Bridge. It was close enough to maintain some pressure and to scotch any possible fresh attempt to raise a counter-force, but not so close as to intimidate the parliament-men. Indeed, as soon as the immediate military presence was withdrawn parliament slackened in its attempt to satisfy the army's material needs; the men got no pay at all during September. For the first time the generals instituted regular weekly meetings of the General Council, which were held on Thursdays in Putney Parish Church from 9 September onward. They served partly as a safety valve for the soldiery's grievances, but the long-interrupted debate on the terms to be offered to the king remained high on the agenda too. At the very first meeting at Putney the rights of the king and his heirs were considered, and Major Francis White, the senior officer-representative of Fairfax's own regiment of foot, questioned whether the king had any rights at all. There was no visible authority in the kingdom now, he declared, but the power of the sword. This was to impugn the parliament's right to even a share in the settlement, no less than the king's, and for saying what he did White was expelled from the General Council, without a voice raised in dissent. The army's commanders were firmly set at this stage against any usurpation of the civil authority. The next weekly General Council approved some modifications to *The heads of the proposals*, whereupon a new edition of them was published by the army's regular printer.

At the end of September the General Council was still committed to the quest for a national settlement by constitutional means, within the basic framework of the ancient constitution. It stayed on this course during the first half of October, though the news of its debates is meagre, and according to some royalist newswriters the agitators were growing restive over the General Officers' persistence with *The heads of the proposals*. But the generals' pressure on parliament was yielding dividends now in better provision for their men's pay and arrears and more secure indemnity for acts committed in war; the soldiers got a whole month's pay in October. Parliament also approved a new establishment for the standing forces in England, which were to number not 6,400, as it had proposed in February, but 26,400. Most members of the General Council could probably see which side their bread was buttered on, for some at least of the leading Levellers were contemplating a future in which there would be no regular army at all – only a provincial militia.

As summer turned to autumn John Lilburne and his Leveller friends became disillusioned with the agitators. They had hoped to indoctrinate them and make them their chief agents in a mass conversion of the soldiery, for in the short term they could see little chance of realising their cherished reforms and constitutional changes except through pressure from the army. But though they had a few strong adherents among the agitators from the start, notably Edward Sexby, Nicholas Lockyer and (for a time) William Allen, we know of very few others whom they won over before the recorded Putney debates began in late October. They had, indeed, slightly more known sympathisers among the officers. Lilburne addressed an open letter to the soldiery in September, advising them not to entrust the same agitators for too long because they were being corrupted by their contact with the army commanders and by the prospect of promotion that this opened up. Standing waters putrefy, he warned them. 'But above all the rest', he wrote, 'be sure not to trust your great officers at the Generall's quarters, no further than you can throw an Oxe', for they had 'by their plausible but yet cunning and subtle policies, most unjustly stolne the power both from your honest Generall, and your too flexible Adjutators.'[12] Fairfax's popularity was unassailable; the great officers whom they should distrust were of course Cromwell, and still more Ireton.

Since the accredited agitators who sat on the General Council were not coming up to snuff, the Levellers set about engineering the emergence of new ones. Lilburne himself claimed to have taken the initiative in this, despite his being still a prisoner in the Tower.[13] But since the army's entry into London the lieutenant of the Tower had been the radical colonel of trained bands, Robert Tichborne, and he had let Lilburne come and go by day pretty much as he pleased. The new agents first made themselves known late in September in five cavalry regiments, but a sixth should be added, namely Fairfax's own regiment of horse, because Edward Sexby, one of its accredited agitators, was closely associated with them from the start, and was an intimate of Lilburne. The new men were commonly known as 'the agents of the five regiments', sometimes as 'the London agents', and when William Clarke began to record the debates at Putney that was as far as they had spread in the army. They met frequently in London – daily in the early stages – and they were committed propagators of Leveller ideas and policies. The interesting question is whether they were ever actually elected by the regiments that they claimed to represent.

[12] J. Lilburne, 'Advice to the private soldiers', dated 8 September 1647, and printed in his *The juglers discovered* (1647), 10–12. This letter was further publicised in *Mercurius Pragmaticus,* 5–12 and 12–19 October 1647.

[13] 'The Tower of London letter-book of Sir Lewis Dyve', ed. H. G. Tibbutt, in *Bedfordshire Historical Record Society* 37 (1958), 90–1.

The army commanders subsequently claimed that they were not. They certainly did not displace the originally elected agitators of the five regiments on the General Council, and those agitators disowned them. Yet they had solid support in at least two of the five regiments, and there was some form of collective choice in a third. Most if not all of them probably did seek some sort of mandate from their fellow soldiers, but there are indications that they were already meeting and acting as a caucus before they did so. Lilburne himself took a hand in briefing them, but their principal organiser and spokesman was John Wildman, a sharp, articulate civilian in his mid-twenties who had had some legal training. The 'agents of the five regiments' were not always the same men, for the signatories of their documents during October and early November numbered not ten but sixteen. Two at least had appeared temporarily as agitators in the past, but two or three contemporary reporters alleged that most were newcomers to the army, probably enlisted since it occupied London in early August.[14]

From their first emergence they – or, rather, their Leveller managers – set themselves up as a rival channel of political expression for the soldiery to that provided by the General Council. They were not slow in producing their first manifesto, which they called *The case of the armie truly stated* and presented to Fairfax on 18 October. It was signed by the agents of the five regiments, and only by them, but though in parts it bears evidence of their contributions its central arguments and its overall thrust show the stamp of a more sophisticated hand. Ever since 1647 that hand has generally been thought to be Wildman's, but whoever wrote it clearly incorporated shreds and patches from the agents themselves. Elsewhere in this volume, however, John Morrill and Philip Baker very plausibly suggest that its main author was more probably Sexby.[15] It is a convincing attribution. Sexby was close to Lilburne, and he was the principal link-man between the old agitators and the new agents. *The case of the armie truly stated* was the opening salvo in a campaign to sow distrust towards the senior officers at headquarters among the soldiery and junior officers generally, and then, through their elected representatives, to turn the General Council away from its quest for a national settlement by mutual agreement between army, king and parliament. The Leveller caucus that directed and spoke through the new agents no longer wished to work within the framework of the ancient constitution, and would very soon show that it was aiming to establish a new one on foundations that can

---

[14] On the emergence and status of the new agents see Woolrych, *Soldiers and statesmen*, 203–6, and Gentles, *New Model Army*, 198–200.

[15] Below, ch. 6. *The case of the armie truly stated is* printed in Don M. Wolfe (ed.), *Leveller manifestoes of the Puritan revolution* (New York, 1944), 198–222. Woodhouse prints the essential parts in *P&L*, 429–36.

fairly be called revolutionary. *The case of the armie* criticised the military grandees severely, and tendentiously, for failing to carry out the promises that the army had made to the nation in its *Solemn engagement,* and accused them of muzzling the agitators and stifling any discussion in the General Council of what was really needed to secure the freeborn people's rights and liberties. It affirmed the supreme authority of the people's representatives, who should be elected at biennial intervals by all the freeborn aged twenty-one or over (males only implied) who had not forfeited their right through delinquency. It ended by upholding the right of the army, with the support of all who concurred with it, in taking whatever action should be necessary to secure its own rights and the people's freedom.

Fairfax and his advisers recognised the seriousness of this challenge and decided that it must be put before the General Council, if only to flush its real authors out into the open and rebut their accusations. *The case of the armie* was consequently reported to the next Thursday meeting on 21 October, but it was not then read and debated. Probably as a preliminary to a full discussion, it was referred to a committee headed by Ireton and consisting of six other field officers, six of the officers elected to represent regiments (or officer-agitators, as we shall henceforth call them) and six soldier-agitators. This committee was briefed to produce a vindication of the public conduct of the army's leadership since June, but it never did so. It did produce a paper of objections to *The case of the armie,* and sent it to the new agents by the hands of Sexby, Lockyer and Allen, along with a friendly invitation to send delegates to next Thursday's General Council on 28 October, to explain their position. When the committee was set up, Cromwell and Ireton probably expected its report to furnish material for disciplinary proceedings against the authors of *The case of the armie.* The reason why its reaction to them was so much milder can be explained by the presence on it of Sexby, Lockyer and Allen. The new agents and their mentors jumped at this opportunity, for which they may have planned, to make the General Council their captive audience. They responded not with a mere defence of their recent manifesto but with an entirely fresh document, drafted for the occasion. This was no less than the original *An agreement of the people,* which was approved by the new agents' meeting on the 27th and brought to headquarters that same day by Trooper Robert Everard of Cromwell's own regiment.

Like *The case of the armie, An agreement of the people* was published over the names of the agents of the five regiments, and of them only,[16] but it is

---

[16] Their names are appended to an address to the public accompanying the first published edition of *An agreement,* not to *An agreement* itself. There are three differences between this list of names and that appended to *The case of the armie:* see Wolfe, *Leveller manifestoes,* 221, 231.

quite different in style and distinct in content. Barbara Taft has argued very plausibly that William Walwyn had a strong, perhaps a dominant, influence in the framing of it.[17] It was not a scheme for a settlement along constitutional lines, analogous to *The heads of the proposals,* for it assumed that the victory of the people in the civil war had wiped the constitutional slate clean. It contained the outline of a *new* constitution, which was to be legitimated not by historic precedent and the existing law but by the personal assent of each and every one of the sovereign people. Since there was never a chance that the present parliament would even consider its proposals, they would have to be implemented, at least initially, by force. The Levellers, needless to say, were looking to the army to supply that force. *An agreement* was more radical and far-reaching in what it proposed than *The case of the armie,* but the fact that both documents appeared over the names of the agents of the five regiments indicates that they were part of the same campaign. The emphasis of *The case of the armie* was more on the grievances of the army as such, since the first need was to persuade the soldiers and as many as possible of the officers to take their political cue from the Levellers and not from Ireton and Cromwell, but it effectively served its purpose of opening the gate to discussion of the larger objectives outlined in *An agreement.* Between them, the two documents aimed to give an altogether new turn to the debates of the General Council, and thereby to change radically the direction in which the army was heading.

It was doubtless because the generals realised how much was at stake that William Clarke, the General Council's secretary, was directed to record the debate on Thursday 28 October, when two civilian Levellers, Wildman and Maximilian Petty, and two of the new agents, one being Everard, came before it to press the case for *An agreement of the people.* So far as we know he had not taken any such record since *The heads of the proposals* were first opened to discussion at Reading. What he now took down, as far as his early form of shorthand permitted, was not so much a debate within the General Council as a confrontation between it and the delegates of a rival organisation whose members were bidding against it for the allegiance of the soldiery.

The spokesmen for the *Agreement* had a deep conviction that their proposals were so self-evidently necessary to secure the freedom of the people that no other commitment or claim to authority should stand in their way. Most (but not all) of what they advocated now seems self-justifying to western liberals, particularly the superior authority of the

---

[17] *The writings of William Walwyn,* ed. Jack R. McMichael and Barbara Taft (Athens, GA, 1989), 30–1.

people's regularly and democratically elected representatives over that of any hereditary interest, and the entrenchment in the constitution of certain rights, such as freedom of religion and equality before the law, so fundamental that not even sovereign parliaments might encroach upon them. But those who bore the responsibility for the army's current incursion into politics had to consider other questions besides that of the inherent justice of what the *Agreement* propounded. Were its proposals likely to find wide enough acceptance amid the circumstances of 1647 to give the country the peace it so badly needed? Did not the best prospect of a lasting peace lie in a negotiated settlement that would command the assent of the army, the king, and at least the independents in both Houses of Parliament? And was not the army in honour bound by the public pledges that it had already made to the nation?

At the very start of the debate on the 28 October, Sexby, with extraordinary boldness, accused Cromwell and Ireton to their faces, saying 'your creditts and reputation hath bin much blasted upon these two considerations', namely labouring to please the king and supporting a parliament that consisted of rotten members. He urged the General Council to consider the proposals now offered to it in the *Agreement* and to join with its authors in supporting whatever they saw 'of reason' in it.[18] Cromwell and Ireton did not seek to reject it *in toto*, for both acknowledged that there were good things in it. But as Cromwell rightly said:

Truly this paper does containe in itt very great alterations of the very Government of the kingedome, alterations from that Governement that itt hath bin under . . . since itt was a Nation . . . How doe wee know if whilest wee are disputing these thinges another companie of men shall gather together, and they shall putt out a paper as plausible perhaps as this?[19]

It was not enough, he argued, to adjudge how far the *Agreement* was just in the abstract; they must consider the probable consequences of implementing it, and 'whether . . . the spiritts and temper of the people of this Nation are prepared to receive and to goe on alonge with itt'. This was a crucial question, since the ultimate legitimacy of the *Agreement* was to rest on its being subscribed by the greater part of the people of England. As Ireton was to say next day, 'If all the people to a man had subscribed to this [the *Agreement*] then there would bee some security to itt, because noe man would oppose', but it was not for the General Council to impose it unilaterally, since 'wee cannott hold to bee a conclusive authority of the kingedome'.[20] Nothing was in fact less likely than the *Agreement* would at that time have commanded universal or even majority assent. No honest royalist could have touched it, and it was scarcely less unacceptable to the

---

[18] *CP,* I:227–8.   [19] Ibid., I:236–7.   [20] Ibid., I:360.

moderate parliamentarians – the majority, at the level of the gentry and upper bourgeoisie – who held the ancient constitution in high esteem and regarded the Levellers' aspirations as subversive of the social order on which it rested. Further down the social scale, but by no means only at that level, the *Agreement* would have been rejected by the growing number of Independents and more radical puritans who believed that God's purpose in granting victory to his people was to bring nearer the establishment of his kingdom on earth. To them, a policy that granted equal rights to saints and sinners alike was an impiety.

Cromwell's other main argument that day was that the army was bound in honour to adhere to the various declarations of its intentions that it had published to the nation since June. Consequently the proper procedure of the General Council was not to go straight to considering the proposals in the *Agreement* on their intrinsic merits, one by one, as Sexby had urged, but first to establish how far they were compatible with the public engagements that the army had already entered into. 'Before wee take this [the *Agreement*] into consideration', he said, 'itt is fitt for us to consider how farre wee are obliged, and how far wee are free.'[21] The long procedural wrangle that ensued makes the first day's debate recorded by Clarke somewhat tedious and repetitive compared with the second, but in insisting on establishing first how far the army was already bound by its engagements, Cromwell and Ireton were not, as Woodhouse thought, stooping to 'the lower tactics of debate' in order 'to kill time and prevent an irrevocable decision'.[22] Mark Kishlansky sees them, far more plausibly, as seeking a procedure that would help them to preserve consensus,[23] but their purpose went further than that. Not only was the army's honour, for which they cared deeply, at stake, but its whole political direction. If its declarations did remain binding, it was under a moral obligation to continue its quest for a settlement by constitutional means in conjunction with its parliamentary allies, at least until its proposals had been thoroughly considered by the parliament and the king. But if Wildman had persuaded the Council that the sole consideration for it was 'whether the thinge [the *Agreement*] bee just or the people's due, and then there can bee noe Engagement to binde from itt',[24] the way would have been open for the army to march into London, as the Levellers wanted it to, and inaugurate a revolutionary settlement by force. Such a course would have torn the army itself apart and alienated most of the political nation.

So when Ireton and Cromwell proposed that a committee be appointed

---

[21] Ibid., I:238–40.   [22] *P&L*, [28].

[23] Mark Kishlansky, 'Consensus politics and the structure of debate at Putney,' *JBS* 20 (1981), 60–3.   [24] *CP*, I:261.

to sift through the considerable bulk of the army's declarations and tabulate the positive commitments contained in them, in preparation for an early debate in full council, it was a constructive move. It did not please Wildman, of course, but it was welcomed by Captain Audley and Lieutenant Chillenden, officer-agitators who were sympathetic to the Levellers' broader aims, if not to all their tactics; they saw it as offering a prospect of genuine reconciliation.[25] The committee was duly appointed, and it covered a broad spectrum, with Colonels Rainborough, Overton, Okey and Tichborne (all men of radical leanings) among its twelve officers and Sexby, Lockyer and Allen among its six agitators. The conciliatory spirit in the meeting was strengthened when Lieutenant-Colonel Goffe moved that before the committee sat next day they should all meet to seek the Lord's guidance in prayer. This was warmly and widely welcomed, for many must have felt with Goffe that 'it hath been our trouble night and day that God hath not been with us as formerly'.[26]

The next morning was therefore set aside for religious exercises, to be held at the quartermaster-general's lodgings in one Mr Chamberlaine's house, and the committee was scheduled to meet in the afternoon. The General Council was to convene again on Monday 1 November to consider its findings. It was part of the committee's brief to confer with the new agents and such advisers as they should bring with them, but Cromwell urged them not to come 'as engaged men uppon their owne resolution', determined 'only to instruct us and teach us'. He hoped for 'an honest and single debate, how wee may all agree in one common way for publique good . . . Butt if otherwise, I despaire of the Meeting; or att least I would have the meeting to bee of another notion, a meeting that did represent the Agitators of five Regiments to give rules to the Councill of Warre [i.e. the General Council of the Army]'.[27]

The whole morning of 29 October was accordingly spent by most members of the council in seeking divine guidance, and they were still at their devotions when Wildman, Petty, Everard and other new agents arrived early in the afternoon to confer with the committee. Finding a much larger company assembled than they had expected, they pressed for an immediate open debate on the *Agreement*. They were strongly supported by Colonel Rainborough, who had probably travelled with them; he had spent the previous night in London, by his own account through indisposition, though his main reason may have been to confer with them.[28] He had a very dubious right to attend the General Council, for he had been appointed vice-admiral on 27 September, and he had been seen there little if at all since then. His regiment had (quite properly) been

[25] Ibid., I:252, 277.   [26] Ibid., I:253.   [27] Ibid., I:270–1, 279.   [28] Ibid., I:287.

given to another officer, but he resented this, and he had twice clashed angrily with Cromwell, once over the latter's opposition to his naval appointment (which turned out disastrously) and again over the question of whether to treat with the king.[29]

One can sympathise with Cromwell for opposing an immediate debate. He had chaired the previous day's General Council until far into the evening, and he and his colleagues had probably spent five hours already in seeking the Lord, which could be quite tiring. Had they even had any food, one wonders? Furthermore, the committee, whose work was in his mind essential before further open discussion took place, had as yet had no chance to meet. But if Cromwell's common sense had prevailed, posterity would have been denied the most famous debate in early modern British history. It is a remarkable piece of fortune that it occurred at all, and that it was recorded. It was entirely unscheduled; it was not held in a formal meeting of the General Council, or in Putney Church, the Council's regular meeting-place; the most famous speaker in it, who argued 'that the poorest man in England is nott att all bound in a stricte sense to that Government that hee hath not had a voice to putt himself under',[30] had a doubtful right to be present at all; and Rainborough might never have got his teeth into the topic of manhood suffrage if Ireton had not committed what John Morrill has called 'the great error of judgement' of raising it, since there is no mention of the franchise in the *Agreement*.[31]

That Friday's debate deserves its fame, for its classic confrontation between the ideal of egalitarian democracy and the conviction that authority should be based on property and precedent, and for the spontaneity and passion with which the arguments were expressed. But one has to ask how it struck most of those who heard it, and how far it was representative of political feeling in the army as a whole. It did go on for a very long time, and for much of that time hardly anyone got a word in except Ireton, Cromwell, Rainborough and Wildman. The heat that it generated clearly dismayed some of the officer-agitators, who tried to set it back on the path of consensus by suggesting compromises, or another committee. Rainborough, whose conversion to Leveller ideas seems to have been very recent, was going beyond most of the party leaders in his devotion to unqualified manhood suffrage, and it would be little more than a year before they and Ireton agreed in the second *Agreement of the people* on a household franchise as a practicable objective. Anyone who strains to hear the voice of the soldiery in the Putney debates should be aware that,

[29] Ibid., I:245n; Woolrych, *Soldiers and statesmen*, 226–7.   [30] *CP*, I:301.
[31] John Morrill, 'The army revolt of 1647', reprinted in Morrill, *The nature of the English revolution* (London, 1993), 326.

apart from one brief interjection by an unnamed agent, the only troopers who spoke that day were Sexby and Everard, and on the other two days recorded by Clarke the only others who opened their mouths were Lockyer and Allen. No agitator of a foot regiment is known to have spoken. Out of just fifty officer-agitators listed in October, twelve spoke in the course of the three recorded days – five of them only once, and very briefly. We should be very cautious about treating the Putney debates, wonderful as they are, as the typical voice of the army.

One outcome of that Friday's confrontation was a new committee, briefed to compare the *Agreement* with the army's public declarations. Despite the presence on it of men of such different views as Cromwell, Ireton, both Rainborough brothers (Major William, the younger, being an elected officer-agitator), Sexby and Allen, it made striking progress over the weekend in finding common ground between the opposed parties. But Wildman and the hard-core Leveller agents were not interested in compromise, and if they paid lip-service to consensus they were seeking it only on their own terms. Two more pamphlets from their camp circulated during the Putney debates. The first, entitled *Two letters from the agents of the five regiments of horse*, was in print by 28 October; it defended *The case of the armie truly stated*, reaffirmed the Levellers' main political objectives, and boldly justified the agitators old and new in acting independently of their officers. The second, *A cal to all the souldiers of the army, by the free people of England . . . justifying the proceedings of the five regiments*, followed just a day later, and has been generally (and plausibly) attributed to Wildman.[32] It contained a violent personal attack on Ireton and a more circumspect one on Cromwell, and it urged the soldiers not only to distrust them but to disobey them. '*Resist the devil and he will fly from you*', it adjured them: 'Hold not parley with them, but proceed with that just work ye have so happily begun, without any more regarding one word they speak.' If Cromwell did not instantly repent and change his course, they should renounce him–'*And with a word ye can create new officers.*' They should set up 'an exact council', draw in well-wishers from outside the army to help them, 'establish a free parliament by expulsion of the usurpers', and assume control of the national finances. 'Be confident that none will oppose, and be as confident that thousands and ten thousands are ready and ripe to assist you.'

These were open incitements to mutiny, and were already bearing poisoned fruit. Fairfax had lately ordered Colonel Robert Lilburne's foot regiment to Newcastle, for sound military reasons, but a party of new agents bearing copies of *The case of the armie* overtook it and urged it not

---

[32] Woodhouse prints excerpts from both tracts in *P&L*, 437–43; the quotations that follow are from 441–3. Italics are in the original.

to let the army be divided. Thereupon its soldiers turned back, held an unauthorised rendezvous and refused to obey their officers. Other regiments were to be in a state of incipient mutiny before the debates at Putney were wound up, and it was not only the army's senior officers who were dismayed. At the General Council's next meeting, on Monday 1 November, news came in that two emissaries of the new agents had persuaded Colonel Lambert's regiment in Yorkshire to elect new agitators, on the ground 'that the officers had broken their Engagements'.[33]

That Monday meeting was the last that Clarke recorded, and Cromwell again presided, as he had on the previous two. Fairfax was reported to be unwell, but one wonders how far his indisposition was diplomatic. He was not at home in the essentially political role of chairing the General Council. Cromwell himself, however, had difficulty in handling this meeting, partly because he opened it by inviting those present to speak of what God had vouchsafed to them in answer to their prayers. That predictably let loose a spate of intemperate opinions, mostly against the king, which were not what he wanted to hear. But he was probably wise to bring them into the open, because nothing was going to be a greater obstacle to rational, open-minded debate than an individual's blind conviction that God had revealed his will to him on a question of secular politics. There were not a few such individuals at Putney, and Cromwell argued against them patiently and earnestly. For himself, he said, 'I cannott say that I have recived any thinge that I can speake as in the name of the Lord', and he warned them against neglecting the light of reason 'uppon the imaginary apprehension of such divine impressions and divine discoveries in particular thinges'.[34] He was respectful and courteous to those who were so sure that they knew God's mind, but he firmly cracked the whip against the subversive agents and pamphleteers who were calling the soldiers to illegal rendezvous and inciting them to disobey the general's orders. 'I have a Commission from the Generall', he said, 'and I understand that I am to doe by itt.'[35] On substantive matters, however, he tried hard to minimise the division between his position and that of the *Agreement*'s supporters. He believed that they were still engaged to leave the settlement of government ultimately to parliament, but granted that parliament needed to be radically reformed, especially in the mode of elections and the distribution of seats.[36] All were pursuing the same end, he claimed, which was to deliver the nation from oppression and slavery and to establish justice and righteousness in it. More strikingly, he granted 'that wee all apprehend danger from the person of the kinge, and from the Lords', and that if the army was free to frame the constitution afresh it

[33] *CP,* I:367.   [34] Ibid., I:376, 379.   [35] Ibid., I:371.   [36] Ibid., I:370.

would set up neither king nor Lords. It was not their intention to preserve the one or the other if they threatened danger and destruction to the people and the public interest. But the generals felt that at the present time the army could not with justice and righteousness set about to destroy either, even though retaining them might pose some hazard to the national interest. The difference between their view and that of the *Agreement*'s promoters, as Cromwell stated it, was that the latter believed that the liberty of the kingdom was totally unsafe if the king and the Lords were retained, so any apparent right they might have must be overridden.[37] He had revealing words for those who were so convinced that there could be no safety while king and Lords continued that they confidently expected God to destroy both. They might be mistaken. 'And though [I] my self doe concurre with them, and perhaps concurre with them upon some ground that God will doe soe, yett lett us, [not] make those things to bee our rule which wee cannot soe clearlie know to be the minde of God.' If God did have a purpose to destroy them, 'yett God can doe itt without necessitating us to doe a thing which is scandalous, or sinne, or which would bringe a dishonour to his name; and therefore let those that are of that minde waite uppon God for such a way when the thing may bee done without sin'.[38] Cromwell, if Clarke has captured his sense correctly, was clearly envisaging a possibility that the king and the Lords might have to go, though God (he thought) had not yet made his will clear regarding them. His attitude had plainly changed since *The heads of the proposals* were first framed, and Charles' temporising response to them probably explains why. The second civil war would clinch his conviction that the king had earned God's wrath. Wildman, by contrast, already felt that there was no way left for mercy towards him, and 'the preservation of the Kinge or Lords was inconsistent with the people's safetie', which must be a law paramount. He and Cromwell were not far apart, however, when he said that 'wee cannott finde anythinge in the worde of God [of] what is fitt to bee done in civil matters'.[39]

After this exchange the debate focused on the king's power to veto bills passed by the people's representatives, and then on the relevant recommendation of the committee, agreed on the previous evening. This did not explicitly mention the royal veto, but it did affirm the power of the Commons to legislate on their own in all matters that concerned commoners and were not reserved by the represented to themselves.[40] It would have been awkward – perhaps unworkable – to preserve a veto solely in matters that specifically affected the interests of the king and the

---

[37] Ibid., I:379–80.   [38] Ibid., I:382.   [39] Ibid., I:384–5.
[40] Ibid., I:407. Though this document is dated 2 November, this clause was probably formulated on the evening of 31 October; see Woolrych, *Soldiers and statesmen*, 252–3.

Lords, but this formulation, with its recognition of entrenched fundamental rights, went some way towards meeting the Levellers' desires, as Rainborough acknowledged.[41] There are hints in the ensuing speeches that Ireton was more attached to the ancient constitution than his father-in-law; he was certainly less conciliatory, and before the record closes he was drawn into a sterile wrangle with Commissary Cowling and Rainborough about the status of the Commons before the Norman Conquest.

Nevertheless, the committee carried on manfully with its search for common ground, and the General Council, having resolved to meet daily and debate all its resolutions one by one, held five more meetings. But no transcript of their proceedings survives, and this may well be because the General Council was becoming more an arena for confrontation than a symposium through which the divisions within the army could be composed. It was certainly difficult to manage, and on 5 November, when Fairfax for once presided and Cromwell was probably attending the Commons, things got badly out of hand. There was pressure to call the army to a general rendezvous, doubtless in the hope of carrying *An agreement of the people* by acclamation, as the *Solemn engagement* had been carried in June; Rainborough had already urged such a course on 29 October. This time he and his allies actually succeeded in getting a letter sent to the Speaker, declaring that reports that the General Council desired parliament to address further propositions to the king were altogether groundless. At this Ireton stormed out of the meeting and refused to return to the General Council until the letter was recalled. By now the Council's public agenda, which concerned the terms of a constitutional settlement for the kingdom, was yielding to a hidden agenda, and not a very well hidden one at that: the question of who was to direct the army, its appointed hierarchy of officers or its Leveller faction. The latter's total numerical strength was probably still not large, but it was spreading. New Leveller-inspired agents were now rapidly appearing in many regiments, perhaps a dozen besides the original five, and in several besides Robert Lilburne's the authority of their officers was slipping.[42] This was causing widespread dismay, and not only among the more senior ranks.

Three things probably persuaded the generals by 8 November that the meetings at Putney must be wound up and the General Council put into suspension. One was the growing threat to the army's unity and discipline, which the debates were doing more to exacerbate than to allay. Another was the intransigent hostility that was being displayed in them towards not only King Charles but monarchy itself. This was dividing not

[41] *CP,* I:391.   [42] Gentles, *New Model Army,* 218, 220–2.

only the army – there were some surprising demonstrations of good feeling towards the king among some of the soldiery in early November – but the Levellers themselves, for John Lilburne was sending friendly messages to him through his fellow-prisoner Sir Lewis Dyve.[43] The radicals' demand that there should be no further dealings with the king not only ran counter to what Fairfax, Cromwell and Ireton believed to be right for the kingdom at this stage, but threatened to inflame public feeling against the army as a whole. But ironically a third factor affecting the generals' decision was almost certainly a sharp suspicion of Charles's own intentions. He was in close and frequent touch with recently arrived commissioners from Scotland, and there were signs that he was meditating escape from Hampton Court. He did in fact bolt just two days after the last meeting of the General Council. It was a matter of urgency therefore to restore the army's old solidarity and discipline.

This was done with remarkable ease, and it results in an apparent paradox. It seems that late in that famous meeting on 29 October a motion was carried, with only three dissentients, to give the vote in parliamentary elections to all men except servants and beggars, and that the General Council confirmed this four days later.[44] Yet within a week, on 8 November, the same General Council formally advised Fairfax to send all the elected officers and agitators back to their regiments until he saw cause to recall them – which he never did. He reported to the Speaker that they had unanimously *offered* to return to their units and do all that they could to restore discipline in them. The explanation is surely that the proponents of the *Agreement of the people* won the debate on the franchise because their case was so persuasive, especially to soldiers who could not see why they should be denied the vote when they had risked their lives for parliament; and because they argued it most eloquently. But they failed when they tried to wrest the soldiers' loyalty from their officers, partly because the solidarity that had been forged across the ranks in battle was generally too strong for them, and partly because of the widely shared ideals between officers and men. Their incitements to mutiny created a backlash, the more so at a time when a national crisis was looming and a military *coup*, such as they aimed at, would have played into the hands of the common enemy. They might score a limited success against Ireton in formal argument, but it was much harder for them to undermine Cromwell's popularity, and impossible to assail Fairfax's. All the little movements of unrest in the army fizzled out in the face of the acclamations that greeted Fairfax at the three rendezvous that he held in mid-November, and the Levellers' attempt to raise a mutiny at the first of them

---

[43] Woolrych, *Soldiers and statesmen*, 230, 247, 263–4.
[44] Ibid., 243–4 for a discussion of the somewhat unclear evidence.

was a very damp squib indeed. The army's unity and discipline were restored in the nick of time, only a few weeks before Charles' Engagement with the Scots set in train the second civil war.

Those of us whose hearts go out to the Levellers for most of their ideals and objectives, and to the courage with which they pursued them, may yet regret their tactics in the autumn of 1647. We may feel it a pity that so much of the direction of their army supporters was assumed at that time by Wildman, who revelled in conflict and conspiracy, and that John Lilburne let his personal animosity against Cromwell and Ireton warp his judgement. We may wonder how the Levellers might have fared if Walwyn had had a larger part in their counsels. As Ian Gentles demonstrates later in this volume, they came closest to achieving a substantial part of their aims when they worked in conjunction with the army leadership, at the time of the second *Agreement of the people*.[45] Whenever they engaged in raising mutiny they did themselves nothing but damage, and in the spring of 1649 the damage was to prove irreparable. But if Ireton and Wildman and Rainborough had all behaved like perfect statemen in 1647, the debates at Putney might have been a dull affair, and posterity would be the poorer.

[45] See ch. 8, below.

5   The army, the state and the soldier in the English civil war

Barbara Donagan

The Putney debates are famous for their impressive and precocious expression of democratic principles. Yet the speakers' democratic claims must be set in the context of their membership of a victorious army conscious of itself as an institution with a strong professional, corporate identity, an institution whose soldiers had earned a special status, yet one that felt its worth undervalued, its codes misunderstood, its just claims neglected, and its survival threatened by civilian power.[1] The 1640s had forced Englishmen to confront new questions about the role of the army in the state, and the speakers at Putney reflected the diversity of their answers. The locus of obedience and loyalty when sovereignty was contested, the uncertain boundaries between civilian and military law, and the proper spheres of civilian and military authority, posed practical as well as theoretical problems. Solutions were difficult and rarely final.

These issues have been less studied than the striking conflict between democratic and conservative visions of a godly state that emerged at Putney. Nevertheless, the participants in the debates were well aware of them, and their broader claims were not clearly distinguished from their conception of the rights, obligations and power of the army. With hindsight we can see that Putney, where soldiers made claims in their dual capacity as soldiers and Englishmen, foreshadowed the impending overt power struggle between military and civilian authority in the state. If for a while we can forget that the army was shortly to purge parliament and then, like the angel in the garden, to expel its residue, we can see that one aspect of its story in the 1640s was its attempt to balance the claims of parliamentary sovereignty in the state and of proper obedience to that sovereign power, with the autonomy of the army in the military sphere. In what follows only a few of the issues relevant to the relations between the state and the army can be addressed. They will include the problems of

---

[1] See Ian Gentles, *The New Model Army in England, Ireland, and Scotland, 1645–1653* (Oxford, 1992), 146–51, on the army's sense of embattlement and its responses in early 1647.

sovereignty (and the related question of where loyalty was due), of jurisdiction, and of the proper division of authority in the state.

The problem of the relation between the state and its army was new to Englishmen for several reasons. In the first place, the country was unaccustomed to a *resident* and *standing* army, to an institution that could dominate its human and material environment by force, and that was responsible to a central authority (unlike, for example, the retine of a feudal warlord). Civil war armies were not comparable either to forces that had been raised for temporary domestic service in times of crisis, or to those raised for overseas service whose unruliness and depredations were at least temporary as they passed on their way to spread mayhem in foreign fields. On the other hand, no army arises *de novo*. Those of the English civil war shared technical and legal attributes with the continental armies with which many of their members had fought.

This civil war was also novel in the way it raised the issue of sovereignty. In the past, civil wars and *coups* had the aim of substituting one *person* for another; in the 1640s there was a transfer of sovereignty from person to institution. For royalists, indeed, there was no more than a shift in emphasis; loyalty only became more intense to a king who in his person headed both state and army. For parliamentarians, however, the constitutional trinity of king, Lords and Commons gradually became a useful fiction and ultimately legally null. In fact, practical acceptance of parliamentary sovereignty long predated the trial and death of the king, and went back to the initial decision to bear arms against him. Much of the reasoning that supported this decision was to return to haunt parliament when those who had upheld it came to perceive members as failing to act as a 'true' parliament should. In both cases the authenticity of the institution, whether monarchical or parliamentary, became a factor that could override the duty of obedience.[2] Parliament's Militia Ordinance and its commisssion to the earl of Essex as captain-general of its army in 1642 marked the beginning of de facto public acceptance of parliamentary sovereignty, for by challenging the king's right to control armed force (a right that was reasserted in his commissions of array), they forced a choice on those responsible for raising troops as to whom they would obey. They gave expression to an alternative loyalty, one to parliament rather than king.[3] Nevertheless, although at Putney the arguments for actually dis-

---

[2] I have discussed these issues in 'Casuistry and allegiance in the English civil war' in Derek Hirst and Richard Strier (eds.), *Writing and political engagement in seventeenth-century England* (Cambridge, 1999), 89–111.

[3] C. H. Firth and R. S. Rait (eds.), *Acts and ordinances of the Interregnum, 1642–1660* (2 vols., London, 1911), I:1–6, 14–16. The ordinance and the commission together placed the country's armed forces under the direction of parliament, for they established the precedence of parliamentary orders over royal commands. This immediately confronted Englishmen with the question of choice as to whom they would obey.

pensing with the king had already become bolder and more overt, the respectable establishment still assumed a constitutional settlement would be reached with the king as titular sovereign.[4] In 1647, as in the earlier years of the war, the real point at issue in discussion of possible settlement with the king was not survival of the institution of monarchy but how power was to be distributed between king and parliament and where ultimate sovereignty was to lie.

A necessary condition for achieving parliament's dominance in the present and maintaining it in the future was possession of the means of force, and proposals for its long-term control of the army remained a vital but contentious element in the fruitless negotiations with the king. Royalists recognised that without a monopoly of armed force the 'Prerogative Royall' could not be preserved and the king would be a mere cipher.[5] Parliament now possessed that monopoly, but in 1647 its control over its own army was endangered: the army might exercise power as an independent third party in the state to reach agreement with the king or, a more immediate danger, it might spin out of control in mutiny and a kind of radical free-fall.[6] If a supple and professional higher command managed to defuse the latter threat by the time-honoured military combination of judicious bending to demands, appeals to a corporate sense of honour and achievement, and sudden flashes of severity, the problems of control of and dependence on the army did not vanish. They were not new in 1647; they remained active issues in 1659.

Once there was an army, and one that was not the servant of a monarchical sovereign power but instead powerfully conscious of its role in overturning that power and sustaining its replacement, what was its role in the state?[7] At Putney its representatives combined universal claims to constitutional rights with particular claims reflecting their corporate interest in redress of grievances specific to the army. The balance of emphasis

[4] See, for example, Ireton's declaration, 'I doe nott seeke, or would nott seeke, nor will joyne with them that doe seeke the destruction either of Parliament or Kinge' (*CP,* I:233). Events were shortly to overcome such principles.

[5] 'What a fine King of clouts shall wee have if these men had their wishes', wrote one royalist, 'his deniall or assent shall be to one and as much purpose, and his Commands of no worth either by Sea, or Land': *Mercurius Pragmaticus* 23 (properly 24), 5 September 1648, 7; cf. John Wildman at Putney, *CP,* I:353; and see Robert Ashton, *Counter-revolution. The second civil war and its origins, 1646–8* (New Haven, 1994), 8.

[6] On fears of 'a private arrangement' between the army and the king, see Robert Ashton, 'The problem of indemnity, 1647–1648' in Colin Jones, Malyn Newitt and Stephen Roberts (eds.), *Politics and people in revolutionary England. Essays in honour of Ivan Roots* (Oxford, 1986), 117–40, at 121–2. See also Gentles, *New Model Army,* 153–4, 170.

[7] We should remember, when speaking of 'the army', that there was no unified military command of all parliamentary forces until July 1647, when parliament voted to place all land forces, including provincial armies and those intended for Ireland, under Fairfax's command. See Austin Woolrych, *Soldiers and statesmen. The General Council of the Army and its debates, 1647–1648* (Oxford, 1987), 165–6; *CJ* V:248; *LJ* IX:338.

between universal claims on behalf of all Englishmen and specific claims on behalf of soldiers fluctuated, but in both cases speakers revealed a belief that the army now had a privileged voice to speak for the nation, as well as a special right to call in the particular obligations owed to it by the state. It stood, so Colonel Harrison's radical regiment proclaimed, for 'England's Freedom and Soldiers' Rights'.[8] The army grandees, however, wanted to unbundle these two sets of claims. If they could support those that would now be regarded as matters of contract and entitlement – pay and benefits such as provision for widows, orphans and the maimed – and could sympathise with claims for indemnity, they were alarmed by those that asserted political rights that would change the character of the state. The latter were outside the domain of the army, they argued, for although the army was the saviour of the state it was also its servant, and in the circumstances of the later 1640s the state was embodied in parliament.

This relationship had been endangered by the divisions of early 1647, when many in the army perceived a presbyterian capture of parliament and feared disbandment as well as neglect of their reasonable claims to pay and indemnity.[9] The crisis was temporarily resolved by the tempestuous events of June and July. The flight of a significant number of members of both Houses and both parties to the protection of the army in the face of counter-revolutionary London mobs, their triumphant return to the city under the wing of the army, and expulsion of presbyterian leaders, all helped to avert a decisive confrontation. Parliament could again be seen as a 'true' parliament of which the army was properly the servant. It remained, however, a servant that had given notice of its power. Meanwhile divisions in the army itself were smoothed over by co-operation between high command and radicals.[10] If that co-operation was not always enthusiastic – Fairfax was later to disavow responsibility for the political stance of the army and for the documents issued in his name after June 1647[11] – for the present a functional unity had been restored within the army and between army and parliament. Participants at Putney, however, were aware of its vulnerability.

If the events of the summer of 1647 had given credence to the idea that

---

[8] Woolrych, *Soldiers and statesmen*, 281; *CP,* I: 352–4; but see John Morrill, 'The army revolt of 1647', in his *The nature of the English revolution* (London, 1993), 325–8, on convergence of interest between soldiers and grandees as a factor in defusing radicalism.

[9] For the events discussed here see, for example, Gentles, *New Model Army*, ch. 6, 140–89; Mark Kishlansky, *The rise of the New Model Army* (Cambridge, 1979), ch. 8, 223–72.

[10] Gentles, *New Model Army*, 176.

[11] 'If you find me carried on with this stream', he wrote, 'I can truly say, it was by the violence of it, and no consent of mine.' His 'general's power [was] broken and crumbled into a levelling faction': Bodleian Library, Ms. Fairfax 36, fols. 4v, 6v. For a sceptical view of Fairfax's dissociation of himself from events, see Firth's comment, *CP,* I:147, n. *a*; see also Woolrych, *Soldiers and statesmen*, 126–33.

a parliament might not be a true parliament, just as a king might not be a true king, and that the obligations of obedience might be loosed in both cases, nevertheless at Putney the higher command, including Cromwell, Ireton and others whose later actions add an ironical gloss to their statements there, were agreed in their representation of the army as the servant and agent of parliament. The hierarchy of obedience they presented – from parliament to commander-in-chief to officers to common soldiers – was necessary if their army was to function effectively. The army might claim that it incorporated the people's interests, but officers, including radicals, had no faith in a people's army or a military collective; discipline and obedience to orders won battles and the hierarchy of obedience ran from parliament to the common soldier. As the General Council resolved at Putney, soldiers owed obedience to their general, for the service of parliament.[12] Yet this conventional view had to coexist with the belief, which was part of international military theory and practice, that there was also an autonomous sphere of military law and action.

The 'official' position as to the army's relation to parliament varied little through most of the 1640s. It succumbed to circumstances at the end of the decade, but even in the 1650s it remained a premiss of debate, and returned to the fore in 1659. Before the war armed force was designed 'for the advancement of His Majesty's service', and when parliament replaced the king, the concept of obedient service remained.[13] Commanders saw their powers as reposed in them by commissions from parliament that imposed obligation and required loyalty; they were 'employed' by parliament, and that employment entailed trust and service. Faithfulness to parliament was as much a matter of personal integrity and honour for parliamentarians as faithfulness to the king was for royalists. In 1642 the earl of Warwick explained his refusal to obey the king's order to give up command of the fleet to a royal nominee thus: 'I resolved not to desert that Charge committed to my Trust . . . but to continue it until I shall be revoked by that Authority that hath entrusted me with it.'[14] In 1644 he was echoed by the earl of Essex, who replied to

---

[12] *CP*, I:412.

[13] See Bodleian, Ms. Fairfax 31, fols. 133v–134, for a pre-war commission (issued to Sir Ferdinando Fairfax as colonel of a trained band regiment in March 1639).

[14] John Rushworth, *Historical collections of private passages of state* (8 vols., 1680–1701), IV:752; and see *A joyful message sent from both houses of parliament to Portsmouth . . . also a royall message sent from the kings maiesty to the earle of Warwick* ([1642]), 4: Warwick commented that in the king's letter 'obeying the Parliament is counted High Treason; a Doctrine I never heard of till this Parliament': *LJ* V:216. In his letter to the king he emphasised the 'weighty trust' placed upon him by parliament: HMC, *Manuscripts of the duke of Portland*, I (1891), 42. Note also Sir John Hotham (before he changed his spots) who explained 'why the Subiect being Commanded by the Parliament ought not to disobey their Commands, though the King commanded the Contrary'. He commended

royalist approaches to negotiate a separate peace, 'I having no authority from the Par[liament] (who having employed me) to treat cannot give way to it without breach of trust.'[15] As lord general and servant of parliament he had no authority unilaterally to commit himself or his army in a matter of public policy. In 1646 Sir Thomas Fairfax displayed similar military rectitude: 'I . . . must not neglect the duty of that trust I owe to the parliament.'[16]

The sense that the army was the agent rather than the master of parliament persisted at Putney. At the first meeting in September an officer from Fairfax's own regiment declared that there was 'now no visible Authority in the Kingdome but the power and force of the sword'. For this he was expelled, and the General Council of the Army pointedly published its 'dislike; and disavow[ed] such principles and purposes'.[17] On 1 November, after Commissary Cowling had declared that 'the sworde was the onelie thinge that had from time to time recover'd our Rightes', Cromwell, in the course of a lengthy rebuttal of radical claims, asserted that the legitimacy of the army depended upon recognition of parliament's authority, and that the army must observe the habits of obedience inculcated by the rules of war. As for the army's officers:

footnote 14 (*cont.*)

loyalty, but warned, '[L]et your Loyalty take its limit from Law.' *A learned speech made by the right worshipfull Sir John Hotham . . . on the 23. of May. 1642* (1642), sig. A3–A3v. See also Robert Ashton, *The English civil war. Conservatism and revolution 1603–1649* (New York, 1978), 167.

[15] Exeter, Devon Record Office, Seymour of Berry Pomeroy Ms. 1392 M/L 1644/54; and see Rushworth, *Historical collections*, V:691–3. Cf. J. S. A. Adamson, 'The baronial context of the English civil war', *TRHS*, 5th ser., 40 (1990), 109–13, who interprets the episode as evidence of Essex's susceptibility to approaches from the king, and of his 'vice-regal' and 'baronial' ambitions. The passage above is the concluding sentence of Essex's brief reply, and cannot be dismissed as boilerplate or taken as encouragement to royalist advances. Note also Essex's refusal of a safe conduct for Henrietta Maria in June 1644: 'he could not obey her Majesties desires, without Directions from the Parliament': Rushworth, *Historical collections* V:684, and see V:668–9. See also Bodleian Ms. Nalson 3, fols. 244, 250, 301, for Essex's insistence on the 'trust', 'duty', and 'honour' he owed to parliament, and Waller's response to the king after his defeat at Cropredy Bridge in 1644: he 'could not treat with his Majesty but by command of parliament', for to do so would make him a 'traitor to . . . [his] cause': Sir William Waller, *Recollections* in [Hannah Cowley], *The poetry of Anna Matilda* (London, 1788), 107–8. Such responses should not be dismissed as suspect merely because they are so clearly 'correct'.

[16] East Sussex Record Office, Danny Ms., no. 100.

[17] 'A declaration from his excellency Sir Thomas Fairfax and the councell of his army, held at Putney, Sept. 9. 1647. Concerning the fundamentall authority and government of the Kingdome' in *A declaration of the engagements, remonstrances, representations . . . from . . . Sir Thomas Fairfax, and the generall councel of the army* (London, 1647), 150. The full title of the 'Declaration' reveals participants' awareness of the constitutional issue at stake. See also Austin Woolrych, 'Putney revisited: political debate in the New Model Army in 1647' in Jones et al., *Politics and people*, 95–116, at 105; and see *CP,* I:lvii, for Major White's later public repentance of his 'rashness'.

itt is their proper place to conforme to the Parliament that first gave them their being . . . how they can take the determination of commanding men . . . without an aucthority otherwise than themselves, I am ignorant of. And therfore I thinke there is much [need] in the Army to conforme to those thinges that are within their spheare . . . Either they are a parliament or noe Parliament. If they bee noe Parliament they are nothing, and wee are nothing likewise.

He went on to argue the need for obedience within the army and the obligation to obey its general. He knew what his commission required but, he implied, others were professionally ignorant and their actions, because destructive of army discipline, were likely to be destructive to the cause. 'I have bin inform'd by some of the Kinge's partie', he concluded, 'that if they give us rope enough we will hange ourselves. [We shall hang ourselves], if wee doe not conforme to the rules of warre'.[18]

As so often with Cromwell, his formulation proved to contain the seeds of future reinterpretations at the behest of God, conscience and circumstance. Nevertheless in it he tied the legitimacy of the army and of the general's authority to parliament, and he linked the exercise of that authority to the rules of war. The first of these – the nature of the general's authority – had a specifically English and constitutional context; thus on 8 November officers and agitators were dispatched to their regiments to bring them to 'obedience to his Excellency for the service of the Parliament and Kingedome'.[19] The second issue moved beyond England to appeal to international norms, and Cromwell accordingly recognised the authority of the laws of war within the army's sphere. Yet the army's authenticity as an institution was dependent on that of the parliament.

By 1652 the relative weight to be assigned to each partner in the alliance had become more problematic. As a member of the Rump observed, it was now a question as to 'whether the soldier shall overcome the parliament or the parliament the soldier'.[20] The immediate outcome nevertheless did not favour parliament. By 1659, however, the old, conventional formulations had regained their power. George Monck condemned the army's assumption of the functions of sovereignty and its exertion of 'force upon the Parliament': 'this poore Common wealth can never bee happy if the army make it selfe a divided interest from the rest of the nation . . . if ever wee are setled, the Parliament must doe it'. The army's 'contempt of authority' could lead only to 'an arbitrary Government by the sword, to enslave the contiences, lawes, and estates of the people'.[21]

---

[18] *CP*, I:369–71.   [19] Ibid., I:412.
[20] Blair Worden, *The Rump Parliament 1648–1653* (Cambridge, 1977), 284.
[21] *CP*, IV:85–7, 90. I am grateful to Robert Landrum for introducing me to Monck's views. See also Sir Charles Firth, *The regimental history of Cromwell's army* (2 vols., Oxford, 1940), I:xxx–xxxiii.

For Monck, too, the army should be the servant and instrument of parliament.[22]

This sounds like a simple story with a happy ending that all right-thinking non-militarists can approve. Yet even in the apparent heyday of such politically correct theory there were strains within both theory and practice.[23] The idea of a delegitimated parliament was already in the air before Putney. The army's *Humble remonstrance* of 23 June 1647 had argued that parliament had subverted its true self by its failure to heed the soldiers. The army would prove 'to be more faithfull to the true interest of Parliaments, and the Kingdom' than parliament, which, by actions as tyrannous and unjust as the 'proceedings of the most Arbitrary Courts' had incurred 'insufferable dishonour'.[24] At Putney, Sexby, while declaring that most of those present 'would loose their lives' for 'a Parliamentarie aucthoritie', feared that they had fought for 'an house which will prove rotten studds, I meane the Parliament which consists of a Company of rotten Members'. Wildman predicted a parliament of ciphers, of 'soe many round Os'. Taken in conjunction with arguments that the injustice of engagements freed men from the obligation to honour them, the way became clear to argue that, when men or institutions were false to their proper roles, there was a higher duty than obedience and keeping faith.[25] The arguments by which a higher duty, comfortingly backed by a divine power, had justified for many members their resistance to a king who had forfeited his right to be considered a true king, were to return to haunt the House of Commons.

There were, of course, areas in which 'the army's engagement in politics', in Woolrych's phrase, was less controversial.[26] The pressure exerted by army leaders in the latter part of 1647 that forced parliament to address many of the soldiers' military grievances was no more than the lobbying and pressure that armies and their commanders habitually

---

[22] Monck's position, however, called up echoes of 1647; army pressure could be exerted over membership, for example, to ensure a 'true' parliament. Compare also Cromwell, cited in n. 23 below.

[23] When Cromwell said that settlement of the kingdom 'belonge[d] to the Parliament', it was with the caveat that the body be 'well composed in their creation and election'. He raised the possibility of a parliament that was 'noe Parliament'. Given a legitimate parliament, however, he was uncertain how far the army should press its case. *CP,* I:369–70.

[24] *An humble remonstrance from his excel. Sir Thomas Fairfax and the army under his command . . . at St. Albans, Iune 23* (1647), 4, 11.

[25] *CP,* I:228, 352, 354. The implications of Wildman's statement (ibid., I:352) that 'the Agents doe declare their principle, that whensoever any Engagement cannott bee kept justly they must breake that Engagement' had alarming social and legal implications that extended far beyond the present quarrel. See Rainborough and 'Buffe-coate' (probably Robert Everard) on the legitimacy of breaking engagements and Ireton on the danger of doing so: ibid., I:242, 271–3.   [26] Woolrych, *Soldiers and statesmen,* 1.

engage in to obtain their real or imagined needs.[27] It was soldiers' larger
political demands and the claim of an intrinsic right to make them that
seemed to threaten both the ancient constitution and hierarchy in army
and state. The title of Austin Woolrych's book, *Soldiers and statesmen*,
suggests that the two roles might be combined. Fairfax, however, representing the traditional view of professional soldiers, was sure that the
army's 'humour of . . . being statesmen' was a destructive deviation from
'their more proper duties of soldiers'.[28] '[T]he considering of what is fitt
for the Kingedome does belonge to the Parliament', said Cromwell at
Putney.[29]

Fairfax, like his officers and men, had a powerful sense of the nature of
the army's proper 'sphere' in the state, of matters in which it should act
autonomously and without civilian interference, and of the vexed border-
lands between the military and the civilian spheres. If the army's corporate pride energised soldiers' claims on behalf of Englishmen's liberties, it
also shaped the force and persistence with which they made particular
demands on their own behalf and defended the army's territory against
civilian incursion. Their sense of themselves as elite and deserving came
only in part from the religious worthiness so often attributed to them.
Soldiers were conscious of 'the great and faithfull services of this Army';
they had 'engaged in this Kingdome and ventur'd [their] lives'; they were
strongly aware of 'the reputation and honour of the Army' as an institution and were sensitive to 'hard thoughts' that 'tend[ed] . . . to [its] dishonour'; and they were victorious: 'Wee have gott the better of them in
the feild'.[30] Even the demand for an end to free quarter came in part
because it rendered the army unpopular and so endangered the putative
bond between the people and their soldiers.[31] On the one hand the army
knew the power bestowed by its monopoly of material force and was not
averse to threatening to use it. On the other hand, it saw itself as neglected
and threatened by civilian authority, which either failed to act to give the
army its due, as in matters of pay, or intervened in spheres that were properly military. Its soldiers had done the state some service, but they met

---

[27] Army leaders attempted to secure parliamentary action on soldiers' 'legitimate' grievances, while at the same time they suppressed recent disorders in the army with all the
severity of military justice: Gentles, *New Model Army*, 219–29. Even as Fairfax excoriated
the agitators and deplored 'the consequences of breaking parliament', he admitted that
soldiers' concerns over arrears were 'just' although he did 'not lik[e] the way' they chose
to seek redress; parliament, through its failure to address the army's legitimate claims
over pay and free quarter, shared the blame for what followed. Bodleian, Ms. Fairfax 36,
fols. 4–5.   [28] Bodleian, Ms. Fairfax 36, fol. 5.   [29] *CP*, I:370.
[30] Ibid., I:42, 47, 56, 272, 295, 322.
[31] Commissary Cowling, speaking of the 'necessities' of the army, said, 'Wee live now uppon
free-quarter, and wee have that against our wills'; he desired that 'wee may not lie as
drones to devoure . . . families': ibid., I:293.

with an 'unworthy requitall . . . from the hands of men, [and were] loaded with reproaches'.[32]

In the rest of this chapter I shall consider two aspects of the larger problem of military–civilian relations. The first relates to the conflict of jurisdiction between military and civilian law and primarily affected individuals; at Putney it found particular expression in soldiers' claims for indemnity for wartime actions. The second relates to conflict between parliament and the army over the latter's claims to act autonomously in matters covered by international conventions of war; such matters might impinge on public policy. Discussion of two 'institutions' of war – plunder and surrender – will illustrate these conflicts in practice, conflicts familiar well before Putney and persistent after it.

The belief that the army was an institution governed by its own laws within its autonomous sphere of activity had a long history, but the potential for conflict was already evident in Essex's commission of 1642, which granted all necessary powers over offences committed by members of the army, 'according to the Course and Custom of the Wars, and Law of the Land'.[33] The two did not always coexist comfortably, and the conduct of war on home ground, between domestic enemies, complicated the application of the laws of war. Essex's commission, it should be noted, was not a grant of the power to impose 'martial law' in the modern sense of suspension of civilian law and extension of military law and authority to civilians, although modern discussions have sometimes been confused by the seventeenth century's promiscuous usage of the term. In the seventeenth century 'martial law' could carry the modern sense, and from time to time, for limited periods, and for certain offences (largely related to security), civilians were subject to trial by courts martial.[34] But martial law also comprehended the laws of war that governed armies, and in the context of the civil war the latter was its everyday meaning. When Cromwell spoke of the rules of war, he meant both the unwritten codes of conduct that guided combatants and the printed articles of war that constituted the formal legal codes of armies.

Army practice tried to reconcile military and civilian justice. Most of the provisions of the printed codes had a straightforward military function; offences against them were tried and punished by well-defined processes of military justice. Others, such as rape or unauthorised destruction of property, directly affected civilians, but were none the less

---

[32] *An humble representation from his excellencie Sir Thomas Fairfax, and the councel of the armie . . . Decemb. 7. 1647* (1647), 5.   [33] Firth and Rait, *Acts and ordinances*, I:16.
[34] For ordinances establishing courts martial for civilians as well as soldiers, see ibid., I:486–8, 842–5.

military crimes tried by military courts and law. In addition, however, the articles made some attempt to mediate between military and civilian jurisdiction in cases that involved both soldiers and civilians. They addressed offences committed by soldiers that had no significant military relevance (for example, non-payment of a debt to a civilian), and attempted to accommodate civilian demands for justice with maintenance of the army's control over its members.[35] In this tricky exercise, both parliamentary and royalist articles of war followed pre-war example. Thus in the section headed 'Of administration of justice', parliamentary articles protected the soldier in non-capital and minor cases, at least in the first resort, from imprisonment and trial by civilians who were less likely to give him a sympathetic hearing. Magistrates were forbidden to imprison soldiers except in capital cases. In 'inferiour cases' such as debt or trespass they were to inform the putative offender's commander, who could either settle the case with the assent of the aggrieved party or give him permission to seek redress 'by due course of law'. The initial source of remedy was thus removed from civilian hands, and appeal to civilian law could come only after a military proceeding. The danger of pro-soldier bias was evident, so provision was made for appeal to the lord general of the army if a commander proved dilatory, lazy or partial. Yet this safeguard, too, was dependent on the discretion of a soldier, not a magistrate.[36]

It was a creaky system with many loopholes, but it tried to provide justice for both citizen and soldier and did not simply replace civilian law by military. Unfortunately it is impossible to know how well the machinery worked. The limited court-martial records available suggest that civilians often bypassed the magistrate and complained directly to officers, and that in such cases the proceedings and the rules of military justice took over in dealing with offenders. They also suggest that cases of offences against civilians such as theft, assault and unauthorised plunder

---

[35] For earlier provisions for co-operation between military and civilian law, see Matthew Sutcliffe, *The practice, proceedings, and lawes of armes, described out of the doings of most valiant and expert captaines, and confirmed both by ancient, and moderne examples, and praecedents* (London, 1593), 339–40. The articles issued for the Scottish campaign in 1640 included provisions governing relations between civil magistrates and army officers for offences committed by soldiers against civilians. *Lawes and ordinances of warre established . . . by . . . the earle of Northumberland, Lord Generall of his Majesties armie and fleet* (London, 1640), sig. D2. Similar provisions were included in the articles of war of both sides in the civil war.

[36] *Laws and ordinances of warre, established for the better conduct of the army, by his excellency the earl of Essex . . . And now inlarged by command of his excellency* (London, 1643), sig. D3v, paras. V, VI; for a similar royalist article, which also allowed a soldier wronged by a civilian to appeal to a civil magistrate, see *Military orders, and articles, established by his Maiestie, for the better ordering and government of his Maiesties armie* (Oxford, [1643]), sig. B3, par. 82.

that satisfied a reasonable standard of proof were severely punished by the army itself. On a single day in July 1644, for example, Sir William Waller's council of war condemned a soldier to hang for robbing a woman, sentenced two men to 'lye neck and Heels together one whole day' (an extremely painful punishment) for plundering a doublet and stealing a pattern for breeches from a tailor, and ordered another soldier to run the gauntlet before being ignominiously discharged for plundering a shirt and an apron.[37]

The problem with military justice in offences against civilians was not so much its usurpation of civilian law as its inability to cope with some cases, the intervention of practical military concerns that led to variable enforcement (not unknown in civilian law as well), and civilian perception that justice was absent or biased. Its deficiencies in addressing civilian grievances resulted in pent-up desire for legal redress once ex-soldiers again became vulnerable to the processes of ordinary law. Soldiers, for their part, feared prosecution under that law for actions that, they claimed, had been done in the course of their professional duties or in cases that merely reflected civilian malice or opportunism. Their anxiety was only partially assuaged by the indemnity ordinances of 1647.[38]

Plunder and unofficial takings were the commonest civilian grievances, and they illustrated the difficulties and unevenness of military law that aroused civilian resentment. Not only was plunder very popular with soldiers, it was also often part of the legitimate rewards of war. Once a feeding frenzy started it was difficult to control, but discipline in civil war armies could in any case never be rigidly and uniformly enforced. Much obviously depended on senior officers' zeal in prosecuting cases. Sir William Brereton, for example, disliked plunder and did all he could to prevent it. In April 1645 he had leading plunderers tried by councils of war. Four were condemned to death and two hanged on the spot, 'which example', he said, 'I endeavour to improve to the terror of all'. Yet many of Brereton's troops continued to believe 'that they might be freebooters in . . . the enemy's country' and many officers – including some of

[37] John Adair, 'The court martial papers of Sir William Waller's army, 1644', *Journal of the Society for Army Historical Research* 44 (1966), 217–19. See also Worcester College, Oxford, Clarke Ms. 21, fols. 2v, 7–7v (bis), 11–11v (bis), 13, 15–16v, 19–22v, 31–32v, 52–53v, and passim. The latter records, dating from 1651 in Scotland and relating to an army of occupation, are more heavily weighted towards cases involving civilians than those for Waller's army in 1644. Both sets of records also include cases in which civilians were punished for offences involving soldiers, such as adultery and robbery. The Scottish cases are published in almost complete form in Godfrey Davies (ed.), 'Dundee court-martial records 1651', *Miscellany of the Scottish History Society*, 2nd ser., 19 (1919), 9–67.
[38] Gentles, *New Model Army*, 121–5; Firth and Rait, *Acts and ordinances*, I:936–8, 953–4, 957–8.

Brereton's – were reluctant to take stringent action.[39] Some had little wish to discriminate too closely between the legitimate and the illegitimate sides of a practice that they themselves engaged in, or to weaken discipline by invoking rules that would either be ignored or would cause discontent among their soldiers. Military justice was selective and discretionary in its application of the harsh penalties at its disposal, and tended to prefer exemplary, *in terrorem* punishment of the few to mass punishment of the many. So even justice such as Brereton's often seemed inadequate to civilians deprived of their particular pound of flesh. Selective, exemplary punishment left too many offenders unpunished and offered little compensation to victims, who had slight sympathy for the flexibility of army justice and little understanding of the military needs that might deflect its course. In addition, the threat posed by armed soldiers deprived of their loot might deter some from even seeking redress. Brereton's statement that he restored goods to owners 'who durst come to claim them' is revealing.[40] To civilians it seemed that plunderers were leniently treated while victims were rarely compensated. Many aggrieved citizens, thirsting for legal satisfaction, saw their opportunity once peace had apparently returned, while soldiers grew correspondingly more anxious.[41]

In terms of military law the crucial distinction was that between actions committed *as* soldiers and those committed *while* soldiers. Civilians often failed to see the difference. Soldiers wanted indemnity for the former, but made no such blanket claims for the latter. Crimes committed in an individual, unofficial capacity remained crimes. They believed, however, that actions performed under orders or in accordance with the normal practices of war should not become grounds for later punitive action under civilian law. Unfortunately the distinction was not always clear, and many actions, such as requisition of horses and cattle, fell into a grey area between the authorised and unauthorised or partook of both.[42] The legitimate easily became illegitimate, while some property simply melted away without trace. As one officer said, denying accountability, 'As for the horses and arms you can expect no other account than (Fortune de la Guerre) they are gone.' That was certainly true of a hogshead of sack

[39] BL Add. Ms. 11331, fols. 25–26v; and see R. N. Dore (ed.), *The letter books of Sir William Brereton, Vol. I. January 31st–May 29th 1645*, Record Society of Lancashire and Cheshire 123 (1984), 297–8, 306–8.
[40] BL Add. Ms. 11331, fol. 25v; Dore, *Brereton letter books*, I:298.
[41] Such concerns do not seem to have been confined to parliamentarians; a spate of pardons issued in Oxford in April 1645 for active royalists suggests similar anxiety about post-war legal liability. Bodleian, Ms. Dugdale 19, fols. 83–84v, 89v–91.
[42] Note Brereton's revealing proviso that only 'very honest men' be employed in a case of officially authorised requisitioning. BL Add. Ms. 11331, fol. 8v; Dore, *Brereton letter books*, I:268.

seized and drunk by parliamentary officers near Ailesbury, and probably of the six barrels of oysters that went with it. Plunder, as Brereton observed, was a 'bottomless bag'.[43]

Many incidents rapidly lost any colour of legitimacy and degenerated into crimes such as highway robbery, extortion and assault. They were imprinted on victims' memory and often preserved in their records to be resurrected when legal opportunity arose; the carrier who lost the sack and oysters, for example, made a 'note where these men live that took my goods', listed the names and directions of six parliamentary officers, and later sought redress.[44] In view of the limited machinery and presumed bias of military tribunals, it is not surprising that 'abused subjects' turned for recourse, once conditions seemed propitious, to the civilian law, which, after all, they had been assured was one of the things the army had been fighting to protect.[45]

The dismay of the army was equally unsurprising. Peace gave plaintiffs the opportunity to pay off old scores, some of which reflected quarrels that had little to do with the war.[46] Furthermore, in the special circumstances of a civil war in which soldiers fought on home ground, the same law would run for enemies and friends once soldiers left the protection of the army, and royalists whose property had been legal game in the war might bring suits. It could not be denied that in the 'late War and publick distractions, there [had] been many injuries done to private persons'. Subsequently many of parliament's faithful servants faced 'a continual vexation for such actions as the exigency of War . . . necessitated'.[47] And an additional ground for anxiety, in the uncertain circumstances of 1647, lay in the presumption that the king would be restored as head of state and then, so the radical John Wildman declared at Putney, 'the Kinge might command his judges to hang them uppe for what they did in the warres'.[48] The army and parliament might be victorious in 1647, but in the longer term soldiers feared another kind of 'victors' justice'.

Even the indemnity ordinances of 1647 were not a sufficient protection.[49] The first, on 21 May, declared that persons who had acted 'by the authority and in the service of the Parliament' were protected from legal

[43] PRO, SP 28/260, fol. 188; SP 28/126, fol. 163; BL Add. Ms. 11331, fol. 25v; Dore, *Brereton letter books*, I:297.   [44] PRO, SP 28/126, fols. 162–3.

[45] *The moderator expecting sudden peace, or certaine ruine* (1642/[43]), 5: 'From hence-forth Robbery shall change its name, and be called no more a crime than borrowing.'

[46] For discussion of the broad range of animosities that found expression through indemnity cases, see Ann Hughes, 'Parliamentary tyranny? Indemnity proceedings and the impact of the civil war: a case study from Warwickshire', *Midland History* 11 (1986), 49–78, at 68–9.   [47] Firth and Rait, *Acts and ordinances*, I:953.

[48] *CP*, I:354.

[49] On indemnity, see Ashton, 'The problem of indemnity', 117–40; Gentles, *New Model Army*, 121–5; Hughes, 'Parliamentary tyranny?', 49–78.

process arising from their actions. If they were none the less prosecuted, proof that they were so acting constituted a sufficient defence. They were not guilty, and judges and juries who found in their favour were themselves indemnified. As further insurance, a large committee (with a small quorum of five) was set up to hear the appeals of those servants of parliament, both military and civilian, who had been prosecuted or who feared prosecution despite the ordinance. Plaintiffs who persisted in their suits in the face of adverse rulings were subject to treble costs and their lawyers to imprisonment.[50] As the army's *Humble representation* pointed out, however, it would be difficult and expensive to prove direct authority from parliament for many actions done in war, and the accused might be caught between the 'Elusions of a Subtle Lawyer' and the perceptions 'of a Country jury'.[51] On 7 June, less than three weeks after the first, a second ordinance drafted specifically for the protection of soldiers (unlike the first) responded to these fears and radically extended the terms of indemnity. It conceded the 'many injuries' committed by soldiers against private persons, but it moved beyond offering a legal defence and mandated 'pardon' and 'oblivion' for actions performed 'by, or for the service of the Parliament', thus pre-empting attempts to initiate suits. As an incentive to compliance, it provided that plaintiffs who persisted in bringing suits must pay the defendants' costs.[52]

The framers of the ordinance admitted that they acted from expediency, and that their purpose was to defuse the 'continual vexation' of the many faithful servants of parliament made apprehensive by prosecutions.[53] Parliament thus, in one view, succumbed to pressure from the army, and deprived civilians of legal redress by placing its soldiers beyond the reach of the law for acts committed both as soldiers and while soldiers. To many contemporaries and some later historians the indemnity ordinances represented a new tyranny. Yet both their protections and their effects were more limited than this suggests.[54] Even the expanded ordinance of 7 June protected only against suits by the king and aggrieved persons, and service to parliament remained the criterion for pardon and oblivion. The ordinances thus offered no protection, for example, for serious felonies such as murder, rape or counterfeiting; they did not intrude on military law; and civilians could still seek to establish that

---

[50] Firth and Rait, *Acts and ordinances*, I:936–8.
[51] *A humble representation of the dissatisfaction of the army* is partially reprinted in John Morrill, *The revolt of the provinces. Conservatives and radicals in the English civil war 1630–1650* (London, 1976), 175. [52] Firth and Rait, *Acts and ordinances*, I:953.
[53] Ibid.
[54] Morrill, *Revolt of the provinces*, 76; see Hughes, 'Parliamentary tyranny?', for a reassessment of this argument. See also G. E. Aylmer, *The state's servants. The civil service of the English republic 1649–1660* (London, 1973), 13–14, 302, 316.

actions had not been performed in the service of parliament.
Furthermore they offered no protection for actions after 7 June 1647, an
omission not repaired until 4 April 1648.[55] In practice, prohibitions, penalties and the extensive removal of soldiers from the reach of the law did
not effectively deter civilians from seeking redress or revenge.

The records of the indemnity committee reveal the limits of protection
and the ingenuity of plaintiffs. Ian Gentles has counted 1,116 cases involving soldiers heard over the eight years of indemnity proceedings from
1647 to 1655, and argues persuasively that these cases that actually
reached the hearing stage 'represented ... only a small fraction of the legal
onslaught with which the parliamentary soldiers had to contend'.[56]
Military cases made up only about a third of those heard by the committee, but soldiers still had ample grounds for anxiety at Putney.[57] By
November 1647 the committee had heard only fifty-eight cases of all
kinds, but thereafter the numbers accelerated to reach a peak monthly
total of 151 in February 1648. By December 1648 it had heard 876
cases.[58] The figures help to explain soldiers' continuing anxiety in
November 1647. Not enough action had yet been taken to reassure them
that the ordinances would prove effective, while the spate of cases that
began in that month indicates the number that had already been brought
before civilian courts. In addition they had no protection for actions done
since June. Soldiers faced a real and immediate threat and urgently felt the
need for benevolent resolution of cases before a sympathetic tribunal.[59]

---

[55] Firth and Rait, *Acts and ordinances*, I:1119–20. This 1648 ordinance also took the first
step towards providing for hearings outside London (in Kent), and for damages for those
wrongly prosecuted. Compare the much more careful and explicit drafting of the Act of
General Pardon and Oblivion of 24 February 1652, which applied to royalists and parliamentarians alike; ibid., II:565–77. It enunciated exceptions from the general pardon,
including murder, piracy, buggery, rape and other felonies, and tried to secure social continuity by avoiding breaks in legal and financial obligations.

[56] Gentles, *New Model Army*, 122. He suggests that there were 'several thousand judicial
prosecutions between 1645 and 1655', but that once the Indemnity Committee had
established its effectiveness a 'large proportion' of suits was dropped. The records of the
indemnity committee are in PRO, SP 24; for a brief description, see Hughes,
'Parliamentary tyranny?', 53.

[57] For the proportion of indemnity cases involving soldiers, see Hughes, 'Parliamentary
tyranny?', 58, and see also 60–2; Gentles, *New Model Army*, 122.

[58] Business declined after December 1648; Gentles suggests that 'procedural sclerosis' had
set in; Gentles, *New Model Army*, 122. See also Ashton, 'Problem of indemnity', 123;
Hughes, 'Parliamentary tyranny?', 58. The act of general pardon and oblivion of 1652
did not stop legal processes initiated before September 1651. Firth and Rait, *Acts and
ordinances*, II:574. Indemnity cases continued until 1655, although the indemnity committee was abolished in 1652; thereafter cases were heard by the Committee for
Compounding: Gentles, *New Model Army*, 121.

[59] Note also the belief that indemnity commissioners were biased against soldiers, in
Humble representation from ... Sir Thomas Fairfax ... Decemb. 7, 1647, 23–4; it proposed the
appointment of commissioners more sympathetic to the army.

Even when soldiers successfully defended themselves they had often been subjected to time-consuming and expensive proceedings, although if they were lucky they might be compensated, as was Richard Price, formerly quartermaster at Nantwich, when he received 15 shillings in damages for unjust and malicious prosecution. And if defences sometimes strained belief, the inventiveness of plaintiffs should not be underestimated, as in the case of the man who contrived to have himself briefly imprisoned so that he could later bring a suit for false imprisonment that 'vexatiously molested and prosecuted' the defendants.[60] Justice may sometimes have been partial, but the processes of law were not vacated by the ordinances for indemnity, and to whatever degree they removed soldiers from the reach of the ordinary law of the land, that removal was nevertheless achieved by the legislation of parliament rather than the fiat of the army.[61]

So far we have looked at the interaction of military and civilian jurisdiction within parliament's own army, which was largely governed by written codified law, whether the army's articles or parliamentary legislation. Military dealings with enemies, however, were governed by the unwritten laws of war and by commanders' practical field judgements. They also impinged on public policy. Here the 'spheres' of army and parliament were more clearly differentiated than in private matters, and here the elements of conflict most clearly emerged. Parliament feared that control of the war would be wrested from its hands and that the army would intrude into civilian affairs. The army defended its conduct of war according to the professional and moral codes of soldiers, and feared that civilian interference would undercut its operations and weaken the hierarchy of military command and discipline, and would also breach the understandings between enemies that shaped the ways in which they behaved to each other.

Such problems are not confined to the seventeenth century. Generals are accustomed to criticism from politicians and the public for acting rashly and precipitately, or alternatively for dawdling and missing opportunities. Armchair strategists second-guess commanders' judgements and civilians worry about the power of the military–industrial complex. Already in the English civil war tensions over lines of authority between the civil state and its soldiers and misunderstandings over military norms and practicalities were familiar. So, for example, the Derby House committee subjected Fairfax to a stream of detailed instructions concerning

---

[60] PRO, SP 24/3, fols. 22v–23, 58–58v, 63.
[61] Compare the presbyterian parliament's attempt to assert a right to override military jurisdiction in military cases in its shortlived ordinance denying courts martial the right to try deserters. Firth and Rait, *Acts and ordinances*, I:957–8; Gentles, *New Model Army*, 380–2.

the disposition of his troops in the dangerous summer of 1648. Fairfax's response may be gauged by their testy complaints of letters ignored and unanswered; in return the committee threatened to use their position as the general's conduit to the House of Commons as a lever to force compliance. Meanwhile civilians criticised his conduct of the siege of Colchester: they wanted dramatic action, not victory by attrition.[62] Static and lengthy operations such as sieges offered particular opportunities for political and bureaucratic intervention whereas the speed of events in pitched battles and rapid marches – Naseby followed by pursuit of the royalists into the south-west, for example – partially insulated men in the field from interference from London. In practice the extent and effectiveness of civilian oversight and criticism varied. Sometimes soldiers and politicians worked in concert, or politicians made suggestions but left the final decision to the man on the spot. At other times their demands were ignored while soldiers got on with their jobs.

Problems extended beyond the higher command, as did awareness of the larger issues involved. The Derby House committee complained to Fairfax in September 1648 that the governor of Oxford, Lieutenant-Colonel Kelsey, neglected and disputed their commands despite his duty to obey. Kelsey, however, took his stand on the nature of military authority, declaring that he would not obey without a command from the lord general, a response that left the committee 'wholly unsatisfied at this deportment'. They argued that it was Fairfax's duty to force Kelsey's obedience to their civilian commands as part of army discipline: the committee, representing parliament, had 'power to give order to the Lord General and to command all the forces of the kingdom'.[63] The starkness of the claim owed much to circumstances, to the political instability of late 1648, and to the fact that parliament was now dealing with a newly (and again) victorious, large, powerful, but no longer acutely needed army that posed a potential threat to the political and social order. Parliament was still trying to assert its civilian supremacy in the state, although the power balance was shortly to move decisively in the army's favour.

The political question could never be forgotten in the 1640s, but such direct and explicit assertion of parliamentary control of the way in which war was to be waged against the enemy, and claims that the soldier owed immediate obedience to parliament regardless of the military mediation of his officers, were relatively rare. Indeed, a habit of confrontation would have sabotaged parliament's war effort. Rather, the issue came up indi-

<hr/>

[62] *CSPD 1648–1649*, 240, 259; BL Harl. Ms. 7001, fol. 186; S. Sheppard, *The yeare of jubile: or, Englands releasment, purchasd by Gods immediate assistance* (London, 1646), 63–4.
[63] *CSPD 1648–1649*, 270–1.

rectly in debates over particular cases. One of the commonest areas of tension was that of the terms of surrender granted after sieges. John Morrill has pointed to complaints that commanders granted royalists 'preferential terms', and he quotes the argument of the Yorkshire committee that such proceedings 'would beget an opinion that the sword hath a power above the Lawe, which will utterly destroy the authority of Parliament'.[64] The irritation of local parliamentarians when local royalists did not get what they deserved is not surprising in the embittered circumstances of divided allegiance, and often longstanding divisions, in besieged towns. Commanders, however, were more certain of where their mandate ran than were local committees. They knew that by the international laws of war they had the power to negotiate surrenders. A moment's reflection shows the practical reasons. Communication with a directing authority in London was clearly impossible when offers and counter-offers were made daily, sometimes hourly, in response to shifting circumstances, and rapid decisions were needed. Negotiations were conducted according to recognised forms and with a recognised menu of options, and the generosity or otherwise of conditions depended on factors that ranged from the length and obstinacy of the defence to the urgency of the commander's need to depart to another scene of action. Commanders had authority over the military methods of achieving surrender and the actual terms negotiated. Fairfax's negotiations with the governor of Bridgewater in July 1645 demonstrated the rapid give-and-take of negotiations that left no time for oversight from London. Nevertheless, the upshot showed a clear awareness of the limits of military powers. His terms took care of the officers and soldiers, but he would not make any long-term settlement for the 'gentlemen' in the town. They were to be disposed of as appointed by parliament; he merely contracted to give them civil usage until parliament should decide on their fate.[65] At York in 1644 the victorious parliamentary commanders had in fact defended themselves against accusations of exceeding their military authority, explaining that parliamentary sequestration orders directed against civilian property were outside their power to negotiate. Instead, the terms promised to the defenders were narrow in scope: '[T]he Generals of the Armies have treated as Generals in reference only to themselves and their Souldiers, and it was not intended to Entrench upon any Ordinances of Parliament . . . The Commissioners of the Treaty . . . had no Order to meddle with any Ordinance of Parliament.'[66]

A sense of their own rights and rectitude did not protect commanders

[64] Morrill, *Revolt of the provinces*, 76, 174–5.
[65] Joshua Sprigge, *Anglia rediviva* (London, 1647), 71–4.
[66] Rushworth, *Historical collections*, V:640.

from criticism, particularly in protracted, visible and politically sensitive cases. The generosity of the terms on which the royalists were allowed to surrender Oxford in 1646 – effectively the formal end of the first civil war – put Fairfax's supporters on the defensive. Parliament had found earlier royalist proposals 'so high' that they were not even debated; the members instead left it to Fairfax 'in what way he thought fit to prosecute the reducing of that Place'.[67] Proceedings were now officially in the military 'sphere' and the outcome was defended on military grounds. Fairfax, it was emphasised, acted with the consent of all his chief officers – the decision was thus both military and collective – and together they reached a pragmatic conclusion. Oxford's nearly impregnable defences and ample supplies would enable the royalists to hold out for six months. On a cost-benefit military analysis it was therefore more beneficial to end the siege early than to expend men and money and tie large forces down in order to achieve a more punitive victory. What followed owed more to the codes of war mutually observed by 'soldiers, Christians and gentlemen' than to civilian oversight. Fairfax, by patient and delicate negotiation, had to persuade the royalist governor Sir Thomas Glemham that his honour allowed him to surrender. Terms finally agreed upon were relatively mild, and the defeated were allowed all the external displays – notably in the ceremony of marching out with horses, arms, colours, drums and trumpets – that publicly asserted their unbroken military honour. The requirement that they abandon these symbols of unbroken honour fifteen miles from Oxford reasserted the fact of defeat but did not detract from the psychological value of the departure.[68] In such a case the details of negotiation and ceremony acknowledged both a sphere of army autonomy and a mutuality of respect and standards between enemies that was suspect to many civilians. It could also render officers who made judgements on the basis of military feasibility vulnerable to accusations of incompetence or half-heartedness in the cause, or of subordinating parliament to military power.

This issue of the right of commanders to negotiate with and impose terms on the defeated had its most controversial expression less than a year after Putney. After the siege of Colchester Fairfax was assailed not only by the royalists but by a suspicious parliament. The siege was long, hard, wet and miserable for all concerned. Feelings were bitter and parliamentarians, already once victorious, were frightened and angry at this return to 'War and Blood'.[69] Fairfax and his council of war had no incli-

---

[67] Ibid., VI:279–80.
[68] Sheppard, *Yeare of jubile*, 63–4; Rushworth, *Historical collections*, VI:280–5.
[69] Rushworth, *Historical collections*, VII:1233. Fairfax used the latter phrase in explaining to the king why he could not intervene on behalf of officer prisoners taken in the Welsh

nation to be generous, and surrender terms were harsh. All senior officers were forced to surrender to mercy only, as distinct from surrendering to quarter; by military convention this left their life or death subject to the general's discretion. Fairfax ordered an immediate court martial for three of the senior commanders, and within hours of the formal surrender of the town Sir Charles Lucas and Sir George Lisle were shot in the castle yard.[70] Despite the impassioned accusations of royalists at the time and since, there is no doubt that Fairfax acted in accordance with the laws of war, although there is also no doubt that his exceptional severity in applying them was a function of the bitterness of the second war. Lucas and Lisle were exemplary victims; they were, as Fairfax observed, 'the Persons pitched upon for this Example' and, as such, victims of a standard form of military justice.[71]

Lucas and Lisle became instant royalist martyrs, which in part explains Fairfax's lifelong defensiveness about his actions, but he also incurred criticism from his own side for the case raised the issue of the proper spheres of army and parliament. When, after the deaths of Lucas and Lisle, he granted quarter to the other senior royalist prisoners, Fairfax had to defend himself against objections that he had usurped the powers of parliament to deal with the defeated. He therefore embarked on the education of parliament as to his own proper powers according to the 'general sense and practice in all Wars', explaining that 'mercy' allowed the general to kill the defeated at his discretion but that 'quarter' obliged him to preserve their lives. Beyond this, however, he recognised a political dimension. His grant of quarter was confined in its application to the immediate context of military action at Colchester; it did not preclude future action by parliament, to whom 'farther Publick Justice and Mercy' belonged, and indeed the commanders at Colchester – Lord Norwich, Lord Capel and Lord Loughborough – and their senior officers were specifically reserved for parliament's disposition: 'I do hereby render [them] unto the Parliament's Judgment, for farther publick Justice and Mercy to be used, as you shall see Cause.'[72] The reservation of *civilian* prisoners for parliamentary disposition was not unusual, as was seen at Bridgewater; after Colchester, however, some *military* prisoners were handed over to parliamentary jurisdiction. For Fairfax, the problem was to balance the

rising, 'it being not in my Power to act farther, the Parliament having Ordered in what way they shall be proceeded against'.

[70] For the extraordinary debate that immediately preceded the deaths of Lucas and Lisle, see *CP,* II:31–9; and see B. Donagan, 'Atrocity, war crime, and treason in the English civil war', *American Historical Review* 99 (1994), 1155–9.

[71] Rushworth, *Historical collections*, VII:1243; BL Harl. Ms. 2315, fols. 11v–12.

[72] BL Harl. Ms. 2315, fols. 10v–11; Rushworth, *Historical collections*, VII:1243, 1247, 1303–4.

army's claim to adhere to the 'general sense and practice in all Wars' with reassurance to parliament that this was not a claim to the supremacy of military over civil power.[73]

In 1649 the balance between military and civilian jurisdiction over the defeated was to swing decisively, if temporarily, away from army autonomy and towards politicisation of procedures. The earl of Norwich and Lord Capel, commanders at Colchester, together with the duke of Hamilton and the earl of Holland, were tried by civil tribunals. After the fall of Pontefract its governor, Colonel Morris, was tried at the York assizes for treason and executed. His protest that as a martial man he should be tried by a council of war was ignored, as was his warning that his fate would become 'a precedent to any soldiers hereafter'.[74] Not only had opponents been relegated from enemies in war to traitors, but the protections of quarter in surrender began to appear as discretionary as mercy had always been.

To many members of the army this was a disturbing development. It not only threatened the mutually beneficial controls that operated between enemies; it also reflected on the honour of the army, and placed the keeping of engagements at the mercy of some flexible ideological or pragmatic higher good. It engaged the speakers at Whitehall in March 1649, where positions ranged from the moral simplicity of the belief 'That the faith and honour of the Army [were] engaged' in keeping promises of quarter and other conditions once given, to the claim of empowerment to act as divine agents regardless of prior engagements: 'God never afforded . . . an opportunity for us to doe justice till now.' Between them lay Lambert's position on the terms granted to Hamilton at his capture: 'hee did not intend hee should bee reserved from the power of the Civill Magistrate', which was glossed at Whitehall to mean that 'the Generall was not impowred to give him life against the Civill aucthority'.[75] It is clear that peace and victory, far from strengthening the autonomy of the army in the practice of the traditional laws of war, increased the pressure to politicise proceedings against defeated enemies and, by reducing the value of bipartisan restraint, to elevate victors' justice over shared codes that had served the interests of soldiers.

Both the urgent anxieties over indemnity and the wider issue of the army's proper relationship to parliament found expression at Putney.

[73] Rushworth, *Historical collections*, VII:1303.
[74] 'An exact relation of the trial and examination of John Morris, governor of Pontefract-castle' in Walter Scott (ed.), *A collection of scarce and valuable tracts . . . of the late Lord Somers* (2nd edn, 13 vols., London, 1809–15), VII:9, 12; Donagan, 'Atrocity, war crime and treason', 1156–63.   [75] *CP*, II:196–8.

Soldiers' conceptions of their 'sphere' of action, of their due as soldiers and of their institutional solidarity were inevitably entwined with the problem of the army's place in the state. Their claims at Putney conflated their rights as soldiers, based on service and military convention, and as Englishmen, derived from abstract principle.[76] At the same time, they were conscious that those civilian Englishmen on whose behalf they claimed rights did not properly understand the soldiers' sphere, did not value their service as they ought, and were prepared to exploit civilian law against them.

The army's claims at Putney, taken collectively, were of two kinds. The first kind, the most dramatic and appealing for later ages, was political, democratic and timeless. The claim that Englishmen's 'liberties' and political rights were a matter of birthright rather than property retains its power to excite and astonish. Claims of the second kind relating to the particular 'rights' and the obligations due to soldiers *as* soldiers, have largely interested later historians as triggers to ideological activism; their intrinsic interest has seemed rooted in the circumstances of a particular time and place. And the justifications and minutiae of proceedings such as surrender have been seen as part of the arcana of military lore and of little concern to those who are not *aficionados* of military history.

Yet the rights of soldiers, the rules of war and the proper relations of army and state have a significance beyond England in the 1640s. Legislative recognition of the state's obligations to its soldiers over pay and indemnity marked the beginning of a new relationship, one in which central government, not king, patron or commander, accepted responsibility for soldiers' welfare. There was a long way to go to the comprehensive reach of modern veterans' benefits conceived as a national duty, but for England the process began in the 1640s. Laws of war remain an embattled ideal. Issues such as surrender terms and treatment of the defeated are still familiar and difficult, and continue to pose the vexed question of whether politics, the laws of war, or the law of the jungle will rule. The processes by which military power moves from supporter to supplanter of civilian government are not unknown today.

Early in the civil war the potential conflict between the army and parliament had been handled by recognition, albeit sometimes grudging, that the army had its own 'sphere', but that it nevertheless remained the servant of parliament. Over time the servant had become a partner, but the partnership was uneasy, unstable and fragile. Its equilibrium was short-lived, and eventually the army's monopoly of physical power could not be denied. The 'grand Juglers, and Leaders of the Army' purged the

[76] Ibid., I:353.

parliament, and in one of the many ironies of the period God and conscience forced the army to exert its power against the parliament of which it had so recently declared itself the servant.[77] The call to follow God and conscience at the expense of earthly engagements was the most subversive sounded at Putney, for it defied the claims for the sovereignty of parliament, for an autonomous, professionally managed army, and for the rule of law. The radicals and idealists who espoused this view, however, were to find as little comfort in the army as they had in parliament.

[77] John Lilburne, *The legal fundamental liberties*, in *CP,* II:264.

6   The case of the armie truly re-stated[1]

John Morrill and Philip Baker

I

The case of the armie truly stated[2] is a document that many have cited but few are at ease with. Historian after historian has taught us that it represents a coming together of radicals in the army and the Levellers; that it was written or at least collated by John Wildman; that it was a shapeless and grumpy document, notable for its lack of both clarity and charity, a veritable darnel-field from within which the pure grain of *An agreement of the people* was then sifted with some difficulty. It was *The case of the armie* which led immediately to special meetings of the General Council of the Army in Putney Church in late October and early November 1647. But it was its digest, *An agreement*, that preoccupied the participants in those debates. *The case of the armie* is at best a document that demonstrates a law of half-intended consequences.

The modern tradition of interpretation stems back at least to S. R. Gardiner, who wrote: 'the dissatisfaction felt in the Army with the policy of their commanders was especially strong in five regiments. These regiments, after cashiering their Agitators, elected new ones, who set themselves, under the influence of Lilburne and his disciples, to prepare a manifesto bearing the title of *The case of the army truly stated*.'[3] C. H. Firth, in his edition of the Putney debates and other materials in *The Clarke papers*, also saw *The case of the armie* as emerging from the 'dissatisfaction

---

[1] This paper benefited much from the lively discussions at the Putney Debates 1647 Conference at the Folger Institute in Washington in October 1997, and from the subsequent thorough commentaries provided in writing by Ian Gentles, Derek Hirst, Mark Kishlansky, Austin Woolrych, Elliot Vernon and Blair Worden. We are grateful to them all, while making it clear that we did take some but not all of the cogent advice given and stand by the chapter as our own readings and not theirs.

[2] The text of *The case of the armie truly stated* can be found in its original form in two reliable modern editions: W. Haller and G. Davies, *The Leveller tracts, 1647–1653* (New York, 1944), 65–87 and D. M. Wolfe, *Leveller manifestoes of the Puritan revolution* (New York, 1944), 198–222.

[3] S. R. Gardiner, *History of the great civil war* (4 vols., London, 1893), III:378.

and suspicion [which] found expression in renewed disturbance in the Army and amongst the Levelling party in general [so that] a certain number of persons, claiming to represent the Levellers of London and other districts, made common cause with the protesting soldiers. The most prominent . . . was John Wildman, a follower of Lilburn's, who was adopted by the Agents as their mouthpiece, and was *probably* [note that unargued "probably"] the author of the "Case of the Army"'. He suggests that *An agreement* was a summary prepared at the same time but presented and printed later.[4]

Introducing the first modern edition of the text in 1944, Don Wolfe suggested that 'though Wildman was *probably* [note that unargued 'probably'] the principal author, differences in style suggest the work of several hands'. He found *The case of the armie* 'a repetitious and poorly organized document, too long and complicated to be read and assented to as a social contract by thousands of soldiers and citizens. Yet it was the necessary bridge between the agitation of the common soldiers for a democratic constraint on Parliament and the composition of the first *Agreement of the People*.'[5]

All this is carefully balanced. But as the Levellers rose in the historical consciousness and as their ideas came more and more to be seen as heroic, so their role in *The case of the armie* became strengthened. Thus William Haller and Godfrey Davies suggested that 'the Levellers and the agitators wanted no settlement short of the full program fathered by John Lilburne. This was made plain in . . . *The Case of the Armie Truly Stated*';[6] while Joseph Frank wrote that '*The Case of the Army* is suffused with Leveller principles' and 'though written largely by Wildman [note the unargued dropping of the "probably"], it was essentially the offspring of all the London Levellers, and to a far lesser degree of the recently-elected Agitators'. Indeed '*The Case* . . . [was] thus the wedge by which Lilburne, Walwyn and Overton finally entered those councils where national policy was actually decided.'[7] H. N. Brailsford thought *The case of the armie* an underachieving Leveller pamphlet, 'long-winded, confused and full of repetitions'; but he also thought 'it was the bridge that leads to *An agreement*'.[8] This is a view followed cautiously but clearly by Gerald Aylmer in his edition of Leveller materials published in 1975.[9]

In the 1970s, Mark Kishlansky, Ian Gentles and John Morrill were

---

[4] *CP,* I:xlvi–xlvii.   [5] Wolfe, *Leveller manifestoes,* 196 and n. 1; and see 46–8.
[6] Haller and Davies, *Leveller tracts,* 13.
[7] J. Frank, *The Levellers* (Cambridge, MA, 1955), 132–4.
[8] H. N. Brailsford, *The Levellers and the English revolution* (London, 1961), 257–9.
[9] G. E. Aylmer, *The Levellers in the English revolution* (Ithaca, NY, 1975), 29–30. Aylmer, however, is cautious about the attribution to Wildman in particular.

prominent in seeking to challenge the nature and extent of Leveller pene-tration of the army, certainly before the high summer of 1647. Morrill argued that Leveller rhetoric was fundamentally opposed to a standing army and that Lilburne's own experience made him suspicious of its leaders and out of touch with its rank and file, while Kishlansky suggested that the dynamics of army relations with parliament could be explained adequately in terms of the army's own sense of its honour, its legitimate demands as an army, and its own experience in war and peace.[10]

These challenges to the idea of a natural and comfortable alliance of interest between the army and the Levellers has led to a softening of the argument, but not to its abandonment. Ian Gentles, in his important book on the New Model, speaks more circumspectly of *The case of the armie* as the work of 'the new agents and their Leveller mentors' although elsewhere he implies that Wildman was a key player in its composition.[11] His characterisation of *The case of the armie* allows for tension between Leveller demands and the self-interests of the army and he implies that *An agreement of the people* is a radical development over and above *The case of the armie*.[12]

By far the most careful recent analysis is that of Austin Woolrych. He has examined all the fragmentary evidence about the emergence of the new agents and laid to rest for all time the idea that they replaced the old adjuta-tors[13] or that they had any formal status at Putney other than as invited guests of a council of which they were not members. His work reveals no evidence of a direct Leveller link, and yet he moves on to assert that '*The Case of the Armie Truly Stated . . .* was the opening shot in a Leveller cam-paign to alter the political direction of the Army.' He offers a specific guide to Wildman's part as co-ordinator of the writing and as the author of the introduction, the conclusion and of the constitutional proposals them-selves, including those for a law paramount and a new franchise.[14]

---

[10] M. A. Kishlansky, *The rise of the New Model Army* (Cambridge, 1979); J. S. Morrill, 'The army revolt of 1647' and 'Mutiny and discontent in English provincial armies 1645–1647', both reprinted in Morrill, *The nature of the English revolution* (London, 1992), 307–58; Ian Gentles, 'Arrears of pay and ideology in the army revolt of 1647' in Brian Bond and Ian Roy (eds.), *War and society* (London, 1975), 44–66.

[11] Ian Gentles, *The New Model Army in England, Ireland and Scotland 1645–1653* (Oxford, 1992), 200, 214. At the latter, he writes: 'after a lame attempt by Wildman to deny that he had a hand in drafting *The Case of the Army'*. We will cite the passage below at p. 115; why Gentles sees this as a lame attempt, given that there is not a shred of evidence for his authorship other than historians' speculations, is not made clear. Having spotted the denial, it is a pity he did not pause to wonder if he had hit on something rather significant!

[12] Gentles, *New Model Army*, 200–4.

[13] We prefer 'adjutators' to 'agitators' because it is a common contemporary usage, and seems to us to proclaim more clearly what they were seen (and saw themselves) as being – that is, *not* 'stirrers-up' but 'assistants'.

[14] Austin Woolrych, *Soldiers and statesmen* (Oxford, 1987), 203–9.

The prevailing view is then that *The case of the armie*, although signed by the agents of five regiments, was essentially a Leveller document that led on, via its digest, to the *Agreement of the people*, to a series of debates at Putney at which Leveller proposals for a new constitutional settlement triumphed over the angry protests of the General Officers. As a result of their defeat at Putney, the generals retaliated by appealing over the heads of the officers and adjutators to the rank and file. Amidst massive recrimination, the grandees persuaded them to sign up to their Remonstrance and they thereby reclaimed political control. Putney was the moment when the Levellers appeared to be in control of the revolution.

This chapter will suggest that in fact there is no evidence that the Levellers wrote or dominated *The case of the armie*, although Leveller ideas do appear in two passages intruded into a document culled from earlier army declarations. It will suggest that if an author or co-ordinator can be suggested, it should be Sexby and not Wildman. It will argue that the extent of the criticism of the generals should not be exaggerated, and that there were fundamental differences between *The case of the armie* (which could be and was the basis of much discussion and consensus at Putney) and the *Agreement of the people* (which was reviled and abandoned at Putney). It will argue that there was much more in *The case of the armie* that was acceptable to the grandees than conventional accounts imply; and that many of the sections assumed to be Leveller-inspired – especially those which have interested historians of ideas most nearly – are more the common coin of army discourse than they are intrusions of distinctively Leveller ideas. It is hoped that this in turn makes the course of events in November 1647 and therefore in the revolution much easier to follow.

II

The title page of *The case of the armie* bears close scrutiny. It is ostensibly an appeal from the agents of five regiments within the army to the whole army. It proclaims itself an *internal* army document: 'THE CASE OF THE ARMIE Truly stated, together with the mischiefes and dangers that are imminent, and some sutable remedies. Humbly proposed by the Agents of five Regiments of Horse, to their respective Regiments and the whole Army. As it was presented . . . unto his Excellency Sir Thomas Fairfax.' The reader is invited to be no more than an eavesdropper on a discussion within the army. There is no Leveller rhetoric here of the agents bringing the concerns of a suffering people to the attention of the army, no attempt to link the mischiefs experienced by the army to the mischiefs experienced by the people. In *form* this is not an overt statement of any alliance of interest between those inside and outside the army.

Below the full title are two biblical quotations. The first is from Deuteronomy 20: 'What man is there that is fearfull and faint hearted? Let him go and returne unto his house, least his brethren's heart faint as well as his heart.' Note the provocative omission of the first half of verse 8, immediately preceding the quotation: 'And the officers shall speak further unto the people, and they shall say, [What man, etc.]' And note that the verse comes from a passage (glossed in many early editions of the Bible as 'rules for the conduct of war') about the need for those in the armies of Jehovah never to flinch or be faint of heart: 'For the Lord your God is he that goeth with you, to fight for you against your enemies, to save you.'[15] Indeed, *The souldiers catechisme* contained a substantial section on valour and courage, including a full citation of Deuteronomy 20:8.[16] Contemporary glosses already recognised this verse as being directly linked to the story of Gideon and the Midianites in the Book of Judges, which provides the second quotation and (perhaps significantly) also appears in the short *Souldiers pocket Bible*: 'And the Lord said unto Gideon, By the three hundred men that lapped will I save you, and deliver the Midianites into thine hand: and let all the other people go, every man unto his place.'[17] The parallel is being drawn with the story of Gideon, who was called from the plough to lead the armies of Israel. Gideon led his 32,000 men to the water and invited them to drink; 22,000 left in terror. Of those that remained, he then sent away all the unvigilant ones who stuck their heads into the river and retained the services of only the 300 who drank water warily from cupped hands. This, too, is doubly interesting. In 1648 Cromwell was to spend much time ruminating on the parallels between himself and Gideon. And there is a studied ambiguity contained in the way the quotation appears. Is it an exhortation to an army *already* winnowed and culled; or is it a call for a fresh winnowing, a new culling out of the unwary and the faint-hearted?[18]

In sum, the biblical quotations at the head of *The case of the armie* reinforce the message that it is a document by and for an army.

The agents are unambiguous that the document is *their* brainchild and is directed as much *at* their own regiments as at the generals and the General Council. It does not claim to be the considered response *of* their

[15] Deuteronomy 20:4. This and all other quotations are from the King James version of the Bible.
[16] *The souldiers catechisme*, 8 April 1644 [BL E. 1186(1)], 22–3. This short book was popular enough to go through a number of later editions.
[17] Judges 7:7. *The souldiers pocket Bible*, 3 August, 1643 [BL E. 1180(2)], 10. The bible itself consists of only sixteen pages, but the books of Deuteronomy and Judges are referred to frequently.
[18] Interestingly, *The souldiers catechisme*, 22, refers specifically to cashiering in its interpretation of Deuteronomy 20:8.

regiments. This makes us consider the precise circumstances in which the new agents emerged and whom they represented. Unfortunately, exhaustive work by Ian Gentles and others has done little to reveal the pre-history of these agents. Suspicions linger in the historiography that they were Johnny-come-latelies to the army, but there is no hard evidence to demonstrate this and some to suggest otherwise.[19] Certainly, soon after the appearance of *The case of the armie*, orders were issued from the army to discharge all recruits to the cavalry since its march on London in August. However, the allegation of a single newsletter – that this represented a purging of subversive elements – has perhaps received too much credence.[20] Problems of over-enlistment are a far more plausible (if mundane) explanation for the decision. The motions of the relevant General Council at which the orders were agreed were largely concerned with the army's material conditions and there is no indication from alternative reports that there was any political motivation for the disbandment.[21] Moreover, the extent to which those orders would have affected the new agents should not be exaggerated as the degree of overlap between them and the old adjutators has gone relatively unnoticed. Two of the eleven signatories of *The case of the armie* had signed earlier documents as adjutators.[22] Indeed, at least eight – perhaps as many as nine – of the men who signed documents in October and November 1647 as 'new' agents were in fact 'old' adjutators.[23] In this, as in so much else, we need to blur categories. Austin Woolrych has demonstrated that there was no solid, fixed membership of the older adjutators; different men speak or sign on different occasions on behalf of their regiments. The new agents represent a new dimension, but not a clean, straightforward break.

Hand in hand with the interpretation of *The case of the armie* as a

---

[19] See Gentles, *New Model Army*, 197 and n. 61, and Woolrych, *Soldiers and statesmen*, 206 and n. 58 for the former view. Their assertions are purely speculative, however, and rely upon the opinions of secondary commentators, some of whom are openly hostile to the army. The specific allegation – that the new agents were recent recruits to the army – is never actually made in the evidence they cite.

[20] *Papers from the armie*, 22 October 1647 [BL E. 411(19)], 4. Both Gentles, *New Model Army*, 202, 207 and Woolrych, *Soldiers and statesmen*, 206 accept this account.

[21] John Rushworth, *Historical collections* (8 vols., London, 1721–2), VII:849–50; *The Moderate Intelligencer*, no. 136, 21–8 October 1647 [BL E. 412(2)], 1333. The fact that the relevant disbandment had still not taken place by December hardly indicates that the army was desperate to rid itself of its most recent recruits.

[22] John Dober (see *CP*, I:140) and William Pryor (see n. 23, below).

[23] Gentles, *New Model Army*, 199, claims the figure to be only five. He excludes Tobias Box (see *A letter sent from several agitators of the army*, 12 November 1647 [BL E. 414(8)], 8 and *CP*, I:438. The reservations of Woolrych, *Soldiers and statesmen*, 277–8, are not convincing), William Michell (see *A copy of a letter sent by the agents*, 11 November 1647 [BL E. 413(18)], 4 and *CP*, I:439), William Pryor (see Wolfe, *Leveller manifestoes*, 221 and *CP*, I:79) and perhaps John Taylor (see *Two letters from the agents of the five regiments*, 28 October 1647 [BL E. 412(6)], 7 and *CP*, I:161).

Leveller document has gone the assumed association of the new agents with the Levellers. We do know that the Levellers had been encouraging 'seduced' soldiers to lay aside their existing adjutators and to elect new ones.[24] But there is only rather dubious evidence that the appearance of new agents was a specific response to that call,[25] or that any known Leveller was involved in their selection. It has been established that in at least one regiment some form of election took place,[26] and while there is good evidence that a proportion of the agents had previous involvement in army organisation, not one of them is known to have been involved in earlier, specifically Leveller activities. The Levellers themselves never claimed any direct involvement in the appearance of the new agents at any point in their careers.[27] All this can only serve to weaken further the direct association made between the Levellers and *The case of the armie*.

Yet the status of the new agents remains equivocal. The signatories of *The case of the armie* were excluded from the meeting of the General Council on 21 October and from the committees set up by the Council over the next fortnight. It even seems possible that although the new agents were encouraged to attend subsequent meetings of the General Council between 28 October and 8 November, most were in fact absent. On one reading only two were present.[28] On the other hand, those *existing* adjutators who publicly aligned themselves with the new agents without having signed *The case of the armie*, such as Edward Sexby and William Allen, were present throughout and one or both of them was appointed to all the Council's committees. The absence of these established adjutators from the list of signatories to *The case of the armie* has been most plausibly

---

[24] See especially, John Lilburne, 'Advice to the private soldiers', in *The juglers discovered*, 8 September 1647 [BL E. 409(22)], 10–11.

[25] For example, the gossip of the royalist prisoner, Sir Lewis Dyve, culled from H. G. Tibbutt (ed.), 'The Tower of London letter-book of Sir Lewis Dyve', *Publications of the Bedfordshire Historical Record Society*, vol. 38 (1958). There is a double-edged approach to this source, admitting that Dyve got things wrong (see Woolrych, *Soldiers and statesmen*, 203), but then treating the remainder of his account as reliable. Woolrych's assertion that as Lilburne himself was Dyve's informant, there is no reason to doubt his initiative with regard to the new agents, seems naïve. While Dyve's first-hand accounts of discussions in the Tower need to be carefully weighed, his reportage of tittle-tattle surely does not.

[26] *A Perfect Weekly Account*, 10–17 November 1647 [BL E. 416(2)], unpag.; Woolrych, *Soldiers and statesmen*, 205 and Gentles, *New Model Army*, 199.

[27] For a full discussion of this, see P. R. S. Baker, 'The origins and early history of the Levellers, c.1635–c.1647', Cambridge Ph.D. thesis (forthcoming). This is not to ignore the later collaboration between *some* of the new agents and the Levellers, although that in itself proves nothing with regard to their origins.

[28] The two referred to by Sexby in his introductory remarks, *CP*, I:226; and see Everard's comments about his attempts to get more to attend, attempts foiled by their absence from the vicinity, *CP*, I:235, 285, 342, and the comments of Edmund Chillenden, *CP*, I:277. But Gentles thinks it possible that two of those appointed to a committee on 9 November *may* have been new agents (Gentles, *New Model Army*, 214 at n. 145; *CP* I:363).

explained by Austin Woolrych. He interprets this as a deliberate attempt to ensure that the views of the new agents would be represented within the General Council of the Army, for if either Sexby or Allen had signed *The case of the armie*, they risked jeopardising their seats on that body.[29] Therefore, under this interpretation of events, the absence of Sexby's name from the document can actually reinforce the possibility of his direct involvement with it.

III

The typography of the first edition of *The case of the armie* reveals quite a lot. No printer is identified, but the design seems to resemble the work of army printers more than most Leveller designs. Moreover, the only name that can be associated with the printing of the earliest new agent pamphlets is that of Robert Ibbitson (or Ibbotson).[30] He was a specialist in the printing of army newsletters, on at least one occasion printed an army-inspired attack on the Levellers, and printed the works of their enemies, and *never* those defending or by the Levellers themselves.[31] It is most likely, therefore, that the agents themselves arranged for the printing of *The case of the armie* through the army's presses. It was almost certainly not sent to a printer regularly used by the Levellers. Not until mid-November did a new agent pamphlet appear with any semblance of a possible Leveller connection. Even then and despite its publication by John Harris, the tract was only a reprint of an earlier pamphlet, leaving at least some grounds on which to doubt the authenticity of its new agent connection.[32]

The publication as an appendix to *The case of the armie* of the letter that the eleven agents had originally handed to General Fairfax along with *The case of the armie* reinforces the claim to internal authorship: 'we the Agents to

---

[29] Woolrych, *Soldiers and statesmen*, 203–4.

[30] Ibbitson is named as the printer of *Propositions of the adjutators of five regiments of horse*, 21 October 1647 [BL E. 411(13)] and *Proposals from nine regiments of horse, and seven regiments of foot*, 4 November 1647 [BL E. 412(23)]. Although the latter contains much of the *Agreement*, it is a reprinting of the document as an official army newsletter (with Gilbert Mabbott's imprimatur), falsely claiming its 'Generall approbation' from the army. Therefore, despite its content, the tract is strictly an army or new agent publication.

[31] See *Papers from the armie*, 3–4, where it seems safe to assume the Levellers are the implied target; *Englands warning by Germanies woe* (printed for John Bellamy), 23 November 1646 [BL E. 362(28)]; John Vicars (ed.), *A summarie or short survey*, 23 November 1646 [BL 669.f.10(101)]; *An apologeticall account . . . of the church . . . of John Goodwin*, 25 February 1647 [BL E. 378(2)].

[32] For Harris see *CP*, I:86n. The relevant tract is reprinted in *P&L*, 452–4, a reprint of *A copy of a letter*, which had appeared on 11 November 1647.

five Regiments of your Horse, have after our weak manner in this our Representation, directed [the document] to our respective Regiments and to the whole Army'.[33] That letter also contains a sustained application of the parable of the servant who hid the pound coin entrusted to him by his lord;[34] and it is generally suffused with the biblical language that characterises much of *The case of the armie*,[35] but not the writings of John Wildman.

Rather, it draws on a biblical language more associated with Sexby's speeches and known writings.[36] The sense of the letter is that the army was a providential instrument driven on by a God-given mission – 'as thereunto called unto by God' – a language alien to Wildman's *Putney projects* as printed only weeks later. This is also close to Sexby's outcries at Putney ('The Lord hath put us into a state . . . that you know not where you are. You are in a wilderness condition . . . I think we that we have gone about to heal Babylon when she would not')[37] but not to anything Wildman says.

The case for Sexby's authorship is considered further below.

IV

There can be no doubt that *The case of the armie* was a composite document. It is full of repetitions and overlaps, with sequences of numbered points being disrupted as they would be if late additions were stitched in from another source. It remains, however, possible to suggest how the document was assembled.

---

[33] Wolfe, *Leveller manifestoes*, 220–1.
[34] In the parable (Luke 19:11–27) a nobleman – who represents the Father – gives one-pound coins to his servants; the first two put their coins to work in the market and return their Lord a rich dividend, while a third, fearful of losing it, wraps it in a napkin and hides it, and on request returns it in due time, only to be reviled by the Lord for his failure to use the money creatively. The agents' gloss on the parable suggests that all men – common soldiers included – were required by God to use those abilities and that power for his service and not to be intimidated into 'silence and forebearance'. Reading the letter, perhaps fancifully but quite strongly, recalls something Murray Tolmie said in his *The triumph of the saints: the separate churches of London 1616–1649* (Cambridge, 1977), 158, about the regimental petitions of May: 'the political organisation of the lower ranks of the army in the spring of 1647 had been essentially a sectarian rather than a Leveller achievement'. The letter of the new agents feels – it can be put no more strongly than that – to have more of the General Baptist mindset in it than anything else. It certainly reminds us of the Bible-saturated language of the agents and helps to indicate the sections of *The case of the armie* in strongly secular language which might have been drafted in.
[35] As in the passage in Wolfe, *Leveller manifestoes*, 210–11.
[36] See, for example *CP,* I:377–8; more contentiously (because it is so much later and may have been co-authored), see *Killing noe murder* (The Netherlands, May 1657) [BL E. 501(4)]. Sexby's authorship is much strengthened by the fact that this tract was published as by his old friend and ally William Allen, who had just resigned from his post in the army in Ireland.   [37] *CP,* I: 377.

	Original[38]	Wolfe[39]	Comment
1. Recriminations			
[a] Preface	1–2	199–200	army-focused
[b] List of Broken Promises	2–7	200–05	army-obsessed
[c] Mischiefs and Evils (I)	*8–9*	*205–07*	*'external' focus*
[d] Mischiefs and Evils (II)	9–13	207–10	army-focused
[e] Link Passage	13–14	210–11	army as 'we'
2. Remedies: Calls for Constitutional Change			
[f] # 1–3 end of Long Parliament	14–15	211–12	close to army declarations
[g] # 4–5 law paramount for elections	15–16	212–15	army text
[h] #4*-5*, 6–12	*16–19*	*215–16*	*linked closely to [c]*
[i] #7*-9* army bread and butter	19–20	217	army bread and butter
[j] Conclusion	20	217–8	army-focused

This scheme commends itself on several grounds. There is a clear shift in the tone and pitch of the document between [b] and [d], with the abandonment of first-person pronouns about the army, with an agenda that is effectively civil, populist, close to much Leveller writing. The headlines in that section [c] are then taken up in [h] – where sections 4*-12 deal with monopolies, prisons, religious freedom, tithes, oaths in court, the reduction of laws to a single volume in English, equality at law, and the restoration of commons to the poor. The strongly secular language of [c] and [h] suggests Wildman, or perhaps army appropriation and adaptation of passages from Leveller tracts. Indeed, [h] displays a remarkably similar content to the thirteen points of the Levellers' *Large petition*.[40] But we would suggest that the bulk of *The case of the armie* – all except for [c] and [h] – is written by and for soldiers: this is based on pronominalisation, on the self-sufficiency of the argument in terms of previous army engagements and declarations, the prioritisation of the army's self-interests, and a consistent biblicism of language.

The central thrust of [a], [b] and [d] is that there has been a failure to honour the commitments of the army, above all those to be found in the Declarations and Remonstrances of 14 and 23 June and 18 August, mainly due to corruption and hardness of heart of the 'rotten studds' in the House of Commons. Yet there is little reason to agree with that tradition of interpretation represented by Ian Gentles when he describes *The case of the armie* as 'a massive indictment of the senior officers'.[41] In the preface there is indeed a pointed comment on how 'the present manner of

---

[38] The pagination is the same in all copies found as is the text. But some versions use a slightly different numbering of points on 15–18. For convenience, this essay follows the numbering of points as given in the most accessible modern edition, that printed in Wolfe, *Leveller manifestoes*.   [39] Wolfe, *Leveller manifestoes*, 199–218.
[40] Reprinted in ibid., 138–41.   [41] Gentles, *New Model Army*, 200.

actings of many at the Head Quarters' meant that 'nothing' had 'been done effectually';[42] but after that, anger is focused on delinquents and corrupt MPs and no specific complaint is made against the generals rather than against the General Council as a whole. Moreover, this reinforces the grounds for suspecting military, as against civilian, authors, with soldiers less obviously inclined openly to attack their officers, as so much of the current output of Leveller literature did. After the list of promises the army had made *to itself* we come down to [e], which is an appeal for an imposed settlement grounded not on an alliance of soldiers and right-thinking citizens but on a renewed pledge of the whole army to act in concert with itself and to the exhortation 'let us never divide each from other till those just demands be answered really and effectually . . . that *our* honour may be preserved unspotted'.[43] That leads into a series of five demands for a dissolution of the Long Parliament within ten months, an immediate purge, a law paramount unalterable by future parliaments fixing biennial elections and a rhetorically vast franchise; that (*pace* months of Leveller argument) all power to make public appointments and call men-in-office to account be concentrated in the House of Commons, and that an enquiry be held into the misappropriation of bishops' lands and other revenues with a view to 'the more easie provision of money for the soldiery'.[44] Any money still owing to them was to come from the sale of dean and chapter lands.[45] After this it lurches off into a discussion of the Leveller agenda exactly as itemised in [c], this lurch consisting of points numbered 4*–12. The previous numbering then resumes, which follows logically on from the discussion of arrears in [g] point 5 – that is, calls for indemnity, provision for army widows and orphans and the maimed, and a strengthening of the financial sanctions against convicted royalists. Thus [e], [f], [g], [i] and [j] hang together as a coherent whole in logical progression, language and army-centredness, with [h] standing out as a self-contained and logical response to [c]. Since most of those sections [e]–[j] are rooted in the past experience of the army with the exception of the arrangements for new parliaments which are embedded within it, they should surely be regarded as a whole as army-generated; and that includes the franchise clause.

If we now take stock of what it is being asked for, it is most fundamentally that private treaties be broken off, especially with the king. The abolition of monarchy is not envisaged[46] but the recall of the king would be the final stage of an imposed settlement, not its precursor. There would

---

[42] Wolfe, *Leveller manifestoes*, 199.   [43] Ibid., 211.   [44] Ibid., 213.   [45] Ibid., 215.

[46] The key point is that a settlement should precede any take-it-or-leave-it offer to the Crown to fit into the interstices of that settlement. *The case of the armie* does not envisage the end of the monarchy – for example, it proposes that arrears are paid out of the sale of the residue of the bishops' lands and the untouched dean and chapter lands and there is a

be an immediate purge of the parliament and urgent action taken by the purged parliament to do two things. The first was that the army's bread-and-butter demands should be addressed so that the burdens on the people at large could be eased. The second was that legislation should be passed that would provide for free elections and for a more equal distribution of seats and a new extended franchise. The elections would be held biennially and on dates which would be forever fixed. In demanding these things, the authors of *The case of the armie* were only going beyond the demands in previous army documents in respect to the arrangements for elections, and there they were in many respects picking up on themes from *The heads of the proposals* (not least the demand for biennial parliaments rather than the normal Leveller demand for annual parliaments). Note that the 'law paramount' related only to the guarantees of elections and that it is presented as a hedge against royal tyranny and not against parliamentary tyranny.

We would thus argue that *The case of the armie* was an army document drawn up by members of the army who felt that the General Council had failed to follow through on the midsummer promises, and that it is a document which includes some half-appropriated Leveller ideas and two 'stitched-in' Leveller sections on economic oppression and its remedies. On this reading the *Agreement of the people* was not an austere and orderly summary of *The case of the armie* but a significant development from it. *The case of the armie* envisaged a purge and an orderly programme of legislation by a purged parliament to prepare for free elections, a just settlement of the army's claims. The *Agreement* implies an immediate dissolution, a national signing-up to a social compact by all those who wished to claim and exercise political rights and freedoms, a social compact at least as concerned to protect against legislative and judicial tyranny as executive tyranny and with a broad list of fundamental civil rights (the 'reserves') withheld from the power of future representatives.

V

Once it is recognised that *The case of the armie* and *An agreement* differ from one another far more than has been recognised hitherto, then a

footnote 46 (*cont.*)

deafening silence where one might have expected to find reference to Crown lands, made all the greater by the addition of the profits of disafforestation as a source of funds. This demand for an imposed settlement and a deferred restoration of the king can be found, in similar form, in the Reading debates. Cromwell's public commitment to a negotiated peace and not an imposed peace had drawn rebukes from the Levellers; but it had not split the Army Council in July and is not treated within *The case of the armie* in a distinctively Leveller way.

series of issues at Putney clarify themselves. We suggest that Sexby is the most likely principal author of *The case of the armie* and Wildman of *An agreement*; that at Putney there is a battle over which should be discussed and that once it became clear to the agents and their *army* sympathisers that the generals were willing to debate the constitutional proposals in *The case of the armie* but not *An agreement*, the road to consensus was reopened and Wildman and his civilian friends in London fell back, frustrated and isolated.

While we cannot be certain who co-ordinated the writing of *The case of the armie*, it was far more likely to have been Sexby than Wildman. It is Sexby who was invited to introduce the discussion and he did so by explaining the agents' answer to the letter from the General Council's committee,[47] and it was he who introduced Wildman and Petty as commentators on, rather than presenters of, *The case of the armie*. Indeed Wildman made clear at Putney that he had only recently been drafted in as an adviser and he seems to show uncertainty as to the pre-history of the document: 'yesterday att a Meeting . . . [with] the Agents of the five Regiments, and having weigh'd their papers, I must freely confesse I did declare my agreement with them'.[48] Furthermore, when Ireton hints that Wildman was the author of *The case of the armie*, the latter's denial reads as actual and not ironic: 'I doe nott know what reason you have to suppose I should bee soe well acquainted with the Case of the Armie'.[49] More generally it seems that Wildman was always keen to discuss *An agreement* while Sexby always speaks to *The case of the armie*. Indeed, it seems most poignant that a new agent pamphlet collected by George Thomason on 28 October – the first day of the Putney debates, when *An agreement* was discussed by the General Council – refers only to *The case of the armie*, making no allusions whatsoever to *An agreement*. In complete contrast, the anonymous, but no doubt civilian, author of *A cal to all the souldiers of the army*, collected by Thomason the following day, wrote of settlement being achieved through 'some substantiall and firme AGREEMENT, for just freedom and common right'.[50] We should perhaps also note that

---

47 *CP,* I:227.   48 Ibid., I:240.   49 Ibid., I:356, 362.
50 *Two letters from the agents of the five regiments*, 28 October 1647 [BL E. 412(6)]; *A cal to all the souldiers of the army, by the free people of England*, 29 October 1647 [BL E. 412(10)], 8 (mispaged 7), capitals as in original. Following Firth's article in the *Dictionary of national biography* and the comments of Maurice Ashley (in his *John Wildman* (London, 1947), 39), this later tract may well have been the work of Wildman. It is particularly similar, both in style and theme, with his later pamphlet, *Putney projects* (30 December 1647 [BL E. 421(19)]), in its vehement attack upon the grandees, allied with an appeal to both soldiers and civilians for immediate action. *A cal* makes a clear and consistent distinction between the army, to whom the tract is addressed, and its civilian author and his allies (8 (mispaged 7)). Thus, and in complete contrast to new agent literature, the plights of John Lilburne, Richard Overton and other civilian prisoners are referred to (2*, 4*

when the debate on the future of the monarchy got bogged down on 1 November, Sexby's close ally William Allen requested that the Council return to a discussion of *The case of the armie*: and only four weeks earlier Lilburne had referred to Allen as 'one of the adjutators for Lieutenant General Cromwell's Regiment, and his officious and extraordinary creature in the imploying all his subtilty and parts'.[51]

We suggested above that the biblical language of *The case of the armie* was more characteristic of Sexby than of Wildman; and there is one more striking parallel in the demand for an interim purge of the parliament. Leveller writing in general, and Wildman's writing in particular, is strongly critical of the Long Parliament and demands that a fixed term be set to its existence. *An agreement*, for example calls for its dissolution on 30 September 1648. The Levellers were later resolutely opposed to Pride's Purge in December 1648. The demand of *The case of the armie* that 'the house be forthwith purged, from al who have forfited their trust, or were unduly elected, but especially that an order be passed forthwith, for the expelling all those from the House, who sate in the late pretended Parliament'[52] looks much more likely to be a restatement of the army's demand for a purge after presbyterian mobs had driven the Speaker and many members from Westminster to army headquarters in late July. It is also very close to the passionate language of Sexby in his first speech at Putney, where he speaks of the parliament as 'a Company of rotten Members' and calls them 'rotten studds' – that is (as Sir Charles Firth surely correctly glosses it), rotten uprights in a lath-and-plaster wall. '[P]rovidence hath bin with us', Sexby reminded them, and now there must be 'expedition' in relation to the king and the parliament.[53] The implication of this speech is that there should be a purge of parliament and a settlement imposed by God's army. What it challenges is the grandees' plans for an orderly transfer of power over the following twelve months as a chastened parliament accepted the wisdom of their proposals and their personal treaty with the king.

If the co-ordinator of *The case of the armie* was Sexby, then his Leveller links need to be carefully scrutinised; and those links – and especially his connection with Lilburne – were not all they have been cracked up to be. Ian Gentles' careful account of him de-emphasises Leveller links and stresses his role as a core activist amongst the first group of adjutators, arranging the purchase of the army's own printing press and distributing

---

footnote 50 (*cont.*)

    (i.e. second pagination)). Moreover, if the tract was by Wildman, it is all the more significant that although there is praise for *The case of the armie*, an 'AGREEMENT' is advocated in its place in order to provide 'a firme establish't certainty of all particulars' (8 (mispaged 7)).   [51] Lilburne, *The juglers discovered*, 8.

[52] Wolfe, *Leveller manifestoes*, 211.   [53] *CP*, I: 227–8.

substantial sums of money on behalf of the General Council.[54] The evidence of Sexby's Leveller links before Putney rests on the exaggerated claims of Pauline Gregg. She wrote that Sexby was 'the chief intermediary between Lilburne and the Army . . . [he] kept copies of Lilburne's pamphlets and was the chief medium for their distribution among the soldiers'.[55] This is based on a complete misreading of a sentence in Lilburne's *The juglers discovered* of late September 1647, which says simply that if Fairfax wants to find out about Lilburne's innocency of the charges made against him by the House of Lords he must read *The freeman's freedome vindicated*, which is now 'with the rest of my books in the hands of Mr Sexby'. This is a rather acid comment, as though it was neither his will nor his preference that Sexby was the custodian of his library, quite likely confiscated when he was imprisoned. There is not a shred of evidence here that Sexby was an intermediary or a promoter of Lilburne's tracts.[56]

There is, furthermore, a tension running through Putney as to the relationship of *The case of the armie* and *An agreement*. We have only to compare Cromwell's harsh language on the latter as dangerously innovative in form and content[57] with his explicit commendation of *The case of the armie*: 'For those thinges that have bin done in the Army, as this of the Case of the Armie truly stated. There is much in itt usefull, and to bee condescended to.'[58] Cromwell appears to have been ready for the kind of settlement envisaged by *The case of the armie* – an orderly handover from one parliament to another and a negotiated settlement with the king – but not that envisaged by *An agreement* – the formal dissolution of all the existing constitutional forms, and the formation of a new social compact (a literal agreement of *all* the people) to put themselves under new forms of government. This is a tension that runs through the franchise debate and even more through the subsequent debate on the future role of the monarchy and on the negative voice. There is only space here to look at one aspect of this, the important debate on the franchise. The wording in *An agreement* is as notoriously understated as the language of *The case of the armie* is ambiguous;[59] but it was not too understated for its import to

---

[54] Gentles, *New Model Army*, esp. 165, 176.

[55] Pauline Gregg, *Free-born John* (London, 1961), 163.

[56] Lilburne, *The juglers discovered*, 1. Despite this, for the acceptance of Gregg's views see Woolrych, *Soldiers and statesmen*, 41, 63–4, which subsequently colour his own account of Sexby's ties with the Levellers at 74, 130, 144 and 203–4.

[57] For his indignant surprise and recognition of the scale of the change, see *CP*, I:236; and cf. his indulgent language about the agents of the five regiments as against his rebuke to Wildman, *CP*, I:277.   [58] *CP*, I:369.

[59] 'that all the freeborn at the age of 21. yeares and upwards, be the electors, excepting those that have or shall deprive themselves of that their freedome, either for some yeares, or wholly by delinquency'. Debate has centred on the comma after 'some yeares'. Does it mean some years by delinquency or wholly by delinquency? Or, wholly by delinquency

be lost on Ireton: 'Itt is said . . . "[that seats will be allocated] according to the number of inhabitants;" and this doth make me thinke that the meaning is, that every man that is an inhabitant is to bee equally consider'd, and to have an equall voice.'[60] There were three principal defenders of the widest possible franchise – the maverick Rainborough, Wildman and Sexby. There is an important distinction between the way Wildman and Sexby approached the question, however. Wildman pitches his response explicitly in terms of the language of *An agreement*: 'Every person in England hath as cleere a right to Elect his Representatives as the greatest person in England. I conceive that's the undeniable maxime of Governement, that all government is in the free consent of the people.'[61] Sexby did not join in until forty-two speeches had been recorded by Clarke, and when the subject had moved from *An agreement* onto the moral high ground. When he does enter the debate it is not to speak up for the poor people, but for the poor soldier.

Wee have engaged in this Kingdome and ventur'd our lives, and itt was all for this: to recover our birthrights and priviledges as Englishmen, and by all the arguments urged there is none. There are many thousands of us soldiers that have ventur'd our lives; wee have had little propriety in the Kingedome as to our estates, yett wee have had a birthright. Butt it seemes now except a man hath a fix't estate in this Kingedome, hee hath noe right in this Kingedome. I wonder wee were so much deceived. If wee had nott a right to the Kingedome, wee were meere mercenarie soldiers.[62]

The key here is that he slips unselfconsciously between the rights of the people and the rights of soldiers.[63] Whenever he says 'we' he means the soldiers and not the people. This rhetoric leads straight through to the compromise agreed the following day in a committee that included the grandees, Rainborough, Sexby and Allen (but not Wildman), that all who had been in arms for the parliament or who had voluntarily assisted the cause with money or supplies were to have the vote; that all convicted royalists were barred for five years and that the rights of all others would

footnote 59 (*cont.*)
   or for some years for something else ? Then there is the status of the 'have or *shall*', especially in relation to 'delinquency'. It cannot even be certain that 'delinquency' here necessarily means 'royalism'. If 'that their freedom' relates to being 'freeborne', it is not clear how that relates to what follows. The only thing we can say for certain is that not much thought had gone into the drafting of this sentence, which points *against* a Leveller-written document, especially in comparison to the coy and radical reworking of the idea of manhood suffrage in the *Agreement*, which is just what one would expect a sophisticated draftsman to do to avoid drawing attention to an incompetent earlier draft.

[60] *CP,* I:299.   [61] Ibid., I:318.   [62] Ibid., I:322–3.
[63] Very much the same can be said, of course, of Rainborough, who behind talk of the 'poorest hee' in fact concentrates on the rights of soldiers: ibid., I:305, 311, 320.

be decided by a parliament voted for by those with an old fixed interest (the forty-shilling freehold) or the new fixed interest (investment in the war).[64] This seems fully compatible with Sexby's language and argument at Putney (and with *The case of the armie*), but not really compatible with the language and argument of Wildman at this time.

VI

All this leaves the exact position of the Levellers during the Putney debates very unclear. As Ivan Roots has pondered, 'what *were* civilian Levellers doing there?'[65] This is an aspect of a much bigger problem: how, quite when and why the Levellers gained a constituency in the army, and why the General Officers put up with it at all. These are issues currently under investigation elsewhere,[66] but a number of preliminary remarks may be made here. First, when Wildman and Maximilian Petty appeared at the General Council of the Army for its final scheduled meeting of October, it is unlikely that alarm bells were instantly set off inside the grandees' heads. They would have seen two civilians and *not* two 'Levellers' before them, as that name was only first appropriated to the group *after* the Putney debates when Ireton had implied that his opponents' arguments threatened a form of political levelling.[67] Furthermore, neither Wildman or Petty would have been immediately identifiable with John Lilburne or Richard Overton, the two authors who had been most outspoken against the grandees, as neither is known to have had any previous involvement with them. If they were allied with anyone, it was far more likely to have been William Walwyn, one of the most vocal critics of Thomas Edwards, whose *Gangraena* the army had also complained against specifically earlier in the year.[68]

Here perhaps lies the key to the civilian involvement with the army. Walwyn had not only attacked the polemics of Edwards, but he was also a prosperous and respected member of his parish, personally involved with many of the meetings and committees that supported the war effort from

---

[64] Ibid., I:364–5.   [65] In his preface to *P&L* (1992), xx, emphasis added.

[66] See Baker, 'The origins and early history of the Levellers'.

[67] Woodhouse's transcription of the relevant speech (123) from the original Worcester College, Oxford, Clarke Ms. 65, fol.83v seems preferable to Firth's (*CP*, I:405) here. See Woolrych, *Soldiers and statesmen*, 275 and Brailsford, *Levellers*, 309 for the first uses of the name 'Leveller'. For a full discussion of the way the term came into use, see Baker, 'The origins and early history of the Levellers', ch. 1. (Ed. note: see also ch. 13, below.)

[68] Baker, 'The origins and early history of the Levellers'; Jack R. McMichael and Barbara Taft (eds.), *The writings of William Walwyn* (Athens, GA, and London, 1989), 18; Woolrych, *Soldiers and statesmen*, 92.

within London. He had never authored an attack upon the grandees and was in fact an ally of the City independent petitioning campaign that explicitly defended the army (and themselves) against presbyterian attack during the summer of 1647.[69] He had yet to put his name to any pamphlets that would have associated him with either Lilburne or Overton. Thus, it is not a surprise to find that Walwyn and leaders of the independent faction within the capital met with Cromwell during mid-1647, and that Walwyn visited army headquarters whilst it resided at Reading in July.[70] Indeed, even the most sceptical account of the Leveller–army relationship sees the two drawing together and sharing common cause during the summer months of 1647,[71] for it was (again) while the army resided at Reading that a 'Mr. Wildman' delivered a paper to Fairfax concerning the purging of independents from the London Militia Committee. As the identical arguments of that paper were adopted by the adjutators during the Reading debates,[72] there is clear evidence for a precedent of army and civilian collaboration. Similarly, there is no reason to doubt Petty's statement during the course of the Putney debates that he attended discussions over *The heads of the proposals*,[73] surrounded, as he was when he spoke, by the principal authors of the document.

Although the process of army politicisation and its internal adjutator organisation functioned quite independently of the machinations of 'well-affected' Londoners, such an obvious haven of support was turned to when need arose. And this constitutes the most likely context for the appearance of the civilian representatives at Putney. Having taken on board some ideas from the Levellers to shore up the raft of traditional adjutator demands, the authors of *The case of the armie* felt the need for those experienced in arguing the cause of parliamentary reform to assist them in presenting a case they were strongly drawn to but had not thought through to any degree.

VII

Perhaps the central puzzle of Putney has always been how the generals could be so outmanoeuvred and defeated in committee and then go to the rank and file and get their overwhelming endorsement for a remonstrance

---

[69] Keith Lindley, *Popular politics and religion in civil war London* (Aldershot, 1997), 395, 396; McMichael and Taft, *Writings of Walwyn*, 391–2.

[70] McMichael and Taft, *Writings of Walwyn*, 391–3.

[71] Mark A. Kishlansky, 'The army and the Levellers: the roads to Putney', *HJ* 22(4) (1979), 795–824, at 812–13, 814–15.

[72] Worcester College Oxford, Clarke Ms. 41, fols. 167, 185; *CP*, I:171.

[73] *CP*, I:351.

that explicitly disowned the Levellers and their programme, yet incorporated the very agreements allegedly wrung from them at Putney. This problem is eased if in fact the following was the sequence of events:

1. A number of existing adjutators and other articulate soldiers became alarmed at the drift of General Council policy towards a negotiated settlement rooted in direct negotiations with the king. They met together and drew up a document, *The case of the armie*, that called the soldiers back to what they believed to be their earlier engagements.

2. In drawing up their programme they drew on 'Leveller' documents for specific parts of *The case of the armie* and perhaps even consulted with supporters of the 'Leveller' movement in London, but such support represented the addition of buttresses that were as much ornamental as load-bearing in function.

3. Although *The case of the armie* was intended to bring the General Council back to fundamentals, it contained just enough explicit criticism of the generals to cause a row and a demand that that charge be retracted. It did not lead to an outright rejection of the substantive demands, because they were in large part compatible with the General Council's stated objectives.

4. When the General Council met on 28 October, the agents presented an emollient letter defending themselves from the charge of seeking to divide the army and then they presented the *Agreement of the people*, which had been written either by Walwyn or more probably by Wildman, whom they called in as expert adviser on particular aspects of *The case of the armie* and at the suggestion of the General Council committee itself.[74] This became the focus of the fierce criticism and denunciation. In the days that followed, the generals and their supporters gave no ground on the specific requirements of the *Agreement*, but indicated that now the question of *their* responsibility for dividing the army had been addressed, they would consider the recommendations of *The case of the armie*.

5. In committee, agreement was reached: the idea of a personal treaty was tacitly dropped; the idea of requiring parliament to introduce reforms intended to remodel parliamentary government and redress

---

[74] The case for Walwyn is suggested by Barbara Taft in her introduction to *Writings of Walwyn*, 30–1. Her argument, that the sweet reasonableness of language and call for a list of natural rights to be withheld from the attention of the legislature allows us to ascribe it to him, is hardly conclusive. But if it was by him, or had been run past him, it would further de-emphasise the link to *The case of the armie* and makes it appear a free-standing alternative to *The case of the armie* rather than its prudent digest.

the soldiers' grievances was accepted and a detailed legislative programme rooted in *The case of the armie* was agreed.[75] The sophisticated
proposals of the *Agreement* – for a dissolution, a social compact and
manhood suffrage – were jettisoned.

6. The five articles agreed by the committee of eighteen at Putney on 30
   October relating to the dissolution of the Long Parliament on 1
   September 1648, the 'secure provision' of arrangements for biennial
   elections, the agreement on the provision for government between
   parliaments and the proposed extended franchise[76] – and the articles
   agreed in the same committee on 2 November and at a committee on
   8 November all derive from or are fully compatible with *The case of the
   armie* and fed straight into the Remonstrance signed by all the regiments during November, presented to the parliament in early
   December and overtaken by the events of the second civil war. They
   are not compatible with *An agreement of the people*.

Yet if Putney restored army unity and if Sexby and other friends of the
agents on the committee that hammered out the Putney compromises
were happy with those compromises, why did they join with some but not
all of the agents in publicly disowning them and denouncing the double-
dealing of the grandees in the declaration signed by the new agents on 11

---

[75] If it is correct to see 1–5 and 7–9 as the agents' (and Sexby's) draft proposals and they are
compared with (a) the committee decisions on 29 October and 2 November (*CP*,
I:363–5, 407–10) (b) the generals' proposals as laid out in the Remonstrance (see
summary in Gentles, *New Model Army*, 223–4) laid before and approved by all the regiments during November, the continuity is very clear:

Case	Putney committee	Remonstrance
dissolution of parl. in autumn 1647	as in *Case*	as in *Case*
purge of MPs now		
army honour to be vindicated	as in *Case*	
law paramount for elections and franchise	yes + religion, indemnity, impressment	
biennial parliaments on wide suffrage	biennial on broad (army) franchise	looser but compatible
public officials accountable to parliament	modified but based on *Case*	
army arrears from church lands, etc.	uncontroversial	close to *Case*
indemnity	uncontroversial	close to *Case*
widows, orphans, maimed	uncontroversial	close to *Case*
strengthening of measures vs. royalists	religion, impressment reserved; no settlement based solely on a treaty betw. King and parl. (the intro. to *Case* demands this but it was not repeated in the articles)	no impressment

[76] *CP*, I:363–5.

November?[77] There are no easy answers to that puzzle. Agreement does not mean trust. Perhaps at Putney itself the unity of the army was maintained or restored but many of those who were party to the accords themselves continued to dislike and distrust one another. Something in the final and poorly recorded days at Putney and in the days that followed made them fall out again, with the most likely culprit being the person of the king. Although the committee agreements ruled out a personal treaty with Charles before a general settlement, great fissures *within* all groups had been revealed by the debates on 1 November with respect to the future powers of the monarchy. Some very strong language was used – the king was twice called a man of blood – and it is hard to avoid the conviction that several participants wished an end to Charles I if not an end to the monarchy. Ireton's passionate commitment to a reduced role but a real role for Charles gathered support amongst some of the officers, adjutators and agents, but others in each group appear to have been attracted to the language of blood guilt. In that respect the escape of the king and his flight to the Isle of Wight, where the governor was Cromwell's cautious friend and confidant Robert Hammond, may have looked to the agents, if not to modern historians, to be too much in the interests of the grandees for coincidence. Perhaps in addition it was the decision to suspend the General Council and to appeal straight to the rank and file at separate (and not a general) rendezvous over the heads of the adjutators and agents which destroyed fragile trust.[78] The Remonstrance seems to be wholly consistent with everything of substance in the decisions of the committee of the General Council that Sexby, Allen and others attended and appear to have supported; and therefore with the substance of *The case of the armie*. But trust had gone.

To add one more layer of puzzlement: why, if he was seen as an incorrigible enemy to the generals, was Sexby employed as such an important intermediary in 1648 between Cromwell and Lilburne and Cromwell and the House of Commons? Why was he then commissioned and made a garrison commander and subsequently a colonel?

Finally, we return to a degree of certainty in addressing why Ireton and

[77] The petition of 11 November (abstracted in *P&L*, 452–4) is especially vehement on the need to exclude the king from all power; and it accuses Ireton of storming out of the General Council on 5 November when a vote was taken to send a letter (itself printed in *CP*, I:440–1) from the Council to the Speaker of the Commons denying that the army wished Parliament to send any further propositions to the king. It is striking that there are no signatures on this petition from any representatives of Rich's regiment, which had been in the forefront of the campaign for *The case of the armie*. The petition of 11 November had many new 'new agents' but lacked the names of several of the old 'new agents'.

[78] *P&L*, 453; *A copy of a letter*, 4. It would seem that the agents believed the suspension of the General Council was only temporary – 'for above a fortnight' (*P&L*, 453) – but nevertheless, this remains an obvious reason for their anger.

Cromwell condemned the agents of the five regiments as well as the Levellers in the Remonstrance read at the three regimental rendezvous in November. On all sides, the Putney agreements became perhaps like the Camp David or Dayton agreements: they were agreed in haste and repented of at leisure. Despite their search for consensus, the grandees and their orders were now openly attacked in new agent literature at a time when the general condition of the army gave them great cause for concern.[79] Moreover, this coincided with a separate outpouring of anonymous pamphlets exhorting the soldiers not to suffer the backsliding of the grandees. It was only now, on the eve of the first rendezvous, that civilian frustration and isolation led to their attempt to hijack the new agent organisation in support of their own and quite separate agenda.[80] And it was precisely because that amounted to an unprecedented development in the context of what had occurred previously at Putney, that the grandees turned against both. Hence, on all sides, trust was at a complete end.

It is thus the suggestion of this chapter that at Putney there was exactly the search for consensus discussed by Professor Mark Kishlansky in his article of eighteen years ago.[81] That search for consensus was destabilised by the thin-skinnedness of the generals about the imputation to their honour and by the radically unacceptable constitutional demands added by and in *An agreement of the people*. If this is correct, then *The case of the armie* may have represented a more viable basis for settlement than has been recognised. When Sir Thomas Fairfax was presented with *The case of the armie*, he is reported to have replied that 'he judged their intentions were honest, and desired that every one of a publique spirit would be acting for the Publique, and that for his part hee . . . thought it meet it should be presented to the Generall Council'.[82] Why can't we take him at his word?

---

[79] *A copy of a letter*, passim. By 8 November Robert Lilburne's regiment of foot had been in a state of open mutiny for more than a fortnight. The same day, Cromwell spoke of the distempers within the army before submitting the motion to send the adjutators back to their regiments: *CP*, I:410–2.

[80] *A cal to all the souldiers of the army*; *An alarum to the headquarters*, 9 November 1647 [BL E. 413(10)].

[81] Mark A. Kishlansky, 'Consensus politics and the structure of debate at Putney', *JBS* 20(2) (1981), 50–69.   [82] Wolfe, *Leveller manifestoes*, 222.

7 Putney's pronouns: identity and indemnity in the great debate[1]

Michael Mendle

Nothing said at Putney is more celebrated than Colonel Thomas Rainboroughs's impassioned outburst about the rights of 'the poorest hee that is in England', a locution as memorable perhaps for its curious idiom as for its sentiments. Putney, though, had other moments of pronomial fire, when the first-person plural, the 'we's' of identity, drove the debate. What occasioned them, how they shaped the concerns that the participants brought to Putney, how they either persisted or evanesced afterwards are themes of this chapter.

The we's of Putney were not unidimensional. Men found themselves arrayed on several axes of solidarity and fissure. The participants were the soldiers of a victorious army, the self-professedly godly, and, in summer 1647, were linked by a common political stance with respect to the parliament. These experiences and commitments were common to most of the men at Putney, and were powerful components of identity. The instinct towards consensus and the acute sensitivity over the army's honour, as Mark Kishlansky has emphasised, were always near the surface in the New Model's discussions.[2] To much the same effect was the response to signs of difference: communal prayer. 'Religion' at Putney did indeed 'bind together' the participants. Yet other forces pulled the same men apart. Some were personal. Thomas Rainborough's resentment of Cromwell may have driven him into the populist camp;[3] the mutual detestation of the two most forward speakers at Putney, Henry Ireton and John Wildman, was not confined to the issues. Other distinctions were social and racial or ethnic (or, better perhaps, pseudo-racial or pseudo-ethnic): Putney, as will be seen, was in good measure a debate over who really constituted the English nation. Most divisive of all

---

[1] I wish to thank John Morrill and Barbara Taft for their helpful critiques of this essay.
[2] Mark Kishlansky, *The rise of the New Model Army* (Cambridge, 1979), chs. 7, 8, Conclusion, and his 'Consensus politics and the structure of debate at Putney', *JBS* 20 (1981), 50–69.
[3] For Rainborough's resentment of Cromwell, who tried to block his appointment as vice-admiral, see Ian Gentles, *The New Model Army in England, Ireland and Scotland, 1645–1653* (Oxford, 1992), 198.

was the menacing prospect of peace, which threatened to pull the godly army apart, indeed to 'civilianise' it. Contributors to this volume, myself amongst them, stress the centrality of the army-as-institution to the proceedings of 1647. But it was the terror of prospective settlement, of peace, that provoked Putney, and the postures men adopted in the debates as well as the topics themselves were those of citizens and civilians. Poised midway between war and peace was the issue of indemnity, the far-from-silent but surprisingly unrecognised partner in all the proceedings.

The debates reveal conflicts not only amongst the participants but also within individuals. Compromise and anger, solidarity and contempt are all present. Somehow all the sensibilities must be kept in the air, a juggling act as difficult as it is needful. The startling anti-monarchism of the 'radicals' at Putney must be read against the same individuals' own outbursts of royalism. What the 'radicals' could often abide in themselves they almost reflexively feared in others. Equally, Ireton's scorn for arguments from the notion of birthright and from natural law must be set against his tacit acceptance of them some months before, when they were trained by radical army-connected scribblers against the parliament.[4] And at Putney, as elsewhere and at other times, identity was a composite of 'we's', often partly unreconciled. Cromwell was general, soldier (as distinct from the former),[5] gentleman, one of the godly. When he and Ireton said 'we', they might mean any of these identities – and also might *not* mean some of them. Those who espoused a populist ideology – men such as Cowling, Allen, Rainborough, Sexby, Wildman – had an identity component that provoked Putney's bitterest passions. They were (or postured as) the 'freeborn' of England. But all save Wildman were also soldiers, and for those who were soldiers, or who spoke for them, the tugs of soldierly and freeborn identity played out in ways that recall the most anguished of Putney's questions: 'Butt I would faine know what the souldier hath fought for all this while?'[6]

The idiom of the 'freeborn' Englishman that seemed so obvious to the agitators and Levellers at Putney and so specious to Ireton was no novelty in army rhetoric. Having its roots in the universalising claims of Cokean common-law ideology, it had an appeal that stretched from Levellers to (as shown below) royalists. It was well established within the inner sancta

---

[4] See below, pp. 128–30.
[5] That is, 'soldier' in the inclusive sense (as it used, for example, by Austin Woolrych in the title of his *Soldiers and statesmen* (Oxford, 1987)), although it is also true and relevant that in the idiom of 1647, 'soldier' was characteristically distinguished from 'officer' – it was a shortened form of 'private soldier'.   [6] *CP*, I:325.

of army 'radical'[7] thought in the summer of 1647. In fact, the notions of that circle can be traced, though briefly, with some precision, because Sexby and his friends had a house organ, the short-lived Oxford-based 'army' press of summer 1647 now usually associated with the names of its two printers, John Harris and Henry Hills. Harris, an Oxford-based actor-turned-printer for Fairfax, later became well known as a somewhat independent London Leveller who published and wrote under various anagramatic forms of his name, of which the most famous was Sirraniho.[8] Hills, a man of extraordinarily volatile opinions, was at this point known primarily, if he was known at all, as a radical sympathiser: in his early teens he had been the postilion (that is, messenger) of the nineteen-year-old John Lilburne.[9]

The press was put together at the insistence of Edward Sexby, who wrote to the agitators on 17 May 1647 that unless a press be 'gott into the Army wee shall bee at a losse'. Sexby had already taken matters into his own hands, as his immediately subsequent remark reveals: 'There wants nothing but money, therefor tell the Officers they must disburse the money.' He reiterated the thought the next day.[10] As its initial offerings seem to be on the fringes, or outside, of official army printing, so probably was the press's early financing.[11] The salient physical features of the books to spring from it suggest that, whatever the source, the level of support was extremely low. The press had only a tiny stock of Roman

---

[7] Though perhaps the term cannot be altogether avoided, in part because it *does* correspond to some contemporary perceptions, the term 'radical' carries many misleading implications of later times. This is in part a reflection of the wistfully conservative or restorative character of much supposedly radical thought, but also, and more immediately, the notion of the freeborn Englishman so dear to the 'radicals' was profoundly integrative and affirmative of a general solidarity.

[8] For Harris see the article on him by Barbara Taft in Robert Zaller and Richard L. Greaves, *Biographical dictionary of British radicals in the seventeenth century* (3 vols., Brighton, 1982), vol. II, *sub nom.* Harris, John. See also Margot Heinemann, 'Popular drama and Leveller style: Richard Overton and John Harris' in Maurice Cornforth (ed.), *Rebels and their causes: essays in honour of A. L. Morton* (1978), 69–92; J. B. Williams (pseudonym for J. G. Muddiman), *A history of English journalism* (London, 1908), 106–7; H. N. Brailsford, *The Levellers and the English revolution* (Stanford, 1961), especially 416, n.4, where Harris is proposed as the author of key issues of *The Moderate*; Joseph Frank, *The beginnings of the English newspaper* (Cambridge, MA, 1961), see index *sub nom.* Harris.

[9] Henry R. Plomer, *A dictionary of the booksellers printers . . . from 1641 to 1667* (repr. Oxford, 1968), 98.   [10] *CP,* I:82–3, 86.

[11] Two payments recorded in the army accounts to Harris in August 1647 seem to refer to the 'official' work that came at the end of the press's brief life. Chequers Ms. 782, fol. 43v (31 August, for £12), fol. 54r (undated, £4 1s.). The entry immediately below the first cited here, £78 17s. to Lt Chillenden for Mrs Coe's printing press, seems to me (*pace* Gentles, *New Model Army*, 486, n.189) to be a distinct transaction, occurring well after the army had arrived in London. Chillenden seems to have been the army council's designated 'point man' in such matters.

type, never had access to italics, and its usual capital I in the text font was a broken J. These features, matched by very poor presswork, are obviously a boon to researchers and, by means of them, a series of soldier-inspired (rather than official publications) stretching from mid-June into late July 1647 can be identified.[12] The first item definitely to be attributed to the press is the agitator-inspired, agitator-signed account of recent events, *A true declaration of the present proceedings of the army*.[13] That appeared, according to two variant title pages, on 12 and 16 June. Within days of the second issue, a second tract issued from the press, *Englands appeale to its own army*, in form not an army publication to the people but the reverse, 'The loud cry of an oppressed kingdome against their oppressors'.[14] From the beginning, it spoke in the idiom of Putney: 'Did we [i.e. the English people] ever thinke you would be mercinary Souldiers, you are not all French and Scotch, sure there is some of you free-borne Englishmen ... What, have you lost your interests and freedomes by fighting for them?' The army, it went on, took up arms neither to defend the king's 'boundlesse prerogative' or the parliament's 'unlimited priviledges, but to maintaine the common liberties of all the free-borne People of England, against all tyrannical usurpations, and uniust oppressions by whomsoever exercised'. The parliament, with its self-perpetuating pressure tactics upon 'counties and Corporations' was clearly the moment's worst offender. Disbandment of the present army would be followed by the erection of another that would 'inslave the People'.[15]

Then came, early in July, the first of three tracts to bear the name of Amon Willbee, *Plain truth without feare or flattery*. Though two London reprints put the initials I.L. on their title pages, John Lilburne never owned up to writing this piece; his friend Richard Overton, who was in a position to know, not only declared that 'until I read it I was as ignorant' of its provenance 'as the Child that is unborne' but then remarked that the parliament had been so devastated by *Plain truth* that it 'had to be

---

[12] The basic spadework was done long ago, and remarkably well for an era lacking modern visual reproduction technology, by Falconer Madan, *Oxford books*, (3 vols., Oxford, 1912), II:449–57. The press continued to operate until the army had moved into London in early August; the last publications were clearly official in character.

[13] BL E. 392 (26); Madan Oxford books, II:449 (no. 1931). Both Woolrych, *Soldiers and statesmen*, 93, n.7, and Gentles, *New Model Army*, 485, n.180, point to the earlier, and similarly titled, *The declaration of the armie under his excellencie Sir Thomas Fairfax* ([London,] 1647) as an earlier instance of agitator publication, which it probably was, and implicate John Harris in its production. That latter suggestion is wholly unverifiable; as Thomason, who was both knowledgeable and scrupulous in these matters, noted, this item [BL E. 390 (26)] was printed in London, with a different and wider range of type than that used at Oxford. This suggests that unless an Oxford version of the item comes to light, the first production of the Oxford Hills–Harris press was *A true declaration*.

[14] ([1647]); Madan, Oxford books, II:450 (no. 1934), not in Thomason, t.p.

[15] *A true declaration*, sigs. A2v, A3.

pictured with the Heeles upward', hinting allusively to another Hills–Harris production, *The antipodes*.[16] *Plain truth*, claiming to be 'printed and published for . . . the poore oppressed, betrayed, and almost destroyed Commons of England' began with a rant against the parliamentary establishment (such as it was) of presbyterian government as an instrument of 'our intended Vassalage and thraldome'. It moved quickly to a rallying cry for all manner of extreme action, 'Wee the free Commons of England, the reall and essentiall body polliticke, or any part of us, may order and dispose of our owne Armes and strength', especially, it continued, the army. Referring to an incendiary broadside of 1642, *A question answered*, much in favour with the Levellers for its suggestion of the legitimacy of self-defence against tyranny, it was a call to resistance.[17]

The drumbeat continued. *The grand informer*, which Thomason bought on 15 July, explored the political theory of the army's fringe. It was a compound of an extreme populist version of the notions that Henry Parker had used in 1642, organised around the maxim *salus populi suprema lex*, and monarchomach theory, here signalled by a reference to the key passage in Calvin's *Institutes* on the responsibility of lesser magistrates. The two were mixed in ways that converged magistracy and popularity in the army. Appeals to equity and natural law to override existing arrangements and, indeed, to make all things possible – what so irritated Ireton at Putney – were luxuriant. The 'people' (often glossed as the 'common people') had always a 'twofold liberty': first, 'of weighing, trying, examining, and judging, by common rules of equity and reason,

---

[16] Richard Overton, *An appeale from the degenerate representative body* (1647) in Don Wolfe (ed.), *Leveller manifestoes of the puritan revolution* (New York, 1967), 171–2. Lilburne never acknowledged authorship of *Plain truth* in his copious self-citations in his margins, and it does not appear in his own authorised bibliography, *The innocent man's second-proffer* (1649) [BL 669. f.14(85)]. Thomason dated his Hills–Harris text on 2 July and added London. But this, clearly an error (or else the press shifted location temporarily, which seems unlikely), probably resulted from Thomason's knowledge that the companion tract of Amon Willbee (here with two l's), the *Prima pars* of *De comparatis comparandis* [BL E. 396(11)] had been already printed in London, despite the claims of its Oxford imprint. See also Madan, *Oxford books*, II:451, 462. Madan suspected but did not definitively assert that *Plain truth* was a production of the Hills–Harris press, apparently because he was working from notes and memory rather than direct comparison with other Hills–Harris pieces he had identified, in which setting the kinship of *Plain truth* with the other tracts is unmistakable. It should be noted that Thomason gives an *earlier* date to *An appeale* (17 July) than to *The antipodes* (22 July). But as Madan notes, in normal circumstances Thomason (though not necessarily Overton) would have seen *The antipodes* a day or two after its Oxford publication. In any event the allusion is unmistakable.

[17] *Plain truth*, t.p., 4, sig. 3 (unpaged). Using Edward Husband's 'Book of Declarations' (*An exact collection* (1643)), 150, the concluding passage alluded to *A question answered*, which was possibly by Henry Parker. On this piece and the Leveller use of it, Michael Mendle, *Dangerous positions* (University, Alabama, 1985), 179, 187–8 and Mendle, *Henry Parker and the English civil war* (Cambridge, 1995), 82–3.

all such orders or decrees as are issued out by the higher powers' and, secondly, of 'non submission' and ultimately resistance to such orders 'upon a serious and judicious debate of the matter in their own thoughts'. If 'those that doe oppress shall have the sole power of determining what is oppression and what is not, it will then follow that all the people of a nation must be absolute slaves, if their Government have a mind to make them so'. So indeed, the 'legislative power' was inferior to 'a people of a land'.[18] There is one other feature of *The grand informer* that cannot be ignored: in tone, style, and argument, it bears a remarkable resemblance to a tract written a decade later, Sexby's *Killing noe murder*. Given Sexby's role in the establishment of the press as well as his argument at Putney, the inference that he wrote *The grand informer* is hard not to draw, although it cannot be proven.

The two remaining productions of the press before it acquired some official commissions were *The antipodes* and *The grand account*. The latter, an exposé of parliamentary financial high jinx which Thomason acquired on 29 July, is sufficiently described by a tag on its title page: 'Let him that stole, steale no more.'[19] *The antipodes*, which Thomason acquired a week before, was in fact signed by I.H. (that is, John Harris) and was his take on the themes of *The grand informer*. It concluded with an appeal to 'you the poore Commons of England' to join with the army against those who 'have abused and daily endeavour to inslave you'. Otherwise 'say farewell, liberty, peace, and all that outward comfort which you may iustly challenge as your Birth-Right, both by the law of God, and fundamentall Institution of this Kingdome'.[20]

Enough has been seen of 'radical' army thought in the summer of 1647 to establish that the claims of birthright, the use of arguments from equity and natural reason, and desperation in tone, language and conclusion – particularly the quickness to find slavery lurking everywhere – were the stock-in-trade of Sexby and his circle in summer 1647. Whatever the army leaders might have thought about such things privately, in so far as the press received official commissions and payments at the end of its brief life, the leaders' attitudes could not have been wholly unapproving.[21] Narrowly construed, the political 'line' of the press was at one with that of army leadership. This is one context in which the debates at Putney must be situated.

---

[18] *The grand informer* (Oxford, 1647), 11, 12, 13.
[19] *The grand account* (Oxford, 1647), t.p. [BL E. 400(18)].
[20] *The antipodes* (Oxford, 1647), 10 [BL E. 399(16)].
[21] The extent to which army funds were used to purchase the acquiescence of the agitators is a topic which would bear investigation. Certainly payments recorded in army accounts are suggestive.

But there is another. These same tracts were also determinedly royalist. Given the enormous struggle of the moment of army and parliament, given too the usual psychology of affection and disaffection, some such development might not be unexpected, and does accord well with contemporary observation of the sentiments of many of the troops.[22] Nevertheless, it might be thought – and the debates at Putney would lead us to think – that Sexby, the Hills–Harris press and the London Leveller interests[23] to be seen just below the surface were the least likely media for the growth of the royalist organism. But exactly the opposite seems to be the case. The 'radical' approach to or rapprochement with royalism was profound, widespread, not least – and in one respect, especially – in the circle around the Hills–Harris press. The warriors of 1642 were now convinced that the king was not the greatest of their problems and perhaps the key to their solution. *Plain truth* derided those in the parliament seeking 'to make the King their scorne, and us their slaves' and to impede reconciliation between king and people.[24] *The antipodes*, for all its populist rage, routinely bracketed king and people as joint victims, even urging 'fellow Souldiers' and those with the 'stigmatised name of Rogue, Anabaptist, Brownist' to 'remember the end of your taking up armes was to defend the Kings Majesty, and to bring offendors to tryall, let them be of what side they will'. The first item in a proposed programme of reform (which included the payment of arrears and indemnity as well as law reform and several kinds of parliamentary reform) was that 'His Majesty be invested in His iust power'.[25] A continuation or concluding section of *The grand account* entitled 'Vox Populi' muttered that while king and parliament had both committed illegalities, 'the Kings Prerogative is a much better Plea, then your priviledge'.[26] Only *The grand informer* (possibly Sexby's work) was silent on the subject, neither hopping upon nor reining in the bandwagon.

After the army occupied London, the need for the press disappeared and, with it, the crude presswork of the severely stinted Hills–Harris press. Hills, who clearly drifted towards power, became an army and then state printer.[27] Harris, though, surfaces in London in 1648 in much the same role as before, as the anagramatic author Sirraniho and as himself, and in other anagramatic guises as the publisher of various other Leveller–royalist collaborations, including tracts by himself and John

---

[22] See Gentles, *New Model Army*, 153, on royalism in the ranks.
[23] *The antipodes*, 16; *Plain truth*, sigs. B1v, C2r.   [24] *Plain truth*, sigs. B3r, C3r.
[25] *The antipodes*, 9.   [26] *The grand account*, 8.
[27] Hills easily survived and prospered in the Restoration; in James II's reign, Hills turned Catholic. This, finally, was too much, and he was run out of London. His son, however, reprinted Lilburne's 1649 trial in 1710, using the same plate that graced his father's 1649 edition.

Wildman on behalf of the presbyterian royalist Sir John Maynard and Maynard on behalf of Lilburne.[28] Indeed, the massive petitioning campaign on Maynard's behalf was a Leveller-managed affair. This ceased in 1649; Harris became a much less equivocal character and it is tempting to suppose that this had something to do with the breaking of his most intimate royalist tie – his wife, Susanna, who was eulogised at her death in 1649 by the royalist astrologer George Wharton. She was

> A *Leveller* in *Folio*, such an one
> As Lov'd to *Levell* an *Usurped-Throne*.
> A *Royallist* besides . . .[29]

From this one might merely conclude that the Harris marriage proves that bedfellows can make for strange politics, but in truth the royalist–Leveller convergence went well beyond the intimate Harris circle. At exactly the moment of inception of the Hills–Harris press, John Lilburne and a gaol-mate, the irrepressible Welsh royalist judge David Jenkins, were thrashing out the issue of indemnity. Practical and political but no less theoretical and constitutional, the Gordian knot of indemnity was a *fils conducteur* running from the summer of 1647 through the debates at Putney: how could troops demobilise, absolutely certain that, once disarmed and disbanded, the forces of retribution and opportunism would not then turn on the soldiers, reclaim their due and much more as well? Constitutions and trust are reciprocals, each supplying the other's deficit: in the summer of 1647, with army mistrust of the parliament at a height, no ordinance of parliament, no matter how airtight its wording, could relieve the soldiers' anxiety.

On Jenkins' telling, he was approached by 'certaine Gentlemen well affected to the Peace of the Kingdome, and safety of the Army' to address 'in writing' whether a parliamentary ordinance for indemnity was consonant with 'the Law of the Land' so as to 'secure them from danger'. Predictably he replied that an ordinance was insufficient protection. Only an act of parliament – which required the king's assent and so a settlement with him – could secure the soldiers, along with 'the payment of Souldiers arrears, and a meet regard to tender consciences'.[30] This remarkable

---

[28] Disguise came naturally to the former actor, but eventually it would kill Harris. He died at the scaffold in 1660, for masterminding a burglary in which he impersonated an officer in order to command soldiers to break into a merchant's house: see *The speech of Major John Harris* (London, 1660).

[29] W.G., *In memorie of that lively patterne of true pietie, and unstained loyaltie, Mrs Susanna Harris, the vertuous wife of Capt. John Harris* (n.p., n.d.). Thomason dated his copy [BL 669. f.15(1)] 27 November 1649 and expanded the printed 'W' of 'W.G.' to read 'Wharton'.

[30] David Jenkins, *The armies indemnity* (1647) [BL E. 390(10)]: Thomason dated 31 May 1647), 1, 5. Jenkins repeated this formula in subsequent tracts, almost as a mantra. In

anticipation of the Declaration of Breda, the voice of a generous royalism, in May and June 1647 must have been a siren song to many soldiers, and apparently, to many 'radicals' no less than to grandees. Lilburne himself gave full voice to the mood in *Rash oaths unwarrantable*, which appeared at the end of May 1647, in which Lilburne declared that Charles in seventeen years of 'mis-government' was not so bad as this 'everlasting parliament'; he had been 'so fenced about with the Lawes of the Kingdome, that it is impossible for a man or Magistrate to be more' while the present parliament cloaked actions contrary to *salus populi* in the idiom of necessity. At the same time, Lilburne also argued for a redistribution of parliamentary seats according to the contribution of each county to the rates *and* for universal manhood suffrage, 'it being a maxim in nature that no man iustly can be bound without his own consent'.[31] If, therefore, a large measure of sympathy for the king and for open-minded royalists and a belief in universal suffrage are immediately and utterly irreconcilable, Lilburne himself was not aware of it. By the autumn, when it seemed to the agitators and their friends outside the army that the army grandees and the parliamentary leadership were uncomfortably similar, another sympathetic royalist prisoner, Sir Lewis Dyve, wrote to the king himself about Lilburne's efforts to ameliorate conditions for his fellow, and royalist, prisoners. Of a meeting between Cromwell and Lilburne, he reported that Lilburne had said that the crimes of the parliament were worse than those of the king, that Cromwell had excused these deviations as the result of 'accident and necessity' and had chastised Lilburne for having fallen prey to 'the infusions of some subtill caveleres with whom he conversed'.[32] It was possible, thus, for a romantic but well-placed and not irrational observer six weeks before the Putney debates to believe that the 'radicals' were *more* royalist than the grandees.

So what happened at Putney? The usual explanation is that the radicalised soldiers felt betrayed by the *The heads of the proposals*, and that the grandees had cut a deal that had jeopardised the soldiers, or at least some of them so believed. There is no reason to argue against this explanation, which itself was thrashed out at Putney, but it leads only to another

what is doubtless an overstatement, Clement Walker, *The history of independencie* (1648) [BL E. 463(19)], 34, claimed that Cromwell and Ireton put the agitators up to demanding an act of indemnity, and consulting 'Judge *Jenkins* for the validity of it'. He also remarked that after Cromwell and Ireton had '*conjur*[ed] *up*' the agitators, the agitators were '*conjured down* by them without requitall'.

[31] John Lilburne, *Rash oaths unwarrantable*, 7, 27, 50.

[32] H. G. Tibutt (ed.), 'The Tower of London letter-book of Sir Lewis Dyve', *Publications of the Bedfordshire Historical Record Society*, vol. 38 (1957), 83 (to John Ashburnham, 21 August 1647), 85–8 (to Charles I, 13 September 1647).

question: how was a settlement with the king that the 'radicals' seemed to have wanted as much as the grandees suddenly a sell-out and betrayal?

From what has been seen, the answer cannot be in the settlement attempt itself. Rather, the concern on all sides was that another 'interest' than their own would settle, or settle first, with the king, and in so doing, constitute or reconstitute the kingdom. This triggered amongst the soldiers (and not just the agitators and agents) anxieties – vague but elemental fears – that were blanks to be filled in as circumstances dictated. In the case at hand, that the apprehensions of betrayal coalesced around the seemingly narrow and certainly self-involved issue of indemnity for the soldiers. But underwriting the distress was something much broader: two vastly different, indeed ultimately incompatible, notions of the king's relation to the body politic. Within one framework, a settlement with the king was the best of all possible worlds; from the other, the worst. In the same way as people in the present age can harbour wildly divergent social stereotypes and narratives, and fit the 'facts' into one framework or the other with lightning rapidity, those who assembled at Putney had quite contradictory understandings of the relation of king and people available to them, and used them to make vastly different constructions of the facts about them. It is not too much to say that the image and even the fate of the monarchy was a function of the implications of how the king settled, and with whom.

In a structural sense, the king's relation to the kingdom can be visualised in two ways: either he is at the apex of the pyramid, but part of it none the less, or he is outside and beyond it all together. In the first case, he is (to use slogans) the first gentleman of England, Arthur surrounded by his Round Table, the supreme embodiment of the principle of nobility. A host of descriptions and narratives follow from this schematisation: the king as but first among equals, with the baronial and aristocratic constitutional implications that are drawn in its train; the king as the keystone of the arch of social hierarchy, with its notions of reciprocal dependency but also of domino-theory collapse. The latter was embodied in slogans such as James I's 'no bishop, no king' and the prophecy of Charles' *Answer to the xix propositions* of the 'dark equal chaos of confusion' attendant upon the Commons' usurpation of the roles of the king and Lords. That itself was an echo of the familiar social nightmare scenarios of the Tudor homilies on obedience and against rebellion. Equally, though, to put the king at the top, but not outside, of the social pyramid made him fair game for those who bridled at other inequalities or inequities, and also made him a focus or kind of code term for all the existing social order.

By contrast, putting the king altogether outside the pyramid brought into play other assumptions, some mystical and even absolutist, some populist. The king who was sovereign equally of duke and villein, who was 'even by God himself' called a god and exercised 'a manner or resemblance of Divine power upon earth' (as James I had put it) could also be the king of the tale of Alfred and the cakes and of Robin Hood. He could sweep away the injustice of his own officers by a wave of his equitable hand, and be the king of the staunchly royalist but also equally banausic young men of Thomas Deloney's wildly popular tales of apprentice derring-do, the adolescent literature of the men of the Putney generation. In Deloney's world, Peachy the Shoemaker's apprentices repeatedly beat up two swashbuckling, cursing, insult-hurling court toughs – cavaliers *avant la lettre* – until the pair begged for mercy. And when Henry VIII learned how the clothier Jack of Newberry defended a serving maid's honour by tricking into marriage the gallant who had deflowered her, the king 'laugh[ed] heartily'.[33]

The question posed by any projected settlement was, thus, in which of the two settings was the defeated king to be placed – or, to put it in the stereotypes of the day, was Charles now to be a Cavalier or a Roundhead king. Was he, to borrow language from *Plain truth without feare or flattery*, to be a king whose power was 'unjust, cruell, irregular, and illegall, defacing and destructive' or, to the contrary, 'just and mercifull, regulated by Law, preservative and corrective'?[34] Was he to be, as the then-royalist Marchamont Nedham put it, 'but a King of Clouts'?[35] The question lies at the heart of the radicals' hopes and fears. The Oxford press edition of *Plain truth* claimed its author to be one Amon Wilbee. One solution to the conundrum behind the pseudonym is that Amon Wilbee is an English declarative sentence, 'Amon will be', which would place us in the middle of the reign of Manasseh (Amon's father), who according to the Chronicler (II Chronicles 33) after years of 'evil . . . like unto the abominations of the heathens' experienced a mid-reign conversion, 'took away the strange gods' and, what is more, walled Jerusalem and 'put captains of war in all the fenced cities of Judah'.[36] No doubt such a vision had an

---

[33] Merritt E. Lawlis (ed.), *The novels of Thomas Deloney* (Bloomington, 1961), 87 (*Jack of Newbury*, ch. 11), 213–18 (*The gentle craft*, Pt 2, ch. 5). Laura Stevenson O'Connell, 'The Elizabethan bourgeois hero-tale: aspects of adolescent social consciousness', in Barbara C. Malament (ed.), *After the reformation: essays in honor of J. H. Hexter* ((Philadelphia, 1980), 267–90, is a useful introduction to Deloney, but minimises the hard edge of social tension of many of the episodes.

[34] *Plain truth*, 4, which at that juncture assumed the truth of the positive case, juxtaposing Charles to the highhanded parliament.

[35] *Mercurius Pragmaticus*, no. 7, 26 Oct.–2 Nov. 1647, 54.

[36] The more modulated version in II Kings 21 does not mention the mid-reign conversion. While Amon, Manasseh's successor, committed new abominations, Amon's son Josiah renewed the reform impulse, relying heavily upon 'the workmen' and 'artificers and builders' (who did the work 'faithfully') to repair the Temple (II Chronicles 34:1, 12; cf. II Kings 22:6, 7).

appeal as much to the likes of Ireton and Cromwell as to the 'radicals', but they, unlike Ireton and Cromwell, had no acceptable monarchical alternative. A king who would protect the powerless from predations – indemnity for disbanded soldiers was closest to hand but hardly the only concern of that nature – was desirable, and a king who would symbolise a community of freeborn individuals, infinitely so. But a king-headed cabal of former, current and new predators was the outcome most to be feared. For those of a contrary disposition, there was the equally potent nightmare of Hydra. A brave man would stand fast until the last head was slain. As Ireton put it repeatedly, until he was convinced that God Almighty would pull down king, Lords and estates, he would defend them. His insistence, late in the third day's proceedings, upon a negative voice for the Lords and the king in matters directly affecting their 'persons or estates' from what Ireton regarded as the otherwise inevitable 'injuries of the Commons' reveals clearly the obverse side of the us-or-them, zero-sum mentality of unbridgeable difference.[37]

Thus the strange families of Putney's 'we's'. Along with the unifying 'we's' of army and faith, the same mouths uttered utterly irreconcilable notions of English particularity, what amounted to two different claim-rights to the kingdom, two different notions of what it was to be English. At its most impassioned and revealing (and to modern sensibilities its least morally edifying), the argument at Putney descended to a pit-brawl over who was *really* English. On one side is the language of the Norman yoke and, shadowing it, a cascade of bitter remarks about the meaning – or, rather, the lack of it – of the spilt blood. Folkish anti-Normanism had recently found an eloquent and not unlearned voice in John Hare, whose *St. Edwards ghost: or, anti-Normanisme* Thomason dated 17 August 1647.[38] Hare's army-connected *Plaine English to our wilfull bearers with Normanisme*, which Thomason purchased on 4 November (the day after he acquired his text of *An agreement of the people*), might also have circulated (like *An agreement*) some days earlier.[39] Hare's language echoed at Putney, providing a connection between lost freedoms and the present possibility of recovery. Buff-Coate (Robert Everard) thought or pretended to think it was universally granted that 'you are resolved every one to purchase our inheritances which have bin lost, and free this Nation from the tyranny that lies upon us'.[40] Rainborough argued that the law

---

[37] *CP*, I:391, 398, see also 403.

[38] On anti-Normanism generally and Hare in particular, Christopher Hill, 'The Norman yoke' in his *Puritanism and revolution* (1968), 50–122 and his *Intellectual origins of the English revolution revisited* (1997), 361–5. Hill asserts that Hare wrote *St. Edward's ghost* in 1642, although it was not published until 1647.

[39] *Plaine English* was published by the London-based, army-connected printer George Whittington.   [40] *CP*, I:239.

restricting the franchise was 'the most tyrannical law under heaven' and wondered 'what wee have fought for' if not to relieve the people from 'the old law of England . . . that inslaves the people of England'.[41] He reiterated that the excluded were 'Englishmen', that they 'ruined themselves by fighting, by hazarding all that they had', and that the outcome of limited suffrage would be that the voting minority would 'make hewers of wood and drawers of water of the other five [parts of the kingdom], and soe the greatest parte of the Nation [would] bee inslav'd'.[42] Sexby followed with similar sarcasm, that while the soldiers fought to 'recover our birthrights and priviledges as Englishmen', Ireton had told them 'there is none'. The 'poorer and meaner', though, had saved the kingdom.[43] As often as Ireton would reply, Rainborough would push his arguments aside with the same refrain: 'I would fain know what the souldier hath fought for all this while. He hath fought to inslave himself, to give power to men of riches, men of estates, to make him a perpetuall slave'.[44] And again, 'I thinke I have nothing att all of what I fought for'.[45] So too Sexby – 'itt were a sad and miserable condition that wee have fought all this time for nothing'.[46]

The agents and their friends at Putney had an inconsistent, somewhat hazy view of the English past, at times (as Ireton noted once) factually self-contradicting. By turns they seemed to want to appropriate and then to repudiate the past. But the one common denominator is that the specifically English birthright that the soldier had sought to recover had been lost at the Conquest. 'Our case', said Wildman, 'is to be considered thus: that wee have bin under slavery . . . Our very lawes were made by our Conquerors'.[47] Commissary Cowling, who fancied himself historically well grounded but whose several utterances can scarcely be reconciled one with another, at least thought the Norman Conquest was a disaster[48] that either extinguished or threatened to extinguish the rights of native Englishmen; not surprisingly, it was Cowling who also put into play the other mythopoeic trope of the dispossessed, the right of the younger son.[49] Whether Cowling and Wildman intended Ireton and Cromwell to be comprehended within or excluded from the umbrella of this first person plural is not clear; what is clear is that it excluded somebody. There was no other point to the utterance.

Against this assault, with its undercurrent of 'us versus them' nativism and contempt for collaborators,[50] was Ireton's callous (and incomprehensibly tactless) assimilation of the case of the propertyless to that of the

[41] Ibid., I:311.   [42] Ibid., I:320; my brackets.   [43] Ibid., I:323.   [44] Ibid., I:325.
[45] Ibid., I:335.   [46] Ibid., I:329.   [47] Ibid., I:319.   [48] Ibid., I:300, 368, 401.
[49] Ibid., I:316.
[50] Cowling, on the social dynamics of the Conquest: 'an Englishman was as hatefull then as an Irishman is now, and what an honour those that were noblemen thought itt to marry their daughters to, or to marry the daughters of any cookes or bakers of the Normans': CP, I:368.

foreigner. His unrelenting ridicule of the claims of birthright (the more painful, perhaps, for the cruel truth of some of his jibes) was literally and, much more poignantly, psychologically alienating. If his opponents had equivocated about English history, sometimes seeing themselves within, sometimes outside, the national story, Ireton did not. He would not allow the propertyless any meaningful role, even as victim. His scornful reduction of the talk of birthright to argument straight from the barrel of the loose cannon of natural law (which it was in part) was tantamount to saying to men about him that they were on the wrong side of the first person plural – that men without lands or trading rights were not those 'who taken together doe comprehend the whole interest of the Kingdome'.[51] The foreigner could claim as much (or, rather, as little) by birthright as the native and, he continued (in a speech that unlike many others Clarke seems to have caught down to the repetitions, rhythms and cadences): 'Wee talke of birthright. Truly [by] birthright there is thus much claime. Men may justly have by birthright, by their very being borne in England, that wee should nott seclude them out of England, that wee should nott refuse to give them aire, and place, and ground, and the freedome of the high wayes and other thinges, to live amongst us.'[52] The question that cries out to be asked, of course, is who is the *we* that should not seclude *them* out of England or refuse *them* air and place and ground to live amongst *us*? In Ireton's single-minded logic, the native without permanent fixed interest would do as the foreigner would, help himself to anything that conduced to his 'better being'.[53]

One army, one faith, but (perhaps) two nations. That was the fissure opened by the discussions at Putney and, of course, the 'texts' provoking them, *The heads of the proposals*, *The case of the armie truly stated* and *An agreement of the people*. The charge that the army grandees had settled the king's affairs (and implicitly the Lords' as well) before those of the army and people must be seen in light of this. It was not a question of prioritising, as if the buffet's treats would be gone before those at the end of the queue got their turn. It was a question, as all the participants at Putney seem to have seen it, of who would have the wherewithal to harm, indeed to destroy, the other.

For Ireton the issue above all others was probably not the matter of the franchise for elections of members of parliament, however impassioned, extended and revealing the discussions over it were, but the maintenance of a limited negative voice for the king and the House of Lords. Yet the two matters were connected in Ireton's logic of the relentless pursuit of

---

[51] *CP*, I:303.   [52] Ibid., I:302.   [53] Ibid., I:308, 325.

interest. A universal franchise, Ireton reiterated at every opportunity, had no other outcome than an anarchic grab by the have-nots of any thing that conduced to their 'better being'. He was no less convinced that unless the king and the Lords possessed a negative voice over matters that directly affected them, the Commons (or the unicameral, kingless representative envisioned in *An agreement of the people*) would help themselves to the others' 'honour, title, estate, liberty, or life'. That way, Ireton insisted, was 'to allow them [king and Lords] nothing'. In rejecting a suspensive veto for the Lords (a compromise promoted in committee), Ireton pushed instead for a right of collective self-exemption 'to protect themselves against the injuries of the Commons'. In Ireton's view, as the Commons had an utter right to whatever needed to be done to promote its own safety, so too had the king and Lords.[54]

For the agents and their friends, however, the settling of the king (and Lords) first was to them the initial step to their own 'destruction', a word that runs throughout the debates. Wildman resisted Cromwell's and Ireton's insistence upon adherence to earlier engagements with the argument that no engagement that led to self-destruction was just, a live issue if the king were restored in 'such a way as hee may bee in a capacity to destroy the people'.[55] Rainborough echoed Wildman: 'itt may bee thought that I am against the Kinge; I am against him or any power that would destroy Gods people'.[56] The future mutineer Lockyer took Wildman and Rainborough to mean that 'destruction is somethinge neere, and the cause of the destruction . . . is the going of the proposalls [i.e. *The heads of the proposals*] to the Kinge'.[57] Ireton characterised such hyperbolic fears as the psychological licence for self-aggrandisement: men 'will imagine any thinge a destruction, if there should be any thinge better'. Cromwell wondered if loose talk of 'destruction' did 'nott give way too much to our owne doubts or feares'.[58] But none of this stilled the 'radicals', and whether or not the fears are credited either objectively or subjectively valid, they are integral to the aims and logic of *An agreement of the people*, and thus to the debates.

The poignancy of the situation was reinforced by a parallel though distinct complex of political notions. As recently examined by Quentin Skinner, the 'neo-Roman theory of free states' included a notion of 'liberty' that included participation in, or consent to the procedure for, the making of laws. In (as Professor Skinner himself describes it) an 'inflammatory' formulation, the antithesis of 'liberty' was 'slavery', for which the threshold condition was not actual mistreatment or loss of civil rights, but the mere prospect of being subject to another's arbitrary

---

[54] Ibid., I:391, 398, 403; see also 405.   [55] Ibid., I:260, 264.   [56] Ibid., I:272.
[57] Ibid., I:275.   [58] Ibid., I:268, 274.

power. He writes of the likes of Harrington and Sidney, but his own words speak as well to *An agreement* and its proponents at Putney:

if you wish to maintain your liberty, you must ensure that you live under a political system in which there is no element of discretionary power, and hence no possibility that your civil rights will be dependent on the goodwill of a ruler, a ruling group, or any other agent of the state. You must live, in other words, under a system in which the sole power of making laws remains with the people or their accredited representatives, and in which all individual members of the body politic – rulers and citizens alike – remain equally subject to whatever laws they choose to impose upon themselves.[59]

It is the condition of 'dependence upon [the rulers'] goodwill' that renders the governed to 'the status of slaves'.[60]

This does much to explain the appeal of *An agreement* and the course of the debate. Only a polity free of control by king and peerage would guarantee the rights of freeborn Englishmen, make them masters of their own fates. The frenzied discussion of the franchise, which Ireton unwisely provoked, played out 'in real time' as it were the historical drama of dependency and subjection, of 'slavery' in the language of Putney's populists as well as of the partisans of the 'neo-Roman theory of free states'. Ireton's insistence that the soldiers fought for the right of the Iretons of this world to make the people's laws for them could only have been received by those who heard it and did not believe it as a humiliation. Almost automatically, Ireton's words reinforced their commitment to a wide franchise, even though some of the 'radicals' did in other settings compromise on the issue, which was fraught with the paradoxical outcomes to be expected of pseudo-independence in a world of dependency. The parallel furore over the participation of king and Lords in the reconstructed polity must be seen in the same light.

The limits of army solidarity were exposed precisely at the moment when the soldiers and officers contemplated their 'civilianisation'. Indemnity was the focus, both practical and psychological, of the many expressions of the fear of 'destruction' attendant upon peace and demobilisation. Distrust of parliament's intentions over indemnity had much to do with the army's sense of menace and thus its own resolve in the summer of 1647; it had likewise been a great motive to work out an army-engineered settlement with the king, when it seemed, as David Jenkins had argued, that an act of indemnity or oblivion was better security for the soldiers than a mere parliamentary ordinance.[61] But when the 'radicals' became con-

---

[59] Quentin Skinner, *Liberty before liberalism* (Cambridge, 1998), 74; see also 70–2.
[60] Ibid., 75.
[61] The theme runs through Jenkins' many writings of 1647; see especially *The armies indempnity* (n.p., 1647).

vinced, or convinced themselves, that the army grandees and their allies were part of the problem rather than its solution – when they switched visions of monarchy – they needed, so to speak, Plan C, another provision for indemnity. *The heads of the proposals* had provided for indemnity through an act of parliament; but a parliamentary act could bind no further than the next occasion to repeal it, and so became merely a kind of opinion poll of the political nation, however that may have been constituted.

The need for an airtight indemnity was what turned bitterness and bromides into action and 'radicals' into radicals. That solution, of course, was *An agreement of the people*, which was more than, but never less than, a constitutional solution to the indemnity problem. It included indemnity amongst the 'reserves', the rights reserved from the otherwise omnicompetent parliament by the sovereign people. Whoever may have been its author or authors, it ostensibly issued from the agents of the five regiments. In the first of two appended letters from the agents, to 'the noble and highly honoured the Free-born People of England', the agents solicited the civilian population's 'joyning with *us* in the agreement herewith sent unto you' (emphasis added). The other appended letter was addressed to the 'Officers and Souldiers under Command of His Excellencie Sir Thomas Fairfax'. It pulled no punches, from its first words placing the *Agreement* in the context of the fears over soldiers' security, which had 'constrained Us [the Agents] to study the most absolute & certain means for your security'. No 'Act of Indemnity' could provide it, since in the succeeding parliament 'a corrupt Party (chosen into the next Parliament by your Enemies meanes)' could undo the act of indemnity of the former, with the certain 'Assistance and concurrence' of the king whom the army had earlier 'conquered'. The agents could 'apprehend no other security, by which you shall be saved harmlesse, for what you have done in the late warre, then a mutuall Agreement between the people & you that no person shall be questioned by any Authority whatsoever, for any thing done in relation to the late publike differences'. Along with a similar soldier-based constitutional provision against impressment, the securing of indemnity was the 'end' for which the *Agreement* was proposed for the soldiers' 'subscription'. While the rhetorical strategy of the letter directed to the civilian population demanded that the agents first share the people's sense of the suffering caused by war ('It's greife and vexation of heart to us; to receive your meate and moneyes, whilest you have no advantage'), the clear purpose of the letter was to explain why 'we have . . . inserted' the indemnity provision into 'this Agreement', and went on to reiterate that parliaments of the old fashion, not bound the constitutional limitation of the 'reserves', could otherwise undo the work of the settlement parliament.

While most modern interest in the debates has understandably focused upon the discussions over the franchise and the place of king and Lords, considered almost as an academic if intense exercise on the best form of government, the passion of both sides and the ugliness in tone and manner there as elsewhere hovered close to the issue of indemnity, which in itself does much to explain it. In an important speech, Wildman summarised the proceedings as his side saw it, finding the most objectionable parts of *The heads of the proposals* to be the apparent continuance of the king's negative voice along with his eventual regaining of control (or partial control) over the militia. This made the parliament 'soe many cyphers, soe many round Os'. That fate was avoided by the *Agreement*, which eliminated the 'great uncertainty' over indemnity. The king could not 'command his Judges to hange them uppe for what they did in the warres'. Equally, the 'Agreement with the people' prevented the abuse of the 'people' by the parliament, an outcome Wildman glossed in narrower terms as 'The parliament shall nott meddle with a souldier after indempnity'.[62]

Wildman's speech clearly rattled Ireton, who called its insinuations (and those of *The case of the armie truly stated*, in which Ireton supposed Wildman to have been implicated) 'as unworthy and as unchristian an injury as was ever done to men that were in society with them'.[63] Reviewing the army's earlier conduct in a way that spoke as well to the *Agreement of the people*, Ireton picked up on a shrewd point made earlier by Cromwell, who had implied that the so-called agreement of the people, even if the 'better' arrangement, would never receive universal assent and so, by the agreement's own logic, could never be a constitutional foundation: 'some Gentlemen are resolved to stick to the worse'. Ireton ventured that 'if all the people to a man' signed on to an agreement, 'there would bee some security to itt'. But an agreement that was favoured primarily by soldiers 'is noe more then our saying our selves that we will bee indemnified'.[64] As Ireton and Cromwell understood, peace can only be made with one's enemy.

William Clarke stopped his labours before the end of the discussions at Putney. Thus the end of Clarke's report of the third day of debate cannot be anything more than a moment *en passant*. Yet there is something almost paradoxically valedictory about the last words spoken on 1 November 1647. After three days of intense discussion, the participants could do little more than make the same tired points one more time – the only difference being

[62] *CP*, I:354–5.
[63] Ibid, I:359; Firth's unnecessary bracketed gloss omitted. For a different view of the authorship of *The case of the armie truly stated*, see ch. 6, above.
[64] *CP*, I:336, 360; see also Ireton at p. 341.

that their tempers were shorter. Ireton grew peremptory with Wildman, telling him of what 'I would nott have you talke'.[65] Wildman soon countered with the assertion that the king could 'by the letter of the present law . . . kill mee, and 40 more, and noe one call him to account for itt', a proposition that made sense only within the most absolutist (or paranoid) constructions of the facts. Ireton's reply surely had a better grasp of the realities: that with the laws reining in the king, and 'the Commons of England bound to obey' its own institution, the House of Commons, no man would believe that the king 'as hee is a single person' would dare so 'to kill this, or that, or any other man'.[66] Yet Ireton's abrasive and at times disingenuous manner undercut his words – when his and Cromwell's bottom-line position was, implicitly, 'trust us',[67] their opponents could find less reason than ever to do so, for the debate had exposed the raw nerves of dependency.

Wildman pursued the argument beyond the confines of Putney. His *Putney proiects*, which Thomason purchased on 30 December 1647, sought to give him the last word. Part of the attack was *ad homines*, a discrediting of Cromwell and Ireton. But it was no less a full-dress justification of Wildman's closing arguments at Putney, through the dissection of monarchy's five 'inslaving' (and wildly absolutist) principles.[68] Wildman's tone necessarily was the same as it was at Putney, dismissive, indeed contemptuous of the meagre leavings of a fundamentally corrupt past, which was little more than a chronicle of victimisation. Yet barely two months later, Wildman (through another easily decoded pseudonym) participated in a massive Leveller campaign on behalf of Sir John Maynard, a presbyterian and royalist who had been one of the eleven members of parliament who were forced to flee the army in August 1647. Maynard's case coming before the Lords, Maynard resisted their claims of jurisdiction over a commoner, a response that naturally drew out a measure of Leveller sympathy. Once again, some royalists and some presumed radicals found a zone of commonality that went well beyond the cynical calculus of shared hatred ('the enemy of my enemy is my friend') and expressed a Cokean consensus about the rights of freeborn Englishmen. Wildman's effort on behalf of Maynard was published for 'Ja. Hornish', that is, John Harris;[69] Maynard returned the favour, speaking in the

---

[65] 'I would nott have you talke of principles of juste Government when you hold that all Governments that are sett uppe by consent are just': *CP*, I:404.   [66] Ibid., I:406.

[67] Ireton's response to the 'what have we fought for' question was that the propertyless would have the benefit of laws made by 'fix't and setled men' (*CP*, I:326); see also *CP*, I: 333.

[68] John Lawmind [pseud.; anagram of Wildman], *Putney proiects* (London, 1647). The principles are introduced on 15–22 and used discursively thereafter.

[69] J. Howldin [pseud.], *The lawes subversion: or, Sir John Maynards case truly stated* (n.p., 1648). Thomason dated this item 6 March 1647/8.

Commons on behalf of John Lilburne; the publisher again was 'I. Harris'.[70] Meanwhile, though, the Levellers apparently did not think their support for a royalist incompatible with their populism. A tiny printed scrap that George Thomason tipped into his collection next to the Leveller petition on behalf of Maynard told the subscription agents to secure the signatures of all sympathisers, whether 'Masters or menservants'.[71]

Wildman's tract on behalf of Maynard was not merely in favour of a royalist; it also repudiated the historical rejectionism of his argument at Putney and in *Putney proiects*, even as it shared those two earlier statements' hostility to the House of Lords. The same laws that Wildman thought nearly worthless at Putney were now great bulwarks of the subject's liberty. The 'established Laws of the Land' were to be treasured,[72] not swabbed away with a brushful of that universal solvent, natural law. Even parliamentary sovereignty had to make a leg before Magna Carta, not as it was a statute (and so subject to repeal), but as it was 'a Declaration of the common Law, or of common reason and equity'.[73] No doubt the exigencies of the moment and political tactics underwrote some of this position-shifting and argument-reversal. But the facility with which those at Putney could slide from the one outlook to another cannot be dismissed as mere opportunism – were it that obvious, it would have been too rank to be worth the investment of time, paper and psychical energy. Rather, participants flipped between the narratives and descriptions available to them, using the ones that resonated with the times and their hearts.

In autumn 1648 Lilburne himself would enter a new phase of royalist sympathy, which if anything would blossom after the king's execution. As he later explained matters, the perpetuation of the monarchy, though not in itself desirable, was necessary as a 'counter-ballance' to the lawless army until the better solution, the second *Agreement of the people*, could be implemented. In the absence of an agreement, Lilburne kept open the possibility that the king (or parliament) might offer a better deal than the army for 'our Freedoms', and thought it probable that without the king, the army would introduce a greater 'slavery' than had been known before.[74] John Hare, whose anti-Normanism laced the anti-monarchical arguments at Putney, was himself more equivocal, providing almost a

---

[70] *A speech spoken in the honourable house of Commons. By Sir Iohn Maynard* (London, 1648).
[71] The slip precedes BL 669. f.11(126), the petition to the Commons on behalf of Maynard that was to be delivered on 18 February 1647/8.   [72] *The lawes subversion*, 23.
[73] Ibid., 13.
[74] *Legall fundamental liberties* (London, 1649), cited in Don M. Wolfe (ed.), *Leveller manifestoes of the puritan revolution* (New York, 1944, repr. 1967), 412; also in William Haller and Godfrey Davies (eds.), *The Leveller tracts 1647–1653* (New York, 1944), 416.

textbook instance of the capacity of a single individual to engage wildly different scenarios. King, nobles, and people, he repeatedly suggested, could *choose* to be Normans or English. William 'surnamed the Conquerour' needed to be 'stript of that insolent Title' which had been imposed on him by 'Norman arrogance and our servile flattery'. But as William could also derive his title from 'Saint *Edwards* legacy' and the acceptance of the English people, so Charles could 'bee pleased to derive his right' from the same English lineage. Similarly, the 'Normane Nobility and Progeny' could repudiate their Norman names and titles. For the rest, a broad cultural campaign was needed to root out the Norman and French presence in language and laws, and to 'make Anglicisme . . . the only soule and habit of all both *Ireland* and great *Britaine*'.[75]

Royalists returned the favour. A curious tract printed entirely in red characters, *The bloody court*, covered the trial and execution of the king and its sequel, the trial and execution of the royalist peers, and in the doing, showed real sympathy for those 'falsely named' Levellers, about whom the author claimed to have some inside information.[76] Clement Walker, the royalist journalist, was also the publisher of John Lilburne's 1649 trial; Walker's *History of Independency* had similarly modulated things to say of the Levellers. Earlier (but also later, since the royalist publisher Richard Royston reissued the item in 1659), Sir Roger Twysden, that archetypal Kentish royalist, found himself writing enthusiastically in favour of Maynard's Leveller-managed campaign against the jurisdiction of the House of Lords over commoners. With modest distancing, Twysden acknowledged himself on the side of Lilburne and Overton. Twysden would neither defend nor attack their 'Railing and Libelling' against the Lords, but did acknowledge them to 'have been great and long sufferers' in a cause he also associated with Maynard and the presbyterian aldermen, 'a noble Knight and four grave Aldermen, who have been Magistrates in one of the famous Cities of Europe'.[77] Twysden dismissed

---

[75] *St. Edwards ghost: or, anti-Normanisme* (London, 1647), 19, 23; the full programme is described 19–23. Charles' triple right coming from a presumed English royal descent (through the Scottish line's marriage into the English), through Edward the Confessor's will, and through 'this Nations admission of the Normane Bloud' is asserted in *Plaine English*, 14, and in *Englands proper and onely way* (London, 1648), 6; see also 4.

[76] *The bloody court; or, the fatall tribunall* (n.p., n.d.). The Wing catalogue apparently considers this item to be a ghost (see entry for B3320), perhaps confusing it with a similarly titled but very different piece attributed to John Gauden, *Cromwell's bloody slaughterhouse* (London, 1660) (G343A). But *The bloody court*, which does not appear in the Thomason collection (*pace* Wing), does appear in a Clarke-collected volume of 1649 tracts (themselves fairly well sorted chronologically) at Worcester College, Oxford (AA. 2.4, item 18).

[77] [Sir Roger Twysden,] *The commoners liberty: or, the English-mans birth-right* (n.p., 1648), 12–13; see also the marginal comments at 9, 21. Royston reissued the old sheets with a new title page in 1659.

Prynne's smear of the Levellers as 'ignorant, sottish Sectaries, illiterate *Ignoramus's*, altogether unacquainted with out Histories and records' as 'not a sincere way of treating the matter in question' when 'of such as have studied the question, foure parts of five' shared their opinion. If the 'chiefest Levelling aymed at the Subiects of England' was that 'the highest Duke should be levell with the lowest beggar', Twysden had aught to say of it than that it brought 'great Peace and happyness'.[78] Justice was 'the undoubted birth-right of every Englishman'.[79] Ireton's babble was the mantra of Twysden and Sexby.

Twysden's remarkable inclusion of himself, Lilburne and Overton in the ranks of the four-fifths of Englishmen who rejected the jurisdiction of the House of Lords over commoners is a reminder that, at Putney and elsewhere, there were many first-person plurals, and, indeed, more than one formula of consensus, just as, indeed, there were many lines of fissure and conflict. If the debates at Putney show how the consensus of the godly army was both shattered and sustained, it also shows that in larger contexts the same identity components could be, and were, differently arranged. There was nothing automatic or permanent about the Leveller hostility to monarchy seen at Putney, nor anything inevitably royalist in the branding of every Leveller position as beyond the pale. The most heated Leveller claims that sparked the Putney debates – the demands for a very wide if not universal franchise, the rejection of any legal distinction of king and peers from commoners, the reduction to the point of abolition of institutional standing for the monarchy and House of Lords – were rooted in a language of the Englishman's birthright that was the *koine* of the kingdom, even if the propositions themselves were not.

Equally, Putney exposed the rawest social nerves of the society of its day. Fears on one side of an anarchic looting expedition undertaken in the name of birthright met fears of an elite sell-out or even a cabal on the other. Two wildly different notions of the entity called England – of the largest 'we' – ripped through the otherwise profound senses of common purpose that had earlier bound the participants together. At bottom the issue sounded strangely like that of 1642, trust of those in ultimate control of the means of retribution. This would recur no less in 1660. One can only wonder what William Clarke, transcribing his 1647 shorthand characters in the early 1660s, made of these debates of perhaps fifteen years before. Did Clarke already perceive in the debates the idiom of lost age, to be preserved in the name of nostalgia? Or did Clarke find something personally immediate in those old discussions? He had served

---

[78] *The commoners liberty*, 4, 5. The second passage cited in this sentence (p. 4) is syntactically troubled; my selection brings out the obvious sense.   [79] Ibid., 1.

the nascent commonwealth as a shorthand secretary at the king's trial in 1649, and his account may have been the one used in the 'official' version. It seems likely he was one of those on the scaffold on the dreadful day.[80] Yet he used his 'book' of trial notes as the Crown's star witness at the trial of the regicides in 1660.[81] He had seen the attempts at settlement in 1647 fail and those of his master Monck succeed in 1660, not least because Charles II absorbed a good part of the army that had opposed him, and convinced the overwhelming preponderance of his former enemies that they had little to fear and much to gain from monarchical restoration. Who was better placed than Clarke to sense the multiple ironies of identity and indemnity in debates he might well have found it prudent to have forgotten?

[80] See ch. 2, above.
[81] *An exact and most impartiall accompt of the indictment, arraignment, trial, and judgment (according to law) of the twenty nine regicides* (London, 1660), 43, 60–1, 71, 74, 84–5, 97.

8 The *Agreements of the people* and their political contexts, 1647–1649[1]

Ian Gentles

The document for which the Leveller movement is best known is the so-called *Agreement of the people*. Between October 1647 and May 1649 the London Levellers and their allies in the New Model Army published three versions of this projected constitution for England. The army also published separately the so-called 'Officers' *Agreement*', which they submitted to the House of Commons on 20 January 1649. In addition, there is a maverick version framed by Lieutenant-Colonel John Jubbes of Colonel Hewson's regiment in December 1648. A native of Norwich, Jubbes professed to be the spokesman of a group of London common councilmen and other citizens who, taking advantage of the evidently positive associations generated by the name, issued *Severall proposals for peace and freedom, by an agreement of the people*. Common to all versions of the *Agreement* was a call for a broadened franchise, electoral redistribution according to population, liberty of conscience in religious matters, the dissolution of the Long Parliament, fresh elections every one or two years, and a list of powers that were reserved by the people to themselves.[2]

The purpose of this chapter is to set the various surviving versions of the *Agreement* in their political contexts and to explore the significance of the alterations that were made between 1647 and 1649.

---

[1] I am grateful to Michael Mendle, Barbara Taft, Philip Baker, John Morrill, Austin Woolrych and Michelle White for their careful reading and criticism of earlier drafts of this essay.

[2] A brief summary of the different versions of the *Agreement* is provided by J. W. Gough, 'The agreements of the people, 1647–49', *History* 15 (1930–1), 334–41. The texts may be found in Don Wolfe (ed.), *Leveller manifestoes of the Puritan revolution* (New York, 1944; repr. London, 1967), S. R. Gardiner, *Constitutional documents of the Puritan revolution* (3rd edn, Oxford, 1906), G. E. Aylmer (ed.), *The Levellers in the English revolution* (London, 1975), and Andrew Sharp (ed.), *The English Levellers* (Cambridge, 1998). Excluded from the present study, for chronological reasons, and also because it was not a product of the Leveller movement, is *The agreement of the general council of officers* (22 Dec. 1659), BL 669. f.22 (31).

The first *Agreement*

In the late winter and spring of 1647 the rank and file of the New Model Army organised themselves to resist the attempt of the Essex peace party – led in the Commons by the conservative presbyterian Denzil Holles – to disband the bulk of the army without paying more than a fraction of the arrears due to it, and to pack the rest off to Ireland to subdue the rebellion there. Agitators were selected in most regiments; the majority of commissioned officers were persuaded or coerced into joining the resistance; and those who did not desert or flee to parliament entered into a Solemn Engagement on 5 June not to disband until their grievances were redressed. These army developments were watched with intense interest by the civilian Leveller movement in London. They supported the agitators' demand to march on London and pull the presbyterian ringleaders from their seats in the House of Commons. However, the higher officers, or grandees as they were coming to be known, proved to be more interested in negotiating a settlement with the king. In consultation with Lords Saye and Wharton, Ireton produced *The heads of the proposals*, which the army laid before Charles in late July.[3] *The heads of the proposals* were at once a handsomer settlement than the English or Scottish parliament had offered the king, and a far more radical one, containing much that would have appealed to the Levellers.

The army experiment in constitution-making was rudely disturbed by the political tempest which erupted in the wake of an attempted counter-revolution in London. On 26 July a presbyterian-inspired crowd invaded and intimidated both Houses of Parliament into passing resolutions to put the London militia committee back into presbyterian hands. The grandees now concurred with the agitators on the necessity for a march on London to put a stop to the counter-revolutionary activities of the leaders of the Essex party and their city allies.[4]

Once in London they found themselves facing a more militant group of agitators or 'agents' claiming to speak for five of the cavalry regiments (those of Cromwell, Ireton, Fleetwood, Whalley and Rich), and representing themselves as the collective authors of *The case of the armie truly stated*. The background and authorship of this pamphlet are analysed in

---

[3] J. S. A. Adamson, 'The English nobility and the projected settlement of 1647', *HJ* 30 (1987), 571–9.

[4] For *The heads of the proposals* and the Essex faction's attempted counter-revolution, see Valerie Pearl, 'London's counter-revolution' in G. E. Aylmer (ed.), *The Interregnum: the quest for settlement, 1646–1660* (London, 1972), 4–56; Ian Gentles, 'The struggle for London during the second civil war', *HJ* 26 (1983), 277–305, at 281–4; and Adamson, 'The English nobility and the projected settlement', 576–8.

chapter 6 by John Morrill and Philip Baker. It is sufficient for the present purpose to note that *The case of the armie* adumbrated some of the key points in the first *Agreement of the people* – a dissolution of parliament, to be followed by biennial parliaments elected by all 'freeborn' adult males. After *The case of the armie* was hotly debated in the army's General Council, the Levellers (chiefly William Walwyn, John Wildman, John Lilburne and Richard Overton) and their agitator friends in the army (chiefly Robert Everard) drafted a new document, which they brought to army headquarters on 27 October. This was the famous *An agreement of the people*, a much more eloquent, lucid and sophisticated text than the sprawling *The case of the armie truly stated*.[5]

On its title page *An agreement* announced the goal of 'a firme and present peace upon grounds of common-right and freedome'. Claiming already to have garnered the support of nine of the twelve horse and seven of the twelve foot regiments of the army, it was now being offered 'to the joynt concurrence of all the free Commons of England'. The root of the recent troubles lay in the infrequency and ineffectuality of meetings of parliament. That problem would be rectified by four measures:

1. electoral redistribution of parliamentary seats 'according to the number of the inhabitants';
2. the dissolution of the Long Parliament on 30 September 1648;
3. parliamentary elections every two years, with parliament to sit for six months;
4. the supremacy of the House of Commons, whose power was to be 'inferiour only to theirs who chuse them'.

The concept of the sovereignty of the people asserted in the fourth clause was made concrete by reference to a number of powers reserved by the people to themselves. The first was 'matters of religion', which were to be left to individual conscience. The second was 'the matter of impressing and constraining any of us to serve in the warres'. Conscription was to be abolished. Thirdly, no one was to be 'questioned for anything said or done' arising from the civil war. Fourthly, everyone was to be treated equally before the law. The fifth reserved power was so vague as to be meaningless for practical purposes: the laws 'must be good and not evidently destructive to the safety and well-being of the people'.

The list of reserved powers was followed by a lengthy address from the newly chosen agents of five cavalry regiments to 'the free-born people of England' apologising for the sacrifices the army had been compelled to require of them. The agents were confident that the *Agreement*, by lodging

---

[5] Austin Woolrych, *Soldiers and statesmen: the General Council of the Army and its debates, 1647–1648* (Oxford, 1987), 214–15.

ultimate power in the people, would put an end to all quarrels and guarantee 'a just and lasting peace'. Their intent was that the *Agreement* should encompass everyone, 'even those that have opposed us'. That was the reason for the guarantee that no one would be questioned for what he had done during the civil war. Why did the authors find it necessary to propose the unprecedented formula of a written constitution, to be literally enacted through the signatures of the people? 'The reason is evident: No Act of Parliament is or can be unalterable, and so cannot be sufficient security to save you or us harmlesse, from what another Parliament may determine, if it should be corrupted.'

Turning to the army, the agents urged that the *Agreement* would be superior to any parliamentary act of indemnity in protecting soldiers from reprisals for what they had done while under arms. The reserve against conscription would also protect their most fundamental freedom: the right not to be compelled to kill or risk their lives for a cause they could not in conscience support. Finally, so grateful would the civilian population be for the *Agreement* that was being set before them that out of their 'abundant love' they would speedily pay the taxes needed to cover the army's arrears and future pay.

When the *Agreement* was presented to the army's General Council in Putney Church on 28 October 1647 the agents tried to put the higher officers on the defensive by accusing them of betraying the interests of the rank and file, as well as the people of England through their servility towards king and parliament. But in the struggle for rhetorical control the grandees were at length able to turn the tables on the radicals. They did this in two ways. First, Oliver Cromwell accused them of being anarchists. Their *Agreement* would entail 'very great alterations' of the government of England. What was to prevent another group of individuals from concocting a very different, but also superficially alluring scheme. 'Would itt not bee utter confusion? Would itt nott make England like one of the Switzerland Country, one Canton of the Switz against another, and one County against another?' In passing, Cromwell made a more telling criticism of the *Agreement*. The proposed constitution was supposedly rooted in the principle of the sovereignty of the people, but he doubted 'whether . . . the people of this Nation are prepared to receive and to goe on alonge with itt'.[6] How, in other words, did the agents or the civilian Levellers know that the people in whose name they claimed to speak would actually be willing to sign their *Agreement*?

Cromwell had a further objection. In *The case of the armie truly stated* the agents had harshly criticised the grandees for failing to live up to the

---

[6] *CP,* I:236–7.

army's engagements of the previous June. But it might turn out that the *Agreement* itself could not be reconciled with the army's engagements. Cromwell's son-in-law, Commissary-General Henry Ireton, then chimed in with the observation that if men could break their engagements whenever they believed them to be unjust, 'this is a principle that will take away all Commonwealth'.[7]

The next day Ireton returned to the rhetorical offensive by construing the demand for electoral redistribution according to population as a call for universal manhood suffrage. This went clean against the fundamental law of the country, according to which only those with 'a permanent fixed interest in this Kingedome'[8] – landowners and merchants – should have a voice in electing the members of parliament. Raising the spectre of communism, he warned that votes for the unpropertied would inexorably lead to the abolition of property. Colonel Thomas Rainborough and others scornfully rejected Ireton's scaremongering, appealing to the right of 'the poorest hee that is in England' to have a say in choosing the government by which he was to be ruled.[9]

Cromwell and Ireton failed to impress many of their fellow officers with the doomsday scenario they attempted to paint at Putney, but their conservative forebodings would have resonated with the members of the House of Commons, and the wider country. The insinuation that the Levellers were anarchists and communists was one that they were never able to shake off.[10] It is interesting that the label 'Leveller' was first applied to them after Putney, by Charles I. Writing in the royalist newsbook *Mercurius Pragmaticus*, Marchamont Nedham reported that the king had christened the army agitators 'by the name of Levellers; in a most apt Title for such a despicable and desperate Knot to be known by, that indeavor to cast downe and level the inclosures of Nobility, Gentry and Propriety, to make us all even: so that every Iack shall vie with a Gentleman and every Gentleman be made a Iack'.[11]

In the army's General Council, though, the Levellers made surprising headway. Ireton's long-winded conservative alarmism not only failed to find a receptive audience; at the end of the day it was counter-productive. The Levellers accepted a tactical compromise, which had the desired effect of winning moderate opinion to their side. With only three officers dissenting, it was agreed that while all who had fought against the king should have the vote regardless of their social status, servants and beggars – meaning wage-earners who lived under their masters' roof and those

---

[7] Ibid., I:242.   [8] Ibid., I:302.   [9] Ibid., I:301.
[10] Jeff D. Bass, '"Levellers": the economic reduction of political equality in the Putney debates, 1647', *Quarterly Journal of Speech* 77 (1991), 427–45, at 429, 435–41.
[11] *Mercurius Pragmaticus*, 9–16 Nov. 1647 [BL E. 414(15)], 70.

who were dependent on alms – would be excluded.[12] In order to avert almost certain defeat at the hands of the lower officers and rank and file, Cromwell moved for an eighteen-man committee of officers and agitators to review the army's declarations and *An agreement of the people* to see if they could be harmonised. The recommendations of the committee, on which both Cromwell and Ireton sat, are an amalgam of grandee and Leveller ideas. The present parliament should dissolve not later than 1 September 1648; future parliaments should be elected biennially, and should meet for six months. Between parliamentary sessions the country should be governed by a council of state with delegated powers. The continuance of the monarchy and House of Lords was tacitly assumed, though with drastically reduced powers. Constituency boundaries were to be redrawn, but whether according to taxation or population was left to parliament to decide. The qualifications for voting were also left up to parliament, with the proviso that all who had fought for parliament before the battle of Naseby, or voluntarily contributed to the war effort, should be included. On the other hand, all who had opposed parliament should be excluded until after the second biennial parliament. Finally, tithes were to be abolished and replaced by a land tax or permanent endowment for the clergy.

The committee's draft bore signs of a compromise between the Leveller *An agreement* and the grandees' *The heads of the proposals*. It silently rejected the Levellers' original and revolutionary concept of an unalterable written constitution brought into being by the signatures of the people. Yet it embraced the almost equally revolutionary concept of powers reserved from parliament – religion, impressment and indemnity for things said or done in the late war. Here again there was compromise – the Levellers' unqualified ban on impressment was modified with the phrase, 'otherwise then for the imediate defence of this Kingdome and keeping the peace within itt'. In other words, only impressment for service outside England was to be banned. Finally, the Levellers had assumed the emasculation, if not outright abolition, of king and House of Lords. The committee's draft also envisaged a House of Commons with greatly enhanced powers, but within the historical framework of a tripartite parliament.[13]

The Levellers could be proud of what they had accomplished in a short

---

[12] The committee's draft, which was in effect the second version of the *Agreement*, was never published, but its contents were reported in *Perfect Occurrences*, 29 Oct.–5 Nov. 1647, BL E. 520(2), 306, and *A copy of a letter sent by the agents of severall regiments . . . to all the souldiers* (11 November 1647) [BL E. 413(18)], 1–2. See also Woolrych, *Soldiers and statesmen*, 243–7, for a valuable discussion of this matter.

[13] *CP,* I:363–7, 407–11.

time: they had won the General Council of the Army to their way of think-ing on several major points. Cromwell and Ireton must have been deeply unhappy at the way the debate had gone.

By 3 November *An agreement of the people* (as presented to the General Council on 28 October) was on the bookstalls in London, carrying the boast of 'the general approbation of the army'.[14] It was as if the laborious work of compromise by the General Council's committee had never taken place. The senior officers now decided that enough was enough. Faced with what was, in effect, a Leveller summons to the soldiery to revolt against their commanders and against parliament, they decided to meet the menace head on. Led by Cromwell, they moved to send the agi-tators back to their regiments with no announced date of recall. In fact an unspecified number of regiments had apparently just petitioned General Fairfax to discharge the agitators.[15] How were the grandees able to impose their will on a group of men, many of whom had recently shown broad sympathy for the Leveller programme? The skeletal character of William Clarke's minutes for the 8 November meeting of the General Council only permit us to guess at the arguments that carried the day. Perhaps Cromwell was able to sway his listeners with an appeal for the restoration of unity. He may also have referred to the increasingly ugly attacks on the king emanating from radical quarters. Equally alarming was the overt royalism being voiced in some regiments.[16] In the end it may have been the promise to hold a rendezvous of the army that won over the majority. Before adjourning, the General Council nominated another eighteen-man committee, only two of whom were rank-and-file agitators, to draft a remonstrance to be offered to the regiments for their approval.[17] It was subsequently announced that the rendezvous would be held on different days in three separate places. This displeased the Levellers, who were hoping to orchestrate a mass demonstration in favour of *An agree-ment of the people*. They still went ahead with their plans to muster civilian support for army militants at the first rendezvous at Ware in Hertfordshire, about twenty-five miles north of London.

On 15 November Fairfax and the other general officers rode to Ware to present the army's Remonstrance to the seven regiments that had been invited to rendezvous there. Already radical officers had been busy dis-tributing copies of *An agreement* and collecting signatures. Upon Fairfax's

---

[14] Wolfe, *Leveller manifestoes*, 225.

[15] The petition does not survive, but was referred to by Cornet Henry Denne in *The Levellers designe* ([24 May] 1649) [BL E. 556(11)], 4. Also, the defeated Levellers later implicitly admitted that the five regiments who had first chosen new agents petitioned to have them sent back. See *Sea-green and blue* ([6 June] 1649) [BL E. 559(1)], 11.

[16] Woolrych, *Soldiers and statesmen*, 263.   [17] *CP,* I: 413.

arrival Colonel Thomas Rainborough presented a petition urging the army to embrace *An agreement*. Fairfax's response was not recorded, but the radical officers were ordered off the field, and some were arrested. The most dangerous moment of the day came when Colonel Thomas Harrison's regiment turned up uninvited and without their officers. Provocatively they wore copies of *An agreement* pinned to their hats, bearing the slogan 'England's freedom, soldiers' rights'. Their defiance collapsed when Fairfax rebuked them and Cromwell tried to rip the papers from their hats. Seeing that none of the other regiments was willing to join their mutiny, they submitted. The day might have turned out differently had Robert Lilburne's regiment, also in a state of mutiny, turned up at the same time as Harrison's instead of some hours later. They too wore *An agreement* in their hats, and when the major of Colonel Pride's regiment rebuked them they began stoning him and broke his head. According to a royalist account a group of officers led by Cromwell waded into their ranks and tore the offending document from their hats. This display of ruthless courage was enough to cow most of the soldiers, and *An agreement* disappeared from view.[18]

Fairfax then resumed his review of the seven regiments, which involved a reading before each regiment of the army Remonstrance. Although *An agreement of the people* had been condemned in the severest terms, several of its clauses were echoed in the Remonstrance: indemnity for all acts committed during the war, 'freedome from pressing according to the first Petition of the Army', the present parliament to be dissolved, future parliaments to meet and dissolve at prearranged times, and provision for 'freedome and equality of Elections . . . to render the House of Commons as neere as may be an equall Representative of the People that are to elect'.[19] Alert observers would not have failed to notice the deliberate ambiguity of the last phrase, which offered no definition of who were 'the People that are to elect'. Another novel idea of *An agreement* was reflected in the requirement that the members of each regiment be required to sign the Remonstrance, to indicate not only their acceptance of its political programme and the authority of the General Council of the Army, but also their obedience to Fairfax and the council of war.

Once the Leveller challenge had been turned back Cromwell revealed to his fellow MPs what he really thought of *An agreement of the people*, and

[18] For an account of the rendezvous at Ware, see Ian Gentles, *The New Model Army in England, Ireland and Scotland, 1645–1653* (Oxford, 1992), 219–24. For a different interpretation see Mark Kishlansky, 'What happened at Ware', *HJ* 25 (1982), 833–9. Kishlansky is dubious about Cromwell's role, and denies that the events at Ware constituted mutiny.
[19] *A Remonstrance from his excellency Sir Thomas Fairfax and his councell of warre* (15 Nov. 1647) [BL E. 414(14)], unpaged.

why he had allowed the Levellers so much free rein in the army. At first he had hoped that:

their follies would vanish, but now when he sees they spread and infected so much he confesses it high tyme to suppress such attempts. And for a more equall representative, because he saw many honest officers were possest with it, he gave waye to dispute about it at the Counsell of war, partly to perswade them out of the unreasonablenes of that representation these London Agents would have, but when he saw, that they would exclude children and servants, yet such as received almes they insisted on as persons competent for electors etc. he saw such a dangerous consequence of that, they which had no interest in estate at all should choose a representation (and they being the most, were likely to choose those of their own condition), that this drive at a levelling and paritye, etc., he could not but disclayme and discountenance such endeavours, and this hath brought so many obloquies upon him and the officers, and he's confident that most of the calumnies raised upon the Army have proceeded from that partie, etc.[20]

Cromwell had conveniently forgotten that at Putney the Levellers had eventually compromised and agreed to exclude those in receipt of alms from the franchise as well as apprentices, servants and beggars. Nevertheless, John Boys' perhaps garbled account of his speech to the Commons reveals that he sincerely believed his own and Ireton's rhetoric about the thrust behind *An agreement of the people*: its 'drive at a levelling and paritye'. Boys' transcript is also valuable for confirming that, initially at least, the Levellers really did advocate something very close to universal manhood suffrage.[21]

The second *Agreement*

Further radical political agitation was temporarily kept in abeyance by the outbreak of the second civil war. Agitation was resumed in September 1648 with the Levellers' 'large petition' to the House of Commons.[22] There was no reference to *An agreement of the people*, but the MPs were taxed for failing to adopt several of its key demands, notably, religious freedom, the abolition of conscription, annual parliaments, free trade and the abolition of tithes. The Levellers' continuing sensitivity to the anarcho-communist slur was expressed in their professed disappointment that the Commons had not yet 'bound your selves and all future

[20] 'The parliamentary diary of John Boys, 1647–8', ed. D. E. Underdown, *BIHR* 39 (1966), 152–3.
[21] See Keith Thomas, 'The Levellers and the franchise' in Aylmer, *The Interregnum*, 57–78, at 70. Thomas authoritatively refutes the argument of C. B. Macpherson that the Levellers, far from being radical democrats, were bourgeois, Lockean liberals, who would have limited the franchise to men of property. See his *The political theory of possessive individualism* (Oxford, 1962), 120–9, 136.
[22] Printed in Wolfe, *Leveller manifestoes*, 283–90.

Parliaments from abolishing propriety, levelling mens Estats, or making all things common'.

More strongly than in the previous year, the Levellers spoke out in favour of the army – its need for regular pay and indemnity. A few days later someone in the army returned the compliment with a statement endorsing the demands of the 'large petition'. Less than two months later the mask of anonymity would be torn off, and the army's endorsement of Leveller demands would become official.[23]

Over the next three months army militants combined with the Levellers to orchestrate an influx of no fewer than thirty petitions, and numerous letters from regiments, garrisons and officers up and down England demanding decisive action from army headquarters. Seventeen of these petitions explicitly supported the Leveller programme.[24] Under this intense pressure, and in the shadow of the royalists' kidnapping and killing of the Leveller spokesman Colonel Thomas Rainborough at the siege of Pontefract in October, the Council of Officers convened at the beginning of November. Its task was to consider the draft Remonstrance almost certainly penned by Henry Ireton. In the midst of its deliberations it received a delegation of London Levellers and radical Independents with the following demands:

1. a constituent assembly made up of representatives from the army and the 'well-affected' in every county to frame a new constitution. The constitution would take the form of an 'Agreement . . . to be mutually signed by the well-affected people and their said Deputies';
2. a definite date for the dissolution of parliament;
3. the army's endorsement of the new constitution or 'Agreement' in its forthcoming Remonstrance;
4. implementation of the Leveller 'great petition' of September. [25]

Restricting eligible signatories to the 'well-affected' would neatly get around the awkward reality that the majority of the English people in the autumn of 1648 were irremediably ill affected. However, the scheme was laid aside owing to the impracticality of organising a constituent assembly in the crisis days of November and December 1648.

John Lilburne proposed to Ireton a committee of sixteen, equally divided among the four factions – Levellers, army, London independents

---

[23] *The demands, resolutions and intentions of the army* ([26 Sept.] 1648) [BL E. 464(41)]. Printed anonymously, the pamphlet bore the initials J.R. (John Rushworth?), and asserted that it had been 'sent from a great commander in the army, and desired to be printed and published in the name of the rest'. I believe the 'great commander' may have been Henry Ireton. See Gentles, *New Model Army*, 267ff.

[24] Gentles, *New Model Army*, 268–9.

[25] John Lilburne, *The legall fundamentall liberties of the people of England* (1649) [BL E. 560 (14)], repr. in Wolfe, *Leveller manifestoes*, 413.

and the 'honest party' in parliament – to thrash out the implementation of the four demands. The committee was duly appointed, but owing to the army's haste to get to London and purge the House of Commons, it made little progress until after Pride's Purge on 6 December.[26] However, the Leveller intervention appears to have borne immediate fruit in that the Remonstrance of the army was amended to endorse a new constitution for England based on *An agreement of the people*. Not only that, the existing political system was to be replaced by a 'supreme council or parliament' elected yearly or biennially, 'with as much equality as may be'.[27] While parliamentary seats should be redistributed according to population, not taxation, the franchise should be denied 'for a competent number of years' to all who had engaged against parliament. Finally, and crucially, only those who subscribed to *An agreement of the people* would be eligible to engage in politics. In noteworthy constrast to what the Levellers had advocated the year before, Ireton in the Remonstrance stipulated that the new constitution would be adopted by parliament, and then made unbreakable by an *Agreement of the people*.

As the army prepared for its revolutionary *coup d'état* against parliament and monarchy, the officers and soldiers took support wherever they could find it. This urgent need to widen the army's political base, combined with insistent pressure from below, explains why Ireton and the other grandees leaned so far in the direction of an *Agreement of the people*. The September to December days of 1648 would see the Levellers attain the pinnacle of their political influence. During that time the grandees would also refashion the *Agreement* and hedge it in with restrictions to make it proof against a royalist recapture of power.

Suggestive of the favourable reception that greeted the Leveller concept in some London circles at that moment is the publication by the New Model Army lieutenant-colonel, John Jubbes, of *Severall proposals for peace and freedom, by an agreement of the people*. Pretending to have emanated from 'many worthy persons of the Common Councel and others of the City of London, on the 11th of this instant December', it re-echoed many of the familiar Leveller demands, but with some interesting twists. All were to be guaranteed equality before the law. Freedom of religion was to be extended even to Anglicans and Roman Catholics. An added note of humanitarianism was struck in the demand 'that the Irish may not still be proceeded against, as to execute cruelty for cruelty'. Parliaments were to

---

[26] Wolfe, *Leveller manifestoes*, 418–19.

[27] *A remonstrance of his excellency, Thomas lord Fairfax ... and of the Generall Councell of Officers held at St Albans the 16 of Nov., 1648* [BL E. 473(11)]. Reprinted in *The parliamentary or constitutional history of England* (commonly known as *Old Parliamentary History*) (2nd edn, 24 vols., London, 1762–3), XVIII:174.

be chosen biennially and were to sit for five months. Parliamentary seats were to be redistributed according to population, with the franchise extended to copyholders worth forty shillings a year, and all others whose personal estate was worth at least £50. Those who had assisted the king in his war were to be excluded from voting for or sitting in the next parliament. No 'free-born person of this nation' was to be liable to impressment for war service, implying perhaps that servants, beggars, apprentices and other 'unfree persons' would still be liable. All who declined to subscribe to the *Agreement* would be denied the protection of the law.[28]

Despite its pretensions, *Severall proposals* was not a Leveller document. Indeed, five months later Jubbes flatly stated 'I am not a Leveller.'[29] In the guise of promoting a radical recasting of the constitution of England, he and his friends were in reality launching a desperate attempt to save the king's life. They acknowledged that the king had been guilty of levying war against parliament, and if he ever again attempted so much as to assert his veto ('negative voice') he ought to be deposed. However, there existed a covenant with 'our brethren of Scotland, whereby mercy is claimed by that nation on his Majesties behalf'. They therefore made the ingenious suggestion that if the king should assent to the *Agreement*, 'that then he may be proclaimed and crowned King again' with a parliamentary revenue adequate to his needs. Furthermore, no one was to be questioned 'for any thing done in reference to the late publique differences'.[30] In a few months' time there was to be an even stronger convergence of royalism and Levellerism than is exemplified by this document, but for the moment the main players ignored it in their pursuit of higher stakes.

Once parliament had been purged, Lilburne's Committee of Sixteen finally got down to work. Within a week they had hammered out a draft *Agreement of the people* for submission to the Council of Officers.[31] On 15 December John Lilburne jumped the gun by publishing, with the help of an obscure printer, his slightly amended version of the Committee of

---

[28] *Severall proposals for peace and freedom, by an agreement of the people, offered unto Commissary General Ireton for the concurrence of the army, by the approbation and consent of many worthy persons of the Common Council and others of the city of London, on the 11th of this instant December* (1648) [BL E. 477(18)], repr. in Wolfe, *Leveller manifestoes*, 313–21. The pamphlet was published anonymously, but its authorship was revealed in May 1649 when Jubbes reprinted it with minor revisions, and acknowledged that he, not a group of worthy London citizens, was its true contriver. See Jubbes, *An apology unto the honorable and other honored and worthy officers of his excellencies the Lord Generals army by Lieut. Col. John Jubbes* ([4 May] 1649) [BL E. 552(28)], 3–20.   [29] Jubbes, *An apology*, 7.
[30] *Severall proposals for peace and freedom*, repr. in Wolfe, *Leveller manifestoes*, 316.
[31] Worcester College Ms. 16 (Clarke Papers), fols. 31–5. I am grateful to Barbara Taft for supplying me with a photocopy of this ms., which contains the untampered-with, and to date unpublished, text of the second *Agreement*.

Sixteen's text of the *Agreement of the people*. He deleted the third article arranging for the election of biennial representatives, and broadened the reserve on religion by deleting the phrase 'professing Christianity'.[32] Egotistically and inaccurately he characterised the latter change as 'mending' the religious reserve 'to the sense of us all but Ireton'.[33] Lilburne knew that he was forcing the hand of the army, but he evidently feared, with reason, that the army would subject it to even more substantial amendment.

In some respects the December 1648 version of the *Agreement* is the most interesting of all, since it shows the Levellers at their most practical and realistic. Closer to the levers of real political power than they would ever be again, they finally grappled with problems of which Ireton and the grandees had long been conscious. Chief among them was the dilemma presented by the estrangement of the great majority of the English people from the revolutionary cause. How could the franchise be radically widened in the manner the Levellers advocated if its almost certain consequence would be the return of a royalist parliament? A second dilemma, already alluded to by Cromwell at Putney, was what to do if the English people, in their mounting conservatism, should simply refuse, in large numbers, to sign the new constitution?

The Levellers had already proposed that only the 'well-affected' should be permitted to devise the new constitution.[34] The second *Agreement* stated that for the purpose of electing their representatives, the people of England ought to be 'more indifferently proportioned', though whether according to population or taxation was not stated.[35] There followed a carefully worked out list of the 300 MPs who would be elected, ranging from fourteen for the boroughs and county of Devon to two for Rutland, and one or two for each of the Welsh counties. The City of London was to see its numbers double to eight, while the borough of Westminster was to decline to one.

Who was to enjoy the right to vote? Evidently a much smaller segment of the population than had been envisaged by *The case of the armie*. The first hurdle to eligibility was the requirement to sign the *Agreement*. All men over the age of twenty-one who made this commitment and were 'not persons receiving Alms, but such as are assessed ordinarily towards

---

[32] Worcester Coll. Ms. 16, fol. 34.
[33] John Lilburne, *Legall fundamentall liberties*, 35. See also Barbara Taft, 'The Council of Officers' Agreement of the People', *HJ* 28 (1985), 172 n.21, 177.
[34] Lilburne, *Legall fundamentall liberties*, 30. See above, p. 157.
[35] *Foundations of freedom; or an agreement of the people: proposed as a rule for future government in the establishment of a firm and lasting peace. Drawn up by severall wel-affected persons, and tendered to the consideration of the Generall Councell of the Army* ([15 Dec.] 1648) [BL E. 476(26)], repr. in Wolfe, *Leveller manifestoes*, 295–7.

the relief of the poor; not servants to, or receiving wages from any particular person' were theoretically eligible. Further excluded, however, for seven years, was anyone who had given aid or comfort to the royalist cause, 'or who shall make or joyn in, or abet any forcible opposition against this Agreement'.[36] The next clause supplied even greater precision to this principle of exclusion for:

> none[37] shall be eligible for the first or second Representatives, who have not voluntarily assisted the Parliament against the King, either in person before the fourteenth of *June* 1645 [the date of the battle of Naseby] or else in Money, Plate, Horse, or Arms, lent upon the Propositions before the end of May, 1643 or who have joyned in, or abetted the Treasonable Engagement in London, in the yeer 1647. or who declared or engaged themselves for a Cessation of Arms with the *Scots*, who invaded the Nation the last Summer, or for complyance with the Actors in any the Insurrections of the same Summer, or with the Prince of *Wales*, or his accomplices in the revolted Fleet.[38]

Anyone who broke these rules would have his estate confiscated, or be imprisoned for a year 'without bayl, or mainprise'.[39]

When the text of the second *Agreement* came to be debated in the Council of Officers, the franchise provisions were approved, apparently without discussion. There was consensus because Levellers and grandees must have seen eye-to-eye on the necessity of freezing the enemies of the revolution out of the political process, at least until the changes that were underway had been consolidated. Indeed, this point was grasped more firmly by Henry Ireton than by his father-in-law Oliver Cromwell. In the Remonstrance of the army the previous month Ireton had agreed to the Leveller demand that the franchise be denied to all who did not subscribe to the *Agreement*. He had hit upon the *Agreement* as the necessary bulwark against the return of monarchy after the New Model Army laid down its arms. That was why in the Whitehall debates Ireton voiced his only recorded disagreement with Cromwell, on the matter of the date of parliament's dissolution. Ireton argued for the last day of April 1649, and for the inclusion of this date in the text of the *Agreement*. Cromwell was for letting parliament set the date for its own dissolution. Ireton's answer demonstrated the depth of his support for the *Agreement*. If parliament was permitted to dissolve itself without having adopted the *Agreement*, he asserted, then parliaments would, most likely, continue to be elected in the old way. He and all his hearers knew that a parliament elected along the old lines would certainly be dominated by royalists. Conversely, if

---

[36] *Foundations of freedom*, 7–8.
[37] Ibid. Wolfe, *Leveller manifestoes*, 297, misprints 'none' as 'more'.
[38] *Foundations of freedom*, 8; Wolfe, *Leveller manifestoes*, 297.
[39] Wolfe, *Leveller manifestoes*, 298.

men were shown that the only way to get rid of the present parliament was through an *Agreement of the people*, they would be deterred from trying to sabotage the new constitution. Ireton's reasoning showed that for him, if not for Cromwell, the *Agreement* was a key pillar propping up the new political scenario that would follow the abolition of monarchy.[40]

It would be only a slight exaggeration to say that the second *Agreement* would have ushered in something more resembling a dictatorship of the well affected than a golden age of democracy. Not only was the vote to be withheld for seven years from all who had supported the king in the civil wars or who had opposed the *Agreement*. The qualifications to become an MP were to be much more stringent. The London Engagement of the summer of 1647 had been adopted at a meeting of royalist and conservative citizens in Skinners' Hall on 21 July. It exhorted parliament to bring the king to London 'without the nearer approach of the army'.[41] The expectation was that once the king was in London popular acclamation would be so overwhelming that parliament would be unable to resist coming to a personal treaty and restoring him speedily to the throne. It was later said that if all who had signed the 1647 Engagement were denied the franchise there would be hardly anyone eligible to vote or hold office in the City. The experience of the municipal elections of December 1648 proves that this was more than a hypothetical point. In that month the Commons passed an ordinance excluding from the municipal franchise all signatories of the 1647 Engagement. The consequence was a revolution in City politics, and a Common Council led by radical militia officers.[42] It is reasonable to suppose that the provisions of the second *Agreement* would have effected an electoral upheaval of similar magnitude in the rest of the country. Indeed, hostile critics at the time attacked the *Agreement* for its electoral restrictiveness.[43] Even friends of the Levellers such as the editor of the radical newsbook *The Moderate* recognised that the *Agreement* would initially disenfranchise a large segment of the people.[44]

To sum up, the authors of the second *Agreement* were driven by Ireton to face up to political realities. It was part of the commissary-general's political ingenuity to see in the *Agreement of the people* a potential bulwark

[40] *CP*, II:170–1.
[41] Corporation of London Records Office, Common Council Journal, vol. 40, fol. 238v.
[42] Gentles, 'The struggle for London', 302–3. It was remarked at the time that so many soldiers had been elected common councilmen 'that they may almost serve for a Council of War' (*Moderate Intelligencer*, 21–8 Dec. 1648 [BL E. 536 (18)], 197).
[43] John Vernon, *The sword's abuse asserted* (London, 1648) [BL E. 477(3)], 17; Clement Walker, *Anarchia anglicana, or the history of independency second part* (1649), 22, 24, 41–2.
[44] *The Moderate*, 14–21 Nov. 1648 [BL E. 473(1)], 154. See also *A warning, or a word of advice to the city of London* ([30 Nov.] 1648) [BL E. 474(6)], 3, for an admission that 'the major party . . . are not to have any vote'.

against a royalist recapture of power. The remaining clauses manifested a similarly hard-headed grasp of political realities. The first *Agreement* had been silent on the question of who was to run the country when parliament was not in session. This vital question was now answered: there was to be a council of state. The separation of the legislative from the executive power was to be safeguarded by the prohibition against members of the council of state, or any army officer or treasurer or receiver of public monies, sitting in parliament. Popular hostility to lawyers was reflected in the stipulation that any lawyer chosen for either parliament or the council of state 'shall be uncapable of practise as a Lawyer, during that trust'.[45]

The list of reserved powers was similar to that found in the first *Agreement*, but with three significant differences. Liberty of conscience was upheld, though the Representative was permitted to undertake 'the instruction or directing of the Nation in a publick way, for the matters of Faith, Worship or Discipline', so long as the public religion was not compulsory and did not promote popery.[46] The promised oblivion for acts committed during the civil wars was modified to exclude 'such as adhered to the king or his interest against the People'. Continuing anxiety about the anarcho-communist smear was revealed in the requirement that 'no Representative . . . shall levell mens Estates, destroy propriety, or make all things common'.[47]

The one departure from political realism was the continuation of the first *Agreement*'s absolute ban on conscription. Why? Because 'every mans conscience [is] to be satisfied in the justnesse of that cause wherein he hazards his life'.[48]

Tacked onto the second *Agreement* were two appendices. The first was a catalogue of items that the Levellers and London Independents would evidently liked to have seen enshrined in the *Agreement*, but which they had reluctantly decided to leave to the next parliament to redress. Their thrust was political, economic and religious libertarianism:

1. the right of the accused not to incriminate themselves;
2. the language of the law to be English;
3. freedom of trade both at home and abroad;
4. abolition of the excise tax and tithes;
5. no imprisonment for debt;
6. abolition of capital punishment except for murder and 'for endeavouring by force to destroy this Agreement';
7. no man to be convicted 'but onely by twelve sworn men of the Neighbourhood';
8. the interest rate on money not to exceed 6 per cent;

---

[45] Wolfe, *Leveller manifestoes*, 299.   [46] Ibid., 300.   [47] Ibid., 300–1.   [48] Ibid., 300.

9. no one to be barred from public office because of his religious opinions.

To this appendix was added a personal wish-list that John Lilburne could not resist publishing, even if he had apparently failed in persuading his fellow committee-men to include it in their appendix. Prominent was his animus against lawyers, 'the chief bane of this poor Nation'. The next Representative should be 'most earnestly pressed for the ridding of this kingdom of those vermine and caterpillars'. Justice should be decentralised by erecting a court in every hundred in the country, and establishing in every county or shire a registry of conveyances, bills and bonds. All local officials should be elected annually by the people. Finally, all base tenures should be abolished.[49]

The 'Officers' *Agreement*

In June 1649 Lilburne tried to maintain that the Committee's document was meant to be final and unalterable. Yet as he and his followers had explicitly stated on the title page of the second *Agreement*, it was being 'tendered to the consideration of the Generall Councell of the Army'.[50] There was no assumption that the army was bound to accept without change the document produced by the Committee of Sixteen. The debate that was held in Whitehall at the very time the king's trial was being prepared produced several modifications. At no time during the debate did any member of the Committee of Sixteen or their clerical supporters object in principle to the officers' scrutinising their draft. It is true that Lilburne and fifteen others published a pamphlet at the end of December 1648 bitterly complaining that the officers were needlessly prolonging the debate with 'tedious disputes and contests' on 'things so essential unto our freedom, as without which we account the Agreement of no value!'. Yet Lilburne had made no claim for the document's unalterability at the first meeting of the Council of Officers in early December.[51] On balance the evidence indicates that Lilburne's later claim should be rejected.

The officers had already met several times and approved most of the *Agreement* before 14 December when William Clarke began keeping detailed notes. All the restrictive provisions regarding the franchise and eligibility for election to the Representative were retained, except the stip-

---

[49] Ibid., 301–3.   [50] Ibid., 293.

[51] Lilburne, *Legall fundamentall liberties*, 35; *CP,* II:78; *A plea for common right and freedom* ([28 Dec.] 1648) [BL E. 536(22)], 3. See also Taft, 'The Council of Officers' Agreement of the People', 173. I am indebted to Barbara Taft and Austin Woolrych for discussing this and other points connected with the *Agreement* with me.

ulation that everyone be required to sign the *Agreement*, which was softened. It was now sufficient that voters or candidates not 'make, or joyne in, or abet any forcible opposition against this Agreement'.[52] The first big stumbling block was the reserve on religion, which was debated for five days. Several lower officers were joined by Wildman, Lilburne and the radical Independent minister John Goodwin in arguing that the civil magistrate ought not to exercise any power over religion. Ireton answered this appeal to principle with an appeal to the need for public peace and order. He also insisted that a measure of latitude should be left to the elected representatives when it came to judging what was necessary to maintain the peace. Ireton's final point was a cogent one. If the *Agreement* was intended to embrace as many of the well-affected people as possible, it should contain no clause that would prevent some of them from signing it. The reserve on religion was such a clause.

Colonel Edward Whalley rammed the point home when he asked his listeners to consider, since the reserve on religion had already divided the army, how it would divide the kingdom. What was the sense in imposing liberty upon the people against their will?

[H]ow can wee terme that to bee an Agreement of the People which is neither an Agreement of the major parte of the people, and truly for anythinge I can perceive . . . nott [an Agreement of] the major parte of the honest partie of the Kingdome? . . . Wee have bin necessitated to force the Parliament, and I should bee very unwilling wee should force the people to an Agreement.[53]

In the end Ireton's stubbornness paid off. The reserve on religion was replaced by an article specifying that Christianity would be 'held forth and recomended, as the publike Profession in this Nation'. No one would be compelled to attend the state church, 'but onely may be endeavoured to be wonne by sound Doctrine, and the Example of a good Conversation'.[54]

The Levellers' absolute ban on conscription was also modified to distinguish between foreign and home service. The magistrate was now empowered to 'take order for the forming, training and exercising of the people in a Military way to be in readinesse for resisting of Forrain Invasions, suppressing of suddain Insurrections, or for assisting in execution of Law . . . provided, That even in such cases none be compellable to goe out of the County he lives in if he procure another to serve in his roome.'[55]

---

[52] *A petition from his excellency Thomas lord Fairfax and the General Councel of Officers of the army, to the honorable the Commons of England in parliament assembled, concerning the draught of an agreement of the people . . . Saturday, Jan. 20* (1649), reprinted in Wolfe, *Leveller manifestoes*, 342.   [53] *CP,* II:84.   [54] Wolfe, *Leveller manifestoes*, 348.
[55] Ibid., p.347; *CP,* II:134.

The officers were deeply divided on the sixth reserve:

That the Representatives intermeddle not with the execution of Laws, nor give judgement upon any mans person or estate, where no Law hath been before provided; save onely in calling to an account and punishing publick Officers for abusing or failing their trust.[56]

Ireton was evidently worried that it might be used to block the trial of the king, the qualifying phrase about punishing public officers notwithstanding. There was, after all, no existing law under which the king could be tried. Lieutenant-General Thomas Hammond, Scoutmaster-General Francis Rowe and all the colonels present and voting supported Ireton. Nevertheless, the lower officers won a narrow victory over their superiors.[57] The motion to delete the sixth reserve was defeated by eighteen to sixteen votes, and it was carried forward as the fifth reserve in the Officers' *Agreement*.

On the next day of debate the officers addressed the thorny question of how to define the sovereign powers of the Representative, not including those that were explicitly reserved to the people. Like the Levellers they were silent on whether the institution of monarchy should be preserved or abolished. In a stunning confirmation of Leveller libertarianism they voted twenty-seven to seventeen that while the Representative should have 'the highest and finall judgment concerning all naturall and civill things', it would not have any power when it came to moral questions.[58] Again the higher officers were overwhelmed by their more numerous inferiors.[59] It must have been a galling defeat for Ireton, but he respected the decision of the majority. The revised version of the article as submitted to the House of Commons on 20 January explicitly excluded 'things Spirituall or Evangelicall' from the Representative's sovereign power.[60]

On 26 December the grandees insisted on reopening the debate on the sixth reserve and *ex post facto* legislation. Although they were again overwhelmed by the more numerous lower officers,[61] they did succeed in deleting the reserve that banned any law which granted special privileges.[62] Three days later the Council of Officers approved the final two reserves without dissent, and then moved to consider the positive articles of the *Agreement*. The article empowering the council of state to summon an emergency session of the Representative was amended to double the

---

[56] Wolfe, *Leveller manifestoes*, 300, 348.
[57] Pride was the one colonel who abstained. Barbara Taft, 'Voting lists of the Council of Officers', *BIHR* 52 (1979), 138–54, at 147.   [58] *CP,* II:139–40.
[59] Taft, 'Voting lists', 148.   [60] Wolfe, *Leveller manifestoes*, 347.
[61] Taft, 'Voting lists', 149.
[62] *CP,* II:156; Taft, 'The Council of Officers' Agreement of the People', 178.

permitted length of the session from forty to eighty days.[63] Another article concerning public credit was amended to eliminate any obligation to royalist creditors. The article against mutiny by the army was broadened to make it a capital offence for anyone to rebel against the Representative's authority.[64]

A high-powered ten-man committee was then named to put the finishing touches on the *Agreement* before presenting it to parliament. The committee's composition was finely balanced, with four conservatives, four radicals and two moderates.[65] Besides making minor changes in the text of the *Agreement*, it drafted 'The form of subscription for the Officers of the Army'. Here the officers were to declare the central articles and reserves 'Fundamentall to our common Right, Liberty, and Safety', and to promise to maintain them 'as God shall enable us'.[66]

A delegation of officers led by Lieutenant-General Thomas Hammond brought the finished version of the *Agreement*, copied out on parchment, to the Commons on Saturday 20 January 1649. After listening to Hammond the Commons ordered the *Agreement* printed, and promised to consider it soon.[67] The fact is, they never did consider it, and the officers never reminded them of their promise. The army's acquiescence in the Commons' spurning of the *Agreement* has prompted the allegation that they did not much care for it in the first place. The debate they staged was merely a sop to the radicals, a tactic for distracting them 'like children with rattles' while the grandees got on with the more serious business of cutting off the king's head.[68]

Undeniably the officers were more preoccupied with the king's trial than with promoting a new constitution for England. Soon they would also have to turn their attention once again to the military threats from Ireland and Scotland. But it was equally true that no one was passionately attached to the *Agreement*. Even the Levellers cared less about the structure of government than about decentralising authority and liberalising the laws. The *Agreement* inspired little public support from those quarters that might have been expected to enthuse over it – London's gathered churches and the army rank and file. The most consistent backing for the

---

[63] *CP* II:155–6; Wolfe, *Leveller manifestoes*, 301, 346–7.
[64] *CP* II:156; Wolfe, *Leveller manifestoes*, 301, 349.
[65] *CP* II:156; Gentles, *New Model Army*, 523, n. 144.
[66] Wolfe, *Leveller manifestoes*, 349–50.   [67] *CJ* VI:122.
[68] Lilburne, *Legall fundamentall liberties*, 35 (repr. in Wolfe, *Leveller manifestoes*, 422). This is the interpretation followed by S. R. Gardiner, *History of the great civil war* (4 vols., London, 1894), IV:295–6; David Underdown, *Pride's Purge* (Oxford, 1971), 199–200; Blair Worden, *The Rump Parliament 1648–1653* (Cambridge, 1974), 76; H. N. Brailsford, *The Levellers and the English revolution* (Nottingham, 1976), 390–1; and Brian Manning, *1649: the crisis of the English revolution* (London, 1992), 177.

Agreement had come from the lower officers. Indeed, their repeated triumphs over Ireton and his supporters may have made the latter lukewarm about the document they had taken so seriously in December 1648. Whatever the reasons, the *Agreement* was politically sidelined, and soon forgotten by everyone except John Lilburne.[69]

The third *Agreement*

The grandees had hoped to soften Lilburne's hostility to them by piloting a bill through both Houses of Parliament to pay him the £3,000 he had been claiming for almost a decade as damages for his sufferings at the hands of the Star Chamber. But there was a catch: the money was awarded in the form of timber from the estates of royalist delinquents in his native county of Durham. In order to prevent the revenue slipping from his grasp Lilburne quit the capital for Durham, before the Whitehall debates were concluded, and did not return until February.[70]

By then the rank and file of the army were seething once again with discontent against parliament and the grandees for neglecting their material grievances. Worried about radical subversion, the grandees asked parliament for permission to punish under martial law any outside agitators who stirred up trouble in the army.[71] This attempt at repression aroused Lilburne to a paroxysm of rage. On 26 February along with several comrades he submitted to parliament a wholesale indictment of the officers' multifarious sins. First they had contaminated the *Agreement of the people* by incorporating many compromises. Lilburne was particularly suspicious of the provision that parliaments should meet for only six months in every two-year period, with an executive council of state carrying on for the other eighteen. In this he was being both inconsistent and unfair. The first *Agreement* had specified that parliament should sit for just under six months 'and no longer', but had been silent on how the country was to be governed during the other eighteen months between parliaments.[72]

Warming to his theme, Lilburne indignantly asked by what right the army was enforcing censorship of the press. And why did the hastily erected council of state include among its members army officers, peers and Star Chamber judges, in flagrant violation of the principles of the *Agreement*? He reserved his harshest words for the higher officers. Ever since the army's Engagement of 5 June 1647 their conduct had been a

---

[69] See also Taft, 'The Council of Officers' Agreement of the People', 179–85.
[70] *CJ* VI:102; *LJ* X:637; Pauline Gregg, *Free-born John* (1961), 258–61.
[71] *CP,* II:200n.; *The justice of the army against evill-doers vindicated* ([5 June] 1649) [BL E. 558(14)], 7–9.
[72] Wolfe, *Leveller manifestoes*, 227. I am grateful to Austin Woolrych for this point.

sorry tale of broken promises and oppression of the rank and file. What was needed was nothing less than a thoroughgoing purge of the high command.[73]

This and other intemperate, reckless attacks on the army leadership by Leveller writers opened an unhealable breach between the two. When at the beginning of March eight troopers circulated a petition demanding the democratisation of the army they were punished by riding the wooden horse, having their swords broken over their heads, and being cashiered from the army. At once they became fresh martyrs in the Leveller pantheon.[74] The vitriolic responses to their punishment, penned by John Lilburne, Richard Overton and Thomas Prince, completed the alienation of the New Model officers from the Leveller cause.[75] In December and January a majority of the Council of Officers had embraced a version of the *Agreement* that was not all that different from the Levellers' 1648 version. In the crisis of April and May the only officer of note to maintain his allegiance to the Levellers was Major John Cobbett.[76]

By allowing unbridled expression to their anger at the grandees the Leveller leaders wrote off any chance to wield meaningful political influence in the future. Before the end of March Lilburne, Overton, Walwyn and Prince were in the Tower awaiting a trial for treason. From this venue they spent the month of April pursuing their efforts to stir up the rank and file to overthrow their officers and implement the Leveller agenda for England.[77] The grandees responded by removing some London-based detachments to the outskirts where they would be less accessible to Leveller propaganda. But when Captain Savage's troopers in Colonel Whalley's regiment were told to move to new quarters in Essex they balked. Seizing the troop's colours they holed up in the Bull Inn, a radical meeting place near Bishopsgate, and defied their commanders' summons to obey orders. Of the six troopers later found guilty of mutiny one – Robert Lockyer – was sentenced to die. It was

---

[73] *Englands new chains discovered* ([26 Feb.] 1649) [BL E. 545 (27)]; repr. in William Haller and Godfrey Davies (eds.), *The Leveller tracts, 1647–1653* (New York, 1944), 161–5.

[74] *The hunting of the foxes from New-market and Triploe-Heaths to White.Hall, by five small beagles (late of the armie.) Or the grandie-deceivers unmasked* ([21 March] 1649) [BL E. 548(7)], repr. in Wolfe, *Leveller manifestoes*, 373–4.

[75] See John Lilburne, *The second part of Englands new-chaines discovered* ([24 March] 1649) [BL E. 548(16)], repr. in Haller and Davies, *Leveller tracts*, 184–9.

[76] *The hunting of the foxes* repr. in Wolfe, *Leveller manifestoes*, 358–83; Lilburne, *The second part of England's new chains discovered*, repr. in Haller and Davies, *Leveller tracts*, 171–89. For the ascription of *The hunting of the foxes* to Overton, see Marie Gimelfarb-Brack, *Liberté, egalité, fraternité, justice! La vie et l'oeuvre de Richard Overton* (Berne, 1979), 379–80. See also Gentles, *New Model Army*, 316–20.

[77] See for example, *The English souldiers standard* ([5 April] 1649) [BL E. 550(1)], probably written by Overton.

widely believed that he had been singled out on account of his promotion of the *Agreement of the people* at Ware in November 1647.[78] His funeral, which reportedly drew about 4,000 mourners, was a remarkable demonstration of Leveller strength in the City. Sea-green ribbons (Colonel Rainborough's colour) were widely worn as a sign of radical allegiance.[79]

On 1 May, four days after Lockyer's funeral, the imprisoned Leveller leaders issued from the Tower the movement's third and last version of the *Agreement of the people*. It contained, in Lilburne's words, the Levellers' 'full and whole desires. . . in reference to civil Government; in the enjoyment of which we should fully acquiesce'.[80] In the preface the authors lamented that for several years the nation had 'drunk deep of the Cup of misery and sorrow', but blessed God that they had done nothing to contribute to that affliction.[81] Despite their imprisonment they trusted that people would not view them as 'wilde, irrationall, dangerous Creatures' for proffering the *Agreement of the people* as the sovereign remedy for the nation's misery.

The promise of the *Agreement* was straightforward: 'to abolish all arbitrary Power, and to set bounds and limits both to our Supreme, and all Subordinate Authority, and remove all known Grievances'.[82] The Representative, which was to be the supreme authority, was increased from the 300 of the second *Agreement*, to 400, but there was no specification as to how the seats would be distributed. The franchise was a 'naturall right' inhering in all men twenty-one years and older except for servants, recipients of alms and those who had served the late king. The latter were only to be excluded for ten years.

Reflecting their deep hostility to the officers of the army the authors laid down that no army officers (as well as receivers of public monies and practising lawyers) could be elected to the Representative. As further safeguards against oligarchical concentrations of power, members of the present parliament were excluded, and future members could not be chosen for the Representative immediately succeeding.

---

[78] Philip Baker has reminded me that there is no evidence dating from November or December 1647 that Lockyer was actually at Ware. His regiment was not there, and if Lockyer had gone to the rendezvous on his own he would have been arrested and his name published.

[79] Ian Gentles, 'Political funerals during the English revolution' in Stephen Porter (ed.), *London and the civil war* (1996), 205–24, at 218–20.

[80] *L. Colonel John Lilburne his apologetical narration* (Amsterdam, 1652) [BL E. 659(30)], 71.

[81] *An agreement of the free people of England. Tendered as a peace-offering to this distressed nation. By Lieutenant Colonel Iohn Lilburne, Master William Walwyn, Master Thomas Prince, and Master Richard Overton . . . May the 1. 1649* [BL E. 552(23)], repr. in Wolfe, *Leveller manifestoes*, 400.   [82] Wolfe, *Leveller manifestoes*, 402.

Parliaments were to be elected annually and to sit for a minimum of four months. There was to be no council of state, but between parliamentary sessions the management of state affairs was to be referred to a 'Committee of their own members'. The Representative was to be omnicompetent, except for those powers reserved by the people to themselves. These were religion, impressment, indemnity (except for those who had 'adhered to the King'), equality before the law, no punishments except as provided by law, no punishment for refusing to incriminate oneself, and all legal proceedings to be limited to six months, to be exclusively in English, and no one to be prevented from pleading his own case.

There followed a number of items that were left to be refined or 'perfected' by the next Representative. The *Agreement* concluded with a random list of items, seemingly thrown together in haste, that were also to be excluded from the enduring powers of the Representative: free trade, the imposition of an excise tax, imprisonment for debt, imposition of tithes, standing armies and capital punishment except for murder 'or for endeavouring by force to destroy this our Agreement'.[83] In addition, the Petition of Right was to be upheld; each parish was to choose its own minister; convictions were to be only by juries of twelve local men 'chosen in some free way by the people'; religion (except for popery) was to be no bar to holding office; the Representative was not to impose any public officer upon the localities. All local officers were to be chosen for a one-year term by those eligible to vote under the *Agreement*. Finally, the Representative was not to have any power to 'level mens Estates, destroy Propriety, or make all things Common'.

Three observations may be made on the third *Agreement*. First, the Leveller leaders, having implicitly recognised the hopelessness of their cause by the spring of 1649, threw realism to the winds and stripped away the qualifying clauses found in the second *Agreement* of the previous December. Secondly, the lineaments of their vision of England stood out not so much as democratic as libertarian and decentralist. Thirdly, fear and hatred of standing armies and self-perpetuating parliaments overrode any worry that a vastly expanded electorate would bring back the monarchy.

The quixotic spirit at the heart of the third *Agreement* is seen in the profound suspicion of all political power. Parliaments were to be dissolved and chosen yearly; no permanent executive, but a temporary committee of MPs was to run the country in the intervals between parliamentary

---

[83] Ibid., 406–9. The *Agreement* did recognise the need for brief transitional arrangements for the excise and for tithes.

sessions. Conscription was not only banned entirely; armies were to be merely temporary bodies whose officers would be chosen by the civilian population from the localities where their regiments were recruited. It was hardly to be expected that a revolutionary army, having waged a bitter fight to achieve power, would consent to see that power thus dissipated. The Levellers' answer for the tendency of all power to corrupt was to distribute it as widely as possible. Power was to be handed to the boroughs, the hundreds and the parishes. Religion, trade and political opinion were to be free.

What was the popular response to the third *Agreement*? Prior to 1 May the Leveller leaders had accused Fairfax and Cromwell of 'treason and murder' for suppressing the mutiny in Whalley's regiment, and promised a popular insurrection if Lockyer was executed. If the publication of the *Agreement* is seen as that call for insurrection it was a failure. In spite of printing 20,000 copies and sending them 'gratis all over England',[84] they were only answered by Corporal (or Captain as he styled himself) William Thompson. On the run for having broken into a house in Essex, Thompson mobilised popular support around the call 'for a New Parliament, by Agreement of the People' in the region around Banbury and Cirencester.[85] He was hunted down and shot in the woods near Northampton, and his 300 followers dispersed.[86]

The leaders of the much larger army uprising that met its end at Burford on 15 May made no public reference to the third *Agreement*, although the writer of the *Moderate Intelligencer* reported that they 'will have the agreement of the people goe forward'.[87] Uppermost in their minds was halting the expedition to Ireland.[88] In a bid to win popular support for their cause they spread word through the countryside that their objective was only to restore 'magistracy, liberty and freedom . . . under fair pretence for Charles the second'.[89] In fact there are many indications of a convergence between royalism and Levellerism in the

[84] Lilburne, *Apologetical narration*, 71.

[85] *England's standard advanced* (6 May 1649) [BL E. 553(2)], 3. A few days later he put forth an enlarged edition of this pamphlet, printing the entire text of the 1 May *Agreement of the people*. *Englands standard advanced in Oxfordshire, or a declaration from Mr. Wil. Thompson . . . May 6. 1649* [BL E. 553 (7)].

[86] *CP*, II:199 and note b; *The iustice of the army against evill-doers vindicated* ([5 June] 1649) [BL E. 558(14)], 7–9.

[87] No. 216 (2–10 May 1649) [BL E. 555(3)], unpag.; entry for 7 May.

[88] For an account of the Burford mutiny see Gentles, *New Model Army*, 333–49.

[89] *Declaration of the Levellers concerning Prince Charles* (17 May 1649) [BL E. 555(26)], 3. This admittedly hostile source must be treated with caution; however, there are enough independent indications that the Levellers were tempted by the royalist option at this juncture, to make the allegation credible. Cf. Thomas Carte, *A collection of original letters and papers . . . from the year 1641 to 1660* (2 vols., London, 1739), I:273; Bulstrode Whitelocke, *Memorials of the English affairs* (4 vols., Oxford, 1853), III:100.

despairing months of the spring and summer of 1649. In *Heaven and earth*, the Leveller sympathiser Captain-Lieutenant William Bray wrote that the king had been more just and merciful than the Rump.[90] In August an apologist for the Burford mutineers denounced the 'Martiall Monarchie' of Cromwell and Ireton, declaring 'we will chuse subjection to the Prince, chusing rather ten thousand times to be his slaves than theirs, yet hating slavery under both'.[91] Among the lead miners of the Peak District in Derbyshire, Andy Wood has discovered a similar mixture of Levellerism and royalism in the summer of 1649.[92] Meanwhile, in London Matthew Rowe wrote to his friend Colonel Michael Jones that the Levellers, by their opposition to the Irish expedition, were giving aid and comfort to Irish papists and acting as unwitting accomplices of the pope.[93]

Conclusion

When the Levellers introduced the first version of the Agreement of the people to the army at Putney in the autumn of 1647, the grandees were able to win a strategic and rhetorical victory against them by zeroing in on the demand for electoral redistribution. While they had issued no explicit call for universal manhood suffrage in the first Agreement Ireton was able to extract the admission that this was what was implied by the redistributing of seats according to population. Having won that point it was not difficult for the grandees to paint the Levellers as men who would subvert private property by handing over power to the propertyless majority. The next step was to smear them as communists and anarchists. Grossly unfair though it was, this smear was a huge propaganda success, so much so that even in the third, and most radical, version of the Agreement the Levellers felt compelled to include a vehement denunciation of those who would level men's estates.[94]

In the autumn of 1648, desperately short of political friends, the higher officers of the New Model Army had turned to the Levellers, hoping to enlist them in the advancement of their projected revolution.

---

[90] *Heaven and earth, spirit and blood, demanding reall commonwealth-justice: or, a letter to the Speaker of the House of Commons. By Captain William Bray* ([29 June] 1649) [BL E. 562(9)], 4.

[91] *The Levellers (falsly so called) vindicated* ([21 Aug.] 1649) [BL E. 571(11)], 10.

[92] Andy Wood, 'Beyond post-revisionism? The civil war allegiance of the miners of the Derbyshire "Peak country"', *HJ* 40 (1997), 23–40, at 38 and n. 62.

[93] National Library of Ireland Ms. 2541 (Cadogan), 649–50; printed in HMC, *Ormond* II (1899), 87–9.

[94] We ought not to assume that the four authors of the third *Agreement* also participated in the drafting of the first *Agreement*. It is possible, as John Morrill and Philip Baker have pointed out to me, that some of the leaders disapproved of the implicit endorsement of universal manhood suffrage in the first *Agreement*.

Collaboration with the army high command produced the version of the *Agreement* that contained a higher quotient of practicality and political realism than any other. Forced to grapple with the brute fact that a broader franchise would produce a royalist parliament, the Levellers acquiesced in a set of electoral qualifications that excluded well over half the adult male population. They also yielded to Ireton's insistence that there be a state church, even if adherence to it was to be voluntary. A council of state was to be erected to act as the executive arm of government between sittings of parliament.

The Council of Officers subjected the second *Agreement* to further modification before putting it to the Rump Parliament on 20 January 1649. The reserve against conscription was changed to allow pressing for home service, while the reserve repealing all legal privileges and exemptions due to degree and birth was dropped. Although the Officers' *Agreement* was not radically different from the second *Agreement* of December 1648, the Leveller leaders were galled by the officers' insistence on seeking parliamentary ratification of the *Agreement* before submitting it to the people.

In their rage at being outmanoeuvred by the grandees the Levellers retaliated with a call for wholesale mutiny in the army. Their poorly judged political intemperance had its predictable consequence: imprisonment in the Tower. From there they issued their third and last version of the *Agreement*. Behind the extremism of the third *Agreement* of 1 May 1649 was a tacit admission of political despair. Gone was the concern for excluding the enemies of the revolution from the franchise. Gone was any worry about how the country was to be defended in the absence of conscription, or governed without a permanent executive. Gone, too, was any care for fostering civil peace through a national church. Even the passion for democracy was muted. Instead, in their repeated demands for the devolution of political power to the localities the Levellers at last showed what moved them most. Front and centre in the third *Agreement* was the quixotic vision of a radically libertarian England, a decentralised federation of the localities.

9   From Reading to Whitehall: Henry Ireton's journey[1]

Barbara Taft

The General Council that began meeting in Putney Church on 28 October 1647 was the second of three army councils that considered proposals for the settlement of the state after the defeat of the king in the first civil war. This essay will trace the army's pursuit of a settlement by following the political journey of Henry Ireton, commissary-general in the New Model Army, member of parliament, close friend and son-in-law of Oliver Cromwell. Tireless in his quest for a reformed constitution, Ireton was the principal draftsman of the army's demands and proposals and a central player throughout the political debates: at Reading in July 1647; at Putney three months later; at Whitehall beginning in December 1648. Focus on Ireton will clarify the positions of the protaganists, expose the fragile unity of the New Model, and cast fresh light on the army's failure to secure a settlement that reconciled individual liberty and political stability.

Ireton brought skills and convictions to the army's councils. The eldest son in a devout Puritan family, he was thirteen when his father died, leaving Henry with four younger brothers and three sisters, a situation that surely enhanced his innate solemnity. After taking the degree of BA at Oxford, in 1629 Ireton entered the Middle Temple where he gained legal and constitutional knowledge that would pervade his political arguments. Edmund Ludlow, who knew Ireton well, noted his diligence and rectitude in public service and his steady concern for justice.[2] Opponents condemned his motives,[3] and many who respected – even admired – Ireton's industry and learning did not like him. His probity may have been tinged with self-righteousness and his forensic talents were often

---

[1] I am indebted to Linda Levy Peck and Michael Mendle for their helpful comments about earlier drafts of this essay.

[2] Edmund Ludlow, *Memoirs*, ed. C. H. Firth (2 vols., Oxford, 1894), I:278–9, 284–9. Except where otherwise noted, the facts of Ireton's life are from C. H. Firth's article in the *Dictionary of national biography*.

[3] E.g. John Lilburne, *The legall fundamentall liberties of the people of England* ([18 June] 1649), 35. Edward Hyde, lst earl of Clarendon, *The history of the rebellion and civil wars in England*, ed. W. D. Macray (6 vols., Oxford, 1888), V:264–5.

marred by certitude. If Ludlow's assertion that Ireton became 'entirely' free of rigid adherence to his own opinion is overstated, the debates reveal that he did become increasingly flexible.

Before Ireton emerged as the army's draftsman in 1647 there are no clues to his ideas about a new constitutional structure. From the early 1630s until the approach of civil war Ireton lived quietly in his native Attenborough where he was regarded as 'a very grave and solid person, a man of good learning, greate understanding'.[4] Although he took no known political actions, as a religious Independent committed to a large measure of toleration he presumably deplored the king's support of Archbishop Laud and his belief that he was accountable 'to none but to God alone'.[5] In 1642 Ireton raised a troop of horse because he preferred war to surrender to a king who violated the rightful power of parliament. Elected to the Commons in 1645, there is no record of Ireton's participation in the House before the quarrel between parliament and the army in 1647.

The conflict began in February, after the departing Scots transferred the king to the custody of the English commissioners. Parliament's subsequent plans for the disbandment of the New Model infantry without adequate provision for arrears of pay and indemnity evoked protests from increasingly concerned regiments. Ireton, observing the dissension from the dual vantage points of army general and member of the House, revealed his sympathy with the soldiers by the end of March when parliament's insulting response to an army petition so angered all ranks that political concerns were added to petitions for redress of professional grievances.[6] The regiments elected representatives – soon termed agitators – to advance their demands. Parliament continued its destructive course and agitators increased in number, influence and denunciations of parliament's abuse of the army. On 25 May the House approved a plan to eliminate New Model infantry by disbanding the regiments one by one at widely diverse places.[7] Four days later, at a large council of war, a petition from determined agitators threatened independent action unless General Fairfax called a rendezvous of the whole army. Ireton led a committee that advised Fairfax to acquiesce and the council approved, 82:4. The unity of soldiers and officers was described as 'incredible'.[8] The unity was

---

[4] Lucy Hutchinson, *Memoirs of the life of Colonel Hutchinson*, ed. James Sutherland (Oxford, 1973), 62.   [5] *LJ* III:879 (26 June 1628).

[6] *The petition of the officers and souldiers in the army* (2 April 1647). *CJ* V:127, 129 (27, 29 March); *LJ* IX:115 (30 March); John Rushworth, *Historical collections* (8 vols., 1721–2), VI:445–7. For Ireton: *CJ* V:132–3 (1, 2 April).

[7] *The apologie of the common souldiers,* dated 28 April, published with *A second apologie* (3 May 1647); *CJ* V:158 (30 April), 183 (25 May); *LJ* IX:207 (27 May).

[8] *Two letters of ... Fairfax ... with the humble advice of the councel of warre ... also, the petition of the private soulderie of the army* ([4 June] 1647). *CP,* I:108–13.

driven by necessity as well as agreement for it is evident that the agitators, who had inflamed troops as they represented them, were in control of a force with which officers must concur or depart.[9]

In the first week in June, two decisive actions marked the army's assertion of political autonomy. Cornet Joyce secured the king from parliament's custody at Holdenby and brought him to Childersley, four miles from Cambridge. The same day, 5 June, the regiments assembled at the rendezvous near Newmarket assented to *A solemne engagement* in which all ranks pledged that the army would not be disbanded or divided until its demands were met. To determine united action a council was established that consisted of the General Officers with two officers and two soldiers elected from each regiment.[10] This general council, as it would be styled, regularised the position of the agitators, bringing them into the command structure. The plan was probably Ireton's. He was a stickler for order, had strongly supported the soldiers at the end of March, the agitators at the end of May, and a month after *A solemne engagement* he would try – vainly – to include agitators in meetings of officers and parliamentary commissioners.[11]

Nine days after the regiments subscribed *A solemne engagement* the army released an outline of a plan for the settlement of the state: *A declaration, or representation,* which was described as 'the Sum and Bottom of the Desires of the Army'.[12] Ireton was the principal draftsman; Cromwell and John Lambert were named as his close associates and the plan was cleared by the council of war.[13] Although larded with the abstract rhetoric of 'fundamentall Rights and Liberties', *A declaration* does not project an ideological revolution. It does propose profound changes within the existing constitutional structure and leaves no doubt that Ireton had given much thought to a settlement. The manifesto also reveals that Ireton had concluded that parliament would not conclude a satisfactory peace with the king.

Asserting the duty of men who 'were not a meere mercinary Army' but citizen-soldiers called forth to secure 'our owne and the peoples just rights, and liberties', *A declaration* proclaims the army's right to

---

[9] Ian Gentles, *The New Model Army* (Oxford, 1992), 168, estimates that of 2,320 officers, 167 dissidents left or were driven out.

[10] *A solemne engagement of the army,* 5 June 1647 ([11 June] 1647), esp. 9.

[11] *CP,* I:148 (2 July).

[12] *A declaration, or representation from . . . Fairfax, and the army* (14 June 1647). Earl of Nottingham to Speaker of the Lords, 15 June, *The parliamentary or constitutional history of England* (24 vols., 1762–3; hereafter *OPH*), XV:453–4.

[13] Bulstrode Whitelocke, *Memorials of the English affairs* (London, 1732), 254. Rushworth to Ferdinando, Lord Fairfax, 15 June, as in *Memorials of the civil war: comprising the correspondence of the Fairfax family,* ed. Robert Bell (2 vols., London, 1849), I:355–6.

resist arbitrary power in accordance with the 'law of Nature and Nations'. Because authority is vested in the office and only ministerially in the person who holds it, *A declaration* proposes to restrict the power of a hereditary king and a parliament that could only be dissolved by its own consent. The Houses are to be purged of men unfit to sit. Within the time set for the duration of this and future parliaments, adjournment or dissolution may only take place by the parliament's consent. Ireton was careful to add that no blame is attached to the 'Worthies' who extended the present parliament to secure the nation's liberties. When the authority of parliament is settled by acts or ordinances with the king's assent, 'the Rights of his Majestie and his posterity may be considered'.[14]

The proposed settlement shifted the balance of power away from the king, who had driven parliament from legislative resistance to civil war; the settlement also disclosed Ireton's awareness that an unbounded parliament would be as undesirable as an unbounded king.[15] Apparently, Ireton assumed that after circumscribing the monarchy the parliament, 'being entrusted, on the people's behalf, for their interest in that great and supreame power of the Common-wealth',[16] would subject itself to the constraints of regular elections from more equally distributed constituencies.

There is no indication that agitators were consulted about *A declaration*, although concluding 'desires' include many of their concerns: the right to petition, legal reform, an act of oblivion, toleration for those who differ from the presbyterian establishment. Agitators also welcomed the concurrent *Heads of a charge* demanding impeachment of eleven members. However, a fortnight later, when army headquarters moved from Uxbridge, fifteen miles from Westminster, to Reading, forty miles away, agitators were not pleased. Parliament had not addressed *A declaration* or the *Charge*[17] and agitators rightly believed that army decisions were taken without input from soldiers elected to a General Council that had yet to meet.

On 16 July the General Council assembled at Reading where Fairfax reportedly presided over more than 100 men. Among the sixty-four named attendees were nineteen officer-agitators and three agitators from

[14] *A declaration*, esp. 4, 5, 9–15 (pagination skips from 6 to 9). An edition printed in Cambridge includes two paragraphs recommending a more equal distribution of seats (*OPH*, XV:455–70, esp. 466).
[15] Cf. *An humble remonstrance from . . . the army* (23 June 1647), reprinted *OPH*, XVI:4–19, esp. 9.   [16] *A declaration*, 10.
[17] *The heads of a charge* (14 June 1647), reprinted *OPH*, XV:470–3; cf. *A particular charge* (6 July 1647), ibid., XVI:70–92. *An humble remonstrance* (23 June).

the ranks: William Allen, Nicholas Lockyer and Edward Sexby.[18] The three soldiers addressed the council the first day; Allen, who also spoke on the 17th, was notably fluent and effective. Cromwell and Ireton led the argument for senior officers.

The opening day was consumed by debate about the agitators' 'petition and representation' of grievances, which called for a march to London to 'putt a speedy period to . . . distractions' as diverse as army pay and the release of John Lilburne and other 'illegally' imprisoned Leveller associates.[19] Cromwell, leading the opposition to the march, proposed appointment of a committee to consider the agitators' representation and promised that Ireton would present a plan of settlement. Ireton opposed the march as a bid for power. The army's purpose, he said, is the securing of the nation's liberties. Before any action '[We should give] . . . some reall tast of that which wee intend . . . and what wee would doe with that power if we had itt in our hands.'[20]

A committee of twelve field officers and six soldier-agitators was named, and when the council reassembled at six o'clock it was evident that they had worked to good purpose 'in the inner Roome'. Cromwell reported that the two demands in the representation that had not been presented to parliament's commissioners were now under way. As for the march, Cromwell conceded that it might 'bee necessiatated' in the end, but he urged the council to await Ireton's plan for a settlement.[21] Ireton explained that in response to a request from the commissioners 'my self and another . . . [were] sequestred or sett apart' to prepare a plan for settlement, for 'Wee doe thinke . . . if ever itt doe come to settle, it must bee by setting downe some thinge that may bee a rule to lay a foundation for the common rights and liberties of the people.'[22] At the day's end, the generals having listened to the complainants at length, it was agreed that the representation would be sent to parliament without the threat of an immediate march to London.[23]

The next day attendees appeared receptive to Ireton's presentation of a draft that would become *The heads of the proposals*. Again noting that he

---

[18] Attendance list of fifty-two officers (*CP,* I:176) collated with October list of agitators (ibid., I:436–9) plus five additional speakers and seven additional committeemen (ibid., I:192–217), for a total of sixty-four names indicates that if reports of 'above 100' in attendance are correct there were some forty unnamed attendees (Rushworth letter, 17 July, ibid., I:214–16); Rushworth to Ferdinando, Lord Fairfax, 20 July, as in *Memorials,* ed. Bell, I:369.

[19] The humble petition and representation of the agitators, 16 July 1647, *CP,* I:170–5.

[20] Ibid. I:177, 179–80 (Cromwell), 177, 179, 182 (Ireton).

[21] Ibid. I:183 (committee), 183–7, 191 (Cromwell) .

[22] Ibid. I:197. 'Another' was Colonel John Lambert (ibid., I:212).

[23] Ibid. I:209–11; Rushworth letters, above, n. 18.

had been 'sequestred' to prepare the draft, Ireton emphasised that he offered it for 'consideration' and twice asked that it 'be referred to a less number that may weigh or consider all things'. William Allen, concurring, observed 'that wee are most of us butt young Statesmen' who need time to deliberate.[24] There is no known contemporary allusion to subsequent Council debate at Reading and the 'perfecting of the proposals' apparently was completed by the committee of twelve agitators and twelve field officers named on 17 and 18 July.[25] How agitators were chosen and who they were is unknown, but the field officers named by Fairfax included Colonels Thomas Rainborough and Thomas Harrison, who had some affinity with radical aspirations. Furthermore, three months later, when Ireton referred to framing the proposals in committee at Reading, he noted that among those present were John Wildman and Maximilian Petty, civilians who spoke for the Levellers at Putney.[26]

There are no records of the committee entrusted with the completion of the proposals but the results again reveal Ireton's realism as well as the importance of committees for the resolution of differences. Always informed and clear-minded, in Council meetings Ireton was frequently irascible or carried away with the pleasure of verbal combat. The products of committee work disclose that his ideas were not immutable and that he recognised that compromise was often essential.

The heads of the proposals presented to the king by 25 July[27] fill out the plan of government sketched in the 14 June *Declaration* – leavened with principles held by army radicals. The king is constrained by parliament and a pre-selected council of state. For ten years parliament holds the sole power to raise money, control the armed forces and appoint the chief officers of state. Parliament is circumscribed by biennial elections and a redistribution of seats in accordance with rates. Toleration is broad and an act of oblivion is mandated.[28] The plan is far more comprehensive than the successive proposals sent to Charles by parliament, all of which

---

[24] Ibid. I:211–13, 214 (Ireton), 213 (Allen).

[25] Ibid. I:216–17. For a contrary view see J. S. A. Adamson, 'The English nobility and the projected settlement of 1647', *HJ*, 30 (1987), 567–602.

[26] *CP,* I:356–7.

[27] *Memoirs of Sir John Berkley*, as in *Select tracts relating to the civil wars in England*, ed. Francis Baron Maseres (2 vols., London, 1815), II:366–7. On 3 August Charles rejected the proposals 'with disdain' (ibid., II:368–9).

[28] For text signed by Rushworth, 1 August, Rushworth, *Historical collections*, VII:731–6 the sixteen proposal articles are followed by a request for speedy response to grievances in the 14 June *Declaration*. Proposals and grievances were published in *A declaration from . . . Fairfax, and his councell of warre. Concerninq their proceeding in the proposalls, . . . together with the heads of the said proposalls, . . . to which are added some further particular desires* ([5 Aug.] 1647).

bounded the king without any countervailing restrictions on parliament.[29]

The heads of the proposals reflect Ireton's convictions, his plans, and his realism. By specifying the powers of parliament its pre-eminence is secured and substantive restraints are placed on the monarchy. At the same time, the explicit inclusion of limited episcopacy, the exclusion of a fixed check on the king's negative voice, and assurance of the royal family's 'personal rights' are retreats from the 14 June *Declaration*, which states that after parliament is reformed and the rights of the people secured by acts assented to by the king, 'the Rights of his Majestie . . . may be considered'.[30] The only known accounts of work on *The heads of the proposals* are reports of alterations responding to the king's objections,[31] and the changes are evidence of Ireton's belief that not only was Charles' support essential to a settlement: the monarchy was a vital component of a reformed constitution.

While Ireton and Cromwell vainly sought the king's acceptance of *The heads of the proposals*, agitators and their followers began moving away from king, generals and *The heads of the proposals* to join beckoning radicals from London. The preceding June, repudiated by parliament, those who would be nicknamed Levellers had turned to the army as the rising political power. On 2 June William Walwyn released the first Leveller petition that asked for a response to 'all the just and reasonable desires' of the army.[32] Walwyn, like Wildman and Petty, was in Reading in early July; all of them probably consorted with agitators. On 6 July agitators presented Fairfax with two papers that anticipated demands in the 16 July representation: the release of Leveller leaders and the disposition of the London militia. John Wildman also protested the militia command in a paper from 'the well affected' in London.[33] As Levellers moved toward the army to gain an ally with power, agitators turned to Levellers to

---

[29] *The constitutional documents of the Puritan revolution, 1625-1660*, ed. Samuel Rawson Gardiner (3rd edn, Oxford, 1906), nos. 57 (Oxford, 1643), 61 (Oxford and Uxbridge, 1644), 66 (Newcastle, 1646).

[30] Above, p. 178; cf. article 14 of *The heads of the proposals*. *The case of the armie truly stated* ([19 Oct.] 1647), 6, notes the backsliding; Ireton denied it (*CP,* I:358–9).

[31] Apparently, Ireton altered two articles opposed by the king before 16 July (Berkley, *Memoirs,* as in *Select tracts,* ed. Maseres, II:363). Cf.: Robert Huntingdon, *Sundry reasons,* as in ibid., II:400–2; John Ashburnham, *A narrative (*2 vols., London, 1830), II:90–2; [John Wildman], *Putney projects* (30 Dec. 1647), 13–15, 31, 39–41, and passim. No hard contemporary evidence refutes Ireton's primacy as principal author of *The heads of the proposals*.

[32] *The Writings of William Walwyn*, ed. Jack R. McMichael and Barbara Taft (Athens, GA, 1989), 27. For petition of 2 June, ibid., no. 19, 291–3, esp. 293.

[33] Ibid., 28–9; Clarke Ms. 41, fols. 164v–167v.

elucidate political aspirations. In October *The case of the armie truly stated* was presented to Fairfax, over the names of hitherto unmentioned 'Agents of five Regiments'.[34] Wildman and the articulate agitator Edward Sexby presumably contributed, but it is clearly the work of several hands – none of whom edited the patchy text to eliminate repetitions and integrate disruptive insertions.

The pervasive complaint of *The case of the armie is* the generals' failure to secure the demands set forth by the army. Specifically, the manifesto deplores the failure to purge the parliament and rectify grievances reiterated in the *Declaration* of 14 June and the *Remonstrances* of 23 June and 18 August.[35] Positive proposals include a firm date for dissolution of the Houses, an immediate purge, and a 'law paramount', unalterable by parliament, to ensure biennial parliaments elected by all the freeborn adult males except those who have lost freedom by delinquency. Additional reforms include religious freedom, equality before the law, reduction of all laws to 'one volume in the English tongue', monopolies, the excise and – inevitably – satisfaction of the army's material grievances.[36] It is evident that the settlement is to be imposed without consultation with the king, and the assertion that the power to legislate and govern resides in 'the peoples representors or Commons assembled in Parliament' indicates that the Commons' power is unrestricted by any negative voice.[37] The constitutional, economic and social proposals in *The case of the armie* were largely derived from reforms sought by Levellers.

Fairfax, recognising that *The case of the armie*'s departure from fundamental concepts in *The heads of the proposals* threatened army unity, immediately stated that *The case of the armie* 'should be presented to the Generall Councell',[38] which had been meeting every Thursday since 9 September in Putney Church. At the Council meeting on 21 October a committee was named to prepare a report on *The case of the armie*. Ireton led eight field officers who were joined by six officer-agitators and six soldier-agitators, including Sexby and Allen. On 27 October the committee was presented with a paper that was subsequently published as *An agreement of the people for a firme and present peace, upon grounds of common-right and freedome*.[39]

Less than a thousand words overall, *An agreement* is devoid of recriminations and grievances and the language is temperate and arresting –

[34] *The case of the armie*, t. p., 23–4.
[35] Ibid., 1–14, esp. 2 and, for *Declaration* of 14 June and *Remonstrances* of 23 June and 18 Aug., 4–7, 8, 10–11, 14; for failure to purge, 6–7, 10–11.
[36] *The case of the armie*, 14–20.   [37] Ibid., 15.   [38] Ibid., 24.
[39] Rushworth, *Historical collections*, VII:849–50. *An agreement of the people* . . . ([3 Nov.] 1647). For the week of 21–7 October, see Austin Woolrych, *Soldiers and statesmen* (Oxford, 1987), 209–15.

certainly not the work of the soldiers who presented it. The substance of the plan was common to all the Leveller penmen but the lucid phrasing of four concise articles and the eloquence of the preamble and conclusion suggest that the final draft was the work of William Walwyn.[40] When published 'As it was proposed by the Agents of the five Regiments of Horse', *An agreement* was followed by a letter 'For the . . . Free-born People of England' that responded to *The case of the armie*'s demand for a paramount law. Because 'No Act of Parliament is or can be unalterable', the people are asked to join the army and subscribe 'this Agreement Wherby the foundations of your freedomes provided in The Case, &c. shall be setled unalterably'.[41]

The first three articles of *An agreement* are clarified versions of specific proposals in *The case of the armie*: redistribution of parliamentary seats according to the number of inhabitants; dissolution of the present parliament by 10 September 1648; biennial parliaments. The heart of the Leveller programme is the final article, which states that the power of the representative 'is inferiour only to theirs who chuse them, and doth extend, without the consent or concurrence of any other person or persons' to all legislative and government power and to 'whatsoever is not expresly, or implyedly reserved by the represented to themselves'. The reserved rights 'are as followeth': freedom of religion; freedom from conscription for war; freedom from questions about conduct during the late war unless excepted by parliament; equality before the law; just laws. The essence of the rights is discernible among the grievances cited in two closely printed pages in *The case of the armie*.[42]

During the General Council debates at Putney from 28 October through 9 November the names of thirty-four speakers and forty-six additional committeemen were recorded; undoubtedly, unnamed observers also were present. Sexby introduced four soldiers, all of whom spoke, as well as Petty and Wildman, who described himself as the 'mouth' of the agents who signed *The case of the armie*.[43] Another effective proponent of soldiers' political rights was Thomas Rainborough, vice-admiral, colonel and member of Henry Marten's tiny republican faction in the Commons. Ireton, supported by Cromwell, led opposing 'Grandees', whom John Lilburne had described as 'proud selfe ended fellowes'.[44]

---

[40] *Writings of Walwyn*, 31, 535.
[41] *An agreement*, t.p., 7–10, esp. 9 (first letter), cf. 13 (second letter). Eight of the ten agents who signed both letters are among the ten agents who subscribed *The case of the armie*.
[42] *An agreement*, esp. art. 4. *The case of the armie*, 14–20, esp. 15, 18–20.
[43] *CP,* I:226–416, passim, esp. 226 (Sexby), 240 (Wildman).
[44] John Lilburne, *Jonah's cry out of the whales belly* ([26 July] 1647), 9.

However much all participants professed their commitment to army unity,[45] the gulf between grandee officers and proponents of *The case of the armie* and *An agreement* proved wide and deep. The fundamental difficulty was the clash between ideologues who desired government by a popularly elected representative prohibited from interfering with the native rights of the sovereign people and advocates of substantial reforms within the traditional structure of government: a king restrained by a parliament restricted by regular biennial elections by men of property.

When the Council assembled on 28 October the division was immediately exposed. Minutes after Sexby 'blasted' Ireton and Cromwell for negotiating with king and parliament, Ireton declared 'againe' his unqualified opposition to 'the destruction either of Parliament or Kinge'. At the same time, initially Ireton was less denunciatory of *An agreement* than was Cromwell. There were, said Ireton, 'thinges really good in itt . . . thinges that . . . I should rejoice to see obtayn'd'. Both generals pointed out that it was essential to consider whether there were pledges contrary to the thrust of *An agreement* among the army engagements so dear to authors of *The case of the armie*.[46] Wildman contended that 'unjust' engagements must give way to 'principles of right and freedome, and the lawes of nature and nations'. Ireton responded that no man could be free of an engagement because he decided it was unjust and warned that 'resort onely to the law of Nature' could destroy all property rights.[47]

Any fellowship engendered by the long prayer meeting that preceded debate on the 29th[48] was dissipated when *An agreement* was read again. Ireton, instead of addressing any of the articles he considered 'really good', immediately asked if the proposals reapportioning parliament 'according to the number of the inhabitants' meant that every male inhabitant 'is . . . to have an equall voice in the election of representors?' Colonel Rainborough assured Ireton that it meant just that, concluding that 'the poorest hee . . . is not att all bound . . . to that Governernent that hee hath not had a voice to putt himself under'.[49] Ireton responded that the right to choose representors was not a natural right; it was a constitutional right, available only to those who had 'a permanent fixed interest in this Kingdome . . . that is, the persons in whome all land lies, and those . . . in whome all trading lies'. Without 'this fundamentall parte of the civill constitution wee shall plainly goe to take away all property'. If, he later

[45] *Two letters from the agents of the five regiments* ([28 Oct.] 1647), 6–7; cf. Rushworth, *Historical collections*, VII:857. *CP,* I:238, 259, 288–9 (Cromwell), 246 (Rainborough), 277 (Chillenden), 288 (Everard and Audley).

[46] *CP,* I:228 (Sexby), 232–3, 241–3 (Ireton), 236–40 (Cromwell).

[47] Ibid., I:241, 260–1 (Wildman); cf. ibid., I:251–2 (Bedfordshire man). Ibid., I:241–2, 263 (Ireton).   [48] Ibid., I:280–6.

[49] Ibid., I: 299–300 (Ireton), 301, 304 (Rainborough); cf. 318 (Wildman).

observed, a man has the right to elect by a right of nature, 'by the same right of nature, hee hath the same right in any goods hee sees'.[50]

Ireton and Rainborough dominated the debate. Ireton argued with great skill and at great length. Rainborough was neither as learned nor as adroit as Ireton, but he was committed to the soldiers' political aspirations and the temper of the meeting was with him. Ireton converted no one, while his lofty view – that men fought 'that the will of one man should nott bee a law, butt that the law . . . should bee by a choice of persons' who were chosen by 'fix't men and setled men that had the interest of this Kingdome [in them]' – was not well received. Sexby, who had asserted that soldiers ventured their lives 'to recover our birthrights and privileges as Englishmen', responded that it appeared 'that wee have fought all this time for nothing'. Had they known, he continued bitterly, 'I believe you would have fewer under your command to have commanded.'[51]

Cromwell, ever mindful of unity, moved towards the middle ground, suggesting that all could agree that the suffrage 'might bee better than itt is' and again proposing a committee, which may have recalled Ireton to the need to blur rather than exacerbate the breach between generals and Levellers, who had evident support among junior officers as well as soldiers. Ireton pointed out that having fought 'for the liberty of Parliaments', he had been the first to press for dissolution of the present parliament and advocate regular elections with a more equal distribution of seats. Now, he asked for a committee to consider extending the vote to 'freemen, and men not given uppe to the wills of others'. Petty, who had supported inclusive suffrage, responded that he now conceived the reason why servants, apprentices and almsmen should be excluded.[52] It was a more meaningful exchange than was immediately apparent.

The debate returned to engagements and Ireton moved from an attack on *The case of the armie* as a threat to unity to the political demands: 'What else is there in this paper [but] that we have acted soe vigorously for [already]?' As for *An agreement*, 'there is butt one thing in this that hath nott bin insisted upon': reapportionment according to inhabitants rather than taxpayers. Ireton agreed that the king 'is bound by oath at his coronation' to accept laws passed by the Commons alone,[53] which opened the way to Petty's assertion that, since he had attended debate on *The heads of the proposals*, God had raised up 'a companie of men that doe stand uppe for the power of the House of Commons . . . and deny the negative voice

[50] Ibid., I:301–3, 307; cf. 327.   [51] Ibid., I:326–7; cf. 333 (Ireton), 322–3, 329–30 (Sexby).
[52] Ibid., I:328 (Cromwell), 333–4, 340–1 (Ireton), 342 and cf. 257–8, 294, 300, 312 (Petty).   [53] Ibid., I:346–51, esp. 348–51.

of King and Lords'. Wildman, after attacking *The heads of the proposals'* provisions for the powers of the king, returned to paramount law: 'There must bee', he said, 'a rule betweene the Parliament and the people, soe that the Parliament should know what they were intrusted to, and what they were nott.'[54] In the longest speech of the day Ireton defended the provisions for the king and underlined the necessity of parliament's participation in any settlement. The only alternatives were the subscription to the *Agreement of the people* by 'all the people to a man' or by the army's acting as the 'conclusive authority of the Kingedome' – which Ireton summarily rejected.[55]

Saturday, 30 October, is noteworthy for the work of the committee that replaced eleven of the eighteen men named on Thursday to confer with others about the *Agreement* and the army's engagements.[56] The new committee retained Cromwell, Ireton, Sir Hardress Waller and Nathaniel Rich, but Colonel Rainborough was joined by five new officer-agitators as well as the six soldier-agitators who again included Sexby and Allen.[57] The committee and the General Council met intermittently through 9 November.[58] There are no records of committee debates, but proposals prepared for the Council reveal that, despite the substantial Leveller majority, men strongly opposed during open debate were able to compromise in the quieter climate of the committee room.

Committee plans for parliament confirmed Ireton's contention that he had long urged proposals demanded by the agitators: dissolution of the existing parliament by 1 September 1648; future parliaments elected biennially to meet for no more than six months, beginning the first Thursday in April; between parliaments government by a council of state and committees named by the outgoing parliament. The limited power of the king was indicated in the provision that he could only call a 'Parliament extraordinary' on the advice of the council of state and such parliaments were to dissolve at least forty days before the next 'Biennial day'. 'Parliament extraordinary', 'Biennial day' and parliament's reform of constituencies 'according to some rule of equality' are all phrases in *The heads of the proposals*. The suffrage compromise reflected the exchange in the debate on the 29th: qualifications for electors and electees were to be determined by the present House, although the committee 'desired' that none who fought for or aided parliament

[54] Ibid., I:351–2 (Petty), 352–6, esp. 354–5 (Wildman).
[55] Ibid., I:356–61, esp. 360.
[56] The original committee (ibid., I:279) apparently never met (ibid., I:286–7).
[57] Ibid., I:363; Woolrych, *Soldiers and statesmen*, 245.
[58] *CP,* I:363–416, 440–2; *Perfect Occurences,* no. 44, 29 Oct.–5 Nov., 307–12; *A Perfect Diurnall,* no. 223, 1–8 November, 1792–6 (corrected pagination).

materially would be denied the vote while none who fought against parliament would be elector or electee until after the second biennial parliament.[59]

The Council meeting on Monday, 1 November, was well along before committee work was considered. Rainborough's motion for committee papers was ignored, and a dispute between Ireton and Wildman about a negative voice elicited Ireton's revelation that a committee meeting Sunday evening had worked out 'several Heads' that could resolve the problem. King and Lords would have veto power over laws affecting their persons or estates and the Lords would retain the right to trial by their peers.[60] Rainborough and Wildman would have none of it. To Ireton's arguments for maintaining the traditional constitution, Wildman responded with *An agreement*'s contention 'that all Governement bee in the Commons'. Rainborough accurately observed that since parliament began waging war aginst the king the Commons had broken the constitution 'againe and againe'.[61]

Before the Council met on Tuesday the committee produced additional articles, beginning with the assertion that the power of the Commons extended to the enactment and repeal of all laws. *An agreement* was further echoed with the inclusion of native rights reserved to the people.[62] Although parliament was to be the instrument of settlement and the structure of government was unchanged, the powers of king and Lords were barely visible and Levellers had advanced many of their primary concerns. Before the end of the day the General Council accepted the substance of all the recommendations and instructed the augmented committee to prepare a declaration including all the proposals for review by the Council and presentation to parliament.[63]

Committee and Council continued to meet, but a comprehensive declaration was never considered.[64] The dismay of the grandees at radical aspects of the settlement was expressed by Cromwell at the Council meeting on 8 November. The generals were no less concerned about rising agitation in the army and, ostensibly responding to Fairfax's plans for a rendezvous, the Council ordered officers and agitators back to their 'distempered' regiments. A committee named to prepare 'what shall bee offer'd to the Regiments att the Rendezvous' included Allen and Lockyer

[59] *CP*, I:363–7; above, pp. 184–5.
[60] Ibid., I:367–406, esp. 374 (Rainborough), 386–91 (Wildman and Ireton).
[61] Ibid., I:391–406, esp. 398 (Wildman), 402 (Rainborough).
[62] Ibid., I:407–9. Equality before the law was not included.
[63] Ibid., I:409–10; Rushworth, *Historical collections*, VII:861; *Perfect Occurences*, no. 44, 310–12; *A Perfect Diurnall*, no. 223, 2–5 Nov. (mispaged).
[64] *CP*, I:440–2; Rushworth, *Historical collections*, VII:861–4; Woolrych, *Soldiers and statesmen*, 259–62.

and four officer-agitators, but Cromwell and Ireton headed the committee with ten likely supporters.[65] The resulting remonstrance was all but certainly completed by Ireton.

Explicit and forceful, *A Remonstrance from . . . Fairfax and his council of warre* was directed to the soldiers. The address states that unauthorised 'Agents', guided by persons not in the army, have spread falsehoods about the lord general and senior commanders and endeavoured to distract and divide the army. Unless discipline is restored the general will resign. If disorder ceases, the general 'will live and die with the Army' to rectify specific grievances of the soldiers, secure regular parliaments and 'render the House of Commons (as near as may be) an equal Representative of the People that are to elect'. 'The People' were not defined, but at three mid-November rendezvous dissension was quickly extinguished. Fairfax was cheered, officers and men accepted the *Remonstrance* and willingly subscribed an appended engagement expressing satisfaction with the generals' programme and promising obedience to superior officers.[66] The ready concurrence of the soldiery indicates that Leveller ideology had not penetrated the ranks to a meaningful extent.[67] Leveller concepts were too abstruse for soldiers primarily concerned with material grievances that could most effectively be alleviated by parliament responding to pressure from generals.

The unity of senior commanders and the lower ranks was not replicated between the contestants in the Council debates. Unlike Reading, where little was recorded that is of enduring interest but open discussion eased the way toward transient agreement with *The heads of the proposals,* the remarkable debates at Putney did not reduce the fundamental cleavage between proponents of reform within the established constitution and idealists committed to government by a single House empowered by the sovereign people. As Wildman observed on 1 November: 'I conceive the difference is as wide as ever.'[68] Nevertheless, however inconclusive, the meetings at Putney are remarkable for the serious consideration of far-reaching proposals. If senior commanders were not persuaded by Leveller argument, junior officers absorbed much of the democratic doctrine – which would be evident a year later when another army council would again try to construct a tenable constitution.

[65] *CP,* I:411–13; Rushworth, *Historical collections*, VII:866.
[66] *A remonstrance from his excellency Sir Thomas Fairfax and his council of war* (14 Nov. 1647), reprinted in *OPH*, XVI:341–5. Woolrych, *Soldiers and statesmen*, ch. 11.
[67] *Papers from the armie* (23 Oct. 1647), 4, doubts 'that there can be in the whole Armie foure hundred men, (. . . amongst one and twenty thousand) that trouble us, or dissent from what is the generall sense of the Army'.   [68] *CP,* I:393.

The second civil war altered the atmosphere and reshuffled alliances. The conflict was brutal and embittering – nowhere more so than at Colchester, where the eleven-week siege ended with two immediate executions supervised by an implacable Ireton.[69] On 17 August, ten days before the siege ended, the Commons had revoked the vote of no addresses to the king that Ireton had strongly supported the preceding January.[70] Ireton had distrusted Charles since the king's escape from Hampton Court in November 1647; his misgivings crystallised by the end of the second war. Parliament's renewal of negotiations with the king convinced Ireton that the army would have to intervene to secure a just peace, but he was not prepared to move immediately.[71] Since Putney, Ireton had recognised that a *rapprochement* with Leveller proposals would be essential to political action by a unified army, yet he may have been disheartened by the prospect of armed intervention against parliament as well as by Fairfax's reluctance to accept its necessity. In September, Ireton's request for a discharge from the army was rejected.[72] Shortly thereafter he withdrew to Windsor, where he prepared a cogent *Remonstrance* that justifies bringing the king to trial by invoking the people's safety, the king's breach of contract and duty, and the 'generall law of reason or Nations' – all witnessed by God's support for parliament's victory in battle.[73]

Lilburne established communication with Ireton during the drafting of the *Remonstrance* and secured the inclusion of plans for another *Agreement of the people*, assurance of inviolable native rights, and consideration of demands in the relatively mild Leveller petition of 11 September.[74] In mid-November Levellers and City Independents agreed that 'the well-affected in every County' would draw up a constitution of government. After several conferences among Levellers, Independents and army grandees, before the end of the month this plan was abandoned and Ireton agreed to Lilburne's proposal for a draft *Agreement* drawn up by a committee of sixteen consisting of four men chosen by and from each of four groups: City Independents; the council of officers;

---

[69] Ibid., II:31–9 (28 Aug. 1648).
[70] *CJ* V:673–4 (17 Aug.); *LJ* X:454 (24 Aug.). *CJ* V:415–16 (3 Jan.); *LJ* IX:662 (15 Jan.). Clement Walker, *The compleat history of independency* (London, 1661), 71.
[71] Berkley, *Memoirs*, as in *Select tracts*, ed. Maseres, II:383–4. Ludlow, *Memoirs*, ed. Firth, I:203–5.
[72] William Clarke, 27 Sept., Clarke Ms. 114, fol. 80; Ireton's letter has not been recovered.
[73] *A remonstrance of . . . Fairfax . . . and of the generall councell of officers* ([22 Nov.] 1648), esp. 4–6, 16–18, 21–2, 61–4; assented to by council of officers, 16 Nov. (*CP*, II:54); presented to Commons, 20 Nov. (*CJ* VI:81).
[74] Lilburne, *Legall fundamentall liberties*, 29–31; *A remonstrance*, 65–70. *To the . . . commons of England . . . the humble petition of divers well affected persons* (11 Sept. 1648).

'honest friends' in the House; and those 'nicknamed Levellers'. During the first ten days of December the army entered Westminster, Colonel Pride purged the Commons, and the drafting committee survived sharp clashes between Lilburne and Ireton, 'principally about Liberty of Conscience, and the Parliaments punishing where no law provides'. On 11 December a text was submitted to the council of officers meeting at Whitehall, where they 'appointed a speedy debate and consideration' of the draft.[75]

The men who attended the Council during the subsequent debates were as diverse as any deliberative assembly in the century. There were no private soldiers, probably because Ireton believed that officer-agitators who attended would defend radical interests – and be less divisive than soldier-agitators had been at Putney. At Whitehall, in addition to uncountable observers, the 160 men recorded as speakers, committeemen or present included thirty-six civilians. Four Levellers – Lilburne, Richard Overton, Walwyn and Wildman – attended on 14 and/or 18 December. At least six clerics spoke on the 14th: Hugh Peter, Joshua Sprigge, Edward Walford and Thomas Collier, chaplains; John Goodwin and Philip Nye, prominent Independents who took opposite positions. William Erbury, a Seeker, spoke six times in January. The officers, who voted on proposed changes and approved the final version of the *Agreement*, counted men from every commissioned rank – generals to subalterns – and their social profile ranged from greater gentry to small tradesmen and men from obscure families who had risen through the merit system in the New Model.[76] The *Agreement* was considered at twelve recorded meetings between 14 December and 15 January.[77] Surviving records include only two reports that are more than fragmentary, but available accounts, together with seven voting lists concerning reserved rights, reveal that junior officers were not pressed to support their commanders. Of the seventy-three officers who cast votes, forty-one were junior officers, all of whom appear to have acted independently.[78]

The committee draft owed much to debates and committee work at

---

[75] Lilburne, *Legall fundamentall liberties*, 30–5. Rushworth, *Historical collections*, VII:1358-61 (11 Dec.). The officers' appointees to the committee of sixteen were named on 28 November (*CP,* II:61).

[76] Barbara Taft, 'The Council of Officers' *Agreement of the people*, 1648/9', *HJ* 28 (1985), 169–85, esp. 174–5, where the figures for clerics are incorrect; *CP,* II:73–132, passim; ibid., 171–80.

[77] *CP,* II:71–186 passim (14 Dec.–13 Jan.); Rushworth, *Historical collections*, VII:1392 (15 Jan.).

[78] Barbara Taft, 'Voting lists of the Council of Officers, December 1648', *BIHR* 52 (1979), 138–54, esp. 142–50.

Putney, which had drawn on *The heads* as well as the 1647 *Agreement*.[79] The present parliament is to be dissolved on or before the last day of April; future Representatives are to be elected every two years; the franchise is extended to adult, male householders who pay poor relief and subscribe to the *Agreement*; the Representative 'of three or four hundred' is reapportioned and the distribution is established.[80] A council of state appointed *by* the Representative is to manage affairs when the legislature is not in session. Essential to Levellers and their allies was the section reserving eight explicit rights to the people. The Representative is forbidden to: (1) interfere with the religious practice of any professing Christianity; (2) impress for war; (3) call any person to account for actions during the wars, except for designated royalists and men accountable for public funds; (4 and 5) enact or continue any law applied unequally; (6) punish without a law or contrary to law; (7) name representatives to lucrative office; (8) 'take away any of the foundations of Common right, liberty, or safety contained in the Agreement'.

There is no record of rancour over secular provisions that were modified,[81] while religion, which had not been debated at Reading or Putney, was the subject of much contention at Whitehall, where the debate on 14 December is scarcely less notable than the franchise debate that distinguished Putney. In response to the question 'Whether the Magistrate have or ought to have any compulsive and restrictive power in matters of religion', John Goodwin spoke bluntly: 'God hath nott invested any power in a Civill magistrate in matters of religion.' Ireton countered that the purpose of government is 'the preserving of humane society in peace', and to this end the magistrate requires authority in spiritual as well as civil matters. No man should be asked to worship against his conscience, but the magistrate must be empowered to punish those who sin against the first table. Chaplains, captains and John Wildman disputed the point. Philip Nye employed some hair-splitting to support Ireton, who cited biblical examples of civil restraint.[82] No agreement was reached and the question was referred to a committee that included officers, clergymen, City independents and Wildman.[83]

At Whitehall as at Putney Ireton led a minority. On 21 December he was defeated, 27:17, on the proposal to give the representative final

[79] 'An agreement of the people of England and the places therewith incorporated for a secure and present peace upon grounds of common right and freedome', Clarke Ms. 16, fols. 31–5. Above, pp. 180, 183.

[80] The distribution list is not in the manuscript draft but 300 constituencies are listed in the text published by Lilburne: *Foundations of freedom; or an agreement of the people* ([15 Dec.] 1648), 4–7.   [81] Taft, 'Voting lists', 140–1; Taft, 'Council of Officers', 175–6.

[82] *CP,* II:71–132, esp. 74–5, 115–18 (Goodwin), 75–7, 120–1 (Wildman), 102, 111, 118–20, 130 (Nye), 79, 107, 113–14, 122, 128–9 (Ireton).   [83] Ibid., II:72, 134–6.

judgement in 'Morall' as well as in 'civil' matters, although he carried a majority opposed to including religion among the reserved rights, 37:12.[84] The second vote enabled him to influence a compromise in the committee that drew up a new article on religion, and the final text of the article is some distance from the draft submitted on 11 December. In the Officers' *Agreement* the magistrate is empowered to confute 'whatever is contrary to sound Doctrine' and, while none are compelled to attend the state church, toleration for Christians does not extend to popery or prelacy.[85] Ireton was defeated in five of the seven votes on the reserves which – except for removal of religion to a separate article and deletion of the fifth reserve (similar to the fourth) – are essentially the same in the officers' text as in the December draft. Ireton vainly opposed the reserve forbidding punishment without or contrary to existing law, perhaps fearing that it would impede punishment of the king and royalist leaders. However, he accepted majority decisions and again demonstrated his understanding of process by working in committee and council to secure a practicable settlement that officers would 'resolve to maintaine'.[86]

The compromise *Agreement* was a viable constitution that was never strongly supported by those who assembled it or those to whom it was addressed. Parliament had no desire to govern constrained by a constitution that decreed biennial elections by an expanded electorate. Nor was the collective body of individuals that Levellers termed 'the people' sufficiently united to assume the responsibility of ultimate sovereignty. Leveller leaders subsequently said that, despite some shortcomings, they would not have opposed the Officers' *Agreement* 'had it been put in execution'.[87] Lilburne, however, had left the council after one day of debate and published his version of the committee draft. Six months later, asserting that the draft had been 'absolute and finall', ready for subscription 'without any more adoe', he bitterly denounced Ireton for securing alterations.[88]

Ireton, since June 1647 the most purposeful proponent of a new constitution, lost the concentration essential to action. Unwonted deference permeates the 'humble Petition' that Ireton prepared to introduce the

---

[84] Ibid., II:139–40 (21 Dec.); Taft, 'Voting lists', 148.

[85] *A petition from ... the general council of officers ... concerning the draught of an agreement of the people ... together with the said agreement presented Saturday, Jan 20* ([20 Jan.] 1649), art. 9; cf. 'An agreement', Clarke Ms. 16, fol. 34. Lilburne deleted 'professing Christianity' in *Foundations of freedom,* 11.

[86] Taft, 'Voting lists', 146–9; Taft, 'Council of Officers', 178–9; *CP,* II:156–7 (5th reserve and committee 'to consider of a forme of conclusion and subscription'). *A petition ... with the said agreement,* articles 8, 9, 10.

[87] John Lilburne, William Walwyn, Thomas Prince, and Richard Overton, *A manifestation* (14 April 1649), 7.

[88] Lilburne, *Legall fundamentall liberties,* 35. For the improbability of Lilburne's contention, see Taft, 'Council of officers', 173.

Agreement to the Rump.[89] No rhetorical humility this time. The absence of any demand for approval of the *Agreement* is a startling contrast to the vigorous *Remonstrance* that had challenged parliament two months before. There is evidence that Ireton's resolve was shaken by Elizabeth Poole, a visionary who on 29 December told the council of 'the presence of God with the Army' and a week later urged the officers to abandon the *Agreement*, which would surrender 'out of your owne hands' the power entrusted to the army by God. Ireton received Mrs. Poole with respect, and it is probable that he also was influenced by millenarian saints such as Thomas Harrison.[90] On 13 January Ireton asked the Council to approve the constitution in order to place power in the hands of those chosen by the people until 'the breaking forth of the power of God amongst men to make such formes needlesse'.[91] Recourse to godly guidance was inevitable for advocates of fundamental reform overtaken by the uncertainty engendered by the imminent trial of the king. On 20 January, the day the Rump received the *Agreement*, Charles's trial began. Ten days later he was executed, and on 7 February the Rump abolished monarchy and vested executive power in a council of state appointed by the House. Ireton was rejected as a member of the council of state[92] and the *Agreement* passed into limbo.

How far had Ireton moved politically? Driven by expediency, he moved a considerable distance. Throughout the wars Ireton fought for religious toleration and a substantial shift of power to a restricted parliament. He promoted precise constitutional proposals in the politicised army where his skilful pen and ready speech reveal an unusual politician: immensely able, occasionally unwise, never duplicitous. At Reading and Putney he defended government by king, Lords and Commons – reordered and restrained yet tried and familiar. After Putney Ireton's realism surfaced as he endeavoured to resolve the tension between individual liberty and a parliament that retained sufficient power to govern. To secure unity with junior officers and men in the ranks he moved steadily leftward, accepting reserved individual rights demanded by Levellers and abandoning the Upper House and a monarchy all but despoiled by a perfidious king. Ireton was prepared to yield much to secure a new settlement before the Rump dissolved itself. Otherwise, he told Cromwell in January, 'If the generality of people could see the end of the Parliament, [they] would . . . looke for a succession of new Parliaments in the old way and old forme of a Kinge agen.'[93] Eleven years later Ireton's prediction was realised.

---

[89] *A petition . . . with the said agreement*, 3–6. The petition was foreshadowed in Ireton's speech on 13 January *(CP,* II:175–6).

[90] *CP,* II:150–4, 163–70 (Mrs Poole). Ibid., 151, 154 (Ireton), 183–6 (Harrison); cf. Ireton at Putney, ibid., I:256–7, 295–8.   [91] Ibid., II:176–7.

[92] *CJ* VI:122 (20 Jan.), 133 (7 Feb.), 141 (14 Feb.).   [93] *CP,* II:170–1 (6 Jan.).

Part 3

Levellers and 'Levellerism' in history and historiography

10   'The poorest she': women and citizenship in early modern England

Patricia Crawford

What does it mean to be absent? There is, as every reader of them knows, a total silence about women's political rights at the Putney debates.[1] To attempt to interrogate women's absence may seem bizarre: why discuss women, when the focus is the debates of a purely male gathering of officers and soldiers? This chapter argues that questions about women's participation in early modern political life were not unthinkable, that the debaters at Putney were using categories that could well have included women, and yet there was no mention of that part of the English nation.

Women could be citizens in seventeenth-century England.[2] The category 'citizens' sometimes excluded women because it could refer to men who bore arms for the defence of their country, but citizens could also be people who lived in a certain territory, the inhabitants.[3] Women were sometimes citizens, 'inhabitants' who had civic duties, as we shall see. Furthermore, according to some, the church itself was a collection of citizens. As an anonymous author explained in 1641, the word church 'doth primarily and properly, signifie a convention of Citizens called from their houses by the publique Cryer'.[4]

---

[1] I wish to thank to Sara Mendelson, with whom I have worked for the last fifteen years on a study of women in early modern England. She has generously shared her research, and many of the ideas in this paper have been developed in discussion with her. Thanks for general discussion about women and citizenship to Ruth Abbey and Philippa Maddern; for comments on this chapter, to Laura Gowing, Ann Hughes, Katharine Massam, Jane Long, Michael Mendle, Maureen Perkins, Judith Richards, Pamela Sharpe and participants at the Folger Conference, 'The Putney Debates 1647', especially Philip Baker, Tim Harris and Lois Schwoerer.

[2] Sara Mendelson and Patricia Crawford, *Women in early modern England, 1550–1720* (Oxford, 1998), 49–58.

[3] http://www.chass.utoronto.ca:8080/english/emed/emedd.html, Early Modern English Dictionaries Database, Thomas Thomas, [Latin-English Dictionary] 1587, TT 87 Oxford, 7387982: 'A citizen, both the man and the woman, of the same citie or countrie: our countrieman, a Burgesse, a freeman'. Citizens and burgesses had voices in parliament; Sir Thomas Smith, *De republica anglorum. A discourse on the commonwealth of England*, ed. L. Alston (Cambridge, 1906), 41–2.

[4] *The presbyteriall government examined; wherein the weaknesse of their grounds are unfolded* (London, 1641), 7.

Political history in general has proved remarkably impervious to feminist questions about women's participation: indeed, Joan Scott has referred to political history as 'the stronghold of resistance'.[5] Sadly, political historians of the early modern period, with certain notable exceptions, have ignored questions of gender.[6] This chapter investigates some of the dominant concepts of historical knowledge.[7] I argue that the exclusion of women from historical accounts occurs in part because of the ways in which historical topics are defined, and institutions, such as parliament or the Church, are selected for analysis. Most institutions of government have been male dominated, so when historians and political theorists write about them, they focus on those who were present, namely men, rather than on those who were absent, women. Thus if a monarch was female, her rule will be discussed, but the broader question of how gender affects all monarchical authority is usually ignored. Similarly, historians may note the presence of women in collective actions, but frequently they convey the impression that women were add-on-extras. Yet women's political agency and the cultural category of gender were in a dynamic relationship. Gender was an important part of social identity, and one whose social parameters and meanings were closely scrutinised by contemporaries; early modern culture endlessly elaborated the distinctions between women and men. Although gender was not the sole category that determined women's social roles, other categories that affected women, such as class and religious affiliation, were themselves inflected by gender.

Rather than beginning with the existing historiographical categories of seventeenth-century political history, and attempting to add a few individual women, this chapter deliberately focuses on women as political agents. It offers another perspective on the political rights of ordinary people that were debated at Putney. The first part of this chapter discusses how we might rethink the subject of politics and women; the second examines very briefly some of the political activities of women,

---

[5] Scott's observation, originally made in 1986, remains true in 2001; Joan Wallach Scott, 'Gender: a useful category of historical analysis' in her *Gender and the politics of history* (New York, 1988), 28–50, at 46; Sara Mendelson, 'The sixteenth and seventeenth centuries: dark ages of women's history', unpublished seminar paper, University of Oxford, 27 January 1981.

[6] Among those exceptions are David Underdown, *Revel, riot, and rebellion. Politics and culture in England, 1603–1660* (Oxford, 1985); Lois Schwoerer, 'Women and the Glorious Revolution', *Albion* 18 (1986), 195–218; Linda Colley, *Britons. Forging the nation 1707–1837* (New Haven and London, 1992); Cynthia Herrup, 'The patriarch at home: the trial of the second earl of Castlehaven for rape and sodomy', *History Workshop Journal* 41 (1996), 1–18; Hilda L. Smith (ed.), *Women writers and the early modern British political tradition* (Cambridge, 1998).

[7] See Lorraine Code, *Rhetorical spaces. Essays on gendered locations* (New York, 1995), 154–5 and passim.

chiefly those of middling and lower social status, to establish the historical context of their claims to citizenship. The conclusion returns to the question of the rights of 'the poorest she', and discusses how women's activities as citizens contexualise the franchise debates at Putney.

Gender and politics

How the history of women and citizenship should be theorised in the seventeenth century is problematic. When people spoke of the franchise or of public participation, they were not usually thinking of women. By the early nineteenth century, when the political rights of citizens to the franchise were again under debate, the gendered nature of the public sphere was so firmly established that the idea that women could be citizens was not generally entertained. Furthermore, by the nineteenth and early twentieth centuries, there seems to have been collective amnesia about women having voted in parliamentary elections in the seventeenth century, although some historians of women recovered substantial evidence about women's rights in the medieval period.[8]

For most twentieth-century historians, including A. S. P. Woodhouse and C. B. Macpherson, the Putney debates had nothing to do with women or their rights: women were not 'men', 'citizens' or 'people' for voting purposes. Woodhouse denied women's involvement in the Women's Petition of 1649 with both a trivialising heading – 'The Female of the Species' – and a footnote.[9] Although M. A. Gibb had found John Lilburne's 'inclusion of woman in his charter of freedom' to be of interest, Macpherson dismissed her comments in a footnote.[10] Certainly no questions about the voting rights of the female sex were raised at Putney. As Keith Thomas observed over thirty years ago, no one so far as we know pleaded for female suffrage during the entire seventeenth century.[11] It is highly unlikely that we *will* find anyone explicitly discussing the female franchise; that was not a seventeenth-century question. The rights of 'the female sex' were only rarely an issue for anyone.

---

[8] Mary Bateson, *Borough customs* (Selden Society, 2 vols., London, 1904 and 1906); Charlotte Carmichael Stopes, *British freewomen* (London, 1894); Rose Graham, 'The civic position of women at common law before 1800' in her *English ecclesiastical studies* (London, 1929), 360–77.

[9] Woodhouse noted in a footnote to the Petition of Women (5 May 1649) that 'It is improbable that this petition was actually composed by the women'; *P&L*, 367.

[10] M. A. Gibb, *John Lilburne. The Leveller. A Christian democrat* (London, 1947), 174; C. B. Macpherson, *The political theory of possessive individualism* (Oxford, 1962), 296n.

[11] Keith Thomas, 'Women and the civil war sects' (1958) in Trevor Aston (ed.), *Crisis in Europe, 1560–1660* (London, 1965), 332–57, at 339. Thomas was one of the first early modern historians to address questions concerning women, and his essays have been enormously influential.

What was at issue during the seventeenth century were rights generally. Many rights in England in 1640 were more properly privileges linked to the ownership of property. Privileges were usually, but not always, based on freehold, which was thought to confer independence and 'a permanent fixed interest' in public affairs.[12] Yet, increasingly, concepts of rights that adhered to the individual were developed. Rights varied according to the context: sometimes they were rights to do something, such as to be a forty-shilling freeholder who elected members of parliament; at other times, rights were more general, negative rights, such as not to be murdered.[13] At the Putney debates, speakers disputed the basis of political rights – property ownership or birthright – and subsequent historians have argued over the degree of radicalism in the soldiers' claims for inclusion in the franchise. Challenging the view of the Leveller claims to universal adult male suffrage, Macpherson argued that the disqualification of servants and alms-takers from the franchise excluded large numbers, thereby reducing the Levellers to possessive individualists, *petits bourgeois*.[14] Subsequently others, particularly Keith Thomas, argued for the genuine democracy of Leveller claims.[15]

The extent to which women were included in the franchise, either as rights-bearing property holders or as independent individuals, is an important question. In this respect, women's citizenship in early modern society was always ambiguous. Several terms are significant in the discussions of female political rights: man and people, freeborn and subject, and finally woman. During the early modern period, there was a legal attempt to clarify language, and to categorise more firmly. For reasons which are not known, much of this classificatory work took the form of the explicit exclusion of women.

The category 'man' or 'mankind' sometimes included women and sometimes excluded them. Sometimes women had birthrights as human beings, as part of 'mankind'; sometimes not. Thus, discussion of 'man's nature' could sometimes refer to human nature, sometimes to that of males only. 'Man' might include women, but the reverse was never true. The legal ambiguity of the term 'man' has persisted into the twentieth

---

[12] *P&L*, 54. See also Jack P. Greene, *All men are created equal. Some reflections on the character of the American Revolution* (Oxford, 1976), 12–17. For a discussion of property as absolute individual ownership, see G. E. Aylmer, 'The meaning and definition of "property" in seventeenth-century England', *Past and Present* 86 (1980), 87–97.

[13] Philip Pettit, *Republicanism: a theory of freedom and government* (Oxford, 1997).

[14] Macpherson, *Possessive individualism*.

[15] Keith Thomas, 'The Levellers and the franchise' in G. E. Aylmer (ed.), *The interregnum. The quest for settlement 1646–1660* (London, 1972), 57–78; Christopher Thompson, 'Maximilian Petty and the Putney debate on the franchise', *Past and Present* 88 (1980), 63–9.

century, despite the attempt to clarify the term in the 1850 Acts Interpretation Act. (The Act declared that 'words importing the masculine gender' were deemed to include females, but women's entitlement to rights was still resisted.)[16]

Were women 'people'? The question was important because people – human beings who were free – had rights. At Putney, the question of property in the person, the inalienable birthrights of free men (as against bondmen or slaves), were discussed. Not all men were 'people' all of the time; sometimes only male heads of household. As Sir Robert Filmer observed in a different context, 'Those that are the people this minute, are not the people the next minute.'[17] Seventeenth-century debates focused on whether 'people' needed to be 'free' in order to exercise their rights. Historians' debates subsequently have been about the meaning of freedom and independence.[18]

Could women be free? It was generally agreed, as a point of pride, that women born in England were not bond but were freeborn, with a property in their persons, as men were. Although there were more people under bondage than Englishmen liked to admit, political commentators from Sir Thomas Smith to Sir Robert Filmer and John Lilburne all claimed that women were born free.[19] As Filmer observed, virgins 'by birth have as much natural freedom as any other and therefore ought not to lose their liberty without their own consent'.[20] Furthermore, in 1583 Sir Thomas Smith had already noted that women in England who were in service had not lost their liberty. Female servants were not under villeinage or serfdom; they were not slaves, 'but serve for the time for daily ministrie . . . and be for other matters in libertie as full free men and women'.[21] In 1646 Lilburne's reading of the creation story made Adam and Eve 'the earthly original foundation' of all subsequent men and women, 'who are, and were, by nature all equal and alike in power, dignity, authority, dominion, or magisterial power one over or above another'.[22] If women were by nature equal to men, how did they lose their freedom? Women lost their liberty when they consented to marriage and placed themselves in subordination to their husbands. Thus the law

---

[16] Jocelynne A. Scutt, *Women and the law. Commentary and materials* (Sydney, 1990), 27–9.

[17] Sir Robert Filmer, *Patriarcha and other writings*, ed. Johann P. Sommerville (Cambridge, 1991), 142.

[18] Macpherson, *Possessive individualism*, discusses Leveller views that man was free, and that property in one's person required certain rights (p. 142). 'All these civil and religious rights were demanded for every one, however dependent by reason of sex or employment. Women were created human beings . . . they were not slaves' (pp. 142–3).

[19] Diarmaid MacCullouch, 'Bondmen under the Tudors', in Claire Cross, David Loades and J. J. Scarisbrick (eds.), *Law and government under the Tudors* (Cambridge, 1988), 91–109, at 91–3. [20] Filmer, *Patriarcha*, 142. [21] Smith, *De republica anglorum*, 137–9.

[22] John Lilburne, *The free-man's freedom vindicated* (London, 1646), in *P&L*, 317.

deemed that married women lacked a property in their own persons, although single women remained legally independent.[23]

To be a 'subject' also varied in meaning. Everyone born in England of an English father was a subject of the Crown. Men, women and children: all were subjects. As subjects, women enjoyed the right to petition the monarch, the parliament and powerful individuals.[24] Nevertheless, there was an extra dimension for women in being 'subject': wives were 'subject' to their husbands.[25]

Finally, the very category 'woman', like the category 'man', was ambiguous, but in a different way. 'Woman' interacted with all four categories previously discussed – man, people, free and subject. Like 'man', 'woman' was not always inclusive; social and marital status could at times exclude. Some women (like some men) enjoyed rights as property holders; they possessed a permanent fixed interest. As we have seen, a woman's rights varied according to her marital status. Whereas to be married and head of household usually improved a man's position as a citizen, by consenting to marriage, to subjection, a woman lost her property rights, some natural rights, and her separate legal existence.[26] Only a single woman or widow, a feme sole, in possession of property had the requisite independence to be deemed free.

Conflicting ideas about doctrines of rights, marital status and property were all interrelated, influencing women's legal and social positions as citizens. Early modern people knew that women's social and legal position was anomalous, despite the contemporary rhetoric about female subordination, so they took care when discussing questions of people's rights to define whom they meant.[27] If contemporaries did not specify whether or not women were included, we may have to turn to the historical context in order to understand women's position more clearly.

Macpherson assumed that women were excluded from the discussion of rights during the 1640s because the Levellers accepted the argument that a man, as husband, father and master, would answer for his

---

[23] Some women later alluded to the issue of slavery when discussing the female married condition: Moira Ferguson, *Subject to others. British women writers and colonial slavery, 1670–1834* (New York, 1992), 24–5.

[24] The *CSPD* records show a long history of women as petitioners; Mendelson and Crawford, *Women in early modern England*, 397.

[25] Margaret Cavendish, duchess of Newcastle, *CCXI sociable letters* (London, 1664), 27.

[26] For single women, see Mendelson and Crawford, *Women in early modern England*, 165–72. In the nineteenth century, Helen Taylor argued that the denial of the franchise to propertied single women was illegal: Helen Taylor, *The claim of Englishwomen to the suffrage, constitutionally considered* (1867; reprinted Garland, New York, 1978).

[27] Cf. Judith Richards, Lotte Mulligan and John K. Graham, ' "Property" and "people": political usages of Locke and some contemporaries', *Journal of the History of Ideas* 42 (1981), 29–51.

household.[28] However, he erred in taking no account of the varied legal position of women; he ignored the feme sole. Seventeenth-century people knew that a propertied single woman could exercise some of her own political rights. Women's rights as citizens emerged, as did those of ordinary men, in a series of relational contexts. 'Citizens' defined their rights through their interactions with others. Their direct actions challenged the claims of political elites to monopolise political power and blurred the boundaries between the public political world and the everyday world of the household. The fluidity of boundaries allowed women some political agency.

Furthermore, the women's actions challenged the discursive construction of the gender order in early modern England. Just as E. P. Thompson defined class relations as interactive, made by the relationships between those above and below,[29] so a range of social relationships between women and men defined the gender order of early modern England. Women were ideally subordinate and obedient to their husbands, responsible for the upbringing of children and care of the household. Yet as Margaret Sommerville has brilliantly shown, ideas about sex and subordination were shot through with contradictions.[30] In certain circumstances, women were expected to disobey. Women's consciences in religious matters could lead them to defy their husbands.[31] Religious belief could take them into public confrontation with the ecclesiastical authorities. A few, such as Anne Askew or Margaret Clitheroe, might resist even to death, and be recognised by their co-religionists as martyrs.

Contemporaries recognised women's rights and duties in a range of public situations. Women's continuing presence in discussion of public issues (despite male claims to monopolise these) established alternative traditions, which were important for women and were also important for society in general, in keeping public issues open for participation by a wider social group. Class, property, custom and belief might each allow claims to female political participation.

Women's activities as citizens

Because women, unlike men, did not write about their ideas of citizenship, the complex surviving evidence about their public participation as

[28] Macpherson, *Possessive individualism*, 126, 296n.
[29] E. P. Thompson, *The making of the English working class* (Harmondsworth, 1968).
[30] Margaret R. Sommerville, *Sex and subjection. Attitudes to women in early-modern society* (1995).
[31] Patricia Crawford, 'Public duty, conscience and women in early modern England', in John Morrill, Paul Slack and Daniel Woolf (eds.), *Public duty and private conscience in seventeenth-century England. Essays presented to G. E. Aylmer* (Oxford, 1993), 57–76.

citizens needs to be interrogated. Social history requires an investigation of the evidence about deeds as well as an analysis of political thought. Yet even accounts of women's actions are to be read with caution, reflecting as they do many of their authors' stereotypical notions of womanhood.

Women of the middling and lower ranks engaged in a range of formal and informal political activities in seventeenth-century England.[32] Being a citizen involved more than the franchise, for parliament was an irregular part of government early in the seventeenth century. Much political activity was at the level of the county, cities and parishes. Local communities were involved in collecting parish rates for the relief of the poor, and disciplining parishioners for their behaviour. The office of constable rotated in many villages, and many treatises on the constable discussed women's eligibility for the office.[33] The very care with which women's ineligibility was sketched out suggests that the matter needed definition. As E.W., *The exact constable*, explained in 1682, no women 'whether Maids or Widows, though House-keepers, and dwelling in Houses, whose Inhabitants used to serve' were fit to be made constables.[34] By 1700 it was deemed unwise to rotate the office by tenure of houses, 'so it may fall upon a woman, (which is not sufferable)'.[35] In towns and cities, civic authorities controlled markets, streets and general order. Even in the eighteenth century, there are records of women serving as churchwardens, and overseers of the poor.[36] Rights to the franchise, which were seldom cogently considered, were only one set of obligations and rights among many.

The most significant formal right of a citizen was the franchise. During the first half of the seventeenth century, as Derek Hirst has shown, there are a number of references to women voting in parliamentary elections.[37] Although it is not always clear on what basis voting occurred, it seems likely that it was confined to single women and widows. Their right to

---

[32] Note that the term 'political' can have an extremely wide meaning. Here I am speaking of public activity (which begs other questions re public/private).

[33] Joan Kent, *The English village constable, 1580–1642. A social and administrative study* (Oxford, 1986), 59. In Norfolk a widow whose husband had 'watched' refused to supply a watch although she had two houses; Norfolk RO, AYL 1/347, ND.

[34] E. W., *The exact constable* (6th edn, London, 1682), 12; *The compleat constable* (London, 1700), 7.

[35] *The compleat constable* (1700), 7; also, [R.G.], *The compleat constable* (4th edn, London, 1710), 8.

[36] Devon Record Office, Farway Churchwardens' Book, DRO 67A/PW1; Kilmington Churchwardens' Book 1721–1828, DRO 5301A/PW1; Sidbury, DRO 2096/P01; Ugborough, Quarter Sessions Order Book, 1697. Thanks to Pamela Sharpe who kindly supplied these references.

[37] Derek Hirst, *The representative of the people? Voters and voting in England under the early Stuarts* (Cambridge, 1975), 18–19. Hirst notes, at p. 19, that in 1623 in New England, the colony's leaders reported that women were denied the franchise 'as both reason and nature teacheth they should be'.

vote in county elections derived from their possession of freehold land worth forty shillings; for borough elections, property qualifications varied. Femes sole who voted in parliamentary elections were wealthier than many of their male neighbours. At the elections for the Long Parliament, some single women who were freeholders sought to express their political preferences by voting. Their rights were challenged.[38] After 1660, women's voting was increasingly unlikely. When in 1678 the borough charter of Richmond was redrawn, the rights of widows and single women were explicitly excluded.[39] By 1690, when George Petyt wrote his *Lex parliamentaria*, he explicitly denied that any woman could vote in parliamentary elections, even if she possessed a freehold.[40]

Oath-taking was another formal public matter, a requirement such as was made of witnesses in court or required of certain licensees, such as midwives or surgeons. In these situations women, irrespective of marital status, were required to take oaths. Other public oath-taking was a test of loyalty. In 1641 the Speaker of the Commons had called for all inhabitants, 'both Householders and others, being of Eighteen years of age and upwards', to take the Protestation. Sara Mendelson has drawn attention to women as well as men swearing the oath.[41] In some parishes, the returns suggest that the entire adult population took the oath. In Cornwall, at St Maby, 195 men swore the oath, and 164 women; at St Tudy, the women were nearly half of those who swore.[42] It is unclear whether parishes imposed the oath on all, or whether women initiated the signing. In other areas, smaller proportions of women were involved. Some returns indicated that the women were widows.[43] In the village of Croston in Lancashire, where women were about 14 per cent of those who signed, the signatories were described as widows and spinsters.[44] Again, in 1643, the parliamentarians imposed two further oaths, a

---

[38] For Worcestershire, *The journal of Sir Simonds D'Ewes*, ed. W. Notestein (New Haven, 1923), 463. Suffolk, BL Harl. Ms. 158, fol. 286v; see also BL Harl. Ms. 165, fol. 8. See further Mendelson and Crawford, *Women in early modern England*, ch. 7.

[39] R. T. Fieldhouse, 'Parliamentary representation in the borough of Richmond', *Yorkshire Archaelogical Journal* 44 (1972), 207–16, at 207–8.

[40] G. P[etyt], *Lex parliamentaria* (1690), 114.

[41] Sara Mendelson, unpublished paper, Oxford, 1989; Mendelson and Crawford, *Women in early modern England*, 397–9. For an invaluable recent analysis of the Protestation returns, see Jeremy Gibson and Alan Dell, *The Protestation returns 1641–42 and other contemporary listings* (Birmingham, 1995).

[42] Mendelson and Crawford, *Women in early modern England*, 397–9; G. A. Foster, 'Early Protestation returns', *Local Population Studies* 59 (1997), 67–8.

[43] For examples where women were noted as widows, see W. F. Webster (ed.), *Nottinghamshire and Derby Protestation returns 1641/2* (Nottingham, 1980), 69; W. F. Webster (ed.), *Lincolnshire Protestation returns 1641–2* (Nottingham, 1984), 48.

[44] Cited in Graham Rogers, 'Custom and common right: waste land enclosure and social change in west Lancashire', *Agricultural History Review* 41 (1993), 137–54, at 142–3.

covenant in June 'to be taken by every Man', and the Solemn League and Covenant in September. Some women subscribed to both.[45] In the London parish of St Mary Magdalen Milk Street, Thomas Case, lecturer, headed the June list, followed by the name of 'Ann his wife'. Women were about one third of the signatories. Later in 1643, in the same parish, women comprised nearly half of the subscribers to the Solemn League and Covenant.[46] In 1696, a similar ambiguity of instructions to 'every Man' would leave scope for female initiative; Sarah Churchill had women courtiers swear a parliamentary bond of association after a Jacobite plot.[47]

Voting and oath-taking were formal matters. Informally, women acted as citizens by participation in economic, religious and political issues in both town and countryside. Their involvement in agrarian collective action has a long history, which historians in recent times have acknowledged.[48] Rarely do we have access to women's voices directly, since their own accounts survive only in the records of prosecuting courts, but we may gain insight into women's underlying concerns by analysing the patterns of their protests. Common rights to graze animals, to glean and to collect firewood were crucial for the survival of poorer families, and remained so during the eighteenth century.[49] Protests against the enclosure of common lands and waste lands, and against the drainage of the fens, were sometimes led by women acting either alone or with men. In 1607 in North Riding a woman, 'Captain Dorothy', led other women to resist their local landowners' attempts to mine coal.[50] Women protested over the lack of food at affordable prices, or when grain was scarce.[51] On some occasions, women were leaders, as was Ann Carter in the riots at

---

[45] In St Olave, Old Jewry, a few married women signed along with their husbands; J. D. Alsop, 'Revolutionary puritanism in the parishes? The case of St Olave, Old Jewry', *London Journal* 15 (1990), 34–5.

[46] Guildhall, Ms. 2597/1, 66v–67, 70–3. Women's names were listed at St Stephen, Coleman St; Guildhall, Ms. 4458/1, part 2, 873–9. Thanks to Phil Baker and Elliot Vernon for these references.

[47] Edward Gregg, *Queen Anne* (London, 1980), 108; Frances Harris, 'Women at court, 1660–1714', paper delivered at North American Conference of British Studies, Chicago, 19 October 1996. Thanks to Dr Harris for allowing me to cite her paper.

[48] Ralph Houlbrooke, 'Women's social life and common action in England from the fifteenth century to the eve of the Civil War', *Continuity and Change* 1 (1986), 171–89; Keith Lindley, *Fenland riots and the English revolution* (London, 1982); Roger B. Manning, *Village revolts* (Oxford, 1988), 96–99; Keith Lindley, *Popular politics and religion in civil war London* (Aldershot, Hants, 1977).

[49] J. M. Neeson, *Commoners: common right, enclosure, and social change in England, 1700–1820* (Cambridge, 1990); Jane Humphries, 'Enclosure, common rights, and women: the proleterianization of families in the late eighteenth and early nineteenth centuries', *Journal of Economic History* 1 (1990), 17–42.   [50] Manning, *Village revolts*, 281.

[51] Peter Clark, 'Popular protest and disturbance in Kent, 1558–1640', *Economic History Review*, 2nd ser., 29 (1976), 365–81; Buchanan Sharp, *In contempt of all authority. Rural artisans and riot in the west of England, 1586–1660* (Berkeley, 1980).

Maldon against the shipment of grain from the area at a time of dearth.[52] Throughout the century, bad harvests precipitated grain riots; in 1693 women rioted in Oxford and in Northampton.[53] Historians have constructed a typology which places the food riot as a lower form of political activity;[54] perhaps it is not immaterial to note that the riot over food was one especially open to women. Since food prices were a women's issue – for were they not responsible for feeding their families? – food riots should be recognised as an important element in women's repertoire of protest.[55] In urban areas, women protested over trade and their livelihoods throughout the seventeenth century. In cities and towns their actions were more visible, as for example were the estimated 4,000–5,000 silk-weavers' wives who besieged parliament in 1697.[56] The law took some account of what was termed female weakness and imbecility, deeming that in case of riot, if women had acted together on their own account, then they would not necessarily be charged. Female rioters used this defence, but if the riot was serious, they were usually unsuccessful. After the Malden riots, Ann Carter was hanged.[57]

In 1642, ordinary women took sides, as did ordinary men, in the conflict between parliament and king, but women expressed their allegiances differently. Although women could not themselves enlist to fight,[58] many supported the soldiers with provisions, helped to fortify particular areas, and donated money and personal possessions to their favoured cause.[59] Others tried to remain neutral, and to discourage their sons from enlisting.[60] During the 1640s and 1650s, a few women published political tracts, engaging in the debates about Church and government. Katherine Chidley's controversial writings are well known. Some women expressed their political views as prophecies from the Lord. Mary Pope addressed

---

[52] John Walter, 'Grain riots and popular attitudes to the law: Maldon and the crisis of 1629' in J. Brewer and J. Styles (eds.), *An ungovernable people. The English and their law in the seventeenth and eighteenth centuries* (London, 1980), 47–84; see also Manning, *Village revolts*, 97.

[53] Max Beloff, *Public order and popular disturbances* (Oxford, 1938), 62–4.

[54] E. P. Thompson, 'The moral economy of the English crowd in the eighteenth century' in his *Customs in common* (Harmondsworth, 1993), 188.

[55] For women's roles in food riots in the later eighteenth century, see John Bohstedt, 'Women in English riots, 1790–1810', *Past and Present* 120 (1988), 88–122.

[56] *HMC Le Fleming*, 346. For further examples, see Beloff, *Public order*.

[57] Walter, 'Grain riots', 77; Mendelson and Crawford, *Women in early modern England*, 44.

[58] Apart from the few women who cross-dressed as soldiers and sailors.

[59] Bulstrode Whitelocke, *Memorials of the English affairs* (4 vols., Oxford, 1853), I:192; Antonia Fraser, *The weaker vessel. Woman's lot in seventeenth-century England* (London, 1984), 163–84; Anne Laurence, *Women in England 1500–1760. A social history* (London, 1994), 241–6. Women in Coventry in 1643 filled up quarrries 'that they might not shelter the enemie': BL Add. Ms. 11364, fol. [18]. Thanks to Sarah Jones for this reference.

[60] 'Some memoirs concerning the family of the Priestleys', in *Yorkshire diaries and autobiographies in the seventeenth and eighteenth centuries*, Surtees Society, 77 (1883), 26.

herself critically to the members of parliament on the basis of her own understanding.[61] Much female activism conformed to and supported the stereotypical notion of women as peace lovers. Very few women ever expressed support for the execution of the king, although some argued that he should be deprived of all political power.[62] Cromwell's sister, Katharine Whitstone, declared herself willing to have saved the king's life with her own: 'truly had I been able to have purchased his life, I am confident I could with all willingness have laid down mine'.[63]

Of all women's public collective actions during the seventeenth century, the demonstrations and petitions during the civil wars are probably the best known. Women's rights to petition had a long history. During the sixteenth and early seventeenth centuries, individual women had petitioned monarchs, powerful courtiers and parliaments. What was new in 1642 was their collective petitioning of parliament. The sources must be read with an understanding of the conventions and stereotypes through which newsbooks and other reports depicted the women's activities.[64] As Ann Hughes' important essay has demonstrated, women petitioners themselves showed awareness of contemporary understandings of gender and chose to represent themselves in acceptable roles within the patriarchal family, as good wives and mothers.[65] Petitioning Parliament was on a different basis from voting. Whereas the franchise was claimed by femes sole with property, married women (femes covert) petitioned parliament *as women*.[66] They justified themselves with whatever rhetorical strategy seemed most appropriate; as Christians, as citizens, and on many occasions when supporting the Levellers, *as wives* and *mothers*.[67]

[61] Mary Pope, *A treatise of magistracy* ([29 Nov.] 1647); Mary Pope, *Behold, here is a word, or an answer to the late remonstrance of the army* ([24 Jan.] 1649); Patricia Crawford, 'Women's printed writings, 1600–1700' in Mary Prior (ed.), *Women in English society 1500–1800* (London, 1985), 211–31.

[62] Lucy Hutchinson, a gentlewoman, was one of the few who was convinced that the king was guilty of blood and therefore should die; Lucy Hutchinson, *Memoirs of the life of Colonel Hutchinson*, ed. James Sutherland (London, 1973), 189–90.

[63] Katharine Whitstone, 16 Feb. 1649, Folger Shakespeare Library Ms. X. c. 53, printed in Patricia Crawford and Laura Gowing (eds.), *Women's Worlds in Seventeenth-century England: A Sourcebook* (London, 2000), pp. 252–4.

[64] Patricia Higgins, 'The reactions of women with special reference to women petitioners' in B. L. Manning (ed.), *Politics, religion and the English civil war* (London, 1973), 179–222, at 179–83.

[65] Ann Hughes, 'Gender and politics in Leveller literature' in Susan Amussen and Mark Kishlansky (eds.), *Political culture and cultural politics in England: Essays presented to David Underdown* (Manchester, 1995), 162–88.

[66] Higgins, 'Women petitioners', 183, 215–17. Ann Marie McEntee, ' "The [un]civill-sisterhood of oranges and lemons": female petitioners and demonstrators, 1642–53' in James Holstun (ed.), *Pamphlet wars: prose in the English revolution* (London, 1992), 92–111. McEntee argues that the concept of citizen was more pronounced in 1649, but this strand was there from 1642, as Higgins pointed out: 'Women petitioners', 216.

[67] Hughes, 'Gender and politics', 170–1.

They referred to themselves as 'the weakest means', and denied that they were seeking to equate themselves with men.[68] Petitioners confidently manipulated negative stereotypes of women: in 1653, in appealing against the act which had imprisoned Lilburne, they declared 'You see the thing is so gross, that even Women perceive the evil of it.'[69] Their ability to deploy a range of identities for political purposes argues for a degree of female political acumen. Positioning themselves as subjects and citizens, from 1641 onwards groups of women regularly demonstrated outside parliament. As Ellen McArthur and Patricia Higgins have shown, the female petitioners were concerned with a range of issues: grievances over trade, complaints of dearth, or their desire for peace.[70]

The surviving evidence about the women's demonstrations of Tuesday 8 and Wednesday 9 August 1643 in favour of peace is greater than usual because MPs suspected that the parliamentary leaders of the peace party were implicated. The demonstrations and counter-demonstrations were organised over the weekend of 5 and 6 August. On Tuesday 'a multitude of women' with white ribbons in their hats besieged the Commons.[71] Laurence Whitacre noted that when a committee went out 'to appease the women they would not be satisfied'. Instead, they beat on the door to try to force it open, and threatened to seize Pym, Strode and others, 'whome they said they would caste into the Thames'.[72] Yonge's description of women was in terms of the predictable stereotypes: 'some say they were Irish, servants & Queens most of them wch came out of Southwark Westminster and other places without the cittie'. Men had accompanied them, and it was thought 'they are put on and backed by some men of wealthe and quality'.[73] On Wednesday the demonstration was reportedly more violent. Estimates of the numbers varied, ranging from two to six thousand, but all accounts agreed that 'from words they fell to blowes'.[74] Troopers came in, many were injured, and a woman was killed.[75] Newsbooks reported variously that the women 'are all of the poorer sort'[76] or 'Oyster wives, and other dirty tattered sluts'.[77] The Commons

[68] *A true copie of the petition of the gentlewomen, and tradesmens-wives, in and about the City of London* ([4 Feb.] 1642 [BL E. 134(17), 7]).
[69] *To the parliament of the commonwealth of England: the humble petition of divers well affected women* ([25 June 1653] [BL 669 f.17(26)]).
[70] E. McArthur, 'Women petitioners and the Long Parliament', *EHR* 24 (1909), 698–709; Higgins, 'Women petitioners'.
[71] BL Add. Ms. 18778, diary of Walter Yonge, fol. 12v; Patricia Crawford, *Denzil Holles, 1598–1680: A study of his political career* (1979), 92–6.
[72] BL Add. Ms. 31116, Whitacre's diary, fol. 69v.
[73] BL Add. Ms. 18778, diary of Walter Yonge, fol. 13v.
[74] *The Parliament Scout*, 3–10 Aug. 1643, 55 [BL E. 64(13)].
[75] BL Harl. Ms. 165, fol. 150r.   [76] *The Parliament Scout*, 55.
[77] *Certaine Informations*, 7–14 Aug. 1643, 231 [BL E. 65(8)].

spent most of the day on 11 August investigating the 'Principall Actors in ye late tumult of women'. All of the leaders they proceeded against were men, including one JP, although a wealthy Lady Brouckner had been named as one involved.[78] Since the Commons believed that the demonstrations emanated from their own disaffected members, they ignored the London women's actions in support of peace negotiations.

In April 1649, women petitioned on behalf of the imprisoned Leveller leaders.[79] Told by an MP that 'it was not for women to Petition, they might stay at home and wash their dishes',[80] the women returned on 5 May with an even more strongly worded petition. They enunciated claims to wider rights in terms of the Christian doctrine of the equality of all before God and their common civil rights:

> That since we are assured of our creation in the image of God, and of an interest in Christ, equal unto men, as also of a proportionable share in the freedoms of this Commonwealth, we cannot but wonder and grieve that we should appear so despicable in your eyes, as to be thought unworthy to petition or represent our grievances to this honourable House. Have we not an equal interest with the men of this nation in those liberties and securities contained in the Petition of Right, and other the good laws of the land? Are any of our lives, limbs, liberties, or goods to be take from us more than from men, but by due process of law . . . ? And can you imagine us to be sottish or stupid as not to perceive, or not to be sensible when daily those strong defences of our peace and welfare are broken down and trod underfoot by force and arbitrary power?[81]

In 1651, a group of women addressed Cromwell demanding reform of the laws relating to debt. The language of *The women's petition* was blunt. Contrary to their expectations, they declared, the execution of the king had not ended tyranny: 'and the Norman laws of the Oppressors still bear Dominion over us'.[82]

Women's petitions referred to the violation of traditional rights and food shortages: 'we are not able to see our children hang upon us, and cry out for bread, and not have the wherewithal to feed them, we had rather dye than see that day'.[83] Appealing to a female tradition of political involvement, they justified their collective actions by the biblical models of Deborah and Jael, and by historical precedents: 'by the British women this land was delivered from the tyranny of the Danes . . . and the over-

---

[78] BL Add. Ms 31116, fol. 69v.
[79] *To the supream authority of this nation . . . the humble petition of divers wel-affected women* [24 April 1649].
[80] *Mercurius militaris, or the people's scout*, 17–24 May 1649, 13.
[81] *To the supream authority of England . . . the humble petition of divers well-affected women* (5 May 1649) [BL 669 f.14(27)].
[82] *The womens petition to . . . General Cromwell* (30 Oct. 1651), BL 669 f.16 (26).
[83] *To the supream authority of England . . . the humble petition of divers well-affected women* (5 May 1649).

throw of Episcopall tyranny in Scotland was first begun by the women of that Nation'. Furthermore, the petitioners of 1649 reminded the MPs that they had contributed to the best of their ability: 'our money, our plate, jewels, rings, bodkins, &c. have bin offered at your feet' (see illustration).[84]

Women were aware of the freedoms and rights of the feme sole. In 1653 a member of parliament told a group of women petitioners that the House could not heed their petition 'they being women, and many of them wives, so that the Law took no notice of them'. The women promptly and properly replied 'that they were not all wives'.[85] Furthermore, they claimed that as they were Christians, conscience and duty authorised their actions.

During the 1640s and 1650s, the number of petitioners and the size of the demonstrations indicates an impressive level of organisation. It was claimed that there were 10,000 supporters of the 1649 petition in support of the Levellers.[86] Newsbooks referred to 2,000–6,000 demonstrators on occasions. A royalist source claimed that 6,000 women subscribed to the 1653 petition,[87] and in 1659, 7,000 supporters were claimed for Quaker women's petition against tithes.[88] Sometimes the women demonstrators wore ribbons: white for peace in 1643, and the Leveller colour, 'sea-green', in 1649.[89] Hostile contemporaries belittled women's initiatives, but we know from other evidence that ordinary women were capable of political initiatives.[90]

The demonstrators and petitioners may not have been the very 'poorest shes'. It is difficult to interpret the evidence about their social status. Sympathetic newsbooks described the women as the wives of prosperous citizens, while others attacked them as oyster wives, fish wives, women 'of the inferior sort'.[91] Here again, worthiness, political rights and voice attached to social status. Also disputed was the level of violence. Some reported that women came to parliament peaceably, with their children, but other newsbook writers depicted the women as aggressive. These differences partly arise from the different kinds of reportage: MPs in their private journals noted some details, newsbooks seeking sales chose

[84] *To the supream authority of this nation, the humble petition of divers wel-affected women* (24 April 1649), 5 (Worcester College, Oxford, AA. 2.4.14).
[85] Bodleian Library Clarendon Ms. 46, fol. 131v.
[86] Higgins, 'Women petitioners', 202.
[87] Bodleian Library Clarendon Ms. 46, fol. 130 (29 July 1653).
[88] Mary Forster and 7,000 Hand-maids of the Lord, *These several papers was sent to the parliament* (1659).
[89] BL Add. Ms. 18778, fol. 12v; *Mercurius Pragmaticus*, 1–8 May 1649, 15.
[90] Mendelson and Crawford, *Women in early modern England*, 380–418.
[91] Higgins, 'Women petitioners', 192 and passim.

From a 1667 pack of playing cards, *The knavery of the Rump*, satirising women as gulled by the preacher into contributing thimbles and bodkins 'for the good old cause'. (By kind permission of the Guildhall Library: Worshipful Company of Makers of Playing Cards collection.)

others. But all male reporters were influenced by contemporary stereo-types of disorderly women.

Throughout the seventeenth century, women claimed informal politi-cal rights as Christians. Religious beliefs could prompt a range of activ-ities. During the 1640s and 1650s some women were part of 'the people' who participated in the political life of the churches. In some London par-ishes, substantial citizens participated in decisions such as the dismissal and appointment of ministers. In 1644 at St Peter's Cornhill, seven women were among the eighty-three parishioners who chose the minis-ter.[92] In the separatist churches, different patterns of lay participation developed. The beginnings were usually informal, as believers gathered at private houses. When the formal covenant establishing a gathered church was made, women were usually signatories.[93] However, women's position under the covenant of a separatist church remained ambiguous. They were admitted as individuals, irrespective of marital status, yet in the enforcement of church discipline, most congregations insisted on the conventional virtues including wifely obedience.[94] Women were expected to speak up in several separatist congregations, although most churches were sensitive about how this should be done. In particular, men disliked any sign that women were exercising authority over them. Women them-selves could be uncomfortable about speaking out. In some congrega-tions, women's rights to be full members of the church were paramount and they shared in decision-making.[95] Sometimes they even voted in Independent and Baptist congregations. In 1653 John Rogers claimed that women enjoyed full voting rights in his Independent congregation in Dublin, although he admitted that some men objected, claiming a 'Soveraignty to themselves'. Rogers' own view was that 'Votes concern all, ergo all must vote.'[96] Female voting rights were also contentious in the Independent congregation in Exeter in 1657.[97] Thus around the time that the franchise was debated at Putney, members of gathered churches were aware of the rights of women as individuals who were church members. In many congregations, women's rights were theoretically unrestricted by their economic position or marital status.

[92] Brian Manning, 'Puritanism and democracy, 1640–1642' in Donald Pennington and Keith Thomas (eds.), *Puritans and revolutionaries. Essays in seventeenth-century history pre-sented to Christopher Hill* (Oxford, 1978), 139–60; Alsop, 'Revolutionary puritanism', 31; Lindley, *Popular politics*, 272.   [93] Crawford, *Women and religion*, 140–3.
[94] Theodore Calvin Pease, *The Leveller movement. A study in the history and political theory of the English great civil war* (Washington, DC, 1916), 143, pointed to the radical argument made in 1646, *Regall tyrannie discovered* [BL E. 370(12)], 11, about the retention of natural rights under the covenant.   [95] Crawford, *Women and religion*, 143–7, 199–200.
[96] John Rogers, *Ohel, or Beth-shmesh* (London, 1653), 463–75.
[97] E.T., *Diotrophes detected* (London, 1658), 11–12, 17–18.

These traditions of female participation seem to have continued in some of the separatist churches in the 1650s and in some cases until later in the century. In the Quaker movement women aspired to leadership. They preached, wrote, testified, travelled and denounced sinners. Quaker women engaged in highly imaginative public street demonstrations. In the Baptist churches, women participated in some aspects of church government, and in the 1690s records indicate that some even voted. In 1694, Maze Pond Baptist Church resolved that 'the Sisters being equaly with the Brethren members of the misticall Body of Christ, his Church, they have equall right Liberty and previledge to voate with them by lifting up of their hands . . . to shew their Assent or dissent for or against any matter or thing that is moued in the Church'.[98] Voting was the individual right of a church member; theoretically, even married women enjoyed a vote.[99]

Women's political partisanship continued after the Restoration, as they took sides in the party conflicts between Whig and Tory. Many supported rival claimants to the throne. Lady Alicia Lisle was executed for her part in giving refuge to men involved in Monmouth's uprising. A spurious publication in her name spoke of her faith in the Protestant religion, and detestation of the evils of popery.[100] Early in the eighteenth century, ordinary women were prominent supporters of the exiled Stuart monarchy, flaunting white flowers on the birthday of the prince of Wales.[101]

Men as well as women could, of course, claim rights as Christians. Specifically gendered were the claims that women advanced on the basis of maternity. Although early modern culture was ambivalent about maternity, one strand was respect and value for women as givers of life and as nurturers. Contemporaries acknowledged women's devotion and care for their children, and many recognised a duty of obedience to mothers as well as fathers. Maternity was significant because it was an experience which many women, albeit differentiated by class, might share. Even if they were not themselves mothers, much of women's sense of themselves as women, different from men, depended upon their maternal potential.[102]

---

[98] Angus Library, Regent's Park College, Ms. 2/4/1, Maze Pond Church Book, 1691–1745, fol. 109, 14 Oct. 1694.

[99] Crawford, *Women and religion*, 119–82.

[100] 'The past speech of Madam Lisle' (1685) in *The dying speeches of several excellent persons* (London, 1689), 25–6.

[101] Paul Kleber Monod, *Jacobitism and the English people, 1688–1788* (Cambridge, 1989), 211, 214, 215.

[102] Patricia Crawford, '"The sucking child": adult attitudes to child care in the first year of life in seventeenth-century England', *Continuity and Change* 1 (1986), 23–52, at 41; Patricia Crawford, 'The construction and experience of maternity in seventeenth-century England' in Valerie Fildes (ed.), *Women as mothers in pre-industrial England* (1990), 3–38.

Maternal rights authorised some women's claims to public as well as private authority. While women could not preach from pulpits about domestic duties, their advice to other women and to children could be published. Mothers prefaced their admonitions with self-deprecatory remarks, but still they claimed authority. Before the civil wars, the genre of maternal advice was a significant component of women's printed writings.[103] Child-rearing gave mothers influence over their children. In gentry correspondence, such as that of the Barrington family in the late 1620s, men acknowledged a duty to listen to their mothers.[104] Some ignored their mothers' political advice unless it coincided with their own views. Bitter letters survive from the countess of Denbigh to her son Basil Feilding, who had chosen the opposite side to his father in the civil war.[105]

Increasingly, mothers fostered in their children a sense of national pride.[106] Women shared the notion that the English nation was elect and, in the eighteenth century, reared their children in patriotism. As Linda Colley has pointed out, not all women's activity as political agents should be seen as oppositional.[107] Yet in their claims to be part of a national group, Englishwomen excluded 'others' from citizenship. Englishwomen denied to slave women and indigenous women in the American colonies the rights which they themselves claimed. Indeed, only the Quakers recognised a Christian obligation to slaves as well as free. Even those colonists who urged the baptism of slaves denied that Christianity offered freedom or civic rights.[108] Mary Astell, who claimed rights for women *vis-à-vis* men early in the eighteenth century, compared women's lot with that of slaves only to draw attention to English women's claims, not to review slavery.[109] Patriotism required that the situation of Englishwomen be superior to that in all other countries.

Whether or not women could exercise a political right during the seventeenth century depended upon a range of intersecting factors,

---

[103] Crawford, 'Women's printed writings', 221–2, 272–3.

[104] *Barrington family letters, 1628–1632*, ed. Arthur Searle, Camden Society, 4th ser., vol. 28 (London, 1983), 73.

[105] Cecilia, countess of Denbigh, *Royalist father and roundhead son. Being the memoirs of the first and second earls of Denbigh, 1600–1675* (London, 1915), 164–5, 181–2.

[106] Linda Pollock (ed.), *With faith and physic. The life of a Tudor gentlewoman Lady Grace Mildmay 1552–1620* (London, 1993), 23–4.   [107] Colley, *Britons*, 289–91.

[108] Morgan Goodwyn, *A supplement to the negro's and indian's advocate* (London, 1681), 7; Morgan Goodwyn, *Some proposals towards promoting the propagation of the Gospel in our American plantations* (London, 1708), 11–12. Here Goodwyn cited the Act of the New York Assembly to the effect that baptised slaves should continue to be bound in service as before baptism.

[109] Mary Astell, *Reflections upon marriage* (3rd edn, London, 1706) in Bridget Hill (ed.), *The first English feminist. Reflections upon marriage and other writings by Mary Astell* (Aldershot, 1986), 76.

which might include social status, property, Christianity, marital status, maternity and nation. Gender influenced all of these other factors. A feme sole might claim her rights as 'man', a property-owner, or even as a citizen and subject; a married women, however, might appeal to the universal rights of Christians, or a citizen who had a right to justice. Some women articulated their rights in theory, while others claimed theirs by their actions.

'The poorest she': women and the Putney debates

During the seventeenth century, women, depending upon their class and marital status, contested their exclusion from public political life, and participated in the exercise of power. They never, so far as I know, advanced claims to participate in politics as feminists concerned about the rights of women; rather, they articulated demands in terms of the conventional rhetoric of Christianity and of their being good wives and mothers. Even the female relatives of the Leveller leaders, Elizabeth Lilburne, Mary Overton and Katharine Chidley, justified their involvement in terms of women's customary roles.[110] Nevertheless, despite the conservatism of their rhetoric, the female culture from which women's arguments developed was significant in allowing a tradition of female activism and in sustaining an alternative view of community.[111]

Yet women were not a monolithic group, and their rights always varied depending upon the context. A crucial distinction was between the independent woman and all others. The rights of the propertied single woman and widow were widely acknowledged in early modern society; all others lived under subjection.[112] The ideal woman, married and dependent, was a minority of the total female population in the seventeenth century, but her legal position as a non-person has been taken as normative by both her contemporaries and subsequent writers.[113]

Women both as individuals and as groups could be present in the political debates of the early modern period; men could not in practice claim exclusive possession of the political sphere. Gentlewomen, middling- and lower-status women all enjoyed access to politics in many different arenas. No responsible adult men could ignore women, for at the basic level of the household they knew that their control over their subordinates

---

[110] Hughes, 'Gender and politics', 176–82.
[111] For female culture, see Mendelson and Crawford, *Women in early modern England*, 202–53.
[112] Carole Pateman, *The sexual contract* (Stanford, CA, 1988), 213; Sommerville, *Sex and subjection*, 174–99.
[113] For futher discussion on this point, see Mendelson and Crawford, *Women in early modern England*, 124–5.

was fundamental to their reputation. Masculinity and authority were inextricably bound together.[114] Women's participation in politics could threaten masculine honour; the spectre of female omnipresence haunted men.

Although no woman's voice was heard in the debates at Putney Church in October 1647, in January 1649, Elizabeth Poole was admitted to the deliberations of the army's General Council to deliver her message from the Lord. Poole was not among the very poorest, for she did not rely on poor relief or charity, but earned her living 'by her hands'.[115] Yet despite her lowly social status, Poole's claim to prophetic power – which the Council examined carefully – gave her a right to be heard. The Putney debates of 1647 took place in an historical context in which ordinary women had some rights to participate in politics as citizens.

Universal political rights admitted the possibility of the inclusion of 'the poorest shes' in the franchise. Although the issue was never explicit, it would not have been unthinkable for the officers and soldiers to discuss the rights of ordinary women as well as ordinary men. But the participants at Putney were not especially interested in women. Their concern was immediate political decisions and the dangers they were in. The issue of universal franchise, of basing government on the consent of human beings irrespective of their property rights, threatened to divide the army. Although I would admit that Cromwell seized upon every issue he could to delay and distract, the question of the female franchise was so clearly already bound up with the fundamental question of rights that it was unnecessary to raise it directly. Cromwell and Ireton knew that the feme sole with property could vote; the Levellers knew that the poorest women could be 'people', citizens possessing some rights, or Christians who enjoyed some share in the government of separatist congregations.

Inherent in the demand for the sovereignty of the people was the role of women. As George Hickes pointed out in 1682, if the supreme power belonged to the people, 'by whose order and authority, or by what Salique law of Nature were Women excluded from it, who are as usefull members of the Commonwealth, and as necessary for humane societies as the men are?'[116] Beyond Putney, later in the seventeenth century, many of women's rights disappeared. Because rights were so interwoven into complex relationships in early modern society, there was no single

---

[114] Susan Dwyer Amussen, *An ordered society. Gender and class in early modern England* (Oxford, 1988); Frances E. Dolan, *Dangerous familiars. Representations of domestic crime in England, 1550–1700* (Ithaca, NY, 1994), 102–6, 119; see also Laura Gowing, *Domestic dangers. Women, words, and sex in early modern London* (Oxford, 1996), 109.

[115] Elizabeth Poole, *A prophecie touching the death of King Charles* (London, 1649), 24.

[116] George Hickes, *A discourse of the soveraign power* (London, 1682), 22.

moment, no specific date at which the reconceptualisation of political theories affected 'women' as a group. Rather, rights altered at different times. Many women never lost a sense of themselves as citizens. During the eighteenth and nineteenth centuries, they sustained what could be termed a 'subterranean citizenship' of involvement with community and public issues based on birthrights, Christianity, maternity and nationalism.

11   The Leveller legacy: from the Restoration to the Exclusion Crisis

Tim Harris

Conventional historiography teaches us that the Levellers disappeared almost as quickly as they came into existence, with the arrest of the Leveller leaders and the defeat of the army mutinies in the spring of 1649 normally taken as marking the effective end of the Levellers as an organised political movement. It took a while for Leveller agitation out-of-doors to fizzle out completely: one thinks in particular of the activity surrounding John Lilburne's trial in 1653, whilst in the mid-1650s some erstwhile Levellers were prepared to engage in plotting with royalist conspirators in the hope that a conditional restoration might lead to the enactment of some their platform.[1] There was also an attempt to relaunch certain aspects of the Leveller programme following the collapse of the republic in 1659, although the issue famously associated with Putney, namely the question of the franchise, was not revived.[2] Yet this was very much the end. Few political narratives covering the period after 1660 contain even an index reference to the Levellers;[3] they have, it seems, disappeared from sight.

Contemporaries, however, were less sure. They saw the spectre of the Levellers in popular political agitation out-of-doors throughout the reign of Charles II. When hundreds of apprentices took to the streets to pull down brothels in Easter Week of 1668, the fact that they marched behind

[1] Pauline Gregg, *Free-born John: a biography of John Lilburne* (London, 1961); G. E. Aylmer (ed.), *The Levellers in the English revolution* (London, 1975); David Underdown, *Royalist conspiracy in England, 1649–1660* (New Haven, 1960); Godfrey Davies, *The restoration of Charles II, 1658–60* (San Marino, CA, 1955), 22; Christopher Hill, *The experience of defeat: Milton and some contemporaries* (London, 1984), 32–6; B. S. Capp, *The Fifth Monarchy men: a study of seventeenth-century English millenarianism* (London, 1972), 106–10.

[2] Austin Woolrych, 'Last quests for a settlement, 1657–1660', in Gerald Aylmer (ed.), *The interregnum: the quest for settlement, 1646–1660* (London, 1974), 183–204, at 192–5; Barry Reay, 'The Quakers, 1659, and the restoration of the monarchy', *History* 63 (1978), 193–213; *The Leveller; or, the principles and maxims concerning government and religion, which are asserted by those that are commonly called Levellers* (London, 1659), 14.

[3] See, for example, Paul Seaward, *The Restoration, 1660–1688* (London, 1991); Geoffrey Holmes, *The making of a great power: late Stuart and early Georgian Britain, 1660–1722* (London, 1993).

green banners (the colour of the Levellers) and made demands for liberty of conscience and further reformation sounded alarm bells for the government, who became convinced that the riots had been instigated by republican conspirators bent on overthrowing the monarchy. The authorities got a similar scare in 1675 when bands of weavers from London's suburbs, wearing green aprons, rose to protest against the use of engine looms; the London weavers, it will be recalled, had formed a mainstay of Leveller support in the late 1640s.[4] And social and political conservatives were convinced they saw levelling implications behind the Whig movement of the Exclusion Crisis, and even suggested that the Whigs themselves were at heart Levellers. One pamphleteer protested that the Exclusion Bill of 1679 gave encouragement 'to the Republican Levellers and Mutineers', and alleged that it 'was Midwiv'd into the World by a notorious Leveller'.[5] Tory rhymesters castigated the Whig leader, the earl of Shaftesbury, as 'A Pestilent Peer of a levelling spirit',[6] and Whig MPs as 'the remains of the Leveling Rump that stink in the House'.[7] The Whig practice of promoting petitions pressing Charles II to let parliament sit so that it could resolve the crisis over the succession and alleviate his subjects' fears about popery and arbitrary government was a phenomenon that came to be dubbed 'Lilburneisme' by one lord mayor.[8] Anti-exclusionist propagandists dismissed the Whig claim to be concerned about liberty and property as a 'specious pretence', since if the Whigs were to get their way, as one Tory pamphleteer warned, 'the whole Kingdom' would 'set up for Levellers and Libertines'.[9]

More generally, the Tory press repeatedly accused the Whigs of seeking to revive the Good Old Cause, of stirring up the rabble, and wanting to destroy all hierarchy in Church and state.[10] Furthermore, some contem-

---

[4] Tim Harris, 'The bawdy house riots of 1668', *HJ* 29 (1986), 537–56; Tim Harris, *London crowds in the reign of Charles II: propaganda and politics from the Restoration to the Exclusion Crisis* (Cambridge, 1987), chs. 4, 8; Richard M. Dunn, 'The London weavers' riot of 1675', *Guildhall Studies in London History* 1(1) (1973), 13–23; H. N. Brailsford, *The Levellers and the English revolution*, ed. Christopher Hill (London, 1976).

[5] [Matthew Rider], *The power of parliaments in the case of succession* (London, 1680), 7, 8.

[6] 'The presbyter has been so active of late', in Nathaniel Thompson (ed.), *A collection of one hundred and eighty loyal songs* (London, 1685), 173.

[7] 'Raree show; or, the true Protestant procession' in Thompson, *Collection of . . . loyal songs*, 317.

[8] Folger Shakespeare Library, Newdigate Newsletter Lc. 732, 16 January 1678/9; Mark Knights, 'London petitions and parliamentary politics in 1679', *Parliamentary History* 12 (1993), 29–46, at 31.

[9] [John Northleigh], *The parallel: or, the new serious association* (London, 1682), 22.

[10] See, for example, 'The convert Scot, and apostate English' (1681), in Thompson, *A collection of eighty-six loyal poems*, 45–54; 'The mad-men's hospital; or, a present remedy to cure a presbyterian itch' (1681), in ibid., 57–60; 'The solicitous citizen; or, much ado about nothing' [n.d.], in ibid., 130–3; *Advice to the city; or, the Whigs' loyalty examined* (London, 1682), reprinted in ibid., 302; [Thomas Durfey], *The Whig's exal-*

poraries saw Leveller principles as underlying some of the Whig tracts they read. For example, the second earl of Bridgewater wrote on the first page of his copy of Edmund Hickeringill's *History of Whiggism* of 1682: 'It is visible to all that read this book that the Author is an Arrant Leveller, and aimes to do all the Mischiefe to Monarchy that he possibly Can.' The tract, incidentally, does not talk about the franchise or about levelling property, but rather maintains that the eldest son can sometimes be excluded from his inheritance, champions parliament, insists that 'The Peoples Welfare is the Supream and Chiefest Law' ('salus populi, suprema lex'), and defends (on these grounds) the parliamentary opposition to Charles I in 1641.[11] Bridgewater was even more alarmed at Hickeringill's sequel, which offers a more explicit justification of resistance when the magistrate breaks the law, writing: 'In this 2d Part the Author endeavours even to outdo himself, in prejudicing as much as he Can all Monarchical Governement, and advancing a Levelling principle.'[12]

In recent years, a few historians have made a more systematic attempt to trace what happened to the Levellers and their ideas after 1660. Thus scholars such as Richard Ashcraft and Gary De Krey have both looked at what erstwhile Levellers or their children and relatives were up to in the Restoration and also searched for parallels between the demands and grievances of Restoration dissidents and the earlier Leveller platform.[13] Although we have learned a great deal from their researches, it remains far from clear whether their findings allow us to talk of a Leveller presence in Restoration England. Few would deny that there was a radical

tation (London, 1682), reprinted in *Poems on affairs of state*, ed. Geoffrey de Forest Lord *et al.* (7 vols., New Haven, 1963–75), III:11; *Heraclitus Ridens*, no. 12, 19 April 1681; William Sherlock, *Some seasonable reflections on the discovery of the late plot* (London, 1683), 2.

[11] [Edmund Hickeringill], *The history of Whiggism* (London, 1682). I am grateful to Michael Mendle for confirming that the hand is that of the second earl of Bridgewater. Bridgewater (1622–86) had been a royalist during the civil war and was a rigid Anglican and fierce opponent of dissent. Although he allied with the country opposition to Danby in the mid-1670s, he joined the new Privy Council in 1679 and did not vote for the Exclusion Bill in the Lords division of 15 November 1680: E. S. de Beer, 'The House of Lords in the parliament of 1680', *BIHR* 20 (1943–5), 22–37, at 37; Andrew Swatland, *The House of Lords in the reign of Charles II* (Cambridge, 1996); *Dictionary of national biography*.

[12] [Edmund Hickeringill], *The second part of the history of Whiggism* (London, 1682).

[13] Richard Ashcraft, *Revolutionary politics and Locke's Two treatises of government* (Princeton, 1986); Gary S. De Krey, 'London radicals and revolutionary politics, 1675–1683' in Tim Harris, Paul Seaward and Mark Goldie (eds.), *The politics of religion in Restoration England* (Oxford, 1990), 133–62; Gary S. De Krey, 'The London Whigs and the Exclusion Crisis reconsidered' in Lee Beier, David Cannadine and James Rosenheim (eds.), *The first modern society: essays in English history in honour of Lawrence Stone* (Cambridge, 1989), 457–82.

opposition to the Restoration regime,[14] though historians disagree over how extensive this was and are prone to bicker over the meaning of the term 'radical'.[15] However, Ashcraft's attempt to associate the platform of Locke and of the Shaftesbury-led Whigs with that of the Levellers has failed to convince most scholars, whilst those erstwhile Levellers (or their descendants) who were active in the Whig movement seem to be doing a number of un-Leveller type things (such as arguing for a restriction of the franchise).

The traditional way of assessing the Leveller legacy, I want to suggest, is too narrowly conceived, and inevitably encourages the conclusion that the Levellers, and what they stood for, all but completely disappeared after 1660. As a result, we not only fail to understand why social and political conservatives feared the possibility of a Leveller revival or thought that the Whigs were, at heart, 'arrant Levellers', but we are even forced to doubt the significance of the Leveller movement in the years 1646–9. For if the Levellers disappeared so quickly, then surely they could not have been that much of a force in the first place. In assessing the Leveller legacy, it is necessary get away from a preoccupation with specific programmes, and especially with the franchise issue, and think about the meaning of the Leveller phenomenon as a social and political movement. It is well known that the Levellers modified or changed their stance on certain specific issues, most notoriously the franchise, for tactical reasons or to meet changing political realities, and that their leaders repeatedly denied that they were levellers in the sense of wanting to destroy property. Contemporaries, however, were concerned about the political levelling implied by the type of activism in which the Levellers engaged: namely, the fact that ordinary men and women were laying claim to have as significant a voice in politics as their social superiors – whether gentry, lords, or

---

[14] In addition to the works cited above, see: Harris, *London crowds*; Richard L. Greaves, *Deliver us from evil: the radical underground in Britain, 1660–1663* (Oxford, 1986); Richard L. Greaves, *Enemies under His feet: radicals and Nonconformists in Britain, 1664–1677* (Stanford, CA, 1990); Richard L. Greaves, *Secrets of the kingdom: British radicals from the Popish Plot to the Revolution of 1688–89* (Stanford, 1992); Jonathan Scott, *Algernon Sidney and the Restoration crisis, 1677–1683* (Cambridge, 1991); Gary S. De Krey, 'The first Restoration crisis: conscience and coercion in London, 1667–73', *Albion* 25 (1993), 565–80; Gary S. De Krey, 'Rethinking the Restoration: dissenting cases for conscience, 1667–1672', *HJ* 38 (1995), 53–83; Gary S. De Krey, 'Reformation in the Restoration crisis, 1679–82' in Donna Hamilton and Richard Strier (eds.), *Religion, literature and politics in post-Reformation England* (Cambridge, 1996), 231–52; Gary S. De Krey, 'Radicals, reformers, and republicans: academic language and political discourse in Restoration London' in Alan Houston and Steven C. A. Pincus (eds.), *A nation transformed?* (Cambridge, forthcoming).

[15] Conal Condren, 'Radicals, conservatives and moderates in early modern political thought: a case of Sandwich Islands syndrome?', *History of Political Thought* 10 (1989), 525–42.

even the king himself. The same implications of political levelling, I shall argue, are found underlying the Whig movement of the Exclusion Crisis. I do not intend to claim that the Whigs, and their supporters, really were Levellers, if only we or they knew it – although we perhaps see greater correspondences between the Leveller and radical Whig programmes than many historians have been prepared to concede. Rather, I wish to suggest: first, that given Tory perceptions of how their divinely ordained, hierarchically structured political order in church and state was supposed to function, the type of activity that the Whigs encouraged did indeed embody a real levelling tendency; and, secondly, that the mass Whig movement of the Exclusion period was, in essence, the same type of socio-political phenomenon as the collective agitation out-of-doors that is first seen in support of parliament, later on behalf of the Levellers, in the 1640s and early 1650s.[16]

Let us begin, then, with the more traditional approach, and look for signs of any concrete links between Restoration protest movements and the Levellers. As mentioned above, there were two, large-scale public disturbances in Restoration London, each lasting several days, where the protesters chose to march behind green banners – the bawdy-house riots of 1668 and the weavers' riots of 1675. I have examined these disturbances in detail elsewhere, but since I have been accused by one reviewer of being too dismissive of the apparent invocation of the Leveller green, a brief re-examination of the relevant evidence is in order here.[17]

The riots of 1668 occurred at a time when the restored regime still felt very insecure: rumours and allegations of underground republican conspiracies abounded, some of them true, many of them unfounded, but nevertheless the government came to believe that it had to be constantly on its guard against any form of dissidence, actual or alleged, that might

[16] The term 'levellers' had originally been coined to refer to those who levelled enclosures, and, occasionally, the term is used in this context after 1660. Thus anti-enclosure rioters in Worcestershire in late-1670, we are told, 'got together under the pretence of Levellers' and proceeded to break down fences and commit various other outrages. See *HMC Le Fleming*, 74; *CSPD, 1671*, 18–19; Max Beloff, *Public order and popular disturbances, 1660–1714* (London, 1938), 76–80; David Underdown, *A freeborn people: politics and the nation in seventeenth-century England* (Oxford, 1996), 122. Unfortunately, space does not permit me to explore contemporary concerns about this sort of levelling here. However, I do see the social levelling of anti-enclosure rioters as a somewhat different phenomenon from the type of political levelling I am concerned with in this chapter (even if contemporaries at times sought to discredit political radicals by accusing them of seeking to level men's estates), and therefore believe that it is legitimate to distinguish the two for analytical purposes.

[17] William Lamont, 'Angels or green aprons? "Popular Toryism" in the late seventeenth century', *History Workshop Journal* 27 (1989), 188–93. For my earlier discussions of these riots, see n. 4 above.

pose a threat to its security.[18] The bulk of the rioters, according to contemporary accounts, were apprentices, and apprentices had gone on the rampage against brothels before – indeed, brothel riots had once been quite common on Shrove Tuesday[19] – but the authorities were particularly alarmed by the overtly political slogans of 1668, when the rioters shouted 'Reformation and Reducement' and threatened 'ere-long they would come and pull White-hall down', insisting 'that if the king did not give them liberty of conscience, that May-day must be a bloody day'. Lord Chief Justice Keeling, who presided over the trials of the ringleaders, was convinced that this was no simple apprentice riot. 'Truly I see scarcely an apprentice among you all' (i.e. among the ringleaders), he observed at one point during the proceedings; he was obsessed with the fact that the rioters marched behind colours – 'Had they any colours?', he asked witnesses – and he voiced the government's insecurities when he made remarks such as 'After all this trouble we have had in this nation, it is a sad thing that a great number of giddy headed people must gather together under pretence of reformation, to disturb the peace of the nation.' Attempting to make such a public reformation, even if merely to rid the land of bawdy-houses, was interpreted by the judges as high treason, because it amounted to a usurpation of the regal authority, and eight of the ringleaders were condemned to death.[20]

There is no doubting the political overtones of these riots. What should be questioned, however, is the government's assumption that the riots were part of a wider design involving ex-Cromwellian soldiers and that they had been stirred up by 'idle persons . . . nursed in the late rebellion'.[21] The government itself could find no firm evidence of a wider conspiracy or plans for a rising on May Day.[22] Moreover, it is difficult to know what to make of the use of green banners. Peter Messenger, one of the alleged ringleaders of the riots, protested in court that 'the rout' had torn off his apron, 'and charged [him] to carry it on a pole'.[23] Yet what else was

---

[18] Greaves, *Deliver us from evil*; Greaves, *Enemies under His feet*; Alan Marshall, *Intelligence and espionage in the reign of Charles II, 1660–1685* (Cambridge, 1994).

[19] Keith J. Lindley, 'Riot prevention and control in early Stuart London', *TRHS*, 5th ser., 33 (1983), 109–10; Ian Archer, *The pursuit of stability: social relations in Elizabethan London* (Cambridge, 1991), 3; Paul Griffiths, *Youth and authority: formative experiences in England 1560–1640* (Oxford, 1996), 151–61.

[20] *State trials*, ed. T. B. Howell (33 vols., London, 1809–26), VI, cols. 879–914 (quotations from cols. 882, 887, 888, 889, 890); Samuel Pepys, *Diary*, ed. R. C. Latham and W. Matthews (11 vols., London, 1970–83), IX:132.

[21] *CSPD, 1667–8*, 310; *London Gazette*, no. 249, 2–6 April 1668.

[22] The one suspect they arrested, who had boasted of his involvement in the disturbances and claimed that he and 40,000 others were ready to rise on 1 May, turned out to have been 'horribly overladen with drink' when he uttered these words, and had witnesses who could testify that he was at work on the days of the riots: PRO, SP 29/239, no. 167.

[23] *State trials*, VI, col. 882.

he to say, given that he was on trial for his life? The court nevertheless found him guilty as charged and passed sentence of execution. Even if he had been telling the truth with regard to this particular, why was it that 'the rout' wanted to use *his* apron as a banner; perhaps it was important that it was green. Justice Keeling, however, was less concerned about the specific colour than the fact that the rioters chose to march behind 'colours', in the military sense – 'we have discovered other colours', he told the jury on one occasion.[24] His concern is easily explained: military colours confirmed the allegation in the indictment that the rioters had marched 'in a warlike manner' and therefore that the ringleaders 'did imagine and contrive war and rebellion'.

What can be said with confidence is that it is not necessary to accept the government's conspiracy theories, since the bawdy-house riots of 1668 are perfectly understandable within an existing tradition of popular political protest – though the riots were no less threatening, subversive or (dare I invoke the term) radical because of that. The disturbances fit into a classic pattern of what might be labelled, in a loose sense, law-enforcement riots. Historians of popular protest have taught that riots were often informed by a belief that the law (or custom) was on the crowd's side, and that in many cases those who took to the streets in protest were simply trying to enforce the law when those in authority proved negligent. There are such legitimising notions, for example, underlying many anti-enclosure riots and food riots.[25] They can be seen again in 1668. Brothels were clearly illegal, yet not only was the government letting these go unpunished but also, given the number of ladies of pleasure at the royal court, almost seemed to be condoning such behaviour. At the same time, the Restoration regime had enacted a severe penal code against the self-styled godly, who worshipped outside the Church of England. The specific trigger for the riots in 1668 was a royal proclamation issued on 10 March calling for a strict enforcement of 'all the Laws now in force against unlawful Conventicles'.[26] The logic of the disturbances thus seems straightforward, and conforms to a classic strategy of

---

[24] Ibid., col. 889.

[25] John Walter, 'Grain riots and popular attitudes to the law: Maldon and the crisis of 1629' in John Brewer and John Styles (eds.), *An ungovernable people: the English and their law in the seventeenth and eighteenth centuries* (London, 1980), 47–84; E. P. Thompson, 'The moral economy of the English crowd in the eighteenth century' in his *Customs in common* (New York, 1991), 185–258; Douglas Hay, 'Poaching and the game laws on Cannock Chase' in Douglas Hay *et al.* (eds.), *Albion's fatal tree: crime and society in eighteenth-century England* (Harmondsworth, 1977), 189–253; J. A. Sharpe, *Crime in early modern England, 1500–1750* (London, 1982), ch. 6; Roger B. Manning, *Village revolts: social protest and popular disturbances in England, 1509–1640* (Oxford, 1988).

[26] *London Gazette*, no. 242, 9–12 March 1667/8; Robert Steele, *A bibliography of royal proclamations of the Tudor and Stuart sovereigns* (3 vols., London, 1910), I, no. 3514.

collective bargaining by riot:[27] if the government was going to clamp down on Nonconformist meeting-houses, the rioters were going to enforce the laws against whore-houses. Keeling understood the logic behind the riots perfectly well: 'we are but newly delivered from rebellion', he said at one point during the trials, 'and we know that that rebellion first begun under the pretence of religion and the law . . . therefore we have great reason to be very wary that we fall not again into the same error'.[28] And in large-scale disturbances of this nature, London crowds frequently divided up into regiments and marched behind different coloured banners or flags – the model here being the London trained bands, not the Levellers. The rioters in 1668 were asking for liberty of conscience, which had been a Leveller demand, but not a demand exclusive to the Levellers; moreover, they were certainly not asking for the full enactment of the Putney programme. We thus reach a dead end in our search for the Leveller connection, if we approach the matter in this way.

We end up being equally frustrated in our attempt to find Leveller connections in the London weavers' riots of 1675. The weavers were protesting against two things: the influx of immigrant weavers from France and the use of mechanised looms for making silk ribbons, both of which represented a threat to their livelihood. Wearing green aprons, to distinguish them from other people, huge bands of weavers assembled in various parts of the metropolitan area over several days in early August and proceeded to fall upon the French weavers, breaking all their materials, and to destroy all the engine looms they could find.[29] The government was initially concerned that the riots might pose a political threat, and the king issued a proclamation warning the weavers 'to forbear any further assembling upon paine of being proceeded against as traitors'.[30] The government was worried, however, less about the intentions of the weavers, whom they recognised were motivated by no other concern than to see the engine looms suppressed, than about the possibility that 'other unquiet spirits and malcontents' might seek to exploit the breakdown in order to cause trouble of their own.[31] Secretary of State Sir Joseph Williamson thought it was a scandal to the government that the riots were not more quickly suppressed, and stated that nobody knew 'where the disorder might have ended', whilst the lord mayor, Sir Robert Viner, warned that people began to 'talke already of other reformations' and feared that it might 'come to that they called in 1641 A Thorough

---

[27] The term was coined by Eric Hobsbawm, 'The machine-breakers', *Past and Present* 1 (1952), 58–62.   [28] *State trials*, VI, col. 884.

[29] For the riot, see Harris, *London crowds*, 191–204; Dunn, 'London weavers' riot'.

[30] PRO, PC 2/64, 490; Steele, *Bibliography*, I, nos. 3615, 3616.

[31] *Calendar of state papers, Venetian, 1673–5*, 448.

Reformation'.[32] One of the weavers interrogated by the Privy Council for involvement in the riots was a Fifth Monarchist, a man by the name of John Mason, who was also accused of speaking 'some desperate words'.[33]

In the end, however, the government determined that the insurrection was 'unpolitically designed', with the king himself acknowledging that the ground was 'no other than what is pretended', and decided not to pursue the rioters on charges of treason. The Fifth Monarchist Mason, it turned out, had been a victim of the riots, having had one engine-loom destroyed.[34] Moreover, before too much is read into the use of green aprons as banners, it needs to be pointed out that the rioters also wore red ribbons in their hats (the badge later adopted by supporters of the duke of York during the Exclusion Crisis).[35] One of the men giving instructions to the rioting weavers at one location, reminding them to 'Meddle only with the looms', in fact wore a blue feather in his cap. Blue ribbons were later to be worn by supporters of the duke of Monmouth during the Exclusion Crisis, but in 1675 Monmouth showed himself to be an enemy of the weavers, and it was troops under his command that were responsible for eventually suppressing the disturbances.[36] With red, blue and green all on display, it seems difficult to sustain the argument that the choice of colours in 1675 was designed to show affinity to a particular political cause. A more likely explanation is that the colours adopted reveal something about the organisational structure behind the disturbances: first, they were intended to make it easy to distinguish between those who were for or against the cause (given the large size of London crowds, it must have been impossible for the participants always to have known, from personal acquaintance, who in the throng was on one's side); and, secondly, they were probably intended to distinguish rank among the rioters (with captains wearing a different colour, perhaps) or to demarcate the different groups or regiments into which the rioters divided.

Let us turn now to the Whig movement of the Exclusion Crisis. That there were erstwhile Levellers, ex-Cromwellian soldiers, and their children and relatives involved in the Whig movement has now been well

---

[32] Longleat House, Coventry Ms. 16, fols. 62, 72, 82.   [33] *CSPD, 1675–6*, 258–9.

[34] BL Add. Ms. 25124, fols. 39, 43; *The diary of William Lawrence, covering periods between 1662 and 1681*, ed. G. E. Aylmer (Beaminster, 1961), 31; Greater London Record Office (London Metropolitan Archive), MJ/SR/1491, rec. 5 (*Oyer et Terminer*) to prosecute and MJ/SR/1493, gaol calendar.

[35] Corporation of London Record Office, Common Council Journal 48, fol. 168; Longleat House, Coventry Ms. 16, fol. 102.

[36] PRO, Assi 35, 116/9, examination of William Guest; PRO, PC 2/64, 490. To confuse matters further, supporters of a Leveller petition of January 1647 chose to wear blue ribbons in their hats. See Walter Frost, *A declaration of some proceedings of Lieutenant Colonel Lilburne* (London, 1648) in William Haller and Godfrey Davies (eds.), *The Leveller tracts, 1647–1653* (New York, 1944), 98, 105.

established. John Wildman, who moved in a radical circle that started gathering around the duke of Buckingham from about 1667, and who was involved both in the Rye House intrigues of 1682–3 and the Monmouth rebellion of 1685, had been at Putney, of course. Another one of Buckingham's entourage was the city radical, Francis Jenks, who was the son-in-law of William Walwyn. Then there were a number of ex-officers and soldiers from the 1640s and 1650s mixed up in the various Whig intrigues of the early 1680s, men such as Colonel Henry Danvers, Major John Gladman, Major Abraham Holmes, John Breman and Richard Rumbold (the last two, at least, can definitely be identified as having once been Levellers).[37] Moreover, prosecutions for seditious words reveal that amongst those who supported the Whigs there were some – it is difficult to know how many – who sympathised with the Good Old Cause and thought Charles II deserved the same fate as his father. In October 1682 a west country man was accused of saying 'that he would fight against the King for the Parliament that voted the Exclusion Bill, as willingly as ever he fought for the old Parliament against Charles I'.[38] A miller from Godalming was accused in 1683 of saying he thought Charles I 'deserved' to be executed 'for running from his Parliaments', an alarming thing to say given that Charles I's son was now likewise running from his parliaments.[39] In the autumn of 1684 a man from Kingston, Surrey, was accused of saying 'Oliver Cromwell's government was better and easier than the King's.'[40]

Nevertheless, despite this radical fringe (and even conceding that this fringe could have been broader than often acknowledged), the Whig movement, taken as a whole, is normally regarded as being a politically and socially much more conservative movement than anything seen in the 1640s. The parliamentary Whigs, in the main, wanted to preserve a strong (albeit Protestant) monarchy, whilst 'the only large-scale demonstrations' of the Exclusion Crisis, namely the pope-burnings of 17 November, John Miller has recently claimed, were nothing like those of the 1640s, but 'smacked more of theatre than of riot; when they were all over, participants and spectators reeled tipsily and innocuously off to bed'.[41] A number of scholars have insisted that any attempts to place figures such as

[37] De Krey, 'London radicals', 138–42; Ashcraft, *Revolutionary politics*, 247–8; Maurice Ashley, *John Wildman, plotter and postmaster: a study of the English republican movement in the seventeenth century* (London, 1947); G. E. Aylmer, 'Locke no Leveller' in Ian Gentles, John Morrill and Blair Worden (eds.), *Soldiers, writers and statesmen of the English revolution* (Cambridge, 1998), 304–22, at 314.   [38] *CSPD, 1682*, 493.
[39] Guildford Muniment Room, LM 1058/1–2 and 1192/2. The accused alleged the prosecution was malicious.
[40] *Historical selections from the manuscripts of Sir John Lauder of Fountainhall. Volume first, historical observations, 1680–1686* (Edinburgh, 1837), 142.
[41] John Miller, 'Public opinion in Charles II's England', *History* 80 (1995), 359–81, at 377.

the earl of Shaftesbury or John Locke in a Leveller milieu falter in the face of the evidence. David Wootton, for example, has reminded us that the constitution they drafted for Carolina adopted a system of government that provided for slavery and hereditary serfdom, whilst Locke's *Report to the Board of Trade on poor relief* of 1695 was scarcely written in the language of the Levellers. John Marshall's brilliant exposition of Locke's views on resistance has shown that, although Locke might have been a revolutionary, he was 'as conservative a revolutionary as a revolutionary could be': his intent was to convince the propertied classes that resistance would not lead to the levelling of the hierarchical ordering of society.[42]

If we take, as our litmus test, attitude towards the franchise, we find that the first Whigs were far removed from the platform advocated by the Levellers at Putney. For example, some draft proposals found amongst the earl of Shaftesbury's papers after his death actually recommended a narrowing of the franchise, on the grounds that a higher property qualification would cut down on electoral bribery. To be fair, Shaftesbury's most authoritative biographer, K. H. D. Haley, has warned against assuming that these proposals reflected Shaftesbury's own views (though interestingly Richard Ashcraft is among those who believe that they did). Nevertheless, Shaftesbury was certainly no democrat, and can be found on a number of occasions during his career defending the privileges of the House of Lords against the Commons.[43] John Wildman, the most famous ex-Leveller turned Whig conspirator – and the man whom John Morrill and Philip Baker have suggested was chiefly responsible for drafting the first *Agreement of the people*[44] – appears to have shifted a long way from the Putney position on the franchise by the time of the Glorious Revolution; it was Wildman, it has now been established, who was the author of a tract of 1689 arguing that the forty-shilling freehold, because of inflation, was too extensive, and that the vote should be restricted to men who possessed freehold land worth £40 p.a.[45] It is true that, in elections to the three Exclusion parliaments, the Whigs tended to do better in the larger,

---

[42] David Wootton, 'John Locke and Richard Ashcraft's revolutionary politics', *Political studies* 40 (1992), 79–98; John Marshall, *John Locke: resistance, religion and responsibility* (Cambridge, 1994), ch. 6 (quotation, 283). See also David McNally, 'Locke, Levellers and liberty: property and democracy in the thought of the first Whigs', *History of Political Thought* 10 (1989), 17–40; Aylmer, 'Locke no Leveller'.

[43] *Some observations concerning the regulating of elections for parliament, found among the earl of Shaftesbury's papers after his death* (London, 1689), 11; K. H. D. Haley, *The first earl of Shaftesbury* (Oxford, 1968), 739–40; Ashcraft, *Revolutionary politics*, 165–6; McNally, 'Locke, Levellers and liberty', 20–3.   [44] John Morrill and Philip Baker, above, 115, 121.

[45] [John Wildman], *Some remarks upon government, and particularly upon the establishment of the English monarchy relating to this present juncture* (London, 1689). For Wildman's authorship, see Mark Goldie, 'The roots of true Whiggism 1688–94', *History of Political Thought* 1 (1980), 214.

more open constituencies, and the Tories in the smaller boroughs. There are also examples of the Whigs championing a broadening of the franchise.[46] Yet the Whig approach to the franchise appears to have been pragmatic; they were interested in electoral victory, not political principle. At the Southwark election of 1681, the Whig candidates, one of whom was the republican Slingsby Bethel, sought to restrict the poll to those who paid poor rates; the Tories defended the right of all householders to vote, and managed to get themselves elected on the more broadly defined franchise.[47] The famous republican ideologue and conspirator, Algernon Sidney, when he stood for the borough of Amersham in 1679 and 1681, argued for a narrowing of the franchise from the inhabitant householders to those paying scot and lot.[48]

Tory propagandists were quick to ridicule the Whig claim that the House of Commons, in pressing for the exclusion of the duke of York, represented the voice of the people by highlighting the existing inequities in the franchise. As one anti-exclusionist writer, who styled himself Captain Thorogood, put it:

> the Parliament as now usually Elected, is not at all the Representative of the People . . . For none have Votes in Elections, but Free-holders of at least forty shillings a Year, and Citizens and Burgesses, and consequently all Lessees for Years, Grantees of Annuities for Years: Men that live upon the Interest, and Product of their Money: The greatest part of the Clergy, all Soldiers, and Seamen, most of the young Nobility and Gentry . . . the whole number of Labourers, Servants, Artificers, and Tradesmen, not residing in, or at least free of Cities and Boroughs, are totally excluded.

What could 'be more unequal, not to say unjust', the author went on to ask, than that 'the far greatest part of the Nation, that are Passengers in the great Ship of the Commonwealth . . . should be debarred their right of choosing a Master or Pilot, to whose Skill or Care they commit their common safety?' Must 'all this be left to the Arbitrary Power and Discretion of such, as by chance, perhaps more than merit, have acquired the Possession of Land, or are free of Boroughs and Cities?' The same author also pointed to the existence of rotten boroughs and the uneven (geographical and demographic) distribution of seats – old Leveller complaints.[49] Other opponents of exclusion used similar arguments to dis-

---

[46] Basil Duke Henning (ed.), *The House of Commons, 1660–1690* (3 vols., London, 1983), I:64–5, 131, 469, 471.

[47] *The tryal of Slingsby Bethel Esq* (London, 1681); Henning, *House of Commons*, I:416; M. D. George, 'Elections and electioneering, 1678–81', *EHR* 45 (1930), 565–8.

[48] *Smith's Protestant Intelligence*, no. 3, 4–8 Feb. 1680[/1]; Henning, *House of Commons*, I:138; Scott, *Algernon Sidney and the Restoration crisis*, 159, 174–5, 183–4.

[49] *Captain Thorogood his opinion of the point of succession* (London, 1679[/80]). For Lilburne's views on rotten boroughs, see Brailsford, *The Levellers*, 114–15.

credit the Whigs. Matthew Rider asked that if people were by nature free from subjection and if sovereignty was not conferred immediately by God but by the people as a trust, 'by what Authority are Free-holders and Freemen only allowed to choose, and be chosen Members of the House of Commons?' For that matter, why were 'Women and Children' not enfranchised, 'who yet upon the aforesaid grounds, have as plausable a pretence to the Government, as the greatest Peers in the Realm'? 'Who gave these Members the power of imposing Poll-moneys, or other Taxes, upon mean Peasants, Servants, Women, and Children, who are undoubtedly the major part of the Nation; and yet were never allowed to have any Vote or Suffrage in the Election of such Members?'[50] In like vein, the high-Anglican cleric, George Hickes, pondered that if sovereignty was in the people, why were women excluded from the government? 'Who gave the men authority to deprive them of their birthright, and set them aside as unfit to meddle with Government; when Histories teach us that they have weilded Sceptres, as well as Men, and Experience shews, that there is no natural difference between their understandings and ours, nor any defects in their knowledge of things, but what Education makes?'[51]

The evidence, looked at in this way, suggests little, if any, connection between opposition groups and political movements in Restoration England and the Levellers. Why did the Tories claim that there was? One obvious answer would be that they were scaremongering. And why not? Such a tactic proved extremely effective, and helped scare people away from the Whigs and encourage them to rally behind the Crown. Yet this is a somewhat blinkered way of looking at the problem. It serves to minimise the significance of the Leveller legacy, forces us to misunderstand the nature of the Tory concerns (which were more genuine than such an interpretation allows), and (by association) invites us to consider that we might have exaggerated the significance of the Leveller movement of the late 1640s in the first place.

Perhaps looking for a revival of some predefined Leveller programme is not the most fruitful approach. Historians have always emphasised the heterogeneous nature of the Leveller movement and its lack of ideological coherence: different types of Levellers stood for different things, and the same Levellers came to adopt different positions as they adapted to changing political realities.[52] Most famously, of course, the Leveller

---

[50] [Rider], *Power of parliaments*, 3–4.
[51] George Hickes, *A discourse of the sovereign power* (London, 1682), 22. Thomas Edwards, *Gangraena*, 3 parts (London, 1646), III:154, made a similar argument against the Levellers, asking that if all men should have the right to vote, why not women and children too.
[52] F. D. Dow, *Radicalism in the English revolution, 1640–1660* (Oxford, 1985), 31.

position on the franchise changed between the first and second *Agreements of the people* (and was to change again later).[53] Contemporary critics did not think the Levellers had a coherent platform. As Marchamont Nedham put it in 1650: 'what these People aime at, and how they would settle, is as hard for me to determine, as in what point of the Compasse the wind will sit next, since they are every jot as giddy and rapid in their Motions'.[54] Moreover, the Levellers themselves always denied that they were levellers, in the sense of wanting to destroy private property rights. Thus it is hardly surprising that the Putney programme was not revived in its entirety in the completely altered political context of the Exclusion Crisis, when it was already apparent that it would be unrealistic to press for it in its entirety by 1648. Nor is it surprising, when the Levellers themselves denied that they were levellers, that the Whigs should be eager to disassociate themselves from insinuations of levelling by protesting a genuine desire to protect property rights.[55]

Let us think, instead, about the essence of the Leveller phenomenon, of its significance and meaning as a social and political movement. Existing accounts of the Leveller phenomenon tend to stress a number of things.[56] The first is that it was a mass movement, perhaps the first of its kind in England to be organised on such a scale, though one that nevertheless tapped into a long-established tradition of popular political agitation and drew on the readiness and ability of ordinary people (especially amongst the urban middling sorts) to organise and to take direct action to protect what they regarded as their rights or their due (either their rights at law or what they perceived to be just and equitable, according to the law of nature).[57] Secondly, it is said, the Levellers developed new techniques of mass propaganda to organise and agitate their supporters amongst the rank and file – cheap print, petitions and demonstrations.[58] It is questionable whether they originated such techniques; Pym and the parliamen-

---

[53] For the successive *Agreements*, see Gentles, ch. 8 above.

[54] Marchamont Nedham, *The case of the commonwealth* (London, 1650), 69.

[55] Cf. F. K. Donnelly, 'Levellerism in eighteenth and nineteenth-century Britain', *Albion* 20 (1988), 261–9, at 267, who shows that although radicals and reformers in the late eighteenth and early nineteenth centuries read Leveller tracts and were influenced by Leveller ideas, they were keen to dissociate themselves from the Levellers because of the negative connotations of the term.

[56] I borrow here from Dow, *Radicalism*, esp. 30–1.

[57] Ian Gentles, 'London Levellers in the English revolution: the Chidleys and their circle', *Journal of Ecclesiastical History* 29 (1978), 281–309, at 281.

[58] Nigel Smith, *Literature and revolution in England 1640–1660* (New Haven, 1994), 131, has suggested that instead of dissecting the Levellers' political thought for its coherence or inconsistency, we might more profitably study Lilburne and his friends as 'clever manipulators of the media opportunities in the 1640s'.

tary opposition used similar tactics in 1641.[59] The Levellers' aim in mobilising the masses, however, was to try to ensure that the voice of the people would be listened to by those in government, and they pursued a number of reform initiatives (famously at Putney, of course) designed to make the voice of the people effective in government and to ensure that ordinary people would not have their rights or justice denied them. Thirdly, then, the Levellers were deeply attached to the principle of popular sovereignty, which as David Wootton has pointed out 'was far more fundamental to their thinking than the franchise or any constitutional question'.[60] For them, *salus populi* should be *suprema lex*. Along with this went various other assumptions: namely, that the representative assembly should have supreme authority, and that the powers of government should be limited by principles of natural justice (that is, laws must apply equally to all; there should be freedom of conscience; all laws 'must be good, and not evidently destructive to the safety and well-being of the people'; juries should refuse to enforce bad law; and if the people's representatives betrayed their trust, the people had the right to resist).[61] What concerned contemporaries was the *political* levelling that this strategy entailed. This was more fundamental to contemporary concerns about the Leveller phenomenon than a perceived threat to property rights (although given that the ownership of property conferred political rights in seventeenth-century England, the two were inextricably bound up in many people's minds). As Marchamont Nedham put it, the Levellers made a 'Plea for Equality of Right in Government'. Discussing the Leveller stance on the franchise and the origins of their nickname, Nedham wrote that because they claim 'all persons have an equality of Right to chuse and be chosen, without respect of Birth, quality, or wealth, all Orders of men being Levell'd in this Particular, therefore the Promoters of this way, are not improperly called Levellers'.[62] A tract of 1659 written in vindication of Leveller principles argued that it was their belief 'that every man ought to be equally subject to the Laws' that led

---

[59] Anthony Fletcher, *The outbreak of the English civil war* (London, 1981); Dagmar Freist, *Governed by opinion: politics, religion and the dynamics of communication in Stuart London 1637–1645* (London, 1997).

[60] David Wootton, 'Leveller democracy and the Puritan revolution' in J. H. Burns and Mark Goldie (eds.), *The Cambridge history of political thought, 1450–1700* (Cambridge, 1991), 412–42, at 433.

[61] Ibid., 412. Cf. *The Leveller*, 5–9, which indentifies the following four maxims as containing 'the sum of all the Levellers Doctrine about our Government': 1. 'the Government of England ought to be by Laws, and not by Men'; 2. 'all the Laws, Levies of Monies, War and Peace, ought to be made by the peoples deputies in Parliament, to be chosen by them successively at certain periods of time'; 3. 'every Man of what Quality or Condition, Place or Office, whatsoever, ought to be equally subject to the Laws'; 4. that there should be a citizen militia, and not a standing army.   [62] Nedham, *Case of the commonwealth*, 70–1.

their political opponents to invent the name Levellers in an effort to discredit them. The author nevertheless proudly reiterated the Leveller commitment to the doctrine 'that the Government ought to be setled upon such equall Foundations of Common Right and freedome, that no man, or number of men, in the Nation, should have the power to invade or disturb the common Freedome, or the common course of impartial justice'.[63]

If the topic is approached in this way, quite a few manifestations of the phenomenon of political levelling in Restoration England are noticeable. Take the bawdy-house riots of 1668 to start off with. For humble tradesmen and apprentices to rise up and instruct the king which laws he should or should not be enforcing, to the point of trying to enforce certain laws (those against brothels) themselves, was indeed a usurpation of the regal authority: the act, by its very nature, placed the common man on a level with the king (even if only temporarily), and in this respect was political levelling. If the reading of the riots as an anti-court protest is correct, then the crowd was trying to hold the royal court accountable to the law, and the belief that the law applied to all, regardless of social status (even the king), was a fundamental Leveller principle. The idea embodied in the riots that ordinary people could exercise the power of the sword, use force themselves to impose justice or even to resist duly constituted authority, was indeed political levelling and a Leveller principle. As George Hickes put it in a sermon of 1682, in the context of challenging what he took to be the Whig belief that power lay radically in the people (another Leveller notion): 'what a great sin it is for the subjects of any government upon any pretence whatsoever, to take up Arms without Authority from the lawfull Sovereign, be it in riots, tumults, or rebellions, or any other illegal meeting howsoever called; for God hath committed the power of the Sword to the lawfull Sovereign onely'.[64] When one group of rioters in 1668 broke open Finsbury jail, in order to rescue some of their fellow apprentices who had already been arrested for their involvement in the disturbances, they told the jailer: 'We have been servants, but we will be masters now' – a remark which, however one interprets it, had frightening levelling implications.[65] The meaning and significance of the rioters' actions in Easter Week 1668 is much more important than the green aprons they marched behind, which are something of a red (or green) herring.

Furthermore, if one looks at the Nonconformist campaign against the penal code, and especially the publications against the second Conventicle Act (1670), one again sees an embracing of Leveller-type

[63] *The Leveller*, 15–16.   [64] Hickes, *Discourse of the sovereign power*, 25.
[65] *State trials*, VI, col. 885.

arguments: an appeal to the principles of natural justice to limit the powers of government, and an articulation of the theory of popular sovereignty. Thus one writer insisted that the Conventicle Act was against the law of God, fundamental law and the law of nature, and therefore ought 'to be esteemed Null and Void, and altogether disregarded, as if there was no such thing in the Nation'.[66] Another maintained that the Conventicle Act, which took away the right to a trial by jury, was against the fundamental laws of the land, which guaranteed people's lives, liberties and properties. By endeavouring to subvert the fundamental laws, parliament had committed the highest treason: 'For our Fundamentals were not made by our Representatives, but by the People themselves; and our Representatives themselves limited by them . . . For no Derivative Power can Null what their Primitive Power hath Established.'[67]

There were similar implications of political levelling in the Whig movement. One should be careful when making generalisations about the Whigs and what they stood for. The Whig movement was a broad church; although the more radical types wanted fundamental constitutional reform, there were many who supported the demand for exclusion (as mentioned above) who nevertheless wanted to preserve strong monarchy in England – they simply wanted to keep it in the Protestant line. Yet the Tories tended to see the Whig movement as a whole, and to make inferences about what the Whigs stood for, from the way the case for exclusion came to be articulated and the tactics and strategies that were adopted in order to bring pressure on the Crown to agree to alter the succession. It was in this way, I wish to suggest, that Tories – given their understanding of how the divinely ordained and hierarchically structured universe was supposed to operate – came to see implications of political levelling behind the Whig campaign. The Whig claim that the king should agree to exclusion because it was the voice of the people, as articulated by their representatives in the House of Commons,[68] was, indeed, a Leveller principle, and it levelled political distinctions between commoners and nobility, and between the king, Lords and Commons. In many respects, Captain Thorogood's and other Tory propagandists' attempts to discredit the Whig position by focusing on the inequities of the franchise prove not how far removed the Whigs were from the Levellers but how close their two positions were: for Thorogood and company the inequities of the franchise were not a problem since they did not believe that

[66] [Nicholas Lockyer], *Some seasonable and serious queries upon the late act against conventicles* (London, 1670), quotation on 9–10.
[67] *The Englishman; or, a letter from a universal friend . . . with some observations upon the late act against conventicles* (London, 1670), 8–11. See also De Krey, 'Rethinking the Restoration'.   [68] E.g. *Vox populi, vox Dei* (London, 1681).

sovereignty was vested in the Commons or that political power was a trust from the people; their criticism of the Whigs only made sense in so far as it was an attack on a levelling position. Sometimes Whig MPs let their constituents know exactly where they stood on these issues. Towards the end of Charles II's reign, Richard Onslow, exclusionist MP for Surrey, was brought before the Croydon quarter sessions for having allegedly gone around various local drinking establishments in 1680 saying things such as 'the fountayne of Authority is in the people and that the King is accountable to them' and that he 'had no power but what he derived from them'.[69] The claim, made by the Whig-dominated Commons, that they, as the people's representative, had the right to change the succession was, at least within the Tory world-view, 'arrant Levellerism'. For as the court Tory Sir Leoline Jenkins insisted, it was 'impossible for subjects to renounce or divest themselves of the allegiance they were borne under'.[70] Matthew Rider, in his attack on the exclusionist movement, complained how 'our designing Levellers' sought to intoxicate 'the Mutinous Multitude . . . with the chimerical conceit of their being the Makers and Creatours of Kings, the very Source and Original of Dominion and Sovereignty, and consequently impower'd, when they think it expedient, to call the King to an account of his actions, and settle the Succession as they please'.[71]

The Whig movement, like the earlier Leveller movement, was a mass movement, where the leaders sought to employ sophisticated techniques of mass propaganda in order to mobilise those out-of-doors – through petitions and demonstrations – and thus put pressure on those who held the reins of power to accede to the demands of those out-of-doors. According to the Tory view, subjects had no right to instruct kings how to rule. All they could do was petition for redress of grievances (so long as they did not do it tumultuously), and hope their case might be favourably heard. As one anti-Leveller tract put it in 1648, 'a Petition is to set forth your grievances, and not to give a rule to the Legislative Power; if you meane it shall be an Edict, which you must compose, and the Parliament must verifie, call it no more a Petition'.[72] Yet the Whig petitions did not simply petition in the above-defined sense; they made demands (that parliament be allowed to sit, or that MPs should vote for exclusion) and backed up these demands with threats (for example, that no taxes should be voted unless the king gave in to the demand for exclusion).[73] In short,

[69] Guildford Muniment Room, 111/10/14/4, 7, 11.

[70] All Souls' Library, Oxford, Ms. 251, fol. 154.   [71] [Rider], *Power of parliaments*, 6.

[72] Frost, *Declaration of some proceedings*, 118.

[73] J. R. Jones, *The First Whigs: the politics of the Exclusion Crisis, 1678–83* (London, 1970), esp. 115–19, 167–73; Mark Knights, *Politics and opinion is in crisis, 1678–81* (Cambridge, 1994), chs. 8–10.

the Whig petitioning campaign *was* Lilburneisme. According to John Northleigh, the Whigs were Levellers because they set up 'the very rabble . . . for the sole Magistrates and Legislators'.[74] The point about Lilburneisme is well illustrated by what happened to the Irish peer, Viscount Clare, when, following the sudden dissolution of the Oxford parliament in March 1681, he promoted a petition at the Ennis Assizes asking the king to call another parliament in England to alleviate people's fears about popery and arbitrary government. By now the political tide was turning; Clare was disgraced by the government for his actions, so that he was reduced to sending begging letters to the lord lieutenant of Ireland, the duke of Ormonde, in an attempt to obtain a royal pardon. 'My sin was a sin of ignorance', he protested; he had believed there really was a popish plot, and thought that parliament could help the king get to the root of the matter. But 'I never thought of siding with any common-wealth or antimonarchical party', he insisted. 'Neither is it my interest to have such as descended for many ages from nobility brought even with the cobbler, so that if my words be doubted, I must be looked upon as a madman if I go against my interest, my inclinations and my duty.'[75] In claiming to see the error of his ways, in other words, this Irish Whig acknowledged the levelling implications of the Whig petitioning campaign.

Let me summarise. I am not trying to argue that the Whigs were, in any literal sense, Levellers, or that they were seeking to revive the Leveller platform. Such a claim could easily be shown to be ridiculous. Indeed, *ipso facto* it strains credibility: the political context was significantly different at the the time of the Exclusion Crisis (when there was a restored monarch with a full complement of his prerogative powers), from what it had been in 1647–9 (when parliament and the army were having to deal with a king defeated in civil war), and the issues facing contemporaries in 1679–81 were also radically different, so that the strategy and goals of the Whigs were inevitably going to be far removed from those of Lilburne and the Levellers. Since the labels we employ as historians have to be meaningful, it obfuscates rather than clarifies to invoke the term Leveller in discussions of the first Whigs; the term Leveller was used as a descriptive label for a particular type of mass political activism that was associated with specific reform initiatives that came to be placed on the agenda in the specific context of the aftermath of the first civil war.

What I am saying, however, is that the Whig movement of the Exclusion Crisis, involving (as it did) an attempt to harness the grievances

---

[74] [Northleigh], *Parallel*, 34.   [75] *HMC Ormonde*, N.S. VI:380.

and concerns of the masses out-of-doors in order to compel those who held the reins of power to bow to the will of the people, implied a type of political levelling (when set against the prevalent assumptions of how the political universe was supposed to be structured in Restoration England) that was, in bare essentials, the same as the type of political levelling that the Levellers had stood for and had earned them their nickname in the first place. Indeed, thinking in terms of the Whig movement as a socio-political phenomenon it was very similar to the collective agitation out-of-doors that is seen first, on behalf of Pym and the parliamentary opposition in the early 1640s, and later in support of Lilburne and the Levellers. I would even go so far to suggest that although Levellerism is not seen in the Exclusion Crisis, Lilburneisme is visible in a meaningful sense. Thinking about the problem in this way, one can begin to appreciate why the Tories were so concerned about the Whig challenge. The alternative conceptual approach to the question of the Leveller legacy I have suggested is fruitful precisely because it helps clarify historical understanding. It also frees us from being too dismissive of the significance of the Leveller movement of the later 1640s. The energies and driving forces behind the Leveller campaign, the articulation by the middling and lower orders (and by their political spokesmen) of a demand that their voice be heard, that their rights and interests be protected, did not evaporate into thin air; these energies were alive and well in Restoration England, they simply came to be channelled in different directions because of the transformed political context.

Confirmation for the validity of the interpretation offered here comes from what might seem a surprising quarter: namely, the defensiveness that certain Tory propagandists showed about possibly being accused of levelling themselves, following their successful attempts in the early 1680s to win over public opinion. Initially, the restored regime had sought to close down what some historians would now refer to as the emerging public sphere of the seventeenth century.[76] To this end, they reimposed strict controls over the press and passed legislation against tumultuous petitioning, they sought to silence political discussion in the taverns and coffee houses, and they dealt firmly with any form of collective agitation out-of-doors that might potentially threaten the political order. By 1680 it was apparent that such tactics had failed; not only had it proved impossible to stop political disputation out-of-doors, but it was also becoming clear that the royal administration was losing the hearts and minds of the people it had to govern. The court therefore changed its

[76] Steven Pincus, '"Coffee politicians does create": coffeehouses and Restoration political culture', *Journal of Modern History* 67 (1995), 807–34.

approach, and launched a deliberate appeal to public opinion, in a self-conscious attempt 'to reduce the deluded Multitude to their Just Allegiance'.[77] Courtiers, Tory MPs and loyal publicists not only promoted a popular propaganda campaign, building on techniques that had first been developed in the 1640s, but even encouraged loyalist demonstrations and popular addresses (not just from members of the local elite, but even from humble groups such as apprentices, tinners, watermen and cooks), some of which could boast thousands of signatories. This was not Lilburneisme. The purpose of the Tory addresses, for example, was to show that the Whigs did not have the masses on their side, but that most people accepted and supported the divinely ordained, hierarchically structured political universe. Moreover, they were addresses, not petitions that made demands of their sovereign. The decision by the government to appeal to those out-of-doors nevertheless reveals a recognition that the voice of the people counted in politics.[78] Indeed, Tory polemicists even went so far as to invoke the motto *salus populi suprema lex* in their propaganda, only claiming that it was the Tories, and not the Whigs, who were truly concerned about promoting the welfare of the people. Thus government licenser of the press, Roger L'Estrange, in his long-running periodical *The Observator*, admitted that government existed for the common good, but denied that this placed sovereignty in the people, or that the people could overthrow the government if they judged it not to be acting for the common good: ' 'Tis the Governours Part, to Resolve, Order, and Appoint, as he sees best for the Common Good; and it is the Subjects Part, to Submit, or Obey.'[79] Or as he put it elsewhere: 'wherein does the Safety of the People consist? but in the Preserving of Order, and Government'.[80]

It was in the context of justifying his efforts to win back the allegiance of the common people, however, that L'Estrange explicitly addressed the issue of whether he, in turn, had been guilty of levelling. It was 'Seditious Instruments', he insisted, that made a 'Seditious People', for the common people were equally capable of being well disposed to the government as they were of being led astray,[81] and those who stirred up the masses were no better than the mob themselves.[82] Man is judged, L'Estrange said, not

---

[77] Thompson, *Collection of . . . loyal songs*, preface.

[78] I have explored these issues in various publications. See, in particular: *London crowds*, chs. 6, 7; 'Understanding popular politics in Restoration Britain', in Pincus and Houston (eds.), *Nation transformed?*; '"Venerating the honesty of a tinker": the king's friends and the battle for the allegiance of the common people in Restoration England', in Tim Harris (ed.), *The politics of the excluded, c. 1500–1850* (Basingstoke, 2001), 195–232.

[79] Roger L'Estrange, *The observator in dialogue* (3 vols. , London, 1684–7), III, no. 196 (31 July 1686).   [80] Ibid., I, no. 209 (21 September 1682).

[81] Ibid., III, no. 151 (6 March 1685/6).   [82] Ibid, III, no. 203 (25 August 1686).

by his pedigree or wealth, but by his 'Life', 'Manners' and 'Intrinsick Value', and his mob was 'made up, out of the Rubbish, of both Great, and Small', and could be found 'In Palaces, as well as Cottages'.[83] It is in the context of developing such a line of argumentation that L'Estrange has the Observator's protagonist, the Trimmer, accuse him of levelling. 'Why, you are upon a Levelling Humour this Morning; as if there were no Difference betwixt Lords, Knights, 'Squires, and Gentlemen; and Cobblers, Broom-men, and the Basest Mechaniques', the Trimmer charges on one occasion.[84] A few issues later, he repeats the allegation: 'You have been Twice or Thrice now . . . upon the Humour of Levelling, and the bringing of All Orders of Men, into a Parity.' 'No, no,' retorts the Observator; 'I am not for Confounding the Degrees; or Breaking the Scale of Upper, and Lower. The Wise, and the Good Men, on the Vulgar side, shall Act still in their Proper Order; and Remain still in the Same Class, as Before.'[85] In the process, one might suggest, L'Estrange reveals the very reasons why the Tories thought they perceived the 'Humour of Levelling' behind what the Whigs stood for during the Exclusion Crisis.

[83] Ibid, III, no. 206 (4 September 1686).   [84] Ibid, III, no. 202 (21 August 1686).
[85] Ibid, III, no. 206 (4 September 1686).

12 Puritanism, liberty and the Putney debates

William Lamont

William Clarke took the minutes at the Putney debates in 1647;[1] Sir Charles Firth recovered them in 1891; A. S. P. Woodhouse produced the most accessible scholarly record of them in 1938. In fact, Woodhouse did more than that: he gave a title and a theme to these debates. Arguably it is Woodhouse, not Clarke and Firth, who has most shaped our ideas about Putney. After Woodhouse, it has proved difficult to think of the Putney debates outside those terms in which he set them. But Putney occupies only a small part of the whole of his volume. He named his volume *Puritanism and liberty*; he chose to juxtapose the Putney debates with the Whitehall debates a year later, whose subject matter was unarguably about the connection between puritanism and liberty; the final two-thirds of his book (179–473) is taken up with extracts from contemporary pamphlets around his theme of 'Puritan Views of Liberty'. In his long and thoughtful Introduction Woodhouse never pretends that the connection between the two is unambiguous. His title and his packaging, however, do his work for him. We view not Putney, but Putney-in-the-company-it-keeps. And Woodhouse chooses that company for us. There is, therefore, a disingenuous element in his argument, that the admitted weaknesses in the Introduction – 'we murder to dissect' – can be redressed by turning to the documents. Since these documents themselves have been selected by the editor for their relevance to his named theme of Puritan views of liberty, there is a circularity at work here which arouses serious misgivings. That theme itself is very much a 1930s tune, one hummed by scholars such as William Haller (*Tracts on liberty in the Puritan revolution* in 1934) and W. K. Jordan (in his four volumes, *The development of religious toleration in England*, from 1932 to 1940).[2] We know that Jefferson was

---

[1] The one thing missing in the otherwise full account of Clarke in his *Dictionary of national biography* entry: X:448–9. The publication date was 1887, four years before his other contribution to history could be appreciated.

[2] *P&L* (1950), [38]; W. Haller (ed.), *Tracts on liberty in the Puritan Revolution 1638–1647* (New York, 1934); W. K. Jordan, *The development of religious toleration in England* (4 vols., London, 1932–40).

influenced by Locke and Harrington; there are times, though, when American historians are tracking down their liberal origins to their source in the Puritan revolution, when we are almost persuaded that Jefferson was steeped in *The collected works of Colonel Rainborough* (if there ever had been such a thing). Certainly it was an eye-opener when a distinguished historian, at a Putney commemoration recently, asked his panel to discuss the reception of Putney in the eighteenth and nineteenth centuries. The answer simply is that there was none, nor could have been, at least until 1891, unless there had been in the interim period a systematic looting of the cupboards in Worcester College, Oxford.

Those who attended the celebration of Putney at the Folger Library in 1997 may have fashioned a different connection altogether: that between puritanism and *illiberality*. They would have seen the spectacle of Washington being taken over by half a million men (and their sons) in baseball caps. They had called themselves the 'Promise Keepers'. These were the anti-gay, anti-abortion religious fundamentalists. A few months on, it was the Rutherford Institute that was behind the campaign against President Clinton.[3] In 1982 it had been established to defend religious liberties under threat from the secular state; in 1998 it saw its function to cleanse the presidency from moral corruption. A recent cartoon reinforces that connection. It depicts the opening meeting of a Puritan reading group: 'OK so every month we choose a book, read it, then we meet to discuss whether it should be burned.'

These might be seen as examples of twentieth-century puritanism on the march, but it would be very easy indeed to find their seventeenth-century counterparts. Think of Thomas Edwards and his *Gangraena*: the knee-jerk conservative reflexes of a Puritan confronting 'the world turned upside down' of the 1640s. Or think of William Prynne – hater indiscriminately of Jews, Quakers, Papists, long hair, plays, health-drinking – and laughter. We know if Edwards and Prynne had been at Putney whose side they would have been on. It would not have been that of Levellers Wildman, Rainborough and Sexby. And then the Putney scenario would have been read straightforwardly as a contest between two opposing Puritan views on liberty. Wildman, Rainborough and Sexby would stand for freedom; Edwards and Prynne would represent bigotry. Still, as a matter of historical fact, Edwards and Prynne were not at Putney; Cromwell and Ireton were. Only, it seems, by eliding

---

[3] The Rutherford Institute thus moves from a concept of negative liberty – freedom from the state – to a concept of positive liberty – purify the White House. This distinction is developed later in this essay. On Rutherford's legacy to the Institute that bears his name, see John Coffey, *Politics, religion and the British revolution: the mind of Samuel Rutherford* (Cambridge, 1997), 11–15. A. S. P. Woodhouse cites Rutherford in his section, 'Puritan views of liberty', for his resistance theories: *P&L*, 199–212.

Edwards/Prynne into Cromwell/Ireton can the antithesis be drawn in that stark form. And it won't do. Professor Woolrych has shown how, at Naseby and again at Bristol, the Long Parliament had deleted whole passages from Cromwell's victory messages, which had put liberty of conscience at the centre of the struggle.[4] One's quarrel (aesthetic as well as historical) is with re-creations of Putney, which represent the Cromwell/Ireton position in agitprop terms, as does Caryl Churchill's *Light shining in Buckinghamshire*.[5] Cromwell/Ireton becomes there indistinguishable from Prynne/Edwards; cast as blinkered champions of repression against the 'liberty' claims of their Puritan opponents. This picture (caricature?) is reinforced by Ireton's emphasis on property against his opponents' demands for a wider franchise (that is how the debates start, after all): Ireton, not only a bigot then, but a bourgeois bigot to boot. But a year on from Putney, Ireton is leader of the pack pursuing the 'man of blood' to his execution. Is there some inconsistency here? Not if one pursues a different tack, and sees 'property' not as the central issue for Ireton but rather as the telling *illustration* of what is for him the important issue. Property, marriage, the constitution itself, were all tied up for Ireton with this core question (which takes up such an inordinate time on the first of what is, after all, only three recorded days of debate): should promises be kept? Students who initially thrill to the *concept* of the debates – the romance of the discovery of the papers, the great set-pieces on the franchise – are often turned off by the *reality*. Those wearisome arguments about what makes a covenant binding, those marathon prayer meetings to resolve issues, the readiness, for Heaven's sake, to listen to each other's *dreams* – they prompt a response something like 'great about the franchise, a pity about the Puritanism'. But when Ireton says at Putney 'if God saw it good to destroy not only Kings and Lords, but all distinctions of degrees – nay if it go further to destroy all property' and then claims 'if I see the hand of God in it I hope I shall with quietness acquiesce, and submit to it, and not resist it',[6] this should not be written off as rhetoric. After all, he was as good as his word. In December 1648 he *was* ready to destroy king and Lords: the 'hand of God' was in Pride's Purge (an intimation which his father-in-law was slower to pick up on, but he too got there in the end). Ireton did not, the cynic might object, get round in the end to destroying 'property' or 'distinctions of degree', but for anti-formalists such as Cromwell and Ireton they were indeed as much 'forms' as were kings or Lords, and therefore were subject to the same pragmatic tests. The difference a year makes is

---

[4] A. Woolrych, Cromwell Day, 1991: 'Oliver Cromwell and the people of God', *Cromwell 400*, ed. P. Gaunt (Cromwell Association, 1999), 54–60, at 56.
[5] London, 1989; originally published London, 1978.   [6] *P&L*, 50.

that Ireton's enemy was 'promise-breaker' John Wildman in 1647, whereas in 1648 his enemy was 'promise-breaker' Charles I.

What Ireton finds offensive in his opponents at Putney is their cocksureness that the 'hand of God' was in what they were advocating, and therefore all previous commitments were void. Hence his outraged response: 'this is a principle that will take away all commonwealths' or 'covenants freely made, freely entered into, must be kept one with another'. In those stark terms it could be represented as promise-keeping versus promise-breaking, and in those stark terms in the course of debate Ireton would, from time to time, represent it. But the polarities can be exaggerated, on either side. Rainborough recognises that engagements *should* be kept: only 'I think under favour that some engagements may be broken'. Cromwell recognises, on the other hand, that unrighteous engagements *should not* be kept: only that 'circumstances' (a weaselly opaque word that) could 'be such as I may not now break an unrighteous engagement'.[7] 'Circumstances' would keep him in Pontefract, while Ireton already in November 1648 could see 'the hand of God' raised against monarchy and Lords. And when that point was reached, all previous obligations dissolved for Ireton, as they had earlier for Wildman and Rainborough. Woodhouse drew attention in his Introduction to the importance among the radical groups at Putney of the phenomenon of 'progressive comprehension': those who now saw the 'new light' could not be bound by what they had previously perceived in the 'old darkness'. Even here the polarities can be exaggerated. Sometimes the contrast is between darkness and light: the classic 'born-again' Christian experience. But Wildman put it more mildly: 'while there is not so clear a light' when a person enters into an engagement that, too, is sufficient reason to take stock. And if the agreement now seems wrong it becomes 'an act of honesty for that man to recede from his former judgment, and to abhor it'.[8]

When on the first day of debate, 28 October, Sexby leads off with an attack on king and parliament, Ireton and Cromwell keep coming back to this question: how far *was* the army free to consider what *An agreement of the people* proposed, in view of previous promises and engagements? Professor Woolrych is right to chide Woodhouse for seeing this as just an exercise in the 'lower tactics of debate'.[9] At the same time Ireton and Cromwell had got what they wanted. Discussion of the content of *An agreement of the people* had been put off for a day, and a committee was appointed to compare the proposals in that document with the army's previous engagements. But

---

[7] Ibid., 11, 26, 32, 16.   [8] Ibid., [44], 10.

[9] A. Woolrych, 'New roads to Putney', unpublished paper, 12; see also his *Soldiers and statesmen* (Oxford, 1987), 223.

what comes across in the debates themselves is the common religious language as well as the divided political perceptions, and this is what gives them
– for all their turgid repetitiveness – their moving quality. Cromwell and
Ireton share many of the intimations of their opponents. Calling a prayer
meeting may indeed merely give breathing-space (a suspicion voiced at the
time), but it is also where 'the hand of God' may be detected. Read
Cromwell's letters in the 1630s and it is easy to see how he would empathise
with the conversion narratives (and dreams) of his opponents; just as, in the
1650s, Cromwell could share the millenarian beliefs (or many of them) with
Fifth Monarchist men – and would still oppose them.

What is difficult in this internal puritan debate is to see 'liberty' at the
heart of it, and then this raises the further question of how far it was
injected into it by 1930s concerns. As early as 1928 A. D. Lindsay, master
of Balliol, had been calling for an accessible modern edition of the
debates for the general reader. This was because 'our modern discussions
of democracy' begin there, he had claimed.[10] Note that it is 'democracy',
not 'liberty', which he was arguing then as its theme. His foreword to the
1938 edition of Woodhouse conveys his overwhelming gratitude at its
appearance. At the same time he was fighting the famous Oxford parliamentary by-election against appeasement. Tom Harrison in his *Picture
Post* report of 5 November 1938 quoted the verdict of one middle-aged
woman voter: 'Lindsay's not right opposing Chamberlain. You could have
understood Labour doing it. But he's supposed to be an educated man.'
In the light of comments like these, is it fanciful to suggest that Lindsay
hailed Woodhouse as a sort of 'Intelligent woman's guide to democracy'?
It was certainly 'something much more complete than I originally dared
to hope'.[11] More complete, because Whitehall is grafted on to Putney by
Woodhouse, and 'Puritan Views of Liberty' are given by him in such generous dollops? He does not say so, and in any case 'democracy', not
'liberty', was his concern in 1938. For his part, Woodhouse, in his
Introduction, had praised Lindsay's own earlier work, *The essentials of
democracy*, for his insight there that the seventeenth-century congregation
was the school for twentieth-century democracy.[12] Lindsay in his turn
commended Woodhouse to those who wished 'to be able to give a reason
for their democratic faith'. And he hoped that it 'would be read so as to
stop the mouths and pens' of the others. Who were they? They were those
'who produce facile refutations of the fundamental ideas of democracy'.[13]

Stopping mouths and pens does not sound like hymns to liberty. Nor
should that be a surprise in 1938. The urgency to get the democratic
message across was what mattered, whether in print or at a by-election

---

[10] *P&L*, [3].   [11] Ibid., [3].   [12] Ibid., [76].   [13] Ibid., [3].

hustings. But in his Introduction Woodhouse had noted that 'there is in Puritanism a possibility of autocracy as well as a possibility of democracy'.[14] When a new edition of Woodhouse was produced in 1950 these remarks were invested with a new meaning. Lindsay provided a postscript then to his original foreword of 1938. The enemy now was not fascism, but an autocracy *that called itself a democracy*. With 'the rise and spread of an entirely new idea of democracy in eastern Europe', Lindsay argued that Woodhouse's study had 'now assumed a new importance'. In that light Putney could be reassessed in 1950. The debates now, he claimed, show 'the fundamental connection between *western* democracy and liberty, and the opposition between democracy and any kind of totalitarianism'.[15] Maybe it was, after all, just a caprice that had led Woodhouse to call his book *Puritanism and liberty* and not 'Puritanism and democracy' – but in these changed circumstances how providential!

Yet there is evidence enough in Woodhouse's own Introduction that he had qualms about the nature of that linkage which had provided him with his title. He recognises that 'a concern for liberty' does not appear to be 'a constant feature of the Puritan mind'; that indeed 'it runs counter to another of the most universally recognised of traits, the passionate zeal for positive reform, with the will, if necessary, to dragoon men into righteousness – or the semblance of righteousness'.[16] This is well put, but it drives a stake through his argument. For his thesis is still that 'liberty' is an important Puritan legacy from Putney. He bases his case upon a taxonomy of religious divisions, which has worn less well than any of the rest of his Introduction. He has to recognise among his Puritan groupings that their common feature was 'the shared ideal of the "holy community"', with its corollary that 'reform must be by coercion'.[17] 'Liberty' only squeezes into his 'Presbyterian/Right' grouping with the claim that 'in the hour of oppression it had been a main plea of every group'. But this is to debase the coinage. 'Liberty' becomes a mere tactic for survival: a universe apart from the precocious anti-Stalinism with which Lindsay would want to invest it in his 1950 postscript to Woodhouse. There is more to be said for 'liberty' in his 'Centre' and 'Left' groupings – there would have to be, if his argument were not to dissolve totally – but even here he acknowledges that the 'Christian liberty' which they advocate frees the individual '*for*, not *from*, the service of God'.[18] It is the most important insight in the whole of Woodhouse's Introduction, but it is not developed by him. The argument dribbles away into a discussion whether this sort of liberty was for the Elect, or for all mankind.

---

[14] Ibid., [84].   [15] Ibid., [3], emphasis added.   [16] Ibid., [51].   [17] Ibid., [36].
[18] Ibid., [67–8], (emphasis in original).

It would not be picked up again until Professor Colin Davis' ground-breaking article of 1992 on the Whitehall debates. It was their juxtaposition to Putney in Woodhouse's ordering of contents that had made 'liberty' seem more of a Puritan concern, it could be argued, than if Putney alone were the object of scrutiny. But Davis shows that even this is illusory. It is true that the Whitehall debates start, not like Putney with the franchise, but with the specific question, 'whether the magistrate have, or ought to have, any comprehensive and restrictive power in matters of religion'.[19] And it stays with that brief. There is no sense of 'liberty' being imposed on a different agenda from the debates themselves (as we may feel is the case with Putney). But the 'liberty' that is being discussed there is no different, in Davis' very careful analysis, from what Woodhouse had found in Putney: it is liberty *for*, not *from*, the service of God. Davis shows that the search there was for 'submission to Christ' and that 'liberty was only a preliminary to that act'. Where though, we may ask, in the seventeenth century would we expect to find Puritans committed to such a concept as freedom *from*: that is to say, the assertion of an autonomous individual will? Only, Davis answers, among the antinomians. He thinks that there were not many of them about. I think there were more than he supposes, but all this matters less than the fact that mainstream Puritans such as Cromwell and Ireton *thought* that there were *more still*. Why Puritans, as much at Whitehall as at Putney, cannot in the final analysis embrace 'liberty' is because of this fear of being overrun by antinomians.[20] I want now to make what seems like a diversion in order to reinforce this central point.

There is another seventeenth-century text which provides an illuminating comparison with Woodhouse. Like Woodhouse, it was published in the 1930s by J. M. Dent (the 1931 Everyman edition was based on a 1925 first publication). Like Woodhouse, it went through several editions, with updated Introductions but an unchanging text (Ivan Roots added bibliographical information to the Woodhouse Introduction in 1974 and again in 1986; Neil Keeble substituted his own Introduction for that of Lloyd Thomas in 1974). That work was Richard Baxter's *Autobiography*, itself abridged from Matthew Sylvester's *Reliquiae Baxterianae* of 1696, by the Reverend J. M. Lloyd Thomas.[21]

[19] Ibid., 125.
[20] J. C. Davis, 'Religion and the struggle for freedom in the English revolution', *HJ* 35 (3) (1992), 507–30, at 519, 523.
[21] The original (incomplete) source is BL Egerton Ms. 2570; published first as Matthew Sylvester (ed.), *Reliquiae Baxterianae* (London, 1696). An abridgement followed: Edmund Calamy (ed.), *An abridgment of Mr Baxter's history of his life and times* (London, 1702, 1713, 1727), then the twentieth-century abridgements: J. W. Lloyd Thomas (ed.),

Baxter was a Puritan who had a real contribution to make to 'liberty'. That is the theme of Lloyd Thomas' Introduction: 'an ascetic figure stepping out of the mists of the seventeenth century and appealing to the sympathies of the modern mind'. Many such sentiments litter his Introduction: he 'speaks directly with the living voice of a contemporary. The speech is of the seventeenth century, the thought is for us and those who shall follow us.'[22] There is perhaps too much stepping out of seventeenth-century mists and into twentieth-century concerns for comfort, but this 1931 perception would in fact be echoed by Neil Keeble in 1974, for whom 'this apostle of charity, moderation and conciliation' was one 'whose breadth of sympathy' invested 'the following pages' with 'their peculiar power and authority'.[23]

And here we insert a rude question: whose 'breadth and sympathy' actually invests the text that follows with authority? Keeble, of course, thought that it was Baxter's, but it was not. It was Baxter's, *as mediated by Lloyd Thomas*. The original manuscript survives only in partial form; the posthumous memoir edited by Sylvester is a shapeless mess. So Lloyd Thomas performed a real service when he cut it down to size. He was scrupulous in putting omission marks when he left things out, and in making clear where he reinserted material from the original that Sylvester had left out (Sylvester had not liked those Baxter aspersions on Charles II's sexual morality). In case anybody should query whether 'personal idiosyncracy of choice' had dictated his selection (do we sense a defensive note here?), Lloyd Thomas warned the reader in his Introduction that he had consulted some Baxter scholars (but he did not say who they were), but conceded that 'no doubt my judgment will be found faulty by some quite competent students of Baxter'.[24] How wrong you were, Lloyd Thomas! For the next seventy years he was given a clean bill of health; Keeble wrote a new Introduction in 1974 but did not tamper with the Lloyd Thomas text.

Doubts began to surface only as more personal details about Lloyd Thomas came to light.[25] He had been a Unitarian minister with a life-long aim to forge closer links with Rome. Baxter was his inspiration. To that end he had founded an organisation called the Free Catholic Movement; to that end he had published from 1916 onwards a monthly magazine, *The Free Catholic*; and to that end he edited Baxter's memoirs.

footnote 21 (*cont.*)

> *The autobiography of Richard Baxter* (Everyman, 1931: first published in 1925); N. H. Keeble, *The autobiography of Richard Baxter* (Everyman, 1974), the same abridgement, but a new Introduction.   [22] Lloyd Thomas, *Autobiography*, vii, xxxvii.

[23] Keeble, *Autobiography*, xxvii.   [24] Lloyd Thomas, *Autobiography*, xxxii.

[25] On which, see Margaret Phelan, 'The Free Catholic Movement', *Baxter Notes and Studies* 2(2) (1994), 20–1.

His movement almost fell apart in 1932 when one of its leading lights decamped to Rome. Lloyd Thomas was expected to follow suit, but didn't, and remained a maverick Unitarian minister until his Birmingham church was destroyed by enemy bombs in 1941.

How Lloyd Thomas systematically rejigged Baxter to suit his ideology will be the subject of another essay.[26] Its findings, however, which are relevant to this essay, is that he excised all passages, obviously, where Baxter expressed his hatred of Roman Catholics and – of even greater relevance to the present argument – of the ideology *of religious liberty* which had, in Baxter's view, provided the essential cover for Papist advances. Two particular omissions are striking in this context. In *Reliquiae Baxterianae*, Sylvester had reproduced Baxter's catalogue of all his Commonwealth writings. Of these, none matched in notoriety his *Holy commonwealth* of 1659. It was the book that he repudiated to save his political skin in 1670; it went with the texts of Milton and Hobbes into Oxford's book-burning of 1683. Lloyd Thomas simply left it out. True, Baxter had pleaded in 1670 that it should now be treated as *non-scriptum*.[27] To have this request honoured as late as 1931 argues, however, for over-literalism, at the very least.

There was an even more revealing omission. Lloyd Thomas left out Baxter's explanation of why it was that he could never support any moves to advance religious toleration, if the beneficiary would be popery. Baxter (in the 1696 edition) had said that he was in favour of 'a certain degree of liberty for Papists'. He would, for instance, never sanction 'cruelty against Papists, any more than others, even when they are most cruel to us'. Yet he would *never* be the one to 'petition for a Papists liberty'. Why? There is a compelling reason why no puritan can ever be the 'introducer of the Papists Toleration': 'God do what he will with us, his way is best, but I think that this is not his way.'[28]

Where have we heard that note before? At Putney, in Ireton's quiet submission to the hand of God, and to other Puritan submissions at Whitehall (in the speakers whom Davis analysed). It is the opposite to a plea for liberty: 'God do what he will with us.' The argument in this essay never has been that Lloyd Thomas or Keeble fabricated an 'ecumenical' Baxter. God's way – which the Puritan is enjoined to follow – was not the insistence upon the perpetuation of trivial differences between Protestants. God's way was to build bridges between Protestants and

[26] 'The religious origins of the English civil war: two false witnesses' in Richard Bonney and David Trim (eds.), *Religious minorities and the rise of pluralism in modern Britain and France* (Peter Lang, 2001).

[27] Richard Baxter, *A holy commonwealth*, ed. W. Lamont (Cambridge, 1994), 251–2.

[28] Sylvester, *Reliquiae Baxterianae*, 3, 36.

Catholics. Baxter truly had a more comprehensive view of common ground between them than his contemporaries had. Not even, in his view, were the Mass and Predestination insurmountable obstacles. But one obstacle was. The papists' political surrender to a foreign jurisdiction was *not* God's way (and Ireton would have said that his opponents' refusal to honour engagements was not God's way either). What Baxter objected to in Hugo Grotius was that *his* ecumenical schemes were not God's way, precisely because they failed to recognise that popery was 'an error in politics'. This conviction is so central to Baxter that Lloyd Thomas' concealment of it, on the systematic scale which I hope to document elsewhere, is to my mind his editorial sin against the Holy Ghost.[29]

In that light, look afresh at Baxter's *Holy commonwealth* – the book which Lloyd Thomas forgot that Baxter had written. Ostensibly its target was James Harrington's *Oceana*, but its real enemy was Sir Henry Vane's *A healing question*; both works were published in 1656. This is clear in the 'Addition to the Preface', which Baxter inserted after the fall of Richard Cromwell in 1659 (for which he blamed Vane's book). Vane's great mistake had been to make 'liberty' the ark of the Puritan covenant. But the 'liberty', Baxter said, 'to preach up Popery, Mahometanism, Infidelity and Heathenism' was what had made Laudianism stink (Puritans had objected not to Laud's rigidity but to his licence). 'Liberty' is what played havoc with family hierarchies and military discipline. It was 'the reign of Satan and not of Christ'.[30] This was the language of Ireton against Wildman. He told one well-meaning correspondent that 'sir HV would not be reconciled by a thousand apologies' and added: 'I never was in danger until I set against the papists. They do all that are seene in nothing.'[31]

Sectarians like Vane were, for Baxter, papists in masks. Their crime was to exalt the autonomous will: their antinomianism was the apotheosis of Puritan commitment to liberty. And also its nemesis in the eyes of their opponents. It is not easy to know the numerical scale of antinomianism, but the fear of its spread gave Baxter's career its symmetry. He began it in 1654 with a pamphlet attacking it: 'All men are naturally of the Antinomian Religion, and that the very work of preachers (when Christ's death and the Promise of pardon and life is once revealed) is principally the cure of natural Antinomianism, and that is that we call the work of conversion'.[32] He ended it in 1691 haunted by the popular reception (he

---

[29] Dr. Williams' Library, *Baxter treatises*, VI, fol. 287.

[30] Baxter, *A holy commonwealth*, 18–40.

[31] Doctor Williams' Library, *Baxter correspondence*, IV, fol. 281.

[32] Baxter, *Richard Baxter's confutation of a dissertation for the justification of infidels* (London, 1654), 288.

thought) given to the reprinting of Tobias Crisp's antinomian sermons from forty years earlier.[33]

It is necessary to separate what Baxter felt about antinomians from what he felt about Ranters. He bracketed the Ranters with 'Vanists', Seekers, Quakers, and Behmenists. These different sects may have had different programmes but their doctrines were the same. Lloyd Thomas faithfully reproduces this taxonomy but characteristically omits Baxter's additional comment that 'the Devil and the Jesuits' were behind the Ranters, and Baxter's crucial rider to this, that even so the Ranters themselves 'were so very few and of short continuance that I never saw one of them'.[34] Professor Davis seizes on the remark as grist to his mill: that Ranterism is in the eye of the beholder. E. P. Thompson chose to combat this argument by eliding Ranterism with antinomianism: it was all there in St Paul and St Augustine, and so the Ranters *did* exist.[35] But this is a *non sequitur*. Just because Baxter hasn't met individual Ranters does not mean that he has not encountered antinomians. Davis thought that there were not many of *them* either, but that is not the point. Baxter may have exaggerated their menace, but the perception that they *were* a menace was one which he shared with many of his fellow Puritans. Davis is right to think that 'liberty' was an alien concept to most Puritans because it exalted the personal will and was therefore tarred with the 'antinomian' brush (and this was a belief that was held irrespective of how many antinomians there actually were).

This detour into Baxter territory brings us back to Putney, and shows us what they have in common. Woodhouse and Lloyd Thomas had both produced seventeenth-century texts for H. C. Dent in the 1930s. The similarities do not stop there. Both were successful in producing texts that endured; Introductions could be added to (in one case wholly rewritten), but there was to be no tampering with the texts themselves. Both provided valuable reinforcement for a historiographical tendency, which was already present in that period, to equate Puritanism with liberty. They did not do it in the same way, though, nor with the same motives. Woodhouse did not impose a vision by playing games with the text; he did it by choosing a title, and by packaging Putney alongside Whitehall and those pamphlets which he had already selected to fit the theme relevant to that

[33] F. J. Powicke (ed.), *The Reverend Richard Baxter's last treatise* (Manchester, 1926), 56.
[34] Sylvester, *Reliquiae Baxterianae*, I:77. Not only Lloyd Thomas dropped this important concession; it is missing from Calamy, *Abridgement*, 102.
[35] J. C. Davis, *Fear, myth and history: the Ranters and their historians* (Cambridge, 1986); E. P. Thompson, 'On the Rant', in G. Eley and W. Hunt (eds.), *Reviving the English revolution: reflections and elaborations on the work of Christopher Hill* (London, 1988), 153–60.

title. He was aware (it is there in the Introduction) of the awkwardness of the fit between the two abstractions. He *might* alternatively have made Puritanism and democracy his title and theme, but the fit there was even worse, as he also recognised. And in 1950 Lindsay could hail Woodhouse's prescience in having plumped for the one concept, rather than the other. Lloyd Thomas' sin is less venial. He cut a swathe through Baxter's text, picking out all the passages that supported a 'liberal' Baxter, and jettisoning the rest. His motives were frankly propagandist. The 'liberal' Baxter stood for reconcilement with Rome (which he truly did believe in, at least on those grounds carefully set out by him); the 'illiberal' Baxter was haunted by popish plots (on grounds also carefully set out by him). By not giving us those grounds in either case, Lloyd Thomas fails to give us Baxter. The paradox which he offers – Baxter's speech is of the seventeenth century, his thought is of ours – is not one at all, because his 'thought' is in fact not his or ours, but Lloyd Thomas'. Lloyd Thomas had wanted to reclaim Baxter's 'liberalism' for his own ecumenical ends; commentators on Putney and Whitehall (as Davis has shown) mistakenly saw these clashes as struggles about liberty. The point is not that Baxter or Ireton or Cromwell were 'illiberal'; they were working upon a different agenda from questions of either liberalism or illiberalism. Ireton will quietly 'acquiesce' in what the 'hand of God' determines; Baxter similarly knows that God does 'what he will with us'. The reflex will be one of suspicion of anything that smacks of the opposite: of the naked assertion of individual will. In that sense the *instinct* is an 'illiberal' one: those are the terms in which Ireton rounds on Wildman for destroying commonwealths, and in which Baxter rounds on Vane for destroying family life. But the 'hand of God' is discerned by Ireton (a year on) in the army's refusal to be bound by covenants with kings; and God wills for Baxter that *doctrinal* differences between Protestants and papists *can* be bridged. In neither case does it mean that these Puritans have become 'liberals', still less that Baxter had taken out a subscription to Lloyd Thomas' *The Free Catholic*.

There *were* some Puritans who can be identified as 'liberals' in our terms, without that identification being hopelessly anachronistic. William Walwyn is one who put liberty at the centre of his agenda; he delighted to call himself an 'antinomian'.[36] Less delighted opponents disliked this emphasis on liberty in men like Walwyn precisely because they associated it with antinomianism; Walwyn *may* have been the part-author of *An*

---

[36] William Walwyn, *Walwyns just defence* (London, 1649), in J. R. McMichael and Barbara Taft (eds.), *The writings of William Walwyn* (Athens, GA, 1989), 395–6: 'I through God's goodnesse, had long before been established in that part of doctrine (called then, Antinomianism) of free justification by Christ alone.'

agreement of the people, and the perception that he had something to do with it may have been part-explanation of what seems to us like an over-reaction on Ireton's part at Putney. Walwyn was not alone, and John Coffey makes an interesting case for adding others like him: Puritans, that is to say, who wanted toleration of all religions on what we would see as pluralistic grounds.[37] But he is making a qualification, not a rejection, of the general argument advanced in this essay, which is that most seven-teenth-century Puritans wanted a godly society, not a pluralistic one.

Woodhouse himself had recognised the power of that contrary impulse in Puritanism: to create a community of like-minded believers. This had been Baxter's own cultural revolution in Kidderminster in the 1650s, one which he went a fair way to exporting across all the other counties in England through his Association of Ministers. This in turn would become the realistic basis for the 'holy commonwealth' programme, which he enunciated in 1659. And he knew quite well what had made that start possible in Kidderminster: a clerical spy system. That was not how he had expressed it, of course; he preferred to speak of 'the zeal and diligence of the godly people who thirsted after the salvation of their neighbours and were in private my assistants'.[38] So much for Lindsay's efforts in 1950 to reinterpret the Puritan *mentalité*; to read the Putney debates by that date as a seventeenth-century *Darkness at noon*. His Puritans were for the most part on the other side of that particular argument. To pretend otherwise is to repeat the mistake of those Victorian Nonconformists who claimed Cromwell for their cause: Blair Worden called their pursuit of the theme of religious toleration 'a monument to Victorian liberalism'.[39] It was for different reasons that their successors of the 1930s assimilated Putney Puritanism to liberalism (after all, until 1891, Putney could not be part of a *Victorian* historical argument). It is fruitless to pick and choose from the words and actions of Cromwell or Ireton or Baxter to see how they measure up to 'liberal' criteria in Victorian times, or in 1938, or again in 1950. No better plea for religious liberty was ever made than Cromwell's rebuke to the Scottish Presbyterians – 'I beseech you in the bowels of Christ think it possible you may be mistaken'[40] – and that too would be recorded by William Clarke during Cromwell's Scottish campaign.[41] And

---

[37] John Coffey, *Persecution and toleration in Protestant England 1558–1669* (London, 2000).

[38] Quoted by Michael Walzer, 'Puritanism as a revolutionary ideology', *History and Theory* 3 (1963–4), 63–5, against an alignment of Puritanism with liberty – or capitalism.

[39] Blair Worden, 'Toleration and the Cromwellian Protectorate', *Studies in Church History* 21 (1984), ed. W. Sheils, 199–233.

[40] Thomas Carlyle (ed.), *Oliver Cromwell's letters and speeches* (4 vols., London, 1897), II:187.

[41] I am grateful to Frances Henderson for this information. We await eagerly her decipher-ing of the later Clarke minutes.

this was of a piece with Cromwell and Ireton questioning their opponents' confidence in tearing up engagements. But Cromwell could tell the governor of Ross that by liberty he did not mean the liberty to exercise the Mass, and could observe of the Cavalier corpses at Marston Moor: 'God made them as stubble to our swords.'[42] To ask which is the *real* Cromwell in all this is one of the most fatuous questions one can ask. They are *all* the real Cromwell. Baxter's original *unedited* memoirs, or even those edited by Sylvester, show a virulent anti-Catholicism which, even by seventeenth-century standards, is breathtaking; but he was brave enough in 1684 to express publicly his scepticism about the belief that the pope was Antichrist.[43] In an essay on George Bernard Shaw, G. K. Chesterton put his finger on the problem: twentieth-century Puritanism was a weak and lukewarm torrent into which had melted down 'much of that mountainous ice which sparkled in the seventeenth century, bleak indeed, but blazing'.[44] That bleak and blazing ice had little to do with 'liberalism'.

Cromwell, like Baxter, harboured more generous impulses to honour the individual conscience than did most of their Puritan contemporaries: hence his continual skirmishes with the Long Parliament during the civil war on this issue, and indeed with successive parliaments throughout the 1650s. He prided himself on being a 'good constable' not an Old Testament Jehovah. Baxter, starting off with hostility to the regicide, was won over, to his surprise, by the freedom which he was permitted under Cromwell to carry out his Kidderminster experiment. But that freedom was permitted in order for Baxter to set up – here's the paradox – an experiment in coercion. Indeed by the end of Cromwell's regime, Baxter had moved from refusing the Engagement in 1650 to yearning for a more interventionist role from the Protector. Baxter's hostility to Quakers and Vanists is well documented, but so too is Cromwell's to atheists or Socinians. These were not blips, in either case, in a 'liberal' programme, since neither *was* pursuing a 'liberal' programme. Both wanted a 'holy commonwealth' as their priority: Baxter recognised, through information provided by their mutual friend John Howe, in Oliver Cromwell a man who could be pushed in a similar direction (and, after his death, even more Cromwell's son).

We are talking about, to use Isaiah Berlin's famous formulation, two concepts of liberty. The negative liberty – freedom from restraint – is what Baxter valued in Cromwell, though only as a step to a positive liberty – freedom to advance a positive goal. Both Cromwell and Ireton sincerely invoke negative liberty against the highhandedness of their Putney

[42] Carlyle, *Letters and speeches*, II:83, I:188.
[43] Baxter, *A paraphrase on the New Testament* (London, 1685).
[44] G. K. Chesterton, *George Bernard Shaw* (London, 1909), 48.

enemies, but their commitment *as Puritans* to positive liberty – as instruments of God's purpose – mean that their basic premises are not different from those of their opponents. The 'hand of God' had not moved against property, they insisted, at Putney, whatever the Levellers said to the contrary. But there could be a time when it would; it certainly did against monarchy a year later. Antinomian Walwyn was by no means the only Puritan to advocate a negative liberty. What marks him out is his *scepticism of positive liberty*: 'if we were in power, we would bear our selves as Tyrannically as others have done'.[45] That is a true Isaiah Berlin perception.

Woodhouse therefore sent out wrong signals when he gave us Putney under the title *Puritanism and liberty*. Lindsay was even more misleading when he hailed Putney as a contribution to the cold war debate. He was actually nearer to the Puritan *mentalité* in 1938 than in 1950, when he let rip his own profound yearning to 'stop the mouths and pens' of opponents who bad-mouthed democracy. They are almost verbatim the sentiments of Puritan root-and-brancher Thomas Wilson in 1641: 'a pious man's greatest care is that . . . vile persons that spake villany may have their mouthes stopped . . . that the purity of discipline, very necessary to the constitution of the Church, may be introduced'.[46] They are what Kidderminster Baxter, unmediated by the good intentions of Lloyd Thomas, would have said; they were what promise-keepers Ireton and Cromwell did say at Putney. Milton had said that 'to be free is the same thing as to be pious',[47] but it's not.

---

[45] William Walwyn *et al.*, *A manifestation* (London, 1649) in McMichael and Taft *Writings*, 334–43, at 341.

[46] Thomas Wilson, *Davids Zeale for Zion* (London, 1641), 15.

[47] John Milton, *Defensio secundum pro populo Anglicano* (1654) in M. W. Wallace (ed.), *Milton's prose* (Oxford, 1963), 407.

Blair Worden

I

As a subject of historical scholarship and controversy the Levellers are a twentieth-century discovery.[1] Over the past hundred years or so they have had a conspicuous, sometimes a prominent position in writings on sevententh-century England. Earlier accounts of them were less ample and less respectful. Both the combination of interest and sympathy inspired by the Levellers in modern times, and the mixture of indifference and hostility induced by them in earlier ones, are reflections of the societies that produced them. This essay will examine modern and pre-modern approaches alike. But it will give more space to pre-modern ones, which evolved or persisted over a quarter of a millennium, than to their more familiar successors. The survey will close around 1960, a date chosen, with unavoidable arbitrariness, as the point at which historical writing ceases to be itself a matter of history and becomes difficult to separate from present-day processes of research and debate.

Pre-twentieth-century attitudes to the Levellers have sometimes aroused disappointment in our own time. In an article in *Past and Present* in 1968, the late Tim Mason reported the preliminary findings of an enterprise of collective research, which unhappily never reached publication, into nineteenth-century attitudes to Oliver Cromwell and the Puritan revolution. Mason and his collaborators compiled a wealth of archival material, and of interpretative suggestions, on which I shall gratefully draw at certain points in these pages. Yet while Mason's team was able to demonstrate the extent and intensity of nineteenth-century interest in Cromwell, it found altogether less evidence of nineteenth-century interest in the Levellers. In the eighteenth century, Mason noticed, the Levellers had attracted less attention still. Why, he and his collaborators asked, had a subject whose importance was self-evident in the modern

---

[1] For the purposes of this essay I use the term 'Leveller' to mean the people in the Puritan revolution who have been called Levellers. A larger account of Leveller historiography than mine, written from a different viewpoint, is Olivier Lutaud, 'Le parti politique "Niveleur" et la première révolution anglaise', *Revue historique* 227 (1962), 77–114, 377–414.

age been so largely ignored earlier? The answer, he hinted, lay in a conspiracy of silence. He urged his colleagues 'to discover by what means the
established order was able to blot out to so great an extent the memory of
. . . the Levellers'.[2]

That was, perhaps, a somewhat loaded injunction. Might it not be
equally well asked why the Levellers, whom few people before the twentieth century thought a worthy subject of historical investigation, have
come to be taken so seriously? That question is no less loaded. Yet how
difficult it is, in examining the historiography of the Levellers, to find
unloaded questions. For that historiography presents us, in a pressing
form, with an issue which no age has faced with less comfort or candour
than ours. What makes an historical subject important? Our discomfort
arises from the present generation's reaction against teleology. If subjects
are to be studied without reference to their long-term significance, or to
their pertinence to the present day, by what criteria do we decide that one
subject matters more than another?

Until very recently the modern interest in the Levellers was unasham-
edly teleological. Not all subscribers to the teleology were admirers of
the Levellers, but many of them were. From the late nineteenth century
a long succession of commentators remarked that the Levellers had
'anticipated' or 'looked forward to' or were 'forerunners of' or 'before-
hand with' later developments of political thought and organisation.[3]
The Levellers were 'far in advance of the age', 'a long way before [their]
time'.[4] They 'had their feet on the main track to the democratic future'
and 'traced the thought patterns of three centuries of their successors'.[5]

[2] T. W. Mason, 'Nineteenth-century Cromwell', *Past and Present* 40 (1968), 187–91, at
190. (Mason implied at that time that the neglect of the Levellers had been merely an
eighteenth-century and not a nineteenth-century phenomenon, but the evidence compiled by his team does not bear him out.) I am indebted to the late Colin Matthew for his
kindness in enabling me to study unpublished material from the 'Nineteenth-century
Cromwell' project, which Mason headed. I have marked with an asterisk those of my references which, directly or indirectly, I have taken from it.

[3] Henry Hyndman, *The historical basis of socialism in England* (London, 1898), 61; J.
Morrison Davidson, *Annals of toil* (4 vols., London, 1896–8), II:222; G. P. Gooch, *The
history of English democratic ideas in the seventeenth century* (Cambridge, 1989), 225; John
Morley, *Oliver Cromwell* (London, 1901), 229, 233; *P&L* (1938), [70]; Christopher Hill,
The English revolution 1640 (London, 1940), 69; D. M. Wolfe (ed.), *Leveller manifestoes of
the Puritan revolution* (New York, 1944), 108; G. M. Young's Introduction (first published
in 1953) to C. H. Firth, *Oliver Cromwell and the rule of the Puritans in England* (1900, repr.
Oxford, 1968), viii; E. P. Thompson, *The making of the English working class* (London,
1963, repr. 1980), 24.

[4] Davidson, *Annals*, II:227; D. W. Petegorsky, *Left-wing democracy in the English civil war*
(London, 1940), 84; cf. Thomas Carlyle (ed.), *Letters and speeches of Oliver Cromwell* (3
vols., London, 1845, repr. 1904), III:435.

[5] William Haller and Godfrey Davies (eds.), *The Leveller tracts 1647–1653* (New York,
1944), 2 (cf. ibid., 48); Wolfe, *Leveller manifestoes*, 108; cf. T. C. Pease, *The Leveller movement* (Washington, DC, 1916), 222.

Writer after writer remarked how 'modern' the Levellers were.[6] Leveller ideas, or the practices of debate that they inspired, were held to have anticipated late eighteenth-century revolutionary thinking in France and America,[7] the arguments of the Luddites and Chartists in Victorian England,[8] the English trade union movement,[9] the Workers' and Soldiers' Councils of the Russian revolution.[10] Leveller (and Digger) ideas and practices were given, or were interpreteted with reference to, modern political labels: socialist,[11] communist,[12] social democrat,[13] anarchist.[14] From the late 1930s it became common for the Levellers to be described as the voice of 'the Left'.[15] Within a Marxist perspective, admittedly, not everything about the Levellers seemed progressive. Their 'forward-looking proposals' had combined with a 'backward-looking' regard for the disintegrating 'village community', and had coexisted, in 'baffling juxtaposition', with a 'backward-looking' resistance to the centralisation of power.[16] In general, however, the Levellers

---

[6] Frederic Harrison, *Oliver Cromwell* (London, 1888), 114; S. R. Gardiner, *History of the great civil war* (London, 1886–91, repr. in 4 vols., 1893), III:379; Davidson, *Annals*, II:227; Gooch, *History of English democratic ideas*, 225; G. M. Trevelyan, *England under the Stuarts* (London, 1904), 281; Pease, *Leveller movement*, 217; Eduard Bernstein, *Cromwell and communism* (English edn, 1930), 95; Hill, *English revolution*, 69.

[7] Harrison, *Oliver Cromwell*, 24; S. R. Gardiner, *Cromwell's place in history* (London, 1897), 40; S. R. Gardiner (ed.), *Constitutional documents of the Puritan revolution* (Oxford, 1889, repr. 1962), li; Gardiner, *Great civil war*, III:379, 387; Davidson, *Annals*, II:227; Morley, *Oliver Cromwell*, 229–30, 233; Trevelyan, *England under the Stuarts*, 281; Pease, *Leveller movement*, 2–4; Bernstein, *Cromwell and communism*, 9–10; Ernest Barker, *Oliver Cromwell and the English people* (Cambridge, 1937), 41; *P&L*, [70]; Petegorsky, *Left-wing democracy*, 40, 244; Wolfe, *Leveller manifestoes*, foreword (by Charles A. Beard) and 108; Joseph Frank, *The Levellers* (Cambridge, MA, 1955), 256. Analogies with the French revolution had also been drawn earlier: Carlyle, *Letters and speeches*, I:258, 435; Edmund Clarke, *Lectures on the public life and character of Oliver Cromwell* (London, 1847), 125; Daniel Wilson, *Oliver Cromwell and the Protectorate* (London, 1848), 140.

[8] Firth, *Oliver Cromwell*, viii (Young's introduction). Cf. *Westminster Review* 8 (1929), 342; cf. Ivan Roots, 'Carlyle's Cromwell', in R. C. Richardson (ed.), *Images of Oliver Cromwell. Essays for and by Roger Howell, Jr.* (Manchester, 1993), 76.

[9] Morley, *Oliver Cromwell*, 221.

[10] H. N. Brailsford, *The Levellers and the English revolution*, ed. C. Hill (London, 1961), 50. Cf. Barker, *Oliver Cromwell*, 36; Hill, *English revolution*, 67–8; R. C. Richardson, 'Cromwell and the inter-war European dictators', in Richardson, *Images of Oliver Cromwell*, 108–23, at 113.

[11] Davidson, *Annals*, II:226; Firth, *Oliver Cromwell*, 240; *P&L*, [99].

[12] S .R. Gardiner, *History of the Commonwealth and Protectorate* (London, 1894–1901, repr. in 4 vols., 1965), I:43–4; J. Morrison Davidson, *The wisdom of Winstanley the Digger* (London, 1904), 14, 16; Trevelyan, *England under the Stuarts*, 40n., 280; Gooch, *History of English democratic ideas*, 206ff.; Bernstein, *Cromwell and Communism*; F. H. Hayward, *The unknown Cromwell* (London, 1934), 26 (but cf. 195).

[13] Davidson, *Wisdom of Winstanley*, 14; Davidson, *Annals*, II:212–13, 224.

[14] Davidson, *Annals*, II:225; Hyndman, *Historical basis of English socialism*, 61.

[15] Barker, *Oliver Cromwell*, 41; *P&L*, [17]; Petegorsky, *Left-wing democracy*; Wolfe, *Leveller manifestoes*, 2.   [16] Hill, *English revolution* (1955 edn), 52; Brailsford, *Levellers*, 537–8.

were the friends of the future. Sometimes the very forwardness of their ideas provided an explanation of their failure – and, at least by implication, of the neglect of their memory over the two centuries and more following their demise.[17]

II

The Levellers have owed their twentieth-century standing principally to socialism – though also, as we shall see, to a tradition of liberalism which has sometimes allied with socialist assessments of the Levellers, sometimes departed from them. Yet the growth of interest in the Levellers was not merely a product of ideological preoccupations. It was the result, too, of developments in historical scholarship. In the period around 1900, when socialist enthusiasm for the Levellers emerged, accounts of the Puritan revolution achieved, under the leadership of S. R. Gardiner and C. H. Firth, an altogether new depth and rigour. The scholarship was mainly the achievement of historians unsympathetic to the Levellers or to socialism where not to both.

It was around 1885 that the modern study of the Puritan revolution was launched. The quarter of a century that begins with that date produced the great narrative works of Gardiner and Firth, Gardiner's *Constitutional documents*, Firth's *Clarke papers*, the *Dictionary of national biography*, and G. K. Fortsecue's catalogue of the Thomason collection. Before that period, attitudes to the Levellers were formed in a world which lacked not only a broad interest in left-wing ideology but also the bibliographical landmarks that the modern student takes for granted. Not everything that was said about the Levellers between the Puritan revolution and the late nineteenth century was unfriendly. Yet those who said friendly things, or who wanted to be fair or accurate, tended to lose themselves in the chronological complexities of the Puritan revolution. When they turned to standard histories of the revolution for guidance, they encountered, and were easily misled by, basic errors of chronology.

Such errors permeated Leveller historiography from its early stages.[18] There were sides to Restoration England that wished to remember the

---

[17] Gardiner, *Cromwell's place*, 38–9, 49–50 (cf. Gardiner, *Constitutional documents*, xlvii, and Brailsford, *Levellers*, 14–15); Frank, *Levellers*, 253, 256.

[18] See, for example, the conflation of events of 1647 with later ones in 'R.B.' (= Nathaniel Crouch), *The history of Oliver Cromwell* (London, 1692, repr. 1698), 43–4; Roger Coke, *A detection of the court and state of England* (London, 1697 edn), 43; Isaac Kimber, *The life of Oliver Cromwell* (London, 1724), 116–17 (cf. ibid., 61); Laurence Echard, *The history of England* (2 vols., London, 1728), II:587; and note Clarendon's confusion about Cromwell and the army mutiny of 1649: W. D. Macray (ed.), *Clarendon's History of the rebellion* (6 vols., Oxford, 1888, repr. 1958), V:130.

Puritan revolution only through distortion and caricature. Few recollections of the period were exact and dispassionate. Most memories succumbed, as recollections of complex events easily do, to conflation. Memories of the Levellers could not easily be checked, for very few pertinent documents were in print. By the end of the seventeenth century not many participants in the civil wars remained alive. Yet if oral memory declined, the years around 1700 produced an expansion of the available printed evidence. It was then that a group of narratives covering the events of 1647–9 was published: the memoirs and histories of Richard Baxter (1696), Thomas Fairfax (1699), Edmund Ludlow (1698–9), Sir John Berkeley (1699), Denzil Holles (1699), the earl of Clarendon (1702) and Major Robert Huntington (1702). For all their prejudices and shortcomings those works at least provided a chronological shape. Meanwhile, in 1701, there appeared the concluding volumes of John Rushworth's *Historical collections*, which supplied a rudimentary account of the army politics of 1647 as well as reprinting the army remonstrances of June of that year and *An agreement of the people* of the autumn.

Yet that spate of publications was short-lived. The eighteenth century added little to it. During the 1740s and 1750s the publication of the *Harleian miscellany* and the *Somers tracts* and the *Parliamentary or constitutional history* made a small number of Leveller and Digger tracts available. Yet over the remainder of the century only a handful of accounts of the Levellers drew on those collections. George Thomason's collection of civil-war tracts, which were open to public inspection from the early 1760s, was equally little used. What seem to us standard texts remained out of view. No one appears to have drawn on *The case of the armie truly stated* before William Godwin in the 1820s. John Lilburne's *Legal fundamental liberties*, a document essential to an understanding of Leveller conduct in the weeks and months before the regicide, seems to have been referred to only once (in the mid-eighteenth-century)[19] before Firth published an extract from it in the *Clarke papers*. In spite of the great movement for parliamentary reform from the late eighteenth century, it was again only with the *Clarke papers* that the Levellers became associated with the issue of the franchise. Only one earlier commentator (writing in 1828) appears to have recognised the Levellers' interest in that subject.[20]

---

[19] In the entry on John Lilburne in the *Biographia Britannica* (7 vols., 1st edn, London, 1747–66).

[20] J. T. Rutt (ed.), *The diary of Thomas Burton* (4 vols., London, 1828), I:49n. Some writers referred to the *Agreement of the people* of May 1649, which (unlike that of 1647) directly calls for an extension of the franchise, but they tended to know the document only through the summary of it in the *Memorials of Bulstrode Whitelocke* (first published in 1682: repr. in 4 vols., 1853, III:25–6), which does does mention that demand. Something might have been detected from ibid., II:226, where, as often, Whitelocke's text is the

Until around 1890 the deficiencies of the available chronology and evidence excluded any sense of the Levellers as a continuous movement. They popped up, seemingly from nowhere, in 1647. They popped up again in 1649. They could be glimpsed plotting from time to time in the 1650s. But there was no spinal narrative to connect those episodes. Until the early twentieth century there was no interest in the intellectual origins or development of the movement. Essentially the Levellers were seen as a military organisation, which had caused agitation and mutiny in Cromwell's army. More – sometimes much more – was written about them with respect to 1649, and especially to the uprising that ended at Burford, than to 1647, the year of the army debates and the first *Agreement of the people*. In relation to 1649 they seemed important because they threatened the new republic. When they figured in accounts of 1647 it was primarily in relation to the rise of Cromwell in the spring and summer, when, it was widely agreed, he had egged on or manipulated or connived with the agitators for his own advancement.[21] Cromwell had come to dominate the historiography of the years following the civil wars. Historians paid little attention to the place of the Levellers in the autumn of 1647 except in remarking on his courage and dexterity in breaking the mutiny at Ware, when the agitation had escaped from his control. They emphasised the same qualities in him in their accounts of the mutiny of 1649.[22] On that theme as on others, the dearth of scholarly enterprise

same as Rushworth's. It was known that the Levellers had aimed at another kind of electoral reform, the redistribution of the parliamentary constituencies, on lines that anticipated the reforms of 1832. But on that subject the bulk of attention was directed towards Cromwell and to the Instrument of Government of 1653, which swept away the rotten boroughs and introduced the principle of the geographical apportionment of representation: John Banks, *A short critical review of the political life of Oliver Cromwell* (Glasgow, 1763), 98; James Burgh, *Political disquisitions* (3 vols., London, 1774–5), I:59; Henry Hallam, *The constitutional history of England* (London, 1827, repr. 1870), 459; T. B. Macaulay, *History of England* (4 vols., London, 1848–55, repr. 1972), I:106; Clarke, *Lectures on . . . Cromwell*, 183.

[21] James Heath, *Flagellum* (London, 1665), 63, 75; James Heath, *A chronicle of the late intestine war . . . to which is added a continuation* (London, 1675), 131; William Dugdale, *A short view of the late troubles in England* (Oxford, 1681), 242; George Bate, *Elenchus motuum* (transl. 1685), pt i, 78, 81 (cf. ibid., 133); Baxter, *Reliquiae Baxterianae* (London, 1696), 61; P. J. d'Orléans, *The history of the revolutions in England* (London, 1711, repr. 1722), 104; Kimber, *Life of Oliver Cromwell*, 38–9, 109; Thomas Gordon (ed.), *The works of Sallust* (1744), 136; William Harris, *An historical and critical account of the life of Oliver Cromwell* (1762), 143; *The parliamentary or constitutional history of England* (24 vols., repr. 1962–3), XV:341–2; Oliver Goldsmith, *An history of England* (2 vols.,1764), II:33, 37; *The political beacon: or the life and character of Oliver Cromwell* (1770), 183; Francis Maseres (ed.), *Select tracts relating to the civil wars in England* (2 vols., 1815), I:xxiv, II:587–8; Royce Macgillivray, *Restoration historians and the English civil war* (The Hague, 1974), 95 (quoting John Hacket); cf. Clement Walker, *The history of Independency* (1649), pt i, 32.

[22] Sir Richard Baker, *A chronicle of the kings of England . . . whereunto is added, The reign of king Charles the First* (1665), 634; Coke, *Detection*, 318; Kimber, *Life of Oliver Cromwell*,

produced an interpretative paralysis. Time and again historians of the Puritan revolution were content to repeat the claims, even the words, of their predecessors.

Cromwell's feats in breaking the Levellers were respected even by some historians of royalist sympathies. For while his memory was largely loathed in the eighteenth century and well beyond it, his critics were sometimes ready to acknowledge the benefit he had conferred on his country by preventing, at critical moments, its descent into anarchy. The Levellers' defeats of 1647 and 1649 were held to be two such moments. Besides, military insurrection was considered a black crime. In general, and in spite of the widespread hostility to the principle of military rule, the Cromwellian army was held in respectful memory, at least from the late eighteenth century. It was commended, even by Edmund Burke, as a disciplined body, composed of sober and reflecting citizens, men of piety, morality, virtue and solid social position.[23] If there were historians who thought that Cromwell's ambition had corrupted it, there may have been more who blamed the Levellers for subverting it.

III

In modern hands 'Leveller' has become a neutral term where not an approving one. It came into being, in 1647, as a smear, which wrongly imputed to the men to whom it was applied a resolve to destroy rank and property.[24] In the Restoration period there were former Roundheads who were aware that the word had not been of the Levellers' own choosing and who were ready, at least up to a point, to come to their defence. Lucy Hutchinson praised the 'honest' and 'sober' men who 'were nicknamed Levellers' (though it would be long before her words were published). She denied, as they had done, the charge that they had 'endeavoured the levelling of all estates and qualities'.[25] Richard Baxter, echoing a complaint by Lilburne himself, wrote that Cromwell had termed Lilburne and his

footnote 22 (*cont.*)

  116–17; Banks, *Short critical review*, 135; Echard, *Complete history*, 591; Harrison, *Oliver Cromwell*, 134.

[23] Edmund Burke, *Reflections on the French revolution*, ed. L. G. Mitchell (Oxford, 1993), 278; William Godwin, *History of the commonwealth of England* (4 vols., London, 1824–8), II:293–4; Macaulay, *History of England*, I:90–1; Robert Vaughan (ed.), *The protectorate of Oliver Cromwell* (2 vols., London, 1839), I:lxxxii; Morley, *Oliver Cromwell*, 221; Trevelyan, *England under the Stuarts*, 280; Frederic Harrison, *Thoughts and memories* (London, 1906), 66–7; cf. Sir Walter Scott (ed.), *Somers tracts* (13 vols., 1809–15 edn), VI:414n.

[24] See Appendix, 280–2.

[25] Lucy Hutchinson, *Memoirs of the life of Colonel Hutchinson* (first published 1806), ed. James Sutherland (London, 1973), 179 (though cf. ibid., 191).

friends Levellers 'to make them odious, as if they intended to level all men of qualities and degrees'.[26]

Royalist writers were mainly less discriminating. In 1665 James Heath described the 'devilish intention' of the Levellers 'by a wild parity [to] lay all things in common'.[27] The long-term victory of that view can be principally attributed to Clarendon's *History of the rebellion*, published in 1702. Clarendon maintained that in 1647 'a new faction' in the Cromwellian army 'were, either by their own denomination or with their own consent, called *Levellers*'. They 'declared that all degrees of men should be levelled, and an equality should be established, both in titles and estates, throughout the kingdom'.[28] Clarendon's account would often be echoed. In the early eighteenth century the Whig writer Paul Rapin de Thoyras, in a work of great influence, reproduced Clarendon's description verbatim (as would Oliver Goldsmith four decades later), while Laurence Echard explained that the Levellers had sought 'to bring all degrees of men to an equality'.[29] In 1754 Hume's *History of England*, a work which exceeded the impact of Rapin's account and matched that of Clarendon's, claimed that the soldiers of 1647 had agreed that 'all ranks of men [must] be levelled; and an universal equality of property, as well as of power, be introduced'.[30] Even thereafter, it is true, we still find occasional voices ready to protest against the uses of the term Leveller by historians of the civil wars, and to recognise the distortions effected by it both during the revolution and in posterity.[31] In general, however, the heavy historiographical artillery of the eighteenth century had done its work. It was supposed through the eighteenth and nineteenth centuries that the men described as Levellers had sought social levelling and that the term therefore fitted them.

Smears can work only if there is a public ready to welcome them. Yet, at least once the seventeenth century is past, it is hard to explain the success of the imputation of social levelling in terms of those anxieties that are sometimes held to have gripped the ruling class or to have shaped its

---

[26] *Reliquiae Baxterianae*, 61.   [27] Heath, *Chronicle*, 131.
[28] Clarendon, *History*, IV:261; cf. VI:76.
[29] Paul Rapin de Thoyras, *The history of England* (1726–31, repr. 4 vols., 1732–47), II:540 (though cf. n. 5 on the same page); Echard, *Complete history*, 587; Goldsmith, *History of England*, II:37.
[30] David Hume, *The history of England*, ed. Henry Stebbing (n.d.), 700. Another register of Clarendon's influence is the persistence of his notion (eventually exploded by William Godwin) that in 1647 the army organised itself into two debating assemblies, one, for the officers, modelled on the House of Lords, the other, for the soldiery, on the House of Commons: Clarendon, *History*, IV:220; Echard, *History of England*, 569; *Political beacon*, 183; Thomas Cromwell, *Oliver Cromwell and his times* (London, 1821), 163–4; Godwin, *History of the commonwealth*, II:303–4; cf. Maseres, *Select tracts*, I:xxi.
[31] Below, 269–70; Caroline Robbins, *The eighteenth-century commonwealthman* (Cambridge, MA, 1959), 240; François Guizot, *The life of Oliver Cromwell* (London, 1854, repr. 1899), 28–9 (cf. William Hazlitt, *Oliver Cromwell* (London, 1857), 140).

ideology. Uses of the term 'Leveller' reveal contempt for Lilburne and the army agitators, but also something close to amusement. What Tim Mason called 'the established order' did not live in dread that the Levellers would come again. Rather, the Levellers seem to have been thought of as faintly ridiculous, even faintly exotic products of broken times. They were deemed worthy of mention when they affected national political events, or in illustration of the folly of the turbulent period they had inhabited, but were not judged entitled to any large space in narratives of those congested years. Still less space was found for the Diggers, who until well into the nineteenth century escaped serious notice.

If there was no dread that the Levellers might come again, there was, it is true, anxiety lest the Puritan revolution might come again. The fear was most often voiced during the Exclusion Crisis, but would sometimes be audible well beyond it, even in the late eighteenth and early nineteenth centuries.[32] That anxiety, however, was focused not on social levelling but on constitutional conflict and religious dissent. Under Charles II it was in relation to the struggles over ecclesiastical conformity and monarchical absolutism that the Puritan revolution offered a mirror to the present and commanded its attention. When the Levellers were mentioned it was normally in connection with those issues, on which they may have been an extreme threat but were rarely a central one. That pattern of discussion persisted through the eighteenth century and beyond it. The Levellers continued to be viewed as fringe manifestations of the two evil tendencies with which the civil wars were normally associated, and which were held by royalist or Tory historians to have infected much, perhaps all, of the Roundhead cause: 'fanaticism' or 'enthusiasm', and 'republicanism'. That picture of the Levellers was based, not on evidence (though evidence could have been found for it), but on fixed images of civil-war radicalism. Again Clarendon was an influential voice. He shaped subsequent thinking first by referring to 'Lilburne, Overton, and other anabaptists and fanatics',[33] and secondly by indicating that the Levellers' hostility to rank and property was of a piece with their 'great malice . . . against the king'.[34] The charge of republicanism proved if anything more effective than that of fanaticism. In 1724 Cromwell's biographer Isaac Kimber described the Levellers as the 'chief actors in the king's death',[35] though in fact they had kept clear of that episode. From the Restoration until the end of the nineteenth century, the

---

[32] W.S. Lewis *et al.*, (eds), *The Yale edition of Horace Walpole's correspondence* (48 vols., New Haven, 1937–83), XXIII:170–1; John Cannon, *The Fox-North coalition* (Cambridge, 1963), 11, 163; Thomas Cromwell, *Oliver Cromwell*, preface.

[33] Clarendon, *History*, IV:241. Cf. Echard, *History of England*, 579; Hume, *History of England*, 700; Carlyle, *Letters and speeches*, II:520.

[34] Clarendon, *History*, IV:261 (cf. Heath, *Chronicle*, 131).

[35] Kimber, *Life of Oliver Cromwell*, 109; cf. *Political beacon*, 167.

Levellers were almost universally associated with antipathy to monarchy. Their social programme – their demands for the end of monopolies and tithes or for the rectification of the legal system – attracted far less attention, though it had been of more consistent concern to them.

IV

In the Restoration period, when former Levellers remained alive, it was easy for upholders of the restored regime to allege that Leveller ideas persisted, too.[36] The government, ever vigilant against conspiracy and ready to exaggerate it, knew that its enemies included a number of men who had had Leveller connections. We might therefore expect government propagandists to have referred frequently to the Levellers' continuing existence. In fact they seem to have used the term only rarely, and far less often than they attacked the persistence of civil-war republicanism and sectarianism. The remnants of the Leveller movement were in truth not much of a threat. Though claims have been made, particularly by Richard Ashcraft, for the influence of Leveller ideas in the reign of Charles II, their presence is hard to pin down.[37] Later, during the revolution of 1688–9, there is a moment when the survival or revival of distinctively Leveller principles does seem visible. A tract, sometimes attributed to John Wildman,[38] referred to 'reservations of liberty . . . ma[d]e' by 'the people' in an 'agreement of the people'.[39] It may have been Wildman, too, who at the same time repeated another distinctive Leveller idea of the 1640s: the proposal that, for electoral purposes, the county unit (which was customarily dominated by leading landowners) be divided into hundreds or wapentakes (where more popular influences might prevail).[40]

Yet if there are those vestiges of Leveller thinking, late seventeenth-

---

[36] Richard Ashcraft, *Revolutionary principles and Locke's Two treatises of government* (Princeton, NJ, 1986), esp. 149–51, 247–51; Richard Greaves, *Deliver us from evil: the radical underground in Britain, 1660–1683* (Oxford, 1986), 90; see also ch. 11 in this volume.

[37] See Gerald Aylmer's critique of Ashcraft: 'Locke no Leveller' in Ian Gentles, John Morrill and Blair Worden (eds.), *Soldiers, writers and statesmen of the English revolution* (Cambridge, 1998), 304–22. (Ashcraft says – *Revolutionary politics*, 160 – that 'one or two' Leveller tracts 'were reprinted' in the 1680s, but does not document his statement.)

[38] Mark Goldie, 'The roots of true Whiggism', *History of Political Thought* 1 (1980), 195–236, at 212.

[39] Scott, *Somers tracts*, 10:198–9; cf. Gardiner, *Constitutional documents*, 333, 334. Compare too the statement, in another tract from the same time which is again perhaps by Wildman (Goldie, 'Roots', 212), that 'all power is originally or fundamentally in the people', with Wolfe, *Leveller manifestoes*, 212.

[40] Wolfe, *Leveller manifestoes*, 298; Blair Worden, *The Rump Parliament 1648–1653* (Cambridge, 1974), 146; Scott, *Somers tracts*, X:196; Goldie, 'Roots', 212; cf. Ben Jonson, *The New Inn*, IV.2.16–17.

century currents of reforming thinking were in general flowing in an opposite direction. There were some concurrences of perspective, it is true, between the Levellers of the 1640s and the radical political reformers of William III's reign, the commonwealthmen: John Trenchard, John Toland and their allies. The commonwealthmen, like the Levellers before them, wrote at a time when the immediate threat to the people's liberties seemed to be posed less by an overmighty king than by an overmighty parliament. In the perception of both groups, parliament was becoming something like a de facto executive. The Levellers would have applauded Toland's claim that the people, who 'delegate' authority 'to their representatives', may 'defend themselves against their legislators' if their 'liberty' is threatened by them. Yet Toland associated that liberty, in a spirit that distances him from the Levellers, with 'property'.[41] The necessary corrective to parliamentary tyranny now seemed to lie in the restriction of legislative power to men of economic substance, whose votes, whether at Westminster or in parliamentary elections, could not be bought. The Levellers' plea for an extension of the franchise was reversed by the radicals of the years after 1688. It was apparently Wildman himself who in 1689 urged the narrowing of the county franchise from the existing freehold of forty shillings to one of forty pounds.[42] The Levellers had hit at 'rich men', but the reformers of the 1690s urged the election of 'rich' MPs.[43] The Levellers had wondered whether servants could safely be given the vote. The commonwealthmen were clear that they could not. 'Citizens', explained Toland, 'will always appear for liberty, but servants for bread.'[44]

Criticism of social injustice did persist within the commonwealth tradition. As late as the 1720s the authors of *Cato's letters* argue for 'equality', for 'popular government', for 'agrarian laws'. They dislike social 'oppression' and men who are 'too rich'. Yet the same authors also distanced themselves from 'all levelling in church and state'.[45] They took their language and principles of social reform not from the Levellers but from James

[41] John Toland, *Anglia libera* (London, 1701), 4–5. Eighteen-century vigilance against the corruption of the people's representatives in parliament did lead the 'patriot' journal *Common Sense*, on 13 October 1739, to quote the attack made on the Long Parliament in Richard Overton's *A remonstrance of many thousand citizens* (London, 1646): see *Gentleman's Magazine* 9 (1739), 536. But the journal did not represent the tract as a Leveller document or mention Overton's protest against social inequality. For 'patriot' use of the Levellers, see also *The Champion* 179 (3 Jan, 1741); cf. John Lord Hewey, *Ancient and modern liberty* (London, 1734), 31–2.   [42] Goldie, 'Roots', 214.

[43] Wolfe, *Leveller manifestoes*, 213; Blair Worden, 'The revolution of 1688–9 and the English republican tradition', in Jonathan Israel (ed.), *The Anglo-Dutch moment* (Cambridge, 1991), 241–77, at 259.

[44] *State tracts* (3 vols., London, 1705–7), II:598 (Toland, *The militia reformed*).

[45] *Cato's letters* (4 vols., London, 1733), II:16; *Cato's letters*, ed. Ronald Hamowy (Indianapolis, 1995), I:30; Thomas Gordon (ed.), *The works of Tacitus* (2 vols., London, 1728–31), I:2, 109.

Harrington, the republican writer of the 1650s. Alongside him in eigh-teenth-century esteem there stood Algernon Sidney, the republican and Whig martyr of 1683.[46] It was Sidney's *Discourses*, not Leveller writings, that James Burgh invoked in 1774 when he argued that MPs were merely 'delegate[s]' from whom their constituents had 'reserved' powers.[47] Toland, the editor of Sidney as of Harrington, probably had Sidney in mind in making his own claims about the 'delegation' of authority to MPs.[48]

Over the first eight decades or so of the eighteenth century the Levellers almost vanished from public discussion. They appeared, of course, in histories of the civil war, but were rarely mentioned outside them.[49] Though the words 'leveller' and 'levelling' were common as pejorative terms, they now had little or nothing to do with the civil-war Levellers. A pamphlet of 1703, called *The Levellers*, was about a proposal to abolish marriage settlements and arranged marriages: there is no sign that the civil-war Levellers entered its author's mind.[50] 'Leveller' and 'levelling' now referred to a principle or proclivity, not to particular people or a particular set of events. They described any impulse towards parity,[51] whether constitutional or social or economic or some indeter-minate mixture of the three. Blackstone's complaint that Locke's princi-ples 'would have levelled all distinctions of honour, rank, offices and property'[52] was one of a host of such allegations. Other meanings or reso-nances were equally devoid of historical reference. Sometimes a 'leveller' was someone who aimed to flatten power or liberty or virtue by tyranny.[53] Sometimes he was a person – as Jeremy Collier put it in 1689 in a passage that would be quoted in the entry on the word in Dr

[46] Blair Worden, 'The commonwealth kidney of Algernon Sidney', *JBS* 24 (1985), 1–40, at 27–37; Worden, 'Republicanism and the Restoration', in David Wootton (ed.), *Republicanism, liberty and commercial society* (Stanford, CA, 1994), 139–93, at 188–93.

[47] Burgh, *Political disquisitions*, I:191.

[48] Algernon Sidney, *Discourses concerning government*, ed. T. G. West (Indianapolis, 1990), 536–9.

[49] One exception may lie in a passage of chapter 19 of Oliver Goldsmith's *The vicar of Wakefield* (noted by Lutaud, 'Le parti politique "Niveleur"', 7). The narrator remembers that there 'was once . . . a set of honest men who were called Levellers'. They maintained that 'we are all originally equal', and naively held that 'all should be equally free'. But the passage is historically unspecific and seems meant to be so. If Goldsmith did have a his-torical occasion in mind it was probably the activity of the agitators in 1647, who in his *History of England* are described in terms close to those of *The vicar*. The *History* does not mention either the Leveller activity of 1649 or the Diggers.

[50] *Harleian miscellany* (8 vols., London, 1744–6), V:416–33.

[51] Cf. Robbins, *Eighteenth-century commonwealthman*, 4 (on 'Leveller' as an eighteenth-century 'missile term'); and John Rule, 'Employment and authority: masters and men in eighteenth-century manufacturing', in Paul Griffiths, Adam Fox and Steve Hindle (eds.), *The experience of authority in early modern England* (London, 1996), 286–317, at 300.   [52] Quoted by Lutaud, 'Le parti politique "Niveleur"', 97.

[53] Edmund Burke, *A letter to a noble lord* (1796), 233 (cf. Thomas Paine, *The rights of man*, ed. Eric Foner (Harmondsworth, 1969, repr. 1985), 172); *Cato's letters* (1733 edn), I:liii–iv.

Johnson's *Dictionary*[54] – of envious disposition, who 'won't allow any encouragement to extraordinary industry and merit'.[55] It was in that last vein that Catharine Macaulay (who herself sought to rescue the civil-war Levellers from the slurs of other historians) complained of 'that general spirit of levelling which pervades modern society', which she thought 'a new circumstance among us', and which she blamed for the recent attacks on her hero Algernon Sidney.[56] Catharine Macaulay was in turn associated by Dr Johnson, on the famous occasion when he mocked her social views by proposing that her footman be invited to dine with them, with 'the levelling doctrine', with the wish to 'level down'.[57] The elasticity of the vocabulary of levelling is demonstrated by its application both to Burke ('the first complete leveller I ever met with', taunted John Thelwall) and Paine (who heard *The rights of man* called 'a levelling system').[58]

So remote had the memory of the seventeenth-century Levellers become that historians of the Puritan revolution found it hard to know how to introduce the subject. Readers, they recognised, could not be expected to have heard of the Levellers and might find their credulity strained by accounts of them. Rapin de Thoyras declared it 'incumbent on me to explain' that there had been a party in Cromwell's army 'called Levellers'.[59] From the late seventeenth century to the early nineteenth, indeed, historians thought it necessary, in reporting the activities of the army agents or of Lilburne's group, to tell their readers that those men had been 'called' or 'named' or 'styled' or 'titled' or 'known as' Levellers.[60] In

---

[54] 1755 edn.
[55] Jeremy Collier, *A moral essay concerning . . . pride* (London, 1689), 42 (cf. 15, 28), as in Collier, *Miscellanies* (London, 1694).
[56] Catharine Macaulay, *History of England* (8 vols., 1763–83), VII:494; cf. Edmund Burke, *A letter from Edmund Burke . . . one of the representatives in parliament for the city of Bristol* (2nd edn, London, 1777), 70.
[57] Boswell's *Life of Johnson*, ed. G. B. Hill and L. F. Powell (6 vols., Oxford, 1934–50), I:447–8 (21 July 1763).
[58] John Thelwall, *Sober reflections on the . . . letter of . . . Edmund Burke* (1796), 15; Paine, *Rights of man*, 172; cf. Peter G. Thomas *John Wilkes: a friend to liberty* (Oxford, 1996), 162. The term flourished in eighteenth-century New England, too: J. R. Pole, *Political representation in England and the origins of the American republic* (London, 1966), 59, 207, 235.
[59] Rapin, *History of England*, II:540. Rapin, admittedly, was writing for a continental as well as an English audience: see Hugh Trevor-Roper's introduction to T. B. Macaulay, *The history of England* (abridged version, Harmondsworth, 1979), 10.
[60] The habit had an existence separate from, though it sometimes overlapped or was fortified by, the wish to explain that the Levellers had not chosen their nickname. For the habit: Coke, *Detection*, 315 (and see Baker, *Chronicle*, 633); Kimber, *Life of Cromwell*, 60; Thomas Carte, *A general history of England* (4 vols., London, 1747–55), IV: 615; Echard, *History of England*, 587; Hume, *History of England*, 700; *Parliamentary or constitutional history of England*, XIX:127 (cf. XIX:186); Goldsmith, *History of England*, II:37; Banks, *Oliver Cromwell*, 40; *Biographia Britannica*, ed. Andrew Kippis (5 vols., London, 1787–93), IV:487.

1763 the index to the *Parliamentary or constitutional history* carried an entry: 'Levellers, who meant by them'.[61]

John Lilburne, it is true, was known about (far more so than any of the other Levellers, to whom the history books gave at best walk-on parts).[62] Yet it was not principally as a Leveller leader or an exponent of Leveller ideas that he was famed.[63] He owed his celebrity rather to the constitutional and legal issues raised by his trials of 1649 and 1653, to his spirited and colourful performances at them, and to the popular clamour they had aroused. The text of the trial of 1649, which had been printed in that year, had been reprinted in William Winstanley's *England's worthies* in 1660 (a work in which Lilburne made his surprising appearance 'not as a Worthy, but as a Wonder').[64] It was printed again in 1710, by a printer who hoped (but failed) to publish a series of Lilburne's tracts,[65] and again in successive editions of the *State trials* from 1719. Interest in Lilburne's afflictions grew in the age of Wilkes,[66] and was strengthened by late eighteenth- and early nineteenth-century concerns about the right to trial by jury.[67] Even so, Lilburne hardly became a household name. In 1817–18 a series of guides to the counties of England passingly referred to him, in connection with places with which he had been associated, as the 'eccentric John Lilburne' or an 'eccentric republican' or a 'sufferer'.[68]

For even the emergence of parliamentary and popular radicalism from the late eighteenth century had brought no wave of interest in the civil-war Levellers. Catharine Macaulay, admittedly, did write

[61] As late as 1896 Morrison Davidson (*Annals*, II:212–13) thought that it was 'not generally known that, during the English Commonwealth, there was a considerable party of Levellers'. Cf. F. W. Cornish, *Life of Oliver Cromwell* (1882), 147; Gardiner, *Cromwell's place in history*, 37.

[62] See especially the enterprising (though mainly derisive) entry on him in the *Biographia Britannica*.

[63] In the eighteenth century other Levellers, and other documents relating to the Levellers, were known about, if at all, in connections other than Leveller ones. Richard Overton's heresy of mortalism was remembered (James R. Jacob, *Henry Stubbe, radical Protestantism and the early Enlightenment* (Cambridge, 1983), 161), but his political pamphlets were not. A pamphlet of 1657, *Killing noe murder*, probably written by a former Leveller (Edward Sexby or William Allen), was reprinted, but as a vindication of tyrannicide, not as a Leveller production.

[64] The entry on Lilburne was dropped in the second edition of 1684.

[65] Theodorus Verax [Clement Walker], *The triall, of Lieut. Collonell John Lilburne* (1649, repr. 1710).

[66] *Gentleman's Magazine*, March 1770, 120; Audrey Williamson, *Wilkes. A friend to liberty* (London, 1974), 67–8.

[67] John Thelwall, *The tribune* (3 vols., 1795–6), III:226ff; Rutt, *Diary of Thomas Burton*, III:504.

[68] *Gentleman's Magazine*, March 1817, 212; October 1817, 326, and supplement to vol. 88(i) (1818), 585. On the matter of Lilburne's standing in the decades around 1800 I dissent from the judgement implied by Robbins, *Eighteenth-century commonwealthman*, 19.

vigorously on behalf of the group which had been 'in derision styled
Levellers', and which had been 'honest to the principles of equal and
general freedom'. The *Agreement of the people* of May 1649 had been 'a
better model than any which had yet been offered to the public', providing as it did for 'the reformation of all the grievances which the people
of England then laboured under, and which to this very day they do at
equal rate sustain'.[69] Yet Catharine Macaulay's was an isolated voice.
The Society for Constitutional Information, whose publications from
1780 were intended to educate the nation in the principle of parliament's accountability to its electorate, introduced its readers to a
wealth of past writing but did not mention the Levellers. If Leveller radicalism was echoed in the late eighteenth century, the echoes were
unconscious. E. P. Thompson, though struck by the resemblances
between the radicalism of the 1640s and that of the 1790s,[70] detected
no influence of the former on the latter. Christopher Hill noted the parallels between the Leveller view of the Norman Conquest and the populist perception of it that surfaced in the 1790s,[71] but there is no sign
that the advocates of that latter sentiment knew that the Levellers had
anticipated them.

If there was no cult of the Levellers in the late eighteenth century, the
words 'leveller' and 'levelling' probably had a wider circulation at that
time, and as fierce a pejorative slant, as at any other period of our history
since the Puritan revolution. Advocates of the rights of man, it was generally alleged, intended to 'level' monarch and subject, rich and poor, the
propertied and unpropertied. 'Levelling' was loosely associated with
republicanism, with sectarian fanaticism, and with envy of wealth.[72] Yet
even now the memory of the civil-war Levellers, to whom so many historians had attributed those very traits, did not surface in contemporary
political discussion. In 1792 John Reeve set up the Association for
Preserving Liberty and Property against Republicans and Levellers. In
devising that title he evidently did not have the civil-war Levellers in
mind. The extensive publications of the Association, which include a
narrative of Puritan rule, contain only one reference (a passing one, in a

[69] Catharine Macaulay, *History of England*, IV:355, V:8. Mrs Macaulay took the text of the
Agreement from *The parliamentary or constitutional history*. I am less sure than Bridget Hill,
The republican virago (Oxford, 1992), 37, that Mrs Macaulay was 'familiar . . . with all the
Leveller manifestoes'.
[70] Thompson, *Making of the English working class*, 26, 34.
[71] Christopher Hill, *Puritanism and liberty* (London, 1958), ch. 3 ('The Norman yoke').
[72] Thomas Holcroft, *A letter to the right honourable William Windham* (1795), 23, 31;
Gentleman's Magazine 1792, supplement, 1199, and April 1794, 312; Geraint H. Jenkins,
'"A rank republican and Leveller": William Jones, Llangadfan', *Welsh Historical Review*
17 (1995), 365–86; cf. F. M. L. Thompson, *English landed society in the nineteenth century*
(London, 1963), 271.

quotation) to the civil-war Levellers.[73] Levelling seems to have been thought of less often as something Englishmen had once tried to do than as the sort of thing foreigners do. The Association for Preserving Liberty and Property pledged itself to thwart 'the rude hands of Russian Levellers'.[74] Burke warned the English against the example of 'the Levellers of France'.[75] When Burke recalled the horrors of the Puritan revolution it was not the Levellers whom he remembered but the language of religious fanaticism and the anti-monarchical preaching of Cromwell's ally Hugh Peter, whom Burke saw as the canting predecessor of Richard Price.[76]

In the early nineteenth century two publications did add a little to public understanding of the civil-war Levellers. In both cases the advance owed as much to the scholarship as to the sympathies of the author. The collection of civil-war tracts edited by Francis Maseres in 1815 not only made a number of contemporary accounts of 1647–9 better known. It provided, in its long introduction, a thoughtful narrative of the army politics of 1647. Then, in the 1820s, there appeared the most impressive and influential account of the period written before Gardiner's, the four-volume *History of the commonwealth* by William Godwin, the first historian to make more than cursory use of the Thomason tracts. Yet Godwin's labours on the Puritan revolution were conducted when his own radical days were past – when he had come, for example, to oppose the movement for the extension of the franchise.[77] He did give much space to Lilburne, but, like many writers before and after him, thought the Leveller leader a violent and self-indulgent demagogue.[78]

Early nineteenth-century voices sympathetic to the Levellers can sometimes be heard. In 1819 we find Coleridge regretting that even in the turbulent times of Cromwell, 'with the exception of a few Levellers', advocates of liberty had demanded only 'freedom for gentlemen'.[79] In 1828 the republican historian J. T. Rutt surmised that the men 'so

---

[73] *Publications printed by order of the Society for Preserving Liberty and Property* (1793), no. 5, 3.

[74] *Proceedings of the Association for Preserving Liberty and Property* (1793), no. 1, 5.

[75] Burke, *Letter to a noble lord*, 238; cf. Burke, *Reflections*, 49.

[76] Burke, *Reflections*, 11, 66 (though cf. 260–1). A friendly use of the term 'Leveller', but one no more historically specific, can be found in Charles Pigott, *A political dictionary* (London, 1795), 69.

[77] William Godwin, *Enquiry concerning political justice*, ed. Isaac Kramnick (Harmondsworth, 1976), 15.

[78] Godwin, *History of the commonwealth*, II:1ff., 22–3, 425, III:56–7, 451n. Cf. Rutt, *Diary of Thomas Burton*, III:503; Alfred Bisset, *The commonwealth of England* (2 vols., London, 1864–7), I:94–6; Gooch, *History of English democratic ideas*, 174; Morley, *Oliver Cromwell*, 290.

[79] S. T. Coleridge, *Philosophical lectures*, ed. K. Coburn (London, 1949), 259–60.

unjustly described Levellers' had 'probably been misrepresented and unjustly censured' and were 'probably the only consistent republicans of their time'.[80] Yet such observations produced no movement of sympathy. 'Leveller' remained a smear. In 1846, when the term was hurled at the Chartists, a Chartist newspaper repudiated it.[81] Few Chartists, and few Victorian republicans, seem to have been interested in the civil-war Levellers. In 1841, it is true, the *English Chartist Circular* reprinted, from the *Harleian miscellany*, a Leveller tract of 1659, in order to dispel 'the atrocious villainy and utter falsehood', perpetrated by 'hireling historians', that the Levellers had been 'ignorant fanatics'.[82] Yet that statement hardly signalled a Chartist embrace of Leveller memory. It was a defensive move, intended to demonstrate the moderation of the Chartists' intentions. The tract of 1659 had itself been a notably moderate document in which the social radicalism that had flourished in the 1640s was barely visible.[83]

The ensuing decades likewise produced little popular sentiment in favour of the Levellers. Around the middle of the century the publications of the French statesman François Guizot did strengthen the chronological foundations on which interest in the Levellers would be based. Yet Guizot, while generally sympathetic to reforming Puritanism, shuddered at the 'anarchical' and 'despotic violence' of the Puritan revolution, which reminded him all too readily of revolutionary happenings in his own land. He found Lilburne's invective 'furious and severe', though he was more troubled by the regicide, that act of 'fanaticism', than by the Levellers.[84] Guizot's researches, like William Godwin's before them, enlarged perceptions of the civil-war period but did not transform them. Neither author created a movement of scholarship. In 1852 H. O. Coxe's catalogue of Oxford college libraries drew attention to the existence of the Clarke manuscripts in Worcester College (though not of Clarke's transcript of the Putney debates). In editing the papers nearly forty years later, Firth found it 'strange that no historian has hitherto thought to make use of them'.[85]

---

[80] Rutt, *Diary of Thomas Burton*, I:49n.

[81] *The Northern Star*, 22 August 1846. (The significance of this and subsequent asterisks is explained in n. 2, above.)

[82] *English Chartist Circular* no. 14 (1841); cf. Roger Howell Jr, ' "Who Needs Another Cromwell?" ' in Richardson, *Images of Oliver Cromwell*, 96–107, at 107.

[83] *Harleian miscellany*, IV:515–21.

[84] François Guizot, *On the causes of the success of the revolution of 1640–1688* (London, 1850), 23–5, 135–6.

[85] *CP,* I:vii. There was apparently a slender exception to Firth's rule: J. B. Deane, *The life of Richard Deane* (London, 1970), 495–6 (a reference I owe to the kindness of Frances Henderson). A moderately sympathetic account of the Levellers can be found in Bisset, *History of the commonwealth*, esp. I:85ff.; on Bisset's work see Davidson, *Annals*, II:228.

V

If the slow course of scholarly discovery is one reason why the Levellers did not attract wider attention before the late nineteenth century, it cannot be the only one. Popular radicals of the eighteenth and nineteenth centuries could easily have discovered more about the Levellers and have made more of them. Why did they not?

By the late eighteenth century some radicals had turned away from all historical models or memories towards timeless and abstract principles of natural or human rights.[86] Yet that explanation hardly suffices. There remained many radical milieux in which the past remained a powerful sanction or inspiration. While the Levellers failed to acquire a following, there were other figures from the seventeenth-century past who succeeded in doing so, and who occupied the territory which we might expect the Levellers to have filled.

First there were the classical and parliamentary republicans James Harrington, Algernon Sidney, John Milton, Edmund Ludlow, Sir Henry Vane. In contrast with the Levellers, most of those writers could conveniently be read in widely available editions. To the writers who did give attention to the Levellers – to Catharine Macaulay, to J. T. Rutt, to William Godwin – Lilburne and his associates were of smaller attraction than the writers in the republican canon. They were of smaller attraction, too, than the heroes of the Rump Parliament: that is, the parliament which had carried out the regicide, the parliament which Milton had championed, the parliament in which Sidney, Ludlow and Vane had sat – and the parliament which had, with Cromwell, crushed the Levellers in 1649 and had exiled Lilburne in 1652. To Catharine Macaulay the rule of the Rump was 'the brightest age that ever adorned the page of history'.[87] The Society for Constitutional Information, which ignored the Levellers, instead promoted works in the classical and parliamentary republican tradition. The same was true of Thomas Spence's journal of the 1790s, *Pig's Meat*, which offered political enlightenment to the labouring classes.[88]

By the early nineteenth century, admittedly, the influence of the seventeenth-century republicans was on the wane. A biographer of Algernon Sidney in 1813 conceded that Algernon's 'political views', 'being chiefly directed at the circumstances of the higher and middling orders of society', could offer no hope to the suffering 'lower ranks'.[89] Yet as late as 1854 we find the *People's Paper* launching a serialisation of a life

---

[86] H. T. Dickinson, 'The eighteenth-century debate on the Glorious Revolution', *History* 61 (1976), 28–45, at 44.   [87] Quoted in Hill, *Republican virago*, 35.
[88] Robbins, *Eighteenth-century commonwealthman*, 322.
[89] G. W. Meadley, *Memoirs of Algernon Sidney* (London, 1813), 214.

of '[Algernon] Sidney the Patriot'.[90] Eleven years earlier the *English Chartist Circular* praised another seventeenth-century writer who had been claimed for the classical republican tradition, Andrew Marvell.[91] It commended his opposition to standing armies, a resonant theme for radicals of the industrial revolution, among whom the enthusiasm of the classical republicans for citizen militias was transmuted into an insistence on the right of the people to bear arms.[92]

The bearing of arms on behalf of the oppressed had become more prominently associated, however, with another seventeenth-century figure: Oliver Cromwell. In the nineteenth century Cromwell became a more potent force in populist political thinking than the classical and parliamentary republicans had ever been. From the early nineteenth century we find calls for a 'second Oliver' to put the oligarchy at Westminster to flight, as Cromwell had smashed the Long Parliament in 1653.[93] Thomas Carlyle's explosive lecture on Cromwell published in 1841, and his edition of *Oliver Cromwell's letters and speeches* in 1845, intensified such sentiment. 'A spirit of Cromwellian might', proclaimed George Harney's *The Red Republican* in 1850, 'is stirring at this hour'.[94] In 1854 the *Northern Tribune* hoped for a leader who 'shall again lead the Ironsides to victory, and sit at England's council-board'.[95] A number of radicals who had earlier had doubts about Cromwell's integrity – and thus might perhaps have been drawn to the Levellers instead – were won over by Carlyle's hero-worship of him. The Chartist Thomas Cooper, a friend of Carlyle, was among them.[96] In 1850, it is true, the republican Joseph Barker regretted Cromwell's suppression of the Levellers at Burford. Yet Barker, following Carlyle, concluded that Cromwell had only been doing his duty.[97] The Levellers were generally held to have got in Cromwell's way. Cromwell, declared Edmund Clarke in a lecture at Manchester in

---

[90] *People's Paper*, 22 July 1854. Cf. *The life of Thomas Cooper, written by himself* (London, 1873), 164; Peter Karsten, *Patriot-heroes in England and America* (Madison, WI, 1978), index entry on Cooper, Thomas.   [91] *English Chartist Circular*, no. 118 (1843).

[92] John Cartwright, *A letter to the electors of Nottingham* (1803), 34–5; *Bronterre O'Brien, The Operative*, 27 January 1839.

[93] Mason, 'Nineteenth-century Cromwell', 77–8; John Dunbabin, 'Oliver Cromwell's popular image in nineteenth-century England', *Britain and the Netherlands V*, ed. J. Bromley and E. Kossman (The Hague, 1975), 141–63, at 148.

[94] *The red republican* (2 vols., 1850–1 repr. 1966), I:frontispiece.

[95] *Northern Tribune* (1854), 413.

[96] *The commonwealthsman: or Chartist advocate*, 12 April 1842 (PRO, HO 45/260); *Life of Thomas Cooper*, 283; Thomas Cooper, *The bridge of history* (1971), 9–10; Dunbabin, 'Oliver Cromwell's popular image', 150–1. For the rise and character of Cromwell's nineteenth-century reputation see, too, Karsten, *Patriot-heroes*, esp. 142–68; Dale Trela, *A history of Thomas Carlyle's 'Letters and speeches of Oliver Cromwell'* (Lewiston, NY, 1992); Blair Worden, 'The English reputations of Oliver Cromwell, 1660–1900' in William Lamont (ed.), *Historians and historical controversies* (1998), 35–48.

[97] Karsten, *Patriot-heroes*, 146.

1846, had been a 'dauntless and inflexible opposer of oppression and arrogance . . . under any name, whether it were of king or priest, peer or commoner, respectable presbyterian burgher or enthusiastic military leveller'.[98]

Cromwell's radical admirers supposed his rule as lord protector to have been a time of working-class prosperity, which the Restoration had cruelly terminated in the interests of the great landowners. From the early nineteenth century there were writers ready to portray the civil wars as a social conflict, waged between a selfish, effeminate and oppressive aristocracy and a manly, upright people. By the end of the century, when the Levellers had acquired their champions, Cromwell would seem the betrayer of the people, but there are only rare glimpses of such feeling earlier in the century. Though he and his fellow Puritan rulers were occasionally charged with levying oppressive taxation or perpetuating social privilege, for the most part Cromwell seemed not the people's enemy but their friend. He had been, remarked the *Northern Tribune* in 1854, 'the first man to draw the sword on the people's side'.[99] Eight years earlier Edmund Clarke's lecture at Manchester explained that Cromwell had 'infused the loftiest energy into the common people, and showed that there was a soul in the plebeian, and a might in his arm, before which the aristocrat and his retainer were as dry twigs before the blast'.[100] Cromwell's admirers viewed him, without any sense of contradiction, as the champion at once of the 'middle classes' and of the 'lower orders' or 'the people'.[101] Only when the bourgeoisie, rather than the aristocracy, came to be seen as the principal enemy of the plebeian class would the Levellers seem the spokesmen of the working class, Cromwell their antagonist.

By the 1880s that process was under way. Nineteenth-century Cromwell was the hero of Nonconformist liberalism. Towards the end of the century Nonconformity was in decline, socialism on the rise. The new attacks on Cromwell were attacks on Nonconformity, too. He was portrayed not only as a representative of the seventeenth-century 'capitalist' and 'profiteering class', not only as a man devoid of 'sympathy with democracy and freedom', but as a forerunner of the hypocritically pious Nonconformists prominent in the Victorian business community.[102] It was against the Cromwellian alliance of 'the chapel' and 'the till', wrote Cunningham Grahame in the *People's Paper* in 1890, that 'honest John

---

[98] Clarke, *Lectures on . . . Cromwell*, vii.   [99] **Northern Tribune*, 413.

[100] Clarke, *Lectures on . . . Cromwell*, 3.

[101] Ibid., 160; Wilson, *Oliver Cromwell*, 140, 178; cf. Thomas Cromwell, *Oliver Cromwell*, 86–7.

[102] Hyndman, *Historical basis of English socialism*, 66; W. C. Abbott, *Writings and speeches of Oliver Cromwell* (4 vols., London, 1937–47), IV:896; Davidson, *Annals*, II:206–7, 213, 222, 227–8.

Lilburne' had led 'the poor' in 'revolt'.[103] In 1899 socialists kept away from the tercentenary commemorations of Cromwell's birth, which attracted so much enthusiasm in the country at large and in which Nonconformists played the leading role.

The way was now open for the rediscovery not only of the Levellers but of the Diggers. The international socialist Eduard Bernstein published his pioneering studies of them in 1895 and 1908. G. P. Gooch wrote about them in 1898 (calling them 'the communists'), as did the socialist L. A. Berens, whose book on Winstanley and the Diggers appeared in 1906.[104] Another socialist, John Morrison Davidson, who had already saluted the Levellers, produced a pamphlet on Winstanley in 1904. There was little unaninimity of approach to the Diggers. Davidson's discussion was resolutely empirical, averse to the continental dogmas of Marxism.[105] He seems to have been unaware of Bernstein's work. Yet it was to Bernstein, as Gooch acknowledged, that 'the honour of discovering Winstanley belongs'.[106] Bernstein, though he worked in England, seems to have had no contact with the British scholarly community until the publication of his book of 1908. Then he received an encouraging letter from C. H. Firth, who sought to have an English translation of it made.[107] By that time, however, the flurry of interest in the Diggers seems to have subsided. Only in 1930 would Bernstein's study become available in English. Even then it had to be given a misleading title, *Cromwell and communism*.

VI

Firth did as much as anyone to make the modern study of the Levellers possible. Yet he was no unstinting admirer of them. Like S. R. Gardiner he thought the Levellers – let alone the Diggers – unrealistic.[108] His research on them faded.[109] Neither Gardiner nor Firth was much interested in the development or composition of the Leveller party. A reader whose knowledge of the Puritan revolution was confined to Gardiner's *History of the great civil war* would not know of the existence of Richard Overton.

In 1891 the first volume of Firth's edition of the *Clarke papers*, with its transcripts of the army debates of 1647, appeared. The revolution in per-

---

[103] *People's Paper* 5 July 1890.
[104] L. A. Berens, *The social problem in the days of the commonwealth* (1898, reprinted from *The new age*); Berens, *The Digger movement in the age of the commonwealth* (London, 1906).
[105] Davidson, *Wisdom of Winstanley*, 26.
[106] Gooch, *History of English democratic ideas*, 206n.
[107] Eduard Bernstein, *My years of exile* (London, 1921), 236–7.
[108] Firth, *Oliver Cromwell*, 473.   [109] Haller and Davies, *Leveller tracts*, 3.

ceptions of army radicalism which it accomplished was not wrought over-
night. Gardiner realistically saw the debate on the franchise at Putney,
which the twentieth century has taken to its heart, as 'a side issue'.[110] The
Putney debates are what everyone remembers about the *Clarke papers*, yet
Firth, though excited by his discovery of them, was concerned to place
them in that broader context of military and indeed national politics
which his edition did so much to illuminate.[111] Early readers of Firth's
edition (not all of whom found the Putney debates easy to follow[112]) were
interested at least as much in the new light it threw on the character and
conduct of Cromwell and Ireton as in its revelations about the Levellers
and army agents.[113]

For the modern picture of the Levellers to emerge, another stage of
historical investigation was necessary. Only when historians took the
Levellers as a subject by itself, and were willing to trace Leveller ideas
systematically through the pamphlet material, would the Levellers
come to be seen to have had a continuous or evolving programme. That
breakthrough was achieved in two publications, both of which seem to
have reached a wide audience. The first was G. P. Gooch's *History of
English democratic ideas in the seventeenth century*, published in 1898,
where a chapter is devoted to the political opinions of the army. Gooch
was no socialist. He sympathised with Ireton's conviction that the
Leveller commitment to natural rights was essentially anarchic. He
regretted that the Levellers had failed to see the necessary role of a
natural aristocracy, a principle that had been grasped by the figure who
for Gooch was the prime reforming thinker of the revolution, James
Harrington.[114]

The second, more ambitious, study was T. C. Pease's *The Leveller movement*, a book whose title proclaimed the new approach which its text
helped to advance. Based on research completed before the Great War, it
was published in 1916. Though declaring a 'prepossession in favour of
the Levellers',[115] Pease was no more a socialist than Gooch had been.
Writing in America, he found liberal rather than socialist virtues in
Leveller teaching. He made no mention of the Diggers except in his bibliography, which described Eduard Bernstein as 'an avowed socialist' who
'distorts his account of the Leveller movement to make it serve as a mere
prelude to communism'.[116] To Pease the significance of the Levellers was

---

[110] Gardiner, *Great civil war*, III:388.   [111] *CP,*I:ix–x.
[112] See the inaccurate summary by Morley, *Oliver Cromwell*, 240; cf. however, Arthur
Patterson, *Oliver Cromwell. His life and character* (London, 1899), 165, 176–7.
[113] Gooch, *History of English democratic ideas*, 158–9, 161; Morley, *Oliver Cromwell*, 233,
236; cf. *CP,* I:lxx.   [114] Gooch, *History of English democratic ideas*, 205–6.
[115] Pease, *Leveller movement*, 6.   [116] Ibid., 372.

that they had sought 'the establishment in England of democratic government limited and bounded by law'.[117] They were the party of constitutional and legal rights.

Pease saw that guiding principle as a virtue. To the Marxist historian
David Petegorsky, a quarter of a century later, the Levellers' preoccupation with 'constitutional mechanisms' was their limitation. Around
1900, socialist historians had tended to regard the Levellers as their
ancestors. By the late 1930s they were viewing them with warier eyes.
What the Levellers lacked, thought Petegorsky, was realistic social and
historical analysis. 'Law, they fail[ed] to recognise, is but the reflection
and crystallisation of the social relationships it is intended to regulate, a
result rather than a cause.' It was the achievement but also the short-
coming of the Levellers, he maintained, that they pointed ahead to
'radical liberalism' and 'liberal democracy'.[118] Petegorsky's study, a Left
Book Club choice, was published in 1940, the year that also produced
the long pamphlet on the English revolution by Christopher Hill that
would soon be republished in the Marxist Textbook series. In Hill's
analysis, to which Petegorsky's is close, the Levellers represented 'the
petty bourgeoisie', a class doomed to division and impotence, being
squeezed as it was between 'the big bourgeoisie' on the one hand and the
landless proletariat on the other. Hill noted the absence of any 'organised working-class movement' to lead 'a frontal attack on the power of
big capital'.[119]

Across the twentieth century it is Marxist or socialist interpretations of
the Levellers that have caught the headlines. Yet alongside them there has
run, less conspicuously, the liberal tradition espoused by Pease. That tradition has been stronger in the United States than in Britain. Its origins
are British none the less. It can be said to begin with S. R. Gardiner's distinction, on which others would soon build, between 'political' Levellers –
Lilburne and his friends – whose aim was liberty and democracy, and the
Diggers, who wanted equality and socialism.[120] Since the Restoration,
historians had generally been content to regard the political and social
levelling of the civil wars as inseparable urges of destruction. Now the two

---

[117] Ibid., 1.
[118] Petegorsky, *Left-wing democracy*, 116, 118–19.
[119] Hill, *English revolution*, 67–9; Petegorsky, *Left-wing democracy*, 83–4, 102, 109, 118–20.
   Nora Carlin has pointed out to me that the bourgeois origins of the Levellers were noted
   by Marx and Engels: Karl Marx and Frederick Engels, *Collected works* (47 vols., London,
   1975–93), VI:321, XXV:19.
[120] Gardiner, *Commonwealth and protectorate*, I:42–4. Cf. Gooch, *History of English democratic
   ideas*, 225; Firth, *Oliver Cromwell*, 239–40; Morley, *Oliver Cromwell*, 291; Trevelyan,
   England under the Stuarts, 282n.; Barker, *Oliver Cromwell*, 41; Hayward, *Unknown
   Cromwell*, 71, 146; *P&L*, [69]; Haller and Davies, *Leveller tracts*, 26; Christopher Hill
   (ed.), *Winstanley. 'The Law of freedom' and other writings* (Harmondsworth, 1973), 49.

were prised apart. Whatever Lilburne's failings, Gardiner reflected, at least he had been no socialist.[121] In Gardiner's estimation the distinction between political and social levelling worked to the Levellers' advantage. In time Marxist history, catching up with the distinction, would turn it to their disadvantage.

In the liberal tradition, and particularly in the United States, two features of the Leveller programme have been especially influential. The first is the principle, which was announced in the *Agreement of the people* of 1647 and which subsequently reappeared in the American Constitution, that the people have rights that they must keep to themselves and away from their representatives. The second is the demand for the abolition of monopolies, that block on free enterprise. To Petegorsky, by contrast, the Levellers' complaints about monopolies revealed the limits of their social sympathies, for monopolies were 'irrelevant to th[e] situation' of the 'propertyless classes'.[122]

The distance between the two traditions need not be exaggerated. On both sides there has been a recognition that the 'individualism' of the Levellers was combined with a sense of communal responsibility.[123] Even so, Leveller individualism has been discussed more indulgently by writers of liberal than of socialist outlook. A. S. P. Woodhouse, writing in 1938, noted that the Levellers had advocated 'free trade' and had held 'a *laisser-faire* ideal of the state'. They looked for 'guarantees against interference with the individual'. They thus looked forward to Bentham and to Mill.[124]

Liberal sentiments on the Levellers' behalf were voiced again in 1944, in the two collections of Leveller tracts which were published in that year and which made a large body of Leveller literature available for the first time since the civil wars. William Haller, introducing one of them, thought that Lilburne had looked to 'free enterprise' as the means 'to satisfy every need that nature plants in the human breast'.[125] The other, edited by Don Wolfe, was introduced by Charles Beard, who claimed that the Leveller manifestoes, anticipating as they did so much that would be

---

[121] Gardiner, *Commonwealth and protectorate*, I:42.

[122] Petegorsky, *Left-wing democracy*, 109.

[123] Gooch, *History of English democratic ideas*, 204; *P&L*, [100] (cf. [70]); Petegorsky, *Left-wing democracy*, 109, 116; Haller and Davies, *Leveller tracts*, 2, 40.

[124] *P&L*, [70–1]. Another line of division in modern historiography has been between those who have detected rationalism or secularity in Leveller thinking (Pease, *Leveller movement*, 217, 358; *P&L*, [18], [82]; Frank, *Levellers*, 245–6; Brailsford, *Levellers*, 537) and those led by Haller (Haller and Davies, *Leveller tracts*, 3) who have emphasised the religious origins of Leveller ideas. The first of those positions had a nineteenth-century ancestry: John Lingard, *A history of England* (8 vols., London, 1819–30), 6:589; R. Vaughan, *Memoirs of the Stuart dynasty* (2 vols., London, 1831), II:183–4; Hazlitt, *Oliver Cromwell*, 140.   [125] Haller and Davies, *Leveller tracts*, 48–9.

said by Locke and Jefferson, 'deserve a permanent place as a fundamental exhibit in the history of constitutional government and liberty in England, the United States, indeed the whole English-speaking world'.[126] In 1955 Joseph Frank's book on the Levellers, written under the shadow of McCarthyism, described the establishment of constitutional and individual rights as their 'central purpose', and noted that 'the battle for an Agreement of the People is still being waged'.[127] In the contention between the liberal and socialist interpretations of the Levellers we see, in microcosm, the enduring twentieth-century debate about the relationship between liberty and equality. Perhaps it is fitting that the 350th anniversary of the Putney debates was celebrated in two places: in Putney Church, with speeches by Christopher Hill and Tony Benn, representatives of the tradition that has looked east to Moscow; and, in the conference from which this book has emerged, in Washington, the capital of the free world.

Appendix – 'The Levellers': the emergence of the term

How did the term 'the Levellers' come into being? John Lilburne and his allies had a clear answer. They maintained that during the army's sojourn at Putney in the autumn of 1647 the army grandees had put the word into circulation, perhaps with the general purpose of discrediting those to whom it was applied, perhaps with the more particular aim of bringing home to Charles I the danger he faced from those trouble-makers and of frightening him into fleeing from his captivity at Hampton Court.[128]

That explanation can be neither proved not disproved. The Levellers' dating of the origin of the term is apparently correct. It is in royalist writing of November 1647 that we find the earliest surviving uses of the term to describe Cromwell's opponents in the army,[129] though whether those uses owed anything to promptings by the army officers cannot be known. A royalist newsletter of 1 November claimed that the five dissenting regiments 'have given themselves a new name, viz. Levellers, for they intend to set all straight, and raise a parity and community in the kingdom'.[130] Ten days later a public declaration left behind by Charles I at Hampton Court explained that the army leaders had been ready to countenance 'the Levellers' doctrine', and that the king had resolved on

[126] Wolfe, *Leveller manifestoes*, vi–vii (cf. 108).

[127] Frank, *Levellers*, 1, 245, 262.

[128] John Lilburne, *An apologetic narration* (1652), 69–70; *Harleian miscellany*, IV:520–1; Haller and Davies, *Leveller tracts*, 1, 424–5.

[129] I dissent from Gardiner's judgement (*Great civil war*, III:380n.) that the term 'must obviously have been in existence before then'.

[130] Bodleian Library, Clarendon Ms. 30, fol. 163v.

his escape after realising that the army intended 'the destruction of the nobility'.[131]

The royalists' deployment of the term 'Leveller', recalling as it did the destruction of enclosures by 'levellers' early in the seventeenth century, seems to have been a calculated move. Hitherto Lilburne's group and the army agitators had been portrayed by their critics as members of an amorphous world of sectarian egalitarianism, where the itch for social parity was regarded as an evil consequence, but only one evil consequence, of a perhaps still more fundamental development, the spread of religious heresy.[132] The royalist propaganda of November 1647 marked a change of tactics. The army was now represented as nurturing a distinctive body of ideas, whose exponents were characterised not by sectarian enthusiasm (though that charge would soon be revived), but by the aim of social parity. The alleged threat to rank and property posed by the soldiery was thus brought into sharper focus.

That strategy became clearer five days after the king's declaration, in an edition of the royalist newsbook *Mercurius Pragmaticus*. Its author, Marchamont Nedham, contrived with characteristic slipperiness both to revive the memory of the destruction of enclosures and to caricature the dissidents' programme of social and political reform. 'We must leave off the name of Adjutators now', he explained, 'and take up a new one', for the king's declaration has fittingly 'christened' them 'Levellers', 'a most apt title for such a despicable and desperate knot to be known by, that endeavour to cast down and level the enclosures of nobility, gentry, and property, to make us all even: so that every Jack should vie with a gentleman, and every gentleman be made a Jack'.[133]

Nedham's characterisation of the Levellers would echo down the centuries.[134] Even so it is hard to tell how much the long-term characterisations of the Levellers would owe to the royalist charges of 1647 and how much to subsequent accounts of that year. The echoes of early royalist propaganda in later writing would not be exact. To posterity the Levellers have seemed a group separate, in aims and character, from the army officers. That was not how the royalists at first described them. Both the king's declaration and Nedham's newsbook sought to tar the officers as well as the agitators with the brush of levelling. (So if, as the Levellers themselves

---

[131] *His maiesties most gracious declaration ... 11 Novemb. 1647* (London, 1647), 2–3.

[132] The anonymous tract *The character of an agitator* ([London], 1647), published on the same day as the king's declaration, recycles that familiar image.

[133] *Mercurius Pragmaticus*, 16 November 1647; cf. Marchamont Nedham, *The case of the commonwealth of England, stated*, ed. P. A. Knachel (Charlottesville, VA, 1969), 96–110.

[134] Historian after historian would describe the Levellers, as Nedham had done, as 'desperate', an adjective which came habitually to be combined with 'furious': Kimber, *Life of Cromwell*, 109, 269; Banks, *Short critical review*, 181; *Political beacon*, 167; Hazlitt, *Oliver Cromwell*, 293.

believed, the officers were themselves responsible for introducing the term, its adoption by royalists rebounded on the army leaders.) Nedham indeed strove to apply the charge of 'levelling' not only to the entire army but to the more radical members of parliament. Both military and civilian leaders of the Roundheads, as described in *Mercurius Pragmaticus*, were 'levelling grandees', bent on 'levelling' church and state.[135] Yet it was on the agitators (or agents) and their allies that the label would stick.

Even on them it did not stick immediately. Though the word Leveller gained circulation in 1648, it found little place in narratives of army politics written at the time. It is not to be found, I think, in Denzil Holles's *Memoirs*, which were written early in 1649 and which have so much to say about the army's insubordination.[136] Only during 1649, under the pressure of fresh developments, did the characterisation pioneered by the royalists two years earlier take wing. The occasion of that development was the rise of the True Levellers, or Diggers, in the spring. The simultaneity of that episode and the army uprising that ended at Burford caused considerable semantic confusion.[137] It did, however, serve to strengthen the identification of Lilburne and his friends with that very cause of social levelling from which they were anxious to dissociate themselves. Ironically, the royalists, who had promoted that identification, now had cause to regret it. Now their propaganda portrayed Lilburne and the army mutineers as friends of liberty – even if headstrong and misdirected ones – against England's new tyranny. It discriminated between their beliefs and the egalitarian absurdities of the True Levellers.[138] As the Interregnum wore on, however, the fragmentation of Lilburne's party, and of all dissident groups, made the distinctions among trouble-makers a matter of declining interest and intelligibility. The various groups and sects tended to be lumped together by their enemies and critics. Philip Skippon's attack, in the parliament of 1656, on 'Quakers, Ranters, Levellers, Socinians, and all sorts' spoke for a trend.[139] So when the Puritan revolution collapsed, and its historiography began, the loose application of the term 'Leveller' was already a habit.

---

[135] *Mercurius Pragmaticus*, 25 February 1648, 18 April 1648, 25 July 1648, 8 August 1648, 17 October 1648. Cf. 3 October 1648; Paul Knell, *A looking-glasse for Levellers* (1648), 13–15.

[136] There is nothing about Levellers in the account of the late 1640s by Thomas May in 1650, and little in that by Sir John Berkeley written in 1651–2 (or in the later *Memoirs* of Sir Thomas Fairfax).

[137] The confusion is most conspicuous in the account of 1649 in Whitelocke's *Memorials*.

[138] That tactic was adopted both by Nedham, whose journalism had already taken opportunities to champion Lilburne against his Roundhead prosecutors before 1649, and by the (formerly presbyterian, now in effect royalist) writer Clement Walker, who observed that 'the grandees' had 'politickly mis-call[ed]' the agitators and their friends 'Levellers': *History of Independency*, pt. ii. 138.

[139] Rutt, *Diary of Thomas Burton*, I:49n.; cf. Christopher Hill, *The world turned upside down* (London, 1972), 192, 205. (Hill's remark (ibid., 91) about the use of the word 'Leveller' in 1647 is misleading.)

14 The true Leveller's standard revisited: an afterword

J. G. A. Pocock

There seems no reason to doubt that debates took place at Putney, or that William Clarke took notes at them, which he later developed into as close a verbatim record as he could achieve. Though the word 'invention' continues to hang over us like Pope's Great Anarch, no one – at least in this volume – has reached the point of suggesting that the manuscripts which lay so long in a cupboard at Worcester College contain a creative fiction by whose means Clarke's solitary genius sought hegemony over others; we still believe that things happen and that archives seek to record them, and Lesley Le Claire and Frances Henderson take us inside Clarke's struggle to construct a record. There ensues a time-lapse of two and a quarter centuries, during which nothing whatever happens in the process by which this history comes to us; but thereafter the creation – it is a better word than 'invention' – of a tradition can be seen taking place. We know it was Charles Firth who edited 'the Clarke papers', A. S. P. Woodhouse who made them the vehicle of 'the Putney debates'. A history with other origins now enters the story, that of 'the Levellers'. We know how this term was employed to discredit a movement of more or less identifiable individuals, though it is less clear how far these adopted a term originally pejorative – as so often happens – to proclaim and identify themselves. As is perhaps not the case with 'the Ranters',[1] we have evidence of a network of people acting together to determine and pursue shared purposes, and we find several of them, known to us independently of the Clarke papers, present at Putney and taking part in debates which appear to have been among officers and soldiers, but in which they intervened as civilians and members of a group we have resolved to term 'the Levellers'.[2] The 'Putney debates' now become an episode in a complex history, made up of the interacting histories of 'the Levellers', 'the agitators', and 'the officers and soldiers' constituting 'the New Model Army'.

The present volume sets out to review and revise this history as it has taken shape during the twentieth century, asking from time to time

---

[1] Lamont, ch. 12, above, 251 and n. 35.
[2] Other than the close analyses contained in this volume (chapters 4, 5, 6 and 8 especially), see most recently Andrew Sharp (ed.), *The English Levellers* (Cambridge, 1998).

whether it can be continued as a narrative employing the above terminology, and whether it is still satisfactory to employ these words as if they denoted reified entities, or groups acting and responding together. Who were 'the Levellers'; was Rainborough one of them; was Sexby; did they call themselves that, and in either case why? These potentially revisionist queries do not arise only – though they do so arise – from the increasing minuteness of an increasingly nominalist historiographical analysis; they have also a dimension of ideology. The history of 'the Putney debates' and 'the Levellers' in the twentieth century has been a history of political faith; there was a creed of democratic socialism (complicated here and there by the presence of those whose socialism was not democratic at all), and a creed of social democracy. Rainborough and the poorest he that was in England became part of the history of these creeds, part of a history of England which socialists thought they could legitimately construct; and the increasing sophistication of historical criticism is not to be separated from the decline of these creeds. The question of what occurred at Putney inescapably merges with – though it does not necessarily entail – the question of whether and in what sense we continue to believe in democracy at all, in an age when globalism abolishes sovereignty and post-modernism identity.

We therefore return to starting-points as minimalist as we can make them: the challenging historical statements that appear to survive all the Occamist razors wielded against them. It continues to be extraordinary that some of the things said (and attempted to be done) at Putney should have been said at all; as it remains extraordinary that we should have this, and only this, record of them. The English civil wars took place in a print culture; much of what we know about 'Levellers' and other 'radicals' is knowledge of the printed pamphlets and declarations they and their adversaries published against one another. Yet 'the Putney debates' were not printed, and played no part in the shaping by print of either a contemporary consciousness of events or a subsequent consciousness of history. They have no history at all in the later seventeenth, the eighteenth or most of the nineteenth century, and do nothing to shape the historical awareness, or the history, of those eras. A historical consciousness, mostly hostile, of 'enthusiasm', antinomianism, and its 'radical' and 'democratic' potential is, it is true, never absent; 'the civil war sects' and 'the Levellers' begin to surface in the nineteenth century, as the contents of the Thomason and other collections become known. But only with Firth, Bernstein, Petegorsky and Woodhouse do 'the Putney debates' begin to modify this context, and both democratic and socialist readings of them appear. The 'Clarke papers' therefore retain a shock value; they do not belong to the history of printed knowledge for centuries, until they sud-

denly appear in it. We may read them as an episode in the history of shorthand, an episode in the history of manuscript and – given a very few
assumptions – an episode in the history of action performed in the instant
before it is recorded. Clarke taking notes at Putney is like Clarke touching
the edge of the axe at Whitehall;[3] he is present at the creation. We may go
on to awareness of the enigmatically private and public mortal he was in
his life and death (Carlyle would have hailed him, as he did Jocelyn of
Brakelonde in his *Past and present*).

It is this sense of immediacy – meaning the absence of mediation by
print or other mechanisms of formed discourse – that makes some of the
things said at Putney extraordinary to us. We are able to believe that
Clarke was attempting, in the raw, to record the attempts of individuals to
articulate their speech, and to some extent their thoughts, also in the raw;
we are looking at speech acts, consciousness and action, at moments of
coming into being. The discovery that Thomas Rainborough was no
Leveller – in the sense that he was not accredited to the meeting as
belonging to that or any invited group – and that his speeches may have
been as infuriating to Sexby and Wildman as they certainly were to
Ireton, heightens this sense of immediacy; perhaps he was speaking spontaneously, and of how many actors in history do we believe that to be true?
It is not often that I find myself slightly to the left of my old friend William
Lamont, but I see more than agitprop in Caryl Churchill's *The light
shining in Buckinghamshire*.[4] I once saw a performance in which the
Putney scene ended with Rainborough and Ireton staring at each other in
exhaustion and mutual defeat; this declared a possibility.

The 'Clarke papers' are dramatically informative, as well as exciting. If
we have to use our imaginations to decide what they may be telling us, it
was Edward Gibbon who once indicated that historical study rested on
the combined exercise of the imagination and the judgement.[5] However,
immediacy can be approached but never finally attained; all speech is in
some degree predetermined. In a history of politics, we tend to privilege
above other predetermining factors membership in a political group with
known aims and programmes; there was a time when all political science
was held reducible to the ascertainment of group interests. We have therefore been accustomed to suppose the existence of more or less militant
parties, termed 'the Levellers', 'the agitators' and so forth, and to read
events preceding, including and following the meetings at Putney as the
history of the attempts of the first-named to make common cause with
the second; alternatively, we suppose 'the officers' – differentiated at

---

[3] Le Claire, ch. 2, above, 30 and n. 36.   [4] Lamont, ch. 12, above, 243.
[5] Georges Bonnard (ed.), *Edward Gibbon: memoirs of my life* (New York, 1966), 99.

times into 'the junior officers' and 'the grandees' – and their interactions with 'the soldiers', or such at least of the latter as have appeared suscepti- ble of political consciousness and organisation, amounting at times to mutiny. Behind such readings – at least in the heyday of democratic and socialist interpretations of the crisis of 1647–9 – there were present some shadowy and some precise concepts of non-elite and class consciousness: the doctrine, that is to say, that individuals derive awareness of the social structure containing them from pressures occasioned by their place within it. Hence Rainborough's 'poorest hee', and still more Sexby's 'soldier that hath fought all this while', were held present at Putney in the just off-stage form of the London crowds who turned out to support Lilburne and the troopers for whom the agitators spoke. All were some- times brought together by the name of 'the English people', of whom democrats and socialists felt confident to speak.[6]

What seems to have happened is that first there arose, and then there faded, a premise and a faith that 'the Levellers' and 'the agitators' – easily collapsed into a single entity – stood for groups larger than themselves, formed and moved by social processes larger than they knew. All history was once written on this premise; but as it has faded, we have come to turn an increasingly searching and merciless light on the constitution of the primary groups themselves. 'The Levellers' did not call themselves that; did they have a name for themselves, and what was their perception of the basis on which they acted together? It is important to ask such questions, if only to dispel facile reifications; but nominalism cannot be pressed so far as to dispel all possibility of co-ordinated action or group identity. The presence of civilians – Wildman and Petty – in what was oth- erwise a council of military men, seems to have been authorised by a per- ception that they came from somewhere and spoke for others; the important discovery that Rainborough did not come from any such authorising group, and may have been speaking only for himself, under- lines the existence of the group to which he did not belong – if at the same time it reminds us that we are looking at a moment when all was in flux, and individuals might find themselves acting in ways, and with associates, undreamed-of months or weeks before.

Nothing in these essays seems to signal the abandonment – only the increasingly minute inspection – of the premise that there existed the individuals designated when the term 'Levellers' is used, that they were endeavouring in London to construct political programmes that we may wish to term 'radical' and to co-ordinate these with demands put forward

---

[6] Brian Manning, *The English people and the English revolution* (London, 1976). The classic exposition of these themes is, of course, H. N. Brailsford, *The Levellers and the English rev- olution* (London, 1961). See Worden, ch. 13, above, 258.

by 'the agitators' (a group more concretely identifiable in so far as we know them to have been chosen by the regiments, and not a mere coalition of the likeminded). The coming together of 'Levellers' and 'agitators' – to use the accepted terminology – seems to have reached a certain point at Putney, followed by a crisis of defeat at Ware and a revival in the very different circumstances of the second civil war. To this extent we retain a scenario traceable back to Firth and even Gardiner, but we are warned not to reify the acting groups or overidentify the behaviour of individuals with their membership in them. Rainborough has become a loose cannon; and the contention that *The case of the armie* is the work of Sexby rather than of Wildman[7] not only makes it less of a 'Leveller' and more of an army document, but raises the question of Sexby himself. For whom or with whom was he acting, and what was the trajectory of his strange life? The behaviour of individuals does not conform to general laws; but *The case of the armie* may still be said to have had more than one author.

No revisionist historiography can prevent our moving from the particular to the general; as a rule it ends merely in the substitution of new for old paradigms at the pole of generality. The important work of Mark Kishlansky[8] probably explains the failure of revolution in the army – the overthrow of leadership by the senior officers would have been a revolution – by demonstrating that the interests of soldiers were in questions of indemnity, pay and demobilisation, and that the emotions of soldiers and officers focused on military honour and solidarity. Hence the failure of the mutinies; it was better to obey the officers than to enter the state of nature. So be it, as it probably was; yet mutiny was attempted. Kishlansky set out to do away with romantic perceptions of the Levellers as leaders of the insurgent masses (still less of the rising bourgeoisie) and cut radical sentiment down to size. Rightly so; but mutiny was attempted. There were soldiers at Ware with *An agreement* in their hats; Cromwell rode them down, but he had to spur his horse to do it. The ghost of insurgency cannot be quite laid; nor can the knowledge that this was an army of civilians, not professionals, and that some of them had had their political consciousness enlarged. The problem is to see into what terrain this enlargement must be followed, and we cannot do that by counting heads.

We are often, and rightly, warned against loose employment of the terms 'radical' and 'radicalism'. But the England of the root-and-branch bill was not unacquainted with the idiom that ascribed 'roots' to structures and problems, and envisaged action beginning at the roots. Even where this metaphor is not in use, there seems no harm in our applying

[7] Morrill and Baker, ch. 6, above.
[8] Mendle, ch. 1, above, 5, 7–8; Woolrych, ch. 4, above, nn. 2, 9; Morrill and Baker, ch. 6, above, 124.

the adjective 'radical' to proposals which seem to identify foundations and to change them; the danger lies in the move from adjective to noun, to such reifications as 'the radicals' or 'radicalism' or to the suggestion that these existed as perceptions in seventeenth-century minds. We may use the adjective of a number of things said and imagined at Putney, notably the proposal that government should rest on the consent of every individual; to say that Ireton or Cromwell perceived the 'radical' character of such proposals is a further use of the idiom on our part. A more formidable problem is that of understanding how some actors in English history at that moment formulated the perceptions and proposals we consider radical: what was it they perceived, how did they come to perceive it, what problems did they encounter as some of them went about translating perceptions into proposals and programmes? That this happened at all is of significance independently of the question how many (or how powerful) they were to whom it happened, but what precisely happened when it did?

'Radical' thinking may be held to consist in the perception that the ruling structure rested on foundations which might have been otherwise – anti-Normanism, for example – or in the affirmation of rights so fundamental as to reside in the individual anterior to any obligation; for example, Rainborough's claim on behalf of 'the poorest hee'. It may next be suggested that where such thinking existed in 1647–9, it existed in an early modern society; that the World Turned Upside Down was indeed the World We Have Lost.[9] We must consider what such a structure was like in order to understand how some intelligences, no matter how few, might arrive at such propositions, and what must be the limits within which they could develop them.

Mention of the World Turned Upside Down reminds us that religious antinomianism is a source of social radicalism; to set the spirit free from ecclesiastical restraints may lead to its emancipation from the secular authority often allied with the latter. We are warned against overestimating the spread of this phenomenon, but its existence is important independently of its extent; that people believed there were Ranters is significant whether there were any or not. It is also significant, however, that the voice of the anarchic seeker is not much to be heard at Putney, and that those who believed the social structure was about to be sanctified and transformed sometimes thought of it in conventionally conservative terms. The present writer is not quite clear why the Levellers should be held responsible for the Promise Keepers and the Idaho militias;[10] the Reformadoes and the presbyterian mobs of 1647 might seem to fill the role better, to say nothing of the General and Particular Baptists who are

---

[9] Mendle, ch. 1, above, 5.   [10] Ibid., 12; Lamont, ch. 12, above, 242.

certainly the Promise Keepers' direct ancestors. During the conference at the Folger Library, I happened to glance at the book being read by my neighbour in a Washington subway train. It said: 'The Bible is a legal document, sealed with the blood of Jesus.' Every one of the debaters at Putney knew what this doctrine meant, and most believed it. The twentieth-century United States was in this respect closer to seventeenth-century England than twentieth-century Britain was. Part of our trouble in coming to terms with the Levellers at Putney and elsewhere is that we see Overton and Walwyn as predecessors of those rather different beings, the anti-Trinitarian Rational Dissenters a century and a half later,[11] who turned a Lockean critique of dogma into an Enlightened equation of religion with free enquiry, and so into a critique of all laws and governments as insufficiently grounded in the liberty of the individual. In the independent United States they remain in the mainstream of a liberal and sectarian culture to this day; in the United Kingdom they were progenitors of the British Left, both Liberal and Labour, which has proclaimed Lilburne and Rainborough symbols of its often more militant agnosticism. In studying the Putney debates we often rediscover that 'history is now and England';[12] it is also now and America.

Antinomian religious beliefs are as compatible with a radicalism (or a populism) of the Right as they are with one of the Left, but in modern (and post-modern) societies there also exists a liberal middle class which will reserve its applause for the Left. This class was altogether lacking in seventeenth-century England. The World We Have Lost consisted of a tissue of authority structures and micro-structures, down at least to the level of the landless poor. It is this omnipresence of authority that must be understood if we are to apprehend the radical thinking that now arose in that world. The central experience of the English civil wars was, in the language then found to describe it, 'the dissolution of government', and the most radical things then done were done in an attempt to reconstitute authority, not to subvert it or even to emancipate the spirit from it. The Fifth Monarchists desired a monarchy, in whose service was perfect freedom. The army manifestoes proclaim that the officers and soldiers are not masterless men, and add that they are not mercenaries but men acting under authority, and therefore possessed of it; if government is dissolved, authority and right (the Latin *jus* denotes both) devolve upon them and it is for them to restore it. Even Rainborough's poorest he, whose consent

---

[11] Knud Haakonssen (ed.), *Enlightenment and religion: rational dissent in eighteenth-century Britain* (Cambridge, 1996); J. C. D. Clark, *The language of liberty, 1660–1832: political discourse and social dynamics in the Anglo-American world* (Cambridge, 1994) and *English society, 1660–1832* (2nd edn, Cambridge, 2000).
[12] T. S. Eliot, *The four quartets*.

must be sought before he places himself under any government, will give that consent and place himself under government. (It is Ireton who fears that he won't.) The problem, in a world where dissolution of government can be imagined absolute but has not absolutely occurred, is whether consent is necessary to those structures of authority that have not yet been dissolved; there are a great many of these, and every speaker has his own reservations. The democracy which must now be envisaged must now decide what it wishes to conserve. Locke was to say it was 'as they think good',[13] but this language may go too far. Even the most convinced antinomian – if antinomianism and conviction are compatible – may have his list of respects in which he is not free to act as he may think good. Rainborough and Ireton differ only because Ireton's scheme of givens is too long for Rainborough, and once they have done debating the principle they can begin to negotiate (though, as others tell them, it may be too late to start).

In these circumstances the radical may find himself demanding that constituted authority perform those acts which in his view will render it legitimate. It is not a strong position, least of all after five to seven years of civil war aimed at the coercion of an otherwise legitimate authority; and the radical oscillates between the extremes of submission to an authority he has not made and the revolutionary substitution of one which he has not made yet. We are frequently assured that the people were royalist at heart, never having desired a dissolution which was the worst thing that had ever happened to them, and that a freely elected parliament, or even an agreement of the people like that called for at Putney, would infallibly have been an agreement to restore the king. It may be so, though we can only talk probabilities; but the curious oscillation of the Levellers between making approaches to the king and demanding the monarchy's reduction to a nullity,[14] may be accounted for by remembering that Charles I was executed for failing to be a king, not (like Louis XVI) for the primary sin of being one. It was G. M. Young, many years ago, who pointed out that had he been another man (or woman), he would have placed himself at the head of the army and led it into London.[15] The freedom of the Spirit might annihilate the monarchy, but might equally transform it. The kingdom would never have been the same again, but it is a universal consensus that anything would have been better than Charles' preferred strategy of sitting still and trying to dictate terms to those who approached him. Levellers and agitators might alike have preferred democratic monarchy to no monarchy at all, and the failure of Putney was not

[13] Locke, *Two treatises of government*, the last words of the text in any edition.
[14] Mendle, ch. 7, above, 131, 134–6, 139; Gentles, ch. 8, above, 172–3.
[15] G. M. Young, *Charles I and Cromwell* (London, 1935).

evident until it became the failure to maintain the later *Agreements of the people*.[16]

Whatever the causes of that failure, it was not out of the question to agree on a new and greatly enlarged electorate; we are compelled to counter-factual speculation only when we begin to wonder what its effect would have been. The exclusion of servants from the franchise made sense in a society where servants were dependents on their masters and service was an employment for the young, from which not a few expected to emerge; the history of the American colonies may be brought in evidence here. The unanswerable question is what a quasi-democracy of smallholders and craftsmen might have achieved in the World We Have Lost, with its social structure based even at the lower levels on magistracy, patriarchy, authority, deference and submission. Squirearchy even more than monarchy is the salient fact of the early modern English social structure, and at Putney it is never directly discussed. Not even Gerrard Winstanley proclaims class war against the gentry and freeholders, and this is the reason why 1649 was not a 1789, 1917 or 1948. Rainborough appeals to us because he can think of human freedom independently of social structure – Ireton thinks it is 'levelling' to do so – but it is perhaps a misleading paradox that the apparent democrats of Putney have lost significance in our eyes as we have ceased to think of history as the social structure in action. To understand what they were saying, and failing to say, we return to social structure as context.

[16] Gentles, ch. 8, above.

Index

agitators, 'adjutators', and/or 'agents', *see* New Model Army
Agreements of the people, 12, 148–74, 291
  first *Agreement*, 1, 7, 8, 12, 14, 15, 33, 67–71, 73–7, 103–6, 114–18, 121–2, 124, 136, 138–42, 149–56, 163, 173, 182–7, 191, 232, 244, 252–3, 256, 261, 279, 287
  second *Agreement*, 72, 78, 144, 156–64, 174, 189–91, 232
  third *Agreement*, 12, 168–74, 270
  see also Jubbes, John *and* Officers' *Agreement*
Allen, William, 62, 65, 67, 71, 73, 109–10, 116, 118, 123, 126, 179, 180, 182, 186–7
Answer to the xix propositions, 134
Ascham, Anthony, 27
Ashcraft, Richard, 221–2, 229, 265
Ashley-Cooper, Anthony, earl of Shaftesbury, 220, 222, 229
Askew, Anne, 203
Association for Preserving Liberty and Property against Republicans and Levellers, 270–1
Astell, Mary, 215
Audley, Captain Lewis, 32, 71
Aylmer, Gerald, 104

Bales, Peter, 40, 46
Barker, Joseph, 274
Barrington family, 215
Barrow, Samuel, 30
Baxter, Richard, 247–55, 260, 262
Beard, Charles, 279–80
Benn, Tony, 280
Bentham, Jeremy, 279
Berens, L. A., 276
Berkeley, Sir John, 260
Berlin, Sir Isaiah, 254
Bernstein, Eduard, 276, 277, 284
Bethel, Slingsby, 230

Blackstone, William, 267
Boys, John, 156
Brailsford, H. N., 104
Bray, William, 173
Breman, John, 228
Brereton, Sir William, 90–2
Bright, Timothy, 40, 41, 44, 46
British Libertarian Alliance, 12
Broucker, Lady, 210
Browning, Robert, 35
Buffe-Coate, *see* Everard, Robert
Burford, mutiny and suppression of Levellers at, 172–4, 261–2, 273, 274, 282
Burgh, James, 267
Burke, Edmund, 262, 268, 271
Burton, Thomas, 43
Butler, James, duke of Ormonde, 237

Cal to all the souldiers, A, 73, 115
Calvin, John, 129
Capel, Arthur, Lord, 39, 99–100
Carlyle, Thomas, 2, 274, 285
Carter, Ann, 206–7
Case of the armie truly stated, The, 9–10, 14, 66–8, 73, 103–24, 138, 142, 149–52, 160, 182–4, 287
Case, Ann, 206
Case, Thomas, 206
Cato's letters, 266–7
Chamberlaine, Mr, 71
Charles I, 7, 30, 34, 35, 43, 58–9, 61, 63, 75–8, 113, 123, 133, 135, 145, 147, 149, 152, 159, 167, 177, 180, 189, 193, 221, 228, 244, 280, 290
  see also Answer to the xix propositions
Charles II, 219, 220, 228, 248, 264
Chartists, 272
Chesterton, G. K., 254
Chidley, Katherine, 207, 216
Chillenden, Edmund, 71
Churchill, Caryl, 243, 285

Churchill, Sarah, 206
Clark, Jonathan, 5
Clarke, Sir George, 23–4, 33–5
Clarke, Samuel, 274–5
Clarke, Sir William, 2, 6, 7, 14, 19–35,
    36–43, 45–50, 53, 65, 68, 70, 73–5,
    118, 138, 142, 146–7, 154, 164, 241,
    253, 272, 283, 285
Clinton, William Jefferson, 242
Clitheroe, Margaret, 203
Cobbett, John, 169
Coffey, John, 253
Coke, Sir Edward, 13, 31
Colchester, siege and surrender of, 96,
    98–9, 189
Coleridge, Samuel, 271
College, Stephen, 13
Colley, Linda, 215
Collier, Jeremy, 267
Collier, Thomas, 190
Comenius, Jan, 40, 41
Conventicle Act, 234–5
Cooper, Thomas, 274
Cowling, Nicholas, 76, 84, 126, 137
Coxe, H. O., 21, 273
Cromwell, Oliver, 10, 14, 24, 29, 31, 44,
    53–4, 56, 62–5, 67–78, 83–5, 87–8,
    107, 117, 120, 123–4, 125–6, 133,
    136–7, 139, 142–3, 149, 151–6,
    160–2, 172, 175, 177, 179, 180,
    183–8, 193, 208, 210, 217, 228,
    242–5, 247, 252–5, 256, 261–2, 264,
    271, 273–7, 287–8
Cromwell, Richard, 250

Danvers, Henry, 228
Davidson, John Morrison, 276
Davies, Godfrey, 104
Davis, J. C., 247, 249, 251–2
Declaration of Dislike, 57
De Krey, Gary, 221
Deloney, Thomas, 135
Derby House Committee, 95–6
Devereux, Robert, earl of Essex, 80, 83–4,
    88, 149
D'Ewes, Sir Simonds, 2
Diggers, 28, 258, 260, 264, 276, 277, 282
Dorothy, Captain, 206
Dyle, Daniel, 44
Dyve, Sir Lewis, 77, 133

Echard, Laurence, 263
Edward the Confessor, 145
Edwards, Thomas, 119, 242–3
Egerton, John, 2nd earl of Bridgewater, 221
Egerton, Stephen, 44

Erbury, William, 190
Everard, Robert, 32, 67, 68, 71, 73, 136,
    130

Fairfax, Sir Thomas, 14, 33, 53–4, 56–65,
    67, 73–4, 76–7, 82, 84, 87, 95–8, 106,
    110, 117, 120, 124, 127, 141, 154–5,
    172, 176, 178, 180–2, 187–9
    Remonstrance from, 188
Feilding, Basil, Lord, 215
Feilding, Cecilia, countess of Denbigh,
    215
feme covert, 208
feme sole, 202–3, 205, 208, 211, 216, 217
Fiennes, William, viscount Saye and Sele,
    61, 149
Filmer, Sir Robert, 201
Firth, Sir Charles, 2, 4, 7, 20–2, 35, 36–7,
    45, 49, 103–4, 116, 241, 259, 260,
    272, 276–7, 283–4, 287
Fleetwood, Charles, 54, 149
Fortescue, G. K., 259
Frank, Joseph, 104, 280
Free Catholic Movement, 248

Gardiner, S. R., 3, 20, 21–2, 103, 259, 271,
    276–9, 287
Gentles, Ian, 5, 8, 94, 104–5, 108, 112, 116
Gibb, M. A., 199
Gibbon, Edward, 285
Gladman, John, 228
Glenham, Sir Thomas, 98
Godwin, William, 260, 271, 272, 273
Goffe, William, 31, 71
Goldsmith, Oliver, 263
Gooch, G. P., 3, 276, 277
Goodwin, John, 165, 190–1
Goring, George, earl of Norwich, 39, 100
Grahame, Cunningham, 275–6
Gregg, Pauline, 117
Grotius, Hugo, 11, 250
Guizot, François, 272

Haley, K. H. D., 229
Haller, William, 104, 241, 279
Hamilton, James, marquess of (earl of
    Cambridge), 39, 100
Hammond, Robert, 123
Hammond, Thomas, 166–7
Hare, John, 136, 144–5
Harleian miscellany, 260
Harney, George, 274
Harrington, James, 28, 140, 242, 250,
    266–7, 273, 277
Harris, John, 110, 127, 130–2, 143–4
    army press of, with Henry Hills, 127–32

Harris, Susanna, 132
Harrison, Maj.-Gen. Thomas, 33, 54, 82, 155, 180, 193
Harrison, Tom, 245
Hartlib, Samuel, 44
Hastings, Henry, Lord Loughborough, 99
Heads of the proposals, The, 11, 61–4, 68, 75, 114, 120, 133, 138, 141–2, 149, 153, 179–82, 185–6, 188, 191
Heath, John, 263
Hewson, John, 148
Hickeringill, Edmund, 221
Hickes, George, 217, 231, 234
Higgins, Patricia, 209
Hill, Christopher, 270, 278, 280
Hills, Henry (the younger), 127, 131
    see also Harris, John, army press of
Hirst, Derek, 204
Hobbes, Thomas, 28, 249
Holles, Denzil, 56–7, 149, 260, 282
Holmes, Abraham, 228
Hopkins, William, 45
Howe, John, 254–5
Hughes, Ann, 208
Hume, David, 263
Huntington, Robert, 260
Hutchison, Lucy, 262
Hyde, Edward, earl of Clarendon, 260, 263–4

Ibbitson, Robert, 110
indemnity, 8, 55, 56, 90–5, 100–1, 113, 132, 134, 140–2, 151, 155, 157, 163, 180
Ingoldsby, Richard, 54
Ireton, Henry, 5, 10, 11, 31, 32, 49, 53–4, 56–7, 61–2, 64–5, 67–6, 69–70, 72–3, 76–8, 83, 118–19, 123, 125–6, 129, 136–40, 142–3, 146, 149, 152–4, 157–8, 160–2, 165–6, 173–4, 175–93, 217, 242–5, 247, 249–50, 252–5, 277, 285, 288, 290, 291

James I, 134, 135
James, duke of York and later James II, 230
Jeake, Samuel, 44
Jefferson, Thomas, 37, 242, 280
Jenkins, David, 132–3, 140
Jenkins, Sir Leoline, 236
Jenks, Francis, 228
Jocelyn of Brakelonde, 285
Johnson, Samuel, 268
Jones, Inigo, 23, 35
Jones, Michael, 173
Joyce, George, 59, 177

Jordan, W. K., 241
Jubbes, John, 148, 158–9

Keeble, Neil, 247–9
Keeling, Sir John, 224–6
Kelsey, Thomas, 96
Kimber, Isaac, 263
Kishlansky, Mark, 5, 7–8, 70, 104–5, 124, 125, 287

Lambert, John, 61, 74, 100, 177
Larnar, William, 13
Laud, William, 27, 29, 46, 176, 250
L'Estrange, Roger, 239–40
Levellers, 1, 3, 9, 11, 12, 13, 28, 53–4, 57, 61, 65–6, 68, 70–2, 73, 76–8, 103–6, 109–10, 112–14, 116, 118–21, 124, 126, 129, 131, 143–6, 148–9, 151–63, 165–7, 169–74, 181, 183, 185–93, 200, 202, 208, 210–11, 216, 217, 283–8, 290
    green colour and, 170, 211, 220, 223–4, 226–7
    historiography of, pre-1960, 256–82
    large Petition of, 57–8, 156–7
    legacy of, 219–40
    origin of term, 280–2
Lilburne, Elizabeth, 216
Lilburne, John, 28, 29, 33, 57–8, 62, 65–6, 77, 78, 103–5, 116, 120, 123, 127–9, 132–3, 144–5, 150, 157, 159–60, 164, 165, 167–70, 179, 183, 189–90, 193, 199, 201, 209, 220, 237–9, 260, 262, 264, 268–9, 271, 272, 273, 275–6, 278–9, 280–2, 286
    1649 trial of, 7, 12–13, 46–7, 50, 145–6, 269
    1653 trial of, 219, 269
Lilburne, Robert, 24, 33, 73, 76, 155
Lindsay, A. D., 245–6, 252–3, 255
Lisle, Lady Alicia, 214
Lisle, Sir George, 99
Lloyd Thomas, J. M., 247–52, 255
Locke, John, 222, 229, 242, 267, 280, 290
Lockyer, Nicholas, 65, 67, 71, 73, 139, 179, 187
Lockyer, Robert, 169–70, 172
Lucas, Sir Charles, 99
Ludlow, Edmund, 175–6, 260, 273

McArthur, Ellen, 209
Macaulay, Catherine, 268, 269–70, 273
Machiavelli, Niccolò, 27
Macpherson, C. B., 199–200, 202–3
Magna Carta, 144
Marprelate tracts, 13
Marshall, John, 229

Marten, Henry, 183
Marvell, Andrew, 274
Maseres, Francis, 271
Mason, John, 227
Mason, Tim, 256–7, 264
Mason, William, 45
Maynard, Sir John, 132, 143–5
Mendelson, Sara, 205
Merchant Adventurers' Company, 58
Messenger, Peter, 224–5
Militia Ordinance, 80
Mill, John Stuart, 279
Miller, John, 228
Milton, John, 19, 27, 44, 249, 255, 273
Monck, George, 24–5, 85–6, 147
Monmouth's Rebellion, 214
Morrill, John, 72, 97, 104–5
Morris, John, 100

Naseby, battle of, 153
National Covenant, 59
Nedham, Marchamont, 27, 135, 152, 232, 233, 281–2
New Model Army, 5, 7–8, 53–7, 59, 149
    agitators, 'adjutators', and/or 'agents' in, 58–60, 62, 64–7, 73, 76, 103, 105, 108–9, 120–1, 149, 154, 176, 178–80, 281, 285–7
    agents of the five regiments, 65–8, 71, 105, 106–7, 110–11, 115, 124, 141, 149–51, 182–3
    officer-agitators, 67, 71, 73, 178, 186, 187
    Declaration (also known as *A representation*), 60, 112, 177–8, 180–2
    General Council of the Army, 1, 53, 60, 62–3, 64–8, 70–2, 74, 76–7, 83, 103, 107–10, 113–15, 119, 121, 123, 151–2, 154, 174, 177–8, 182, 186–7, 217
    Humble remonstrance (23 June 1647), 86, 93, 112, 182
    Solemn engagement, 59, 60, 67, 76, 149, 168–9, 177
    see also Heads of the proposals
Newcastle, Propositions of, 63
Norman oppression or Norman yoke, 31, 136–7, 210, 270, 288
Northleigh, John, 237
Nye, Philip, 190, 191

oblivion, *see* indemnity
Officers' *Agreement*, 148, 164–8, 174, 190–3
Okey, John, 71
Onslow, Richard, 236

Overton, Mary, 216
Overton, Richard, 13, 28, 57, 104, 119–20, 128–9, 145–6, 150, 169, 190, 264, 276, 289
Overton, Robert, 71
Owen, Sir John, 39

Paine, Thomas, 268
Parker, Henry, 27, 129
Parliamentary or constitutional history, 260, 269
Pease, T. C., 3, 277–8
Pepys, Samuel, 25, 41, 44
Percy, Algernon, earl of Northumberland, 61
Petegorsky, David, 278–9, 284
Peter, Hugh, 190, 271
Petty, Maximilian, 68, 71, 115, 119, 120, 180–1, 183, 185, 286
Petyt, George, 205
Phillips, John, 44–5
Pitson, James, 29
Poole, Elizabeth, 193, 217
Pope, Mary, 207
Pottinger, Henry, 2, 20–1
Price, Richard, quartermaster, 95
Price, Richard, 271
Pride, Thomas, 155, 190
Pride's Purge, 158, 190, 243
Prince, Thomas, 169
Promise Keepers, 242, 288–9
Protestation, 205
Prynne, William, 21, 146, 242–3
Putney debates,
    manuscript text of, 3, 31, 36–9, 45–50, 241, 272, 283, 285
    printed texts of, by
        Aylmer, Gerald, 4
        Firth, C. H., 2, 4, 7, 21, 36–7, 49, 241, 272, 276–7, 283
        Lutaud, Olivier, 4
        Woodhouse, A. S. P., 3–4, 7, 22, 49, 241, 247, 283;
            see also Woodhouse, A. S. P. *and* Lindsay, A. D.
Pym, John, 209, 232

Rainborough, Thomas, 1, 29, 31–2, 48, 63, 71–3, 76, 118, 125–6, 136–7, 139, 152, 155, 157, 170, 180, 183–7, 242, 244, 284–91
Rainborough, William, 73
Ranters, 283, 288
Rapin de Thoyras, Paul, 263, 268
Reading, debates at, 2, 4, 7, 39, 68, 120, 175, 178–80, 188, 191, 193

Reeve, John, 270
reformadoes, 62–3
Rich, Henry, earl of Holland, 39, 100
Rich, Jeremiah, 45
Rich, Nathaniel, 149, 186
Rich, Robert, earl of Warwick, 83
Rider, Matthew, 231, 236
Rogers, John, 213
Roots, Ivan, 118, 247
Rowe, Francis, 166
Rowe, Matthew, 173
Roytson, Richard, 145
Rumbold, Richard, 228
Rushworth, John, 24, 28, 30, 41, 43, 48, 260
Russell, Conrad, 5
Rutherford Institute, 242
Rutt, J. T., 271–2, 273

St John, Oliver, 61
Sams, Eric, 6, 22, 37
Savage, John, 169
Scott, James, duke of Monmouth, 227
    see also Monmouth's Rebellion
Scott, Joan, 198
Selden, John 11
Self-Denying ordinance, 54
Sexby, Edward, 10, 11, 29, 32, 65–7, 69–71, 73, 86, 106, 109–11, 115–19, 122–3, 126–7, 130–1, 137, 146, 179, 182–6, 242, 244, 284–7
Shelton, Thomas, 25, 37–41, 45, 46–7, 50
shorthand, 6, 7, 36–48
Sidney, Algernon, 140, 230, 267, 268, 273–4
Sirraniho, see Harris, John
Skinner, Quentin, 14, 139–40
Skippon, Philip, 54, 56, 282
Smith, Sir Thomas, 201
Smyth, John, 43
Society for Constitutional Information, 273
Solemn engagement of the army
    see New Model Army
Solemn League and Covenant, 56, 59, 61–2, 206
Somers tracts, 260
Sommerville, Margaret, 203
Souldiers catechism, The, 107
Souldiers pocket Bible, 107
Spence, Thomas, 273
Sprigge, Joshua, 9, 190
Stapleton, Philip, 56
Strode, William, 209
Stubbs, Henry, 20

Sylvester, Matthew, 247–9, 254

Taft, Barbara, 68
Thelwall, John, 268
Thomas, Keith, 199–200
Thomason, George, 115, 129–30, 144
Thomason tracts, 2, 28, 34, 259–60, 271, 284
Thompson, E. P., 203, 251, 270
Thompson, William, 172
Thorogood, Captain, 230, 235
Tichborne, Robert, 64, 71
Tickell, Thomas. 34
Tironian notae, 40, 42
Toland, John, 266, 267
Trenchard, John, 266
Tuck, Richard, 11
Two letters of the agents of the five regiments, 73
Twysden, Sir Roger, 145–6

Van Dyke, Anthony, 34
Vane, Sir Henry, the younger, 61, 250, 252, 273
Vertue, George, 34
Villiers, George, 2nd duke of Buckingham, 228
Viner, Sir Robert, 226

Walford, Edward, 190
Walker, Clement, 145
Waller, Sir Hardress, 186
Waller, Sir William, 90
Walwyn, William, 13, 28, 57, 68, 78, 104, 119–21, 150, 169, 181, 183, 190, 228, 252–3, 255, 289
Ware, mutiny or disturbance at, 14, 33, 77–8, 154–5, 170, 261–2, 287
Webb, James, 35
Wentworth, Sir Thomas, earl of Strafford, 27, 29
Whalley, Edward, 149, 165, 169, 172
Wharton, George, 132
Wharton, Philip, Lord, 61, 149
Whitacre, Laurence, 209
White, Francis, 64
Whitehall, debates at, 2, 4, 7, 39, 161, 164, 168, 175, 190–2, 241, 245, 247, 249, 251–2
Whitstone, Katherine, 208
Wildman, John, 9, 29, 66, 68, 70–3, 75, 78, 86, 92, 103–6, 111–12, 115–16, 118–19, 121, 125–6, 131–2, 137, 139, 142–4, 150, 165, 180–4, 186–8, 190–1, 228, 229, 242, 244, 250, 252, 265, 266, 285–7

Willbee, Amon, 128–9, 135
William I, 145
Williamson, Joseph, 226
Willis, John, 41, 45
Wilson, Thomas, 255
Winstanley, Gerrard, 28, 276, 291
Winstanley, William, 269
Wolfe, Don, 104, 279
women, citizenship and rights of, 197–218
    see also feme sole
Woodhouse, A. S. P., 3, 4, 7, 45–6, 49–50, 70, 199, 241, 244–7, 251–3, 255, 279, 283–4
    see also Putney debates
Woolrych, Austin, 5, 8, 33, 46, 86–7, 105, 107, 110, 243
Wootton, David, 229, 233
Worcester College, Oxford, library of, 20, 22–4, 35
Worden, Blair, 253

Yonge, Walter, 209
Young, G. M., 290